KING'S COLLEGE LONDON
MEDIEVAL STUDIES

XIII

GAUTIER D'ARRAS

ILLE ET GALERON

edited and translated by

PENNY ELEY

KING'S COLLEGE LONDON
CENTRE FOR LATE ANTIQUE & MEDIEVAL STUDIES
1996

ISSN 0953-217X
ISBN 0 9522119 5 5

A catalogue record for this book is available
from the British Library

Printed in England
on acid-free recycled paper
by
Short Run Press Ltd, Exeter

TABLE OF CONTENTS

ACKNOWLEDGEMENTS

I gratefully acknowledge a grant in aid of publication from The Vinaver Trust, and thank the Director of the Trust, Professor Peter Field, for his helpful comments on the specimen pages I submitted for consideration.

I would also like to thank the Executive Editor of the King's College London Medieval Studies, Professor David Hook, for all his help in the preparation of this volume; Dr Karen Pratt for her unfailing encouragement and scholarly collaboration ever since we first mooted the idea of editing and translating Gautier's works (her companion volume, *Eracle*, is currently in preparation); Professor Glyn Burgess for his comments on and corrections to sections of the text and translation; and my husband Adrian, for his support during the years when I wondered if this project would ever come to fruition.

INTRODUCTION

Gautier d'Arras is known to us as the author of two octosyllabic romances, *Eracle* and *Ille et Galeron*. Until the middle of this century, his works suffered from a bad press from critics who compared them unfavourably (and in many cases unfairly) with the romances of his more famous contemporary, Chrétien de Troyes. Ferdinand Lot referred to *Ille et Galeron* in 1896 as 'cet ennuyeux récit' (p. 585), while Maurice Wilmotte, writing in 1940, described Gautier himself as a 'fruste paysan' and a 'babillard sentencieux' (p. 113). A move towards more generous re-assessment of Gautier's work began in the 1950s, but even as late as 1968 the noted critic Jean-Charles Payen felt able to dismiss him as 'un réaliste qui sacrifie au snobisme' (p. 346) and 'un écrivain consciencieux quoique sans génie' (p. 349). Nowadays, it is more generally accepted that Gautier was a writer of considerable talent, with a particular gift for observation and psychological analysis, whose work deserves to be better known and more widely studied.

The Author

There is little hard evidence which would allow us to make a convincing identification of the author of *Ille et Galeron*. He refers to himself in the Prologue as 'Gautiers' (l. 23), and again in the closing lines as 'Gautier d'Arras' (l. 6592). This latter appellation could indicate either that he lived and worked in Arras, or that he was a native of Arras who had moved away, and had then adopted the name of his home town as a cognomen. Cowper (1949, 1954) proposed identifying our author with a certain Gualterus de Atrebato (or Atrebatensis) who appears as a witness on over a hundred documents associated with the court of Philippe d' Alsace, count of Flanders. The earliest of these documents is dated 1160, and the latest 1184. According to Cowper, Gualterus probably belonged to the family of the châtelains of Arras, and appears to have owned property at Baudimont.

However, as Fourrier (pp. 180-83) and Renzi (1964, pp. 13-16) pointed out, the evidence for this theory is by no means conclusive. In the first place, Gautier is an extremely common name, and at any given time in the later twelfth century there would have been dozens of individuals who could legitimately have referred to themselves as Gualterus de Atrebato. The existence of a poet and a knight of the same name at the same period does not prove that they were one and the same person. Secondly, the social status of Cowper's Gualterus does not appear to be consistent with some of the statements made by the poet Gautier. Both *Eracle* and *Ille et Galeron* contain passages of fulsome praise of patrons on whom the poet is clearly dependent for a living. The Prologue to *Eracle* contrasts the meanness of certain nobles with the generosity of count Thibaut de Blois, who never fails to reward his musicians and *trouvères* appropriately. The precise details which are given of the way in which the rewards were distributed suggest that Gautier had benefitted personally from the count's *largesse*. It is hard to imagine the land-owning son of a châtelain including himself amongst the court entertainers lining up to receive payment for their services. Moreover, both poems contain references and allusions which indicate that their author had been educated as a *clerc*, rather than as a member of the secular nobility. *Eracle* demonstrates a level of knowledge of biblical and other sacred texts which would have been unusual for a *chevalier*. *Ille et Galeron* reveals a degree of familiarity with vernacular literature (the *chansons de geste*, Wace's *Brut*, Marie de France's *Lais* and the *romans antiques* to name but a few examples) which suggests that Gautier was himself a professional practitioner. A thirteenth-century *Miracle de Nostre Dame* (MS Arsenal 3518, folio 96b) names Gautier alongside Chrétien de Troyes and Benoît de Sainte-Maure (themselves both *clercs* and *trouvères*) as one of the *bons menestrels* of the past.

Resumé of *Ille et Galeron*

Lines 1-134
Prologue. The poet praises the empress Beatrice, in whose honour he intends to compose a *lai* about Galeron and Ille, son of Eliduc.

Lines 135-873
The story is set in Brittany, which is ruled by Duke Conain. When Ille is ten years old, Eliduc dies, and Ille is dispossessed by Hoel and forced into exile at the French court, where he is welcomed because of his father's past service to the king. Ille grows up and becomes a knight, and serves the king so well that the monarch offers him lands in France. Ille refuses, and asks instead for the king's help in recovering his inheritance in Brittany. With ten French knights, he sets out for Brittany, where he has arranged to meet his two uncles. A traitor passes information about the rendez-vous to Hoel, who attacks Ille's uncles with a large force of knights. Ille arrives in the middle of the battle; with his help Hoel's force is routed, and two of Hoel's nephews are killed. Ille's return is welcomed by his relatives and the local population, and news of his success reaches Conain and his beautiful sister Galeron.

Lines 874-1580

Ille is received at Conain's court, and he and Galeron fall in love, despite the difference in rank between them. The poet hints that the course of their love will not run smoothly. Galeron's would-be suitor Rogelion joins forces with his uncle Hoel to attack Ille on his return from court. Ille achieves a decisive victory, as a result of which Conain makes him seneschal of Brittany. Ille and Galeron suffer the torments of love in secret: he feels unable to approach her because of her rank; her natural modesty prevents her from saying anything to him. The situation is resolved when Conain decides to give his sister in marriage to his new seneschal, after obtaining the consent of both parties. The wedding angers three of Galeron's powerful suitors, who march on Brittany, but are ambushed and taken prisoner by Ille.

Lines 1581-2010

With all opposition effectively neutralised, Ille enjoys a period of unclouded happiness with Galeron, during which his virtues are recognised throughout Brittany. One day, at the end of a tournament, he undertakes a final joust, and is wounded in the left eye. Ashamed to reveal his injury to Galeron, in case she rejects him, he takes refuge in a distant manor and refuses to see anyone except his chaplain. Galeron obtains entry to his chamber by deception, and reassures him of her continuing love for him. Unable to believe that a great lady could still love a man of relatively humble birth once he had been disfigured, Ille leaves secretly and makes his way to Rome, where the elderly emperor faces an invasion by Byzantine forces. On discovering Ille's departure, Galeron sets out to find him, but her route takes her in an entirely different direction.

Lines 2011-3148

Ille presents himself to the emperor as a poor mercenary, and is taken into the army, where his appearance excites general ridicule. He silences his critics by distinguishing himself on the battlefield, and his valour and tactical sense win the admiration of the Roman seneschal. When the seneschal is killed, the remaining barons beg Ille to replace him, which he agrees to do on a temporary basis, subject to confirmation by the emperor. Under his leadership the Roman army wins a long and hard-fought battle, and the Byzantine emperor is forced to flee Italy. Meanwhile, Galeron, having searched in vain for her husband, decides to go to Rome to seek penance from the pope for the sin of pride, which she believes was instrumental in driving Ille away from Brittany. She takes humble lodgings in Rome and lives a devout and blameless life, earning her living as a seamstress.

Lines 3149-3979

News of Ille's victory reaches Rome, where the emperor's daughter Ganor begins to be attracted to him. On Ille's return to the court, he is confirmed as seneschal, and Ganor falls hopelessly in love with him. Ille only has thoughts for Galeron, who he knows has not been seen in Brittany since his departure, but remains unaware that she too is now in Rome. The emperor confides in the pope his intention to marry Ganor to Ille, and asks the pope to take the news to the seneschal. Ille refuses the offer of Ganor's hand, and on being pressed for an explanation, reveals his past history. At the pope's suggestion, he sends messengers to Brittany to look for Galeron, on the understanding that if they fail to trace her, he will marry Ganor. The messengers return without Galeron, and a date is set for the wedding, much to Ganor's delight.

Lines 3980-4902

On the morning of the wedding-day, Galeron hears for the first time that Ille is in Rome and about to marry the emperor's daughter. Afraid that she will be committing a sin if she does not act before the marriage is celebrated, she waits at the church door and makes herself known to Ille when he arrives. She asks his permission to enter a convent, leaving him to marry Ganor. On hearing that she still loves him, Ille decides to give up Ganor and return to Brittany with his wife. The news of Ille's imminent departure is greeted with despair in Rome; Ganor is distraught. On taking his leave of her, Ille promises to return if she should ever need his help, and is overcome by pity for her plight.

Lines 4903-5395

Ille returns to Brittany, where he and Galeron receive a joyful welcome, after which he swiftly restores peace to his dukedom. News of the rejoicing reaches Rome, to the great dismay of the emperor and Ganor. Ille and Galeron have two sons, Acarin and Garsion. During the traumatic birth of their third child, a daughter, Galeron vows to become a nun if her life is spared. On recovering from her confinement, she takes the veil, leaving Ille alone and distraught. Memories of Ganor's grief at his departure from Rome help him to overcome his own grief at losing Galeron.

Lines 5396-6124

After the death of her father Ganor refuses to marry the emperor of Constantinople, who responds by attacking her possessions. Ganor sets out secretly for Brittany to ask Ille for help; he, meanwhile, has heard of her predicament, and sets out for Rome, pretending that he is going on a pilgrimage to Compostela. In Vienne, Ille discovers that Ganor has gone to Brittany to look for him. The news fuels his incipient love for Ganor; the conflict between this new love and his first love for Galeron is expressed in the image of a knight besieging a tower defended by a crossbowman. He continues towards Rome, and comes across a castle which is being besieged by the emperor. During a battle between besiegers and defenders, Ille and his men launch a surprise attack, and the enemy is routed. Ille is welcomed by the defenders, who tell him that Ganor has disappeared. Ganor returns sadly to Rome, having been told that Ille has gone to Compostela.

Lines 6125-6592

When Ganor persists in her refusal to marry the emperor, she is betrayed by ten of her men, who plan to hand her over to the invader when she leaves Rome to inspect her forces. Their treachery is revealed to Ganor by a loyal member of the party, who then slips away to warn the army. On hearing the news, Ille sets out to rescue Ganor, and they are joyfully reunited. Ganor punishes the traitors and marries Ille. The new emperor rewards his companions, and devotes himself to the protection of the empire. Ille and Ganor have four children, including three sons who later distinguish themselves by their prowess, and live out their days happily together.

The Manuscripts

Ille et Galeron has come down to us in two manuscripts, which present different versions of the text. MS P (Bibliothèque nationale, fonds français 375) is a large volume dating from the late thirteenth century, written in three different French hands. It contains *Ille et Galeron* and twenty-two other vernacular works, including three of the *romans antiques*, and two romances by Chrétien de Troyes (a detailed description of this MS is given by Léopold Constans on pp. 27-31 of volume VI of his SATF edition of the *Roman de Troie* (Paris: Firmin Didot, 1912)). The volume consists of 346 folios; *Ille et Galeron* occupies folios 296 recto (apart from the first 25 lines of column 1) to 309 verso, and is written in four columns throughout. On the majority of the folios the columns are of sixty lines each; folio 306 verso has columns of fifty-nine lines, while folio 307 recto and verso has columns of fifty-six lines (except for the fourth column of 307 verso, which has fifty-seven lines). The text of *Ille et Galeron* in P contains numerous scribal errors and omissions; errors are often found in clusters (e.g. folio 298[r] columns a-c, 303[r] column b, 304[v] column a), which may suggest that the scribe, in addition to being careless, may have been working from an original which was damaged or otherwise difficult to read in places. MS W, now at the University of Nottingham, formerly belonged to Lord Middleton of Wollaton Hall, and was first brought to the attention of scholars in 1911 by W. H. Stevenson's, *Report of the Manuscripts of Lord Middleton preserved at Wollaton Hall, Nottinghamshire* (London: Historical Manuscripts Commission, 1911; a full description of the MS is given on pp. 221-35). It is written in a thirteenth-century French hand, and contains a variety of vernacular romances, *chansons de geste* and fabliaux. W is a carefully-produced MS, which presents a far less obviously corrupt text of our romance than P.

The Texts

The extent of the difference between the two versions of the poem cannot be gauged simply by comparing their lengths (P contains 6,592 lines, while W has 5,835). In total, there are 1,182 lines in P which do not appear in W; W also contains 425 lines which are not in P. Although minor variations are to be found throughout the romance, in general terms P presents more extended versions of the prologue, Ille's initial exploits, the early stages of his relationship with Galeron, and parts of the first war in Italy, while W gives a more detailed account of the abduction and rescue of Ganor, and a fuller version of the epilogue. The two MSS differ significantly in the way they describe the crucial episode in which Ille loses his left eye. In P, this incident is located at a tourney: after overcoming all his opponents, Ille undertakes a final joust against a newcomer so as to make his victory complete in the eyes of his *amie*. This act of bravado results in his being injured by the unknown knight. In W, on the other hand, Ille loses his eye in the course of a war, after being attacked by one of the defenders of a castle he is besieging.

There are also important differences between the MSS where references to the poet's patrons are concerned. Both versions include a prologue dedicating the work to 'l'empererris de Rome', who can be identified with Beatrice of Burgundy, daughter and heiress of count Renaud III of Burgundy, who married the Holy Roman Emperor Frederick Barbarossa in 1156. P includes more fulsome praise of the empress than does W; W includes eight lines which do not figure in P, in which the poet signals his intention to make up for lost time after having made her acquaintance later than other poets. P has a very brief epilogue, in which the poet names himself, but makes no further reference to his patron. W, on the other hand, ends with thirty lines which are not in P, which introduce a second dedicatee, 'le bon conte Tiebaut', who is praised as being the empress' equal in nobility of both words and deeds. *Eracle* also contains a dedication to a count Thibaut, and mentions that he is the son of another count of the same name, who is now dead. These individuals must realistically be one and the same person, who can be none other than Thibaut V, count of Blois from 1152 (when he succeeded his father Thibaut IV) until his death in 1191. These lines further inform us that *Ille et Galeron* was begun for Beatrice and finished for Thibaut (W lines 5828-30).

The epilogue in W also contains a reference to Gautier's other extant romance:

> Galters d'Arras qui s'entremist
> D'Eracle, ains qu'il fesist ceste uevre. (W 5805-06)

Together with the double dedications (*Eracle* was apparently begun for Thibaut, and finished for Count Baudouin of Hainault), these lines have led to a considerable amount of speculation about the relationship between the two works. Both Becker and Cowper (in the Introduction to his edition) propounded theories of intercalated composition, according to which Gautier would either have written *Ille et Galeron* during two separate periods, alternating it with the writing of *Eracle* (Becker), or in one period, after he had begun *Eracle*, but before he finished it (Cowper). Becker's theory rests largely on an unwarranted emendation of W 5806, and has been contested by Fourrier (pp. 186-87). Cowper's is more plausible, since *s'entremetre* can have the sense of 'to undertake', and does not necessarily imply completion of a task (although it may do).

It is worth noting, however, that these arguments are all couched in terms of a single entity which their authors call *Ille et Galeron*. The existence of the two different versions of the poem has so far had little impact on discussions of the relative chronology of Gautier's works (or, indeed, their dating). It is nonetheless important to try to clarify the relationship between the versions preserved in MSS P and W before formulating theories about their composition. Is it possible to establish whether one of the two versions represents an adaptation of the other? If so, is there any evidence as to whether the adaptation was made by a *remanieur* or by the author himself?

When we consider these questions in more detail, it soon becomes apparent that if W represents an abbreviated and revised version of P, or, conversely, if P represents an expanded and revised version of W, then the adaptation was expertly done, by someone who had a detailed knowledge of the poem and a genuine understanding of the characterisation of the protagonists. In the majority of cases where the MSS diverge for more than half-a-dozen lines, it is impossible to tell simply by comparing the two texts whether a cut or an expansion has been made: both MSS present seamless narratives which are entirely logical and internally coherent. So, for instance, if W ll. 428-29 and 574-75 represent points at which P has been abbreviated, the cuts have been skilfully made, and no-one reading W without reference to P would suspect that anything has been removed. Likewise, if P 4225-55 represents an expansion of W, there is nothing in either text or context which indicates that these thirty-one lines might have been added at a later date.

In a small number of instances, however, the text of one MS contains an awkward transition or an inconsistency which seems to betray the activities of a *remanieur*. If we exclude inconsistencies which can be explained in terms of a simple scribal error such as the omission of a single couplet, we find that such passages occur almost exclusively in W. One characteristic example is to be found in the account of the preliminaries to the marriage of Ille and Galeron. In both MSS, after Ille has proved his worth by bringing peace to Brittany, Duke Conain decides to reward the seneschal by giving him his sister in marriage (P 1408-27; W 870-79). In P, Conain then approaches Galeron to ascertain her feelings about marriage; without knowing of his intentions, she promptly declares that the only man she would be prepared to marry is Ille. Having reassured his sister that the seneschal is indeed the man he has in mind, Conain then approaches Ille with his offer, without telling him that Galeron has already agreed to the match. When Ille replies that he cannot believe that Galeron would deign to accept him, Conain offers to plead the seneschal's cause for him, provided that Ille will be duly grateful if he succeeds. Smiling to himself over his little game, Conain sends for Galeron, and shows Ille how effective an advocate he is by securing her immediate agreement to a wedding (P 1408-522). In W, on the other hand, this episode does not contain the first interview between Conain and Galeron, but starts with the duke's approach to Ille. In this version, too, Conain smiles at Ille's gloomy assessment of his chances of being accepted (W 914), but his reaction is puzzling, and quite unmotivated: why should Conain smile, when he is no wiser than Ille about Galeron's true feelings, and when we have been told less than forty lines earlier that he is seriously concerned that Galeron might not wish to marry Ille (W 876-78)? The only reasonable explanation for Conain's smile in W is that this scene represents an abbreviated version of an original similar to P: the forty-seven lines of Conain's conversation with Galeron have been cut, but the abbreviator has overlooked the detail of the smile in the scene which he has retained.

The central episode of the loss of Ille's eye also contains an inconsistency in W. In this version, Ille is injured while fighting in a war about which we are told nothing beyond the basic statement 'Un jor estoit en une guerre' (W 981). The absence of information about the war is in itself slightly curious: on every other occasion when Ille becomes involved in warfare, whether in Brittany or in Italy, we are given a wealth of circumstantial detail about the warring parties, the geographical location, and the reasons for the conflict. Moreover, Ille's involvement in a war close to his own territories in Brittany (he is easily able to travel while injured to one of his *manoirs*) appears to be a direct contradiction of the statement made in W 776-82 (P 1202-09) that he had brought peace to the whole of Brittany, and was so firmly in control that no-one there dared to oppose him. It is worth noting in this regard that on the only other occasion when Ille has to fight locally after his marriage, it is made clear that his opponents come from outside Brittany and are actively invading Conain's territory. In P, no such inconsistency arises: Ille loses his eye while participating in a tourney, which would be a normal form of sport and military exercise for knights during peace-time. Moreover, the P version of this episode is more consistent with the later characterisation of the hero. In one of his conversations with the pope, Ille reveals that he deliberately courted death on the battlefield (ll. 3734-36), suggesting an impulsive, desperate streak in his make-up which fits well with the idea of the foolish excess of his final joust. In this instance, too, the inconsistencies in W can be best explained in terms of this version's being an adaptation of an original similar to P (on possible reasons for altering the context of Ille's injury, see below, pp. xxi-xxii).

If this is the case, and if therefore all the passages in which W diverges significantly from P represent alterations to an original, it is worth reiterating that the majority of these alterations have been made in such a way as to make the hand of the *remanieur* well-nigh invisible. The degree of skill involved, and the level of familarity with the text which this implies, lends weight to the suggestion made by Fourrier and others that the *remanieur* was none other than Gautier himself. This hypothesis has the additional advantage of enabling us to make sense of the existence of the second dedication, to Thibaut de Blois, which is found in the epilogue of W, but not in that of P. We may imagine Gautier composing an initial version of *Ille et Galeron* for the empress Beatrice, hoping that her links with the house of Blois-Champagne, with whom he was connected, would encourage her to look favourably on his work. Some time later, perhaps because the first version had not attracted the attention he had hoped for, Gautier undertook (or supervised) the creation of a second version, which he dedicated to Thibaut de Blois. While the switch to a second patron does not necessarily imply a breakdown in relations with the first, it is not hard to imagine why the first *Ille et Galeron* might not have found favour with the empress. Gautier appears to invite the identification of Galeron's brother Conain with the real-life Duke Conain IV of Brittany (see note to l. 157). By the same token, Ganor, who is the daughter of an emperor and eventually becomes empress of Rome, could well have been identified with Beatrice, herself an empress whose ancestors included four Holy Roman emperors (a point which

xv

Gautier stresses in his prologue; see also the note to l. 5586). Now, for all her beauty and nobility, the picture of Ganor which emerges from the romance is by no means entirely flattering: she is portrayed on various occasions as impatient, jealous, vengeful and self-destructive. In comparison with Galeron, she must certainly be perceived as flawed (if psychologically more realistic than her rival). While this may make her an interesting figure in the eyes of modern criticism, it might not have endeared her to an empress whose public image, if Gautier's prologue is to be believed, was one of discretion, dignity and self-restraint.

A number of the minor differences between P and W, which are probably to be attributed to the activities of scribes rather than to the author, also shed some light on the question of the relationship between the two MSS. We have already noted that W is the work of a careful scribe who has avoided many of the careless errors committed by the scribe of P. The work of this scribe (or possibly of one of his predecessors) appears to have included a series of attempts to clarify an original which he found obscure, and whose readings were closely related to those of P. W contains a number of obvious *lectiones faciliores*, which are discussed in the notes to ll. 828, 2172, 4201 and 5168. On several occasions, it also presents simpler versions of passages which seem at first sight to be obscure in P, but which prove on closer inspection to be cogent, and sometimes quite subtle, ideas expressed in elliptical language (see notes to ll. 961, 1052, 1361 and 1919). In at least one instance W's attempted clarification of a difficult passage succeeds only in introducing an internal contradiction where none exists in P (see note to l. 5293).

There is also some evidence that the scribe of W may have been working from an original which already contained some of the errors present in P. Two possible instances of this are discussed in the notes to ll. 3838 and 4755. Another example is to be found in a complex passage which likens the struggle between Ille's growing affection for Ganor and his original love for Galeron to a man besieging a high tower defended by a crossbowman (P 5618-55; W 4712-51). Having introduced the siege imagery, Gautier then goes on to gloss his own text, explaining that Ille's heart is represented by the tower, his first love for Galeron (who is now a nun) by the defender, and his love for Ganor by the assailant, who attempts to prove that love for a nun has no place in the heart of a secular nobleman. It is useful to compare the unamended text of the two MSS at this point.

P 5639-5655	W 4733-4751
Et veut mostrer par argumens	Mostrer li vielt par argumens
Et prover k'amors de nonain	Et mostrer qu'amors de nonain
N'a droit en cuer de castelain,	N'a droit en cuer de castelain,
De duc, de conte ne de roi,	De duc, de conte ne de roi,

Ains torne mout a grant desroi
C'on l'i suefre, c'on l'i consent.
Illes s'en deut, Ille s'en sent.
L'autre amors est fors a confondre
Ne ne set soussiel que respondre,
Mais itant dist qu'ele est tenans
Par droit; tex est ses convenans;
Et ceste qui noiens devint
Des lors qu'ele none devint:
De castel c'a a faire none?
Mais fille a roi qui taut et done,
Et la none son sautier lise
En l'abeïe et en l'eglise!

Et torne molt a grant desroi
Et li offre c'on li consent.
Ylles s'en dielt, Ylles s'en sent.
Mar vit la tençon qui tant dure,
Qui tant est fors et aspre et dure.
L'altre amors est fors a confondre
Ne ne set sosiel que respondre;
Mais tant dist que ele est devens
Par droit, tels est ses convenens.
Et ceste qui none devint,
Des l'eure que ce li avint,
N'a de castel que faire none,
Mais fille qui li tolt et done;
Et la none sen sautier lisse
En abeïe ou en eglise.

Initially, W appears to offer the more coherent text, while P 5650-51 ('Et ceste qui noiens devint/ Des lors qu'ele none devint') are clearly corrupt. However, closer inspection suggests that the scribe of W found this passage problematic, and did not fully grasp the sequence of ideas it represents. In W, 'l'altre amors' (which is Ille's love for Ganor, as opposed to his *amor entiere* for Galeron) is taken to be the subject of 'set' in l. 4743 and 'dist' in l. 4744. This creates a logical inconsistency: the idea that this love is difficult to overcome (l. 4742) does not tally with the subsequent statement that it is at a loss to find a suitable response. And what is it that this love might be seeking to respond to (l. 4743)? The only argument put forward in the preceding lines is its *own* contention that love for a nun has no place in Ille's heart.

The inconsistency becomes even more pronounced in the following couplet. The word *convenens* implies a formal agreement or legal contract: the idea of the second love having a legal right to its position *outside* Ille's heart ('devens' l. 4744) is quite illogical, when the whole thrust of the argument is that this love, represented by the besieger, is trying to force home its claim to be *inside* as the sole lawful occupant. These lines make sense only if the subject of *set* and *dist* is the first love, and if, as in P, they represent the response of the present incumbent to the forceful arguments put forward by the rival claimant. From the point of view of logic and internal consistency, P's 'qu'ele est tenans' (l. 5648) has to be the correct reading. W's 'qu'ele est devens' looks like a scribal emendation stemming from a failure to grasp the fact that this passage represents a debate between the two loves, rather than a simple statement of the position of the second (the use of the phrase *mostrer par argumens* in P 5639 and W 4733 implies a dialectic). *Ceste* in the following couplet marks a change of speaker, as the second love puts forward a pragmatic counter-argument: irrespective of legal niceties, what use is a fortified tower (a man's heart) to a nun? It is not unreasonable to suggest that 'soussiel' in P 5647 may represent a corruption of *ciele*, and that in the original the progress of the debate was clearly marked by means of the opposition between *c(i)ele* and *ceste*. If the scribe of W was working from a copy which already contained this error, then his confusion as to which statements should be attributed to which of the two loves becomes more understandable.

The same line of reasoning can be applied to W 4748-51, which again are less than satisfactory as they stand. There is an awkward repetition of the noun *none* in l. 4748, when the sense of the sentence requires that it should end with the infinitive *faire*, while l. 4749 is clearly inadequate in terms of both syntax and meaning: who is this *fille*, and why should she be giving anything to, or taking anything from the nun? P is obviously corrupt at this point: the repetition of the rhyme word without change of meaning in ll. 5650-51 indicates a scribal lapsus. The most plausible reconstruction of the original here, as in so many other instances, is that suggested by Löseth, who emended P 5650 to read 'Et ceste, que a noient vint'. The confusion apparent in W is readily explained if we assume that the scribe was working from a MS which contained the same error as P. His previous misreading of the debate between the two loves precluded his emending the text along the same lines as Löseth, which requires that *ceste* and the subject of the verb *(de)vint* be seen as two different people. Instead, he concluded that the correct ending for the line in his original which corresponded to P 5650 had been transposed to the following line, reinstated it, and then adjusted the equivalent of P 5651 to make as much sense of the passage as he could.

While the question of the relationship between the two MSS of *Ille et Galeron* is unlikely ever to be conclusively resolved, the evidence we have found seems to point to the following scenario. Gautier initially composed the longer of the two versions of the poem for Beatrice of Burgundy; some time later, he revised the work, perhaps as a result of a frosty reception from the empress, and added a second dedication to Thibaut de Blois. In order to account for the existence of mistakes common to both versions, which we posited above, we must assume that the shorter version was adapted from a MS which already contained a small number of scribal errors (if the original was sent to Beatrice, then at least one other copy must have been made at an early date for Gautier's own use), and that these errors were not corrected when the adaptation was made. If the *remanieur* was Gautier himself, it might seem strange that he allowed such errors to stand. However, the process of adaptation is unlikely to have involved a line-by-line revision of the text. Gautier may well have decided in advance which sections of his narrative needed revising, and then concentrated his attentions on the relevant portions of his own MS, without checking the rest in detail. A *tour de force* such as the siege image quoted above would surely not have figured in his list of passages which could be revised or abridged. Both versions were then re-copied (how many times is not clear), in a process which ultimately produced the existing MSS P and W. P is the work of a scribe who was himself careless, or did not take it upon himself to try to correct the careless errors of others. The scribe of W was much more diligent, and tried to correct passages which he found unclear, either because his original was corrupt, or because he did not fully appreciate the complexity of Gautier's style.

If this scenario is accurate, then it might be seen as lending support to a theory of intercalated composition of *Eracle* and *Ille et Galeron* similar to those outlined above. Since the reference to *Eracle* having been composed (or undertaken) before *Ille* is found only in W, it might be argued that in fact the first version of *Ille* was written before *Eracle*, and that *Eracle* was composed during the period that elapsed between the appearance of the longer and the shorter versions of *Ille*. Such a theory might be attractive, were it not for the fact that both versions of *Ille* contain an unmistakable allusion to the action of *Eracle* (P 180-184 and W 120-124; see the note to l. 184). This passage begins with the second line of a couplet, and is so closely integrated into the thematic context that it is highly unlikely to have been interpolated into either MS at a later date. This being so, we must conclude that both versions of *Ille* postdate *Eracle*, and attribute the absence of any explicit reference in P to Gautier's authorship of *Eracle* either to scribal carelessness or to authorial modesty which had been overcome by the time the second version of the poem was completed (for an alternative hypothesis, see the note to l. 6592).

The Dating of *Ille et Galeron*

In the absence of biographical details about the author, we have to rely almost entirely on the internal evidence of the text to estimate the date at which it was written. Gautier's references to his patrons provide a firm *terminus a quo* and *terminus ad quem* for both versions of the text. Line 69 of the prologue mentions the coronation of the empress Beatrice, which took place in Rome on August 1st 1167, eleven years after her marriage to Frederick Barbarossa. Beatrice died on November 15th 1184, so it is reasonable to assume that the version of the text preserved in MS P was completed before that date. The second dedication in the epilogue of W to Count Thibaut de Blois must likewise have been composed before the death of Thibaut V in 1191. Various arguments have been put forward in an attempt to establish a more precise dating for *Ille et Galeron*, and two main theories have emerged, both of which also take account of evidence for the dating of *Eracle*. According to Foerster and Calin, the dedication in *Eracle* to Baudouin of Hainault was intended for Baudouin IV, who died in 1171. *Eracle* would therefore have been composed before that date, with *Ille* following shortly afterwards. The second theory, supported by the arguments of Sheldon and Heinermann, assumes that *Eracle* was dedicated to Baudouin V, who ruled from 1171 until his death in 1195. This later dating for *Eracle* was favoured by Becker, allowing as it does for *Ille* to have been started after 1167, without *Eracle* then having to be fitted in before 1171. According to this theory, *Ille* was not completed until the late 1170s or early 1180s. Although he was not convinced by the case for intercalated composition, Fourrier also favoured a later dating for *Ille*, as he did for other romances such as *Partonopeus de Blois*.

Attention has been focused in particular on the meaning of the word *ja* in l. 69 ('Rome le vit ja coroner'). In his 1891 edition, Foerster suggested that *ja* implied that the coronation was a recent event; Settegast, on the other hand, followed by Fourrier, argued that *ja*, used in conjunction with the simple past tense, always had the sense of modern French *jadis*, that is 'in the distant past'. The best guide to its meaning in l. 69 would seem to be Gautier's own usage in similar grammatical contexts elsewhere in the poem. Of the nine equivalent occurrences of the word, two (ll. 64 and 4859) refer to events in the life of Christ, and so could be taken to indicate the distant past. In two more instances *ja* has to be translated by the ambiguous phrase 'in the past', since there is no clear location in time of the events described. In the first of these (l. 104), *ja* is equivalent to 'once upon a time', and as such is a marker of the distance between the real world of the prologue and the fictional world of the *lai* rather than of precise temporal distance. The second (l. 1924), forms part of Ille's lament following his injury, when he recalls having heard a *respit* about woman's fickleness, and could equally well evoke a recent or a distant memory. The remaining five occurrences of *ja* with the simple past all refer explicitly to recent events. Ille's first response to his disfigurement contains the following lines:

> «E las! ja vic je ja tel eure,
> Se je morusse a droit n'a tort,
> Que Diex fust blasmés de ma mort.»   (1710-12)

Whether God would have been blamed by Galeron or by the people of Brittany is not clear, but in either case such a response to his death would only have been appropriate *after* the military exploits which brought him recognition at Conain's court, and those exploits in turn can only be of relatively recent date, since Ille is still a young man at this point. During his conversation with the pope, Ille uses *ja* to refer to his marriage to Galeron (1. 3667), which took place the same year he lost his eye and moved to Rome (ll. 3680-81), where he is still a relative newcomer. When Galeron makes herself known to Ille in Saint Peter's, she uses the phrase *je fui ja ta bone amie* (1. 4194). She also tells him that she has been in Rome for under four years, and it is clear from the first section of the narrative that she had not been Ille's *amie* for long before they were separated. *Ja* is used again with the simple past in ll. 5361 and 5401 when Ille, now in Brittany, remembers Ganor's love for him and his military success in Rome. It is explicitly stated in the same speech (ll. 5371-73) that barely four years have elapsed since the period he is evoking: *ja* can only indicate the recent past in this context. The balance of evidence therefore seems to be against interpreting 1. 69 as a reference to the distant past, and there would seem to be some grounds for concluding that Beatrice's coronation was still a relatively recent event when Gautier began to compose *Ille et Galeron*, which would give a likely date of composition for the first version in the early 1170s.

There may be some support for this in the fact that Conain IV of Brittany, certain events of whose life are echoed in the portrayal of Galeron's brother Conain (see note to 1. 157), died on February 20th 1171. It would have been tactless, to say the least, to narrate the death of the fictional duke Conain (which occurs during Ille's exile in Rome) while his real-life counterpart was still alive. Equally, the audience would have been more likely to understand the allusions to Conain IV if his failures as a ruler were still relatively fresh in their memories.

The other arguments put forward by Fourrier for a later dating are based on possible allusions in the text to political events in the 1170s and 1180s, none of which is entirely convincing. He links the mention of the *popelicans* or heretics in 1. 1247 to renewed condemnation of the Cathar heresy following the third Lateran Council of 1179, arguing that Gautier's criticism must have coincided with a resurgence of the Cathar threat (pp. 195-97). However, the Cathars had attracted periodic denunciations from the ecclesiastical authorities from as early as the eleventh century. Moreover, if, as Fourrier claims, the weavers of Champagne were particularly well-disposed towards Catharism in the second half of the twelfth century, then a writer working in the cultural milieu of Blois-Champagne could have found good reason to condemn the heresy at any time. Fourrier also argues that the different circumstances in which Ille loses his eye in P and W are conditioned by contemporary reality. For him, the displacement of this central event from a tourney in P to a war in W is a response to the emphatic reiteration by the same Lateran Council of earlier papal bans on tourneys (p. 197). This may well be the case, but it does not provide evidence for the original date of composition of *Ille*, only of the W version of the text. If, as we have argued, the P version is the original, and if this version was composed before the mid 1170s, then a date of around 1180 for the revised version is entirely possible, allowing as it does for Gautier to have taken account of responses to his romance before reworking it for a second patron.

This dating for P also provides us with an alternative (or complementary) explanation for the switch to a second patron. From 1174 to 1178 the empress Beatrice accompanied her husband on his expedition against the Lombard League in Italy, where communication with the Blois-Champagne milieu was much more difficult than it was during the previous six years, which the imperial couple had spent in Germany and Burgundy. If Gautier had composed the first version of *Ille* and presented it to Beatrice in the early 1170s, hoping for her continued patronage, then her departure for Italy in September 1174, on what promised to be a lengthy campaign, would have been quite a blow. It is quite possible that the second dedication in *Ille* reflects Gautier's rueful realisation that he was more likely to be remembered and rewarded by a local patron, whose generosity he had already had reason to celebrate in verse, than by one who travelled as extensively as Beatrice, and who might be absent for considerable periods of time from the circles in which he could hope to encounter her.

The Language of *Ille et Galeron*

A number of critics, notably Heimer and Hüppe, have studied *Ille et Galeron* from a linguistic point of view, reaching very similar conclusions about the language of the author. Examination of the rhymes and scansion reveal no more than a handful of dialectal features which can be attributed to Gautier himself. Both MSS provide strong evidence that, even though he was in all probability a native of Arras, Gautier strove to write in the standard literary language of his day and to exclude Picard traits from his romance. The picardisms present in both MSS can be attributed almost exclusively to the scribes, rather than to the author; of the two MSS, W has a more pronounced dialectal flavour than P. Some of the features of P which are characteristic of the dialects of the Northern region are listed below.

1. *C* followed by *a* gives [k] (spelt *c* or *k*) rather than *ch*, e.g. *kace* 376, 441; *caitif* 345; *cambre* 966, 1675; *cambrelenc* 1740, 3167; *car* 509, 1249; *kaïr* 708 (note also *cose* 339, 458; *coisist* 443).

2. Latin *c* + *e* or *i* gives [tʃ] (spelt *c* or *ch*) rather than [ts], e.g. *chi* passim; *merchi* 284, 2253 (twice as frequent as *merci*); *ochis* 619, 2433; *cier* 324; *mesciés* 405

3. The unstressed form of the feminine article and pronoun is often *le* rather than *la* in the singular, e.g. 2, 43, 69; likewise, but less frequently, the possessive adjectives *me* (3900, 5482, etc.) and *se* (143, 224, etc.) are found alongside *ma* and *sa*. The absence of distinction between masculine and feminine forms of the unstressed pronoun in the oblique case in this region leads in turn to *li* being used for *la* in the nominative singular, e.g. 3074, 3081, 4097, 4322.

4. *A* + [ɲ] gives *agne* not *aigne*, e.g. *Bretagne: adagne* 1683-84; *Bretaigne: montagne* 1985-86; *plagne* (= *plaine*)*: plagne* (from *plaindre*) 5662-63

5. On the model of *faç* (1350, 6527), the first person singular of the present indicative sometimes ends in *-c: commanc* 1520, 6249; *cuic/quic* 1561, 1847, etc.; *manc* 4900; *muç* 5383; *prenc* 6093; *renc* 4496, 6094; *senc* 4797; *vienc* 2023; there are also two examples in the simple past: *oc* 3696; *vic* 1710.

6. The triphthong *-eau* is differentiated to *-iau* in *biax* 200, 257, 284, etc.; *damoisiaus* 6288; *lionchiax* 674; *nouviaus* 199, 258; *roiaus* 4782, etc. *Aqua* > *iaue* in 4014.

7. The intervocalic group *-ml-* is retained without an interconsonantal glide and represented by *-nl-*, e.g. *tranle: ensanle* 570-71, *sanle: ensanle* 730-31.

8. The stressed form of the first person singular pronoun is *jou* in 1365, 1943, etc.

9. The analogical form of the possessive *vo* occurs in 3755 (nominative singular), 4021, 4743, 4744, 6079.

10. *Locum* is represented by *liu* 940, 1932, 2254, etc. and *lius* 1312, 1753, etc., as well as by *leu* 1627, 5921 and *leus* 924, 1673, indicating reduction of the triphthong *ieu* to *iu*.

11. Tonic free [o] before *r* is represented by *eu: leur* 330, 413, 488, etc.; *eure* 213, 3417, 4466; *honeur* 83, 1481, etc., but also by *o: lor* 81, 184, 333, etc.; *ore* 924, 3420, 4026; *onor* 37, 2477, etc..

12. The first personal plural ending is *-omes* in 3854, 5008, 5178, 5179, 5987, 5990 and 6080. However, this ending became quite widespread in the twelfth century, and provided a useful alternative to *-ons* in terms of scansion (*savomes* in 3854 is followed by *savons* in 3855, and *volomes* in 5987 by *veons* in 5988). The form *poiemes* (*pouvoir*) occurs once, in 5726.

Also worthy of note are the rhymes *double: torble* (1859-60, 3724-25, 5225-26), indicating metathesis of *r*; three examples of a vocalic interconsonantal glide in forms of the verbs *avoir* and *savoir: saverés* 1442, *averiés* 4275, and *averés* 4520; and two examples of the preservation of final *t* in the past participle: *toloit* 2649 and *valut* 3249.

Style and Versification

In terms of style, *Ille et Galeron* has many features in common with other Old French romances of the period. Gautier was clearly influenced by the teaching on rhetoric which formed part of the education of a *clerc*, and makes use of a wide variety of figures of style to embellish his narrative The prologue alone contains instances of metaphor, metonymy, simile, hyperbole, anaphora, chiasmus, *frequentatio* (expressing the same idea in various ways), antithesis, and personification. Elsewhere in the text we find examples of alliteration (ll. 1708-09), *annominatio* (the grouping of etymologically related terms, as in l. 4827ff), *distributio* (expressing a whole by means of enumeration of its parts, as in ll. 1290 and 4916-21), paronomasia (l. 678), prosopopoeia (presented as indirect speech in ll. 5646-56), sequences of rhetorical questions (ll. 4723-34), and many other forms of amplification. Figures of speech involving repetition are particularly common in *Ille et Galeron*. They range from the ornamentation of a single line with *annominatio* and alliteration, as in 'Vilenie vient de vil leu' (l. 1616), through couplets in which only the rhyme word varies:

> «Com malement il nos baillissent,
> Com malement il nos traïssent!»   (2775-76)

to extended use of anaphora in a battle scene:

> Illes les plaisse, Illes les fiert,
> Illes les destruist et requiert,
> Illes lor perce lor escus,
> Illes les fait tous irascus,
> Illes lor fausse lor haubers,
> Illes les fait chocier envers.   (742-47)

Complex combinations of rhetorical devices are particularly striking in the monologues attributed to the three main characters, and in the dialogues between Ille and Galeron and Ille and Ganor.

Gautier frequently makes use of personification to dramatise the attributes of his hero: in ll. 3800-21, for example, Ille is described as having Honour as his chamberlain, and as being able to reconcile the conflicting demands made on him by two other members of his court, Justice and Compassion. A number of critics have commented on the author's skilful handling of metaphors, which range from the fleeting picture of the rich man as an angler, setting hooks for those he wishes to cultivate (l. 4202), to fully-developed images which may extend over many lines of verse. As we have already seen, the conflict between Ille's love for Galeron and his feelings towards Ganor is described at length in terms of the siege of a high tower defended by a crossbowman (ll. 5617-55); Ganor's unrequited passion for the hero is represented by a tunic of sorrow created by Love, whose skirt is made of suffering, and whose seams are made of pain (ll. 6262-74). Although he does make use of some conventional similes, such as likening a warrior on the battlefield to a wolf attacking its prey (ll. 595-98), Gautier also has a talent for finding vivid and imaginative comparisons. Ille's grief after Galeron's retirement to the convent is likened to a hangover which can be cured only by a 'hair of the dog' (in other words another love), although the remedy is likely to prove much harder to come by than in the case of wine (ll. 5321-34).

Gautier makes very little use of description in *Ille et Galeron*, which is perhaps surprising given his inventiveness in other areas, and given that rhetorical training placed considerable emphasis on techniques of describing people and places as part of the process of amplification. Unlike the poets of the *romans d'antiquité*, and unlike his contemporary Chrétien de Troyes, Gautier does not give us detailed physical descriptions of his protagonists. The account of Ille's early years in France ends with a hyperbolic statement about his physical and moral qualities, but no more is said about his appearance than that he is one of Nature's finest creations (ll. 252-55). The most detailed portrait we are given of the hero consists of three lines (ll. 3317-19) evoking Ganor's response to his arrival at court in Rome after his first defeat of the Greek emperor. Likewise, Galeron is simply described as 'mout [...] bele creature' (l. 144), while Ganor is presented as 'la fille au roi, la bele' (l. 3285): in both cases, the young woman's beauty is taken for granted, and no further details are provided. *Ille et Galeron* contains none of the elaborate descriptions of castles, palaces or scenery which characterise other romances of the period. When landscapes and buildings are depicted in this text, the descriptions are strictly functional: they present information crucial to an understanding of the plot, rather than providing an opportunity for the poet to demonstrate his learning. When Ille returns to Italy, he takes lodgings with a loyal *castelain* in a castle which is described as being situated in an out-of-the-way place, on a rocky outcrop which no-one can approach:

> Li castiax ert en une roche:
> Nus n'i avient, nus n'i aproce,
> Nus home n'i puet siege tenir
> Ne aprocier ne avenir;
> Li castiax ert en un destor. (5712-16)

These details are not simply decorative: they are essential if we are to understand how the hero manages to keep his return secret and so maintain the element of surprise in his attack on the Greek army. Offord's comparative study of the vocabulary of *Ille et Galeron* and Chrétien's *Cligés* reveals a much more restricted range of lexemes relating to the natural world, physical characteristics, arms and military equipment in *Ille*, whereas the two works are very similar in terms of the range and variety of abstract vocabulary relating to emotions and moral concepts. This confirms the view that Gautier is less interested in the external appearance and surroundings of his protagonists than in their motivation and psychology (see below, pp. xxxviii-xl).

The *Artes Poeticae*, which reflect the training received by vernacular writers, also recommend the use of proverbs and proverbial expressions to support a line of argument. Schulze-Busacker (1981, 1985) has identified some fifty passages in *Ille et Galeron* which make use of formulae which can be related to items in the various modern collections of medieval proverbs. These proverbial expressions lend a moralising flavour to the text by linking the particular events of the narrative to general 'laws' of human behaviour encapsulated in traditional formulae. Sometimes proverbs are explicitly signalled as such, as in Ille's conversation with Ganor after his first victory over the Greeks has silenced his earlier critics:

> «Amis, fait el, or aient honte
> Cil qui desfirent vostre conte!
> Mout sevent dire et petit faire.
> – France pucele deboinaire,
> L'en a sovent dit et retrait
> Que mout a entre dit et fait.»   (3339-44)

More often, though, they are integrated into narrative or direct speech without an introductory formula, and their form is adapted to the linguistic and thematic context. Two or more proverbs may be combined in one passage in order to give added weight to an assertion, as in ll. 1253-69. Of particular interest is the way in which two proverbs are shown to have a decisive influence on the course of the narrative. Ille's initial reaction to the loss of his eye is coloured by thoughts of Galeron's social position, and by a popular saying about woman's love:

> [...] crient mais qu'ele ne l'adagne
> Et k'ele l'ait mais en despit,
> Si se crient mout de ce respit:
> «Tant as, tant vax, et je tant t'aim.»   (1684-87)

Shortly afterwards he is visited by his wife, and is faced with a crucial decision: should he accept Galeron's assurances that his disfigurement makes no difference to her feelings for him, and remain in Brittany; or should he go into voluntary exile before she has the chance to reconsider and reject him? Once again, his thinking is guided not only by his awareness of his own social inferiority, but also by the received wisdom of the day, as expressed in another proverb:

> «Jou oï ja dire un respit
> que feme a mout le cuer volage
> et mue sovent son corage.»   (1924-26)

The irony of Ille's situation is that while this may be true (in the eyes of Gautier's audience, at least) where the majority of women are concerned, he is married to an exceptional individual, who will ultimately give the lie to this *respit*. Only later, in Rome, will Ille be able to recognise that Galeron is not to be judged according to time-honoured views of female behaviour.   So while Gautier frequently uses proverbial expressions in an entirely conventional fashion to support his narratorial generalisations, he also exploits two such formulae in a much more original way, to demonstrate that there is always an exception to every rule. The effect of this is not to question the validity of the *respits*, but to set Galeron apart from other women, and by doing so to enhance the status of the man who wins her.

The frequency with which Gautier cites proverbial expressions, and the way he uses the *respits*, both suggest that for him such formulae were more than just ornaments of style.   The compressed, elliptical discourse of proverbs seems to correspond to a basic habit of mind in our author, whose own discourse is occasionally elliptical to the point of obscurity for modern readers (see the notes to ll. 4463, 5293, 5651, and 6024). Gautier has a fondness for pithy formulations which give a single verse the force of a punch-line, even at the expense of a certain syntactical clarity. When the Roman knights who accompanied Ille back to Brittany return with fulsome praise of his duchess, the emperor accuses them of disloyalty: they think more of Galeron's gifts of jewels than they do of Ganor. They promptly reproach their master for his small-mindedness with a succint riposte:

> Li rois respondi as barons:
> «Vencus vos a tos covoitise!
> – Sire, mes faites: 'grant francise'!»   (5166-68)

Couplets, too, often take on the quality of aphorisms, as in Ille's exhortation to the Roman knights whom he sees leaving the field after he had been injured:

> «Preu sont li malvais d'autre part
> De çou que vos estes coart.»   (3011-12)

Ille et Galeron is written in octosyllabic rhyming couplets, the characteristic form of twelfth-century romance. According to Warren, Gautier makes relatively sparing use of the *couplet brisé* (only some 20% of sentences in *Ille et Galeron* end in mid couplet), and is more conservative in this respect than Chrétien de Troyes. The influence of *Eneas* can be seen in a number of passages of dialogue where the speakers' words occupy alternate lines or hemistiches. The first of these two techniques is used to good effect during Ille's conversation with the pope, to convey the urgency of the pontiff's questioning:

> «Et si vos di je nonperuec
> Que tex offres ne fu mais onques.
> – Por coi le refusés vos donques?
> – Biax sire, assés i a por coi.
> – Quel cose donc? Dites le moi.» (3661-65)

The second adds drama and intensity to Ille's exchange with his host in Vienne, as he learns that Ganor has gone to Brittany to seek his help:

> Aprés souper a dit: «Biax sire,
> Savés me vos noveles dire
> De cex de Rome, u laide u bele?
> – Oïl, sire! Leur damoisele
> Se herberga chi l'autre soir.
> – Puet c'estre voirs? – Oïl, por voir.
> Au duc de Bretaigne est alee
> Tout coiement, a recelee.
> – Que quiert ele? – Biax sire, aïe,
> Si com en l'ome u plus se fie.» (5580-89)

Like his contemporaries, Gautier does not observe a regular alternation of masculine and feminine rhymes, and mixes *rimes suffisantes*, *rimes riches* and *rimes léonines* throughout the work. *Rimes redoublées* are very uncommon: in addition to the example of ll. 6357-60 quoted above, we find ll. 6399-401 which all rhyme in *-ors*, and there are two sequences of couplets rhyming in *-erre* and *-ere* (ll. 526-29 and 3840-43; *tere* rhymes with *guerre* in ll. 1401-02). There is a small number of minimal rhymes, which are effectively no more than assonance, such as *aé: duceé* (ll. 3079-80) and *i a: crea* (ll. 3199-200).

One interesting feature of the text is the way in which homonymic rhymes are used to reinforce rhetorical effects at key points in the story. Such rhymes are rare in purely narrative passages: 49% of all instances are found in direct speech, while a further 26% occur in passages of authorial comment or intervention. In certain episodes the frequency of homonymic rhymes is significantly higher than the average: there are ten occurrences in the 400 lines of the central reunion scene in St Peter's church (the average frequency is one such couplet in 58), and within this episode, four homonymic rhymes in the 47 lines of Galeron's first speech to Ille (ll. 4113-59); there are also three occurrences in the 63 lines of Ganor's second speech to Ille during their parting scene (ll. 4711-73). Like other plays on words, homonymic rhymes demand extra mental effort on the part of the audience to distinguish different meanings in identical sets of phonemes. Requiring the audience to make that extra effort at more frequent intervals than usual can be an effective foregrounding device, intensifying the impact of moments of high drama.

Ille et Galeron and the *Chronique de Nantes*

In an article published in 1896 Ferdinand Lot noted a curious parallelism between the names of some of the protagonists of Gautier's romance and those of individuals involved in an incident in the early history of Brittany, recorded in the *Chronique de Nantes*. The *Chronique* tells how Hoel, illegitimate son of Alain Barbetorte, count of Nantes, declared war on Conan, count of Rennes, in an attempt to acquire the title of duke of Brittany. Conan responded by sending Galuron to assassinate Hoel in 981, and then seized Nantes and had himself proclaimed duke instead. Lot suggested that the presence of the names Hoel, Conan (or Conain) and Galuron (Galeron) in both works indicated that Gautier was familiar with the *Chronique*, and that the first 1,500 lines of the romance were loosely modelled on it. While the combination of the three names is certainly unusual, it does not necessarily prove that Gautier was consciously echoing Breton history in *Ille et Galeron*. The names Conain and Hoel were quite common in the ruling families of north-west France in the early Middle Ages. By Gautier's day four dukes of Brittany had borne the name Conain; the last of these, Conain IV, had been at war with his uncle Hoel, count of Nantes, in the early 1150s. Gautier had no need to go back to the *Chronique de Nantes* to find a Conain and a Hoel on opposing sides in a conflict in Brittany. There remains the question of Galuron/Galeron, which Foerster had already identified as a man's name of Celtic origin. If Gautier had consciously been using the *Chronique* as a source, it is hard to see why he should have chosen to give his heroine the name of a man, and an assassin to boot. It is far more likely, as Renzi (1967) argues, that he had encountered the name somewhere without registering its gender associations, and chose it simply because of its Celtic sound, to add an additional Breton flavour to his poem.

Ille et Galeron and *Eliduc*

The question of the sources of *Ille et Galeron* becomes more complex and more interesting when we move on to consider the relationship between Gautier's romance and Marie de France's *Eliduc*. The two works are closely related, as can be seen from a summary of Marie's narrative. Eliduc, a Breton knight, enjoys a privileged position at the court of the king of Brittany. His enemies succeed in turning the king against him; unable to see the king to defend himself, he decides to leave Brittany for a while. Before embarking on his journey, he assures his wife that he will remain faithful to her. Once in England, Eliduc comes to the aid of an elderly king, who is being besieged by a neighbouring ruler, and leads his men to victory. He then enters the king's service for a period of one year. During this time, Eliduc falls in love with the king's daughter and heiress, Guilliadun, who returns his love. Meanwhile, the king of Brittany finds himself under attack, and, realising that he had been misled over Eliduc, he sends for the knight to help him. Eliduc obtains the permission of the king to return to Brittany, and agrees privately with Guilliadun that he will come back and take her away with him once his year's service to her father is up. Having brought peace to Brittany, Eliduc returns secretly to England and takes Guilliadun on board his ship. As they approach the coast of Brittany, a terrible storm threatens to sink the ship; a sailor accuses Guilliadun of bringing misfortune upon them because she is with a married man. On hearing the truth about her lover, she falls to the ground, apparently lifeless. Having brought the ship safely to land, Eliduc takes the body to a hermit's chapel, but is unable to bury it because the hermit himself has died. He leaves the body and returns home, but continues to visit the chapel. Disturbed by his behaviour, his wife has him followed; she then takes advantage of his absence at court one day to visit the chapel herself, where she rightly guesses that the body is that of her husband's *amie*. Her attendant kills a weasel which runs over the body; as they watch, its mate appears and revives it with a woodland plant. Seizing the plant, Guildeluec uses it to revive the young woman, and then takes her home. Seeing Eliduc's joy at finding his *amie* alive, Guildeluec asks his permission to retire to a convent. Eliduc then marries Guilliadun; after many happy years together, they also decide to enter religious houses.

Critical opinion has been divided over whether Gautier's poem represents a re-writing of Marie's *lai*, or whether both works derive more or less independently from a common source which told the story of 'the man with two wives', and featured a protagonist called Eliduc. In the prologue to *Eliduc*, Marie tells us that the story comes from an ancient Breton *lai* which used to be called after its hero, but has now changed its title, and is currently known by the names of its two heroines:

> D'eles deus ad li lai a nun
> Guildeluec ha Gualadun. (*Eliduc* 21-22)

Gautier's source was certainly a *lai*: he describes *Ille et Galeron* in the prologue as a *lai*, and later contrasts it with other *lais* which are too fanciful to be taken seriously:

> Grant cose est d'Ille a Galeron:
> N'i a fantome ne alonge
> Ne ja n'i trovereés mençonge.
> Tex lais i a, qui les entent,
> Se li sanlent tot ensement
> Com s'eüst dormi et songié. (931-36)

Line 931 also gives the work a Breton title (*a* represents Celtic *ha*, 'and') which appears to be modelled on *Guildeluec ha Gualadun*. This does not prove that Gautier knew Marie's *lai*, since her prologue presumably quotes an accepted Breton title for the story, which Gautier could have found in another source. It is nonetheless suggestive, as is the existence of a number of close parallels between episodes in *Ille et Galeron* and the first half of Marie's *lai*.

When Eliduc arrives in England, he comes to the aid of an elderly king who is under attack by another king to whom he has refused to marry his daughter and heiress. The first time Ille arrives in Rome the elderly emperor is at war with another emperor who has designs on his territory; on his second visit, the emperor of Constantinople has invaded Italy again because the Roman emperor's daughter is refusing his hand in marriage. When Eliduc rides out to battle, he is accompanied by fourteen English knights – the same as the number of Breton knights who travel with Galeron on her long journey to look for Ille. After Eliduc's decisive victory over his new master's enemies, a messenger is sent ahead to inform the king of his success, and the monarch honours the knight by coming down from his fortress to greet him. When Ille returns to Rome after defeating the emperor of Constantinople, a messenger precedes him with the good news, and begs the emperor to disregard protocol and come out to greet the man who has saved his empire; this the emperor duly does. Likewise, when Eliduc announces to Guilliadun his intention to return to Brittany, she faints, and he holds her in his arms, lamenting, until she comes round. Faced with the same news, Ganor also faints, and Ille, 'qui mout tres durement s'en deut' (l. 4776), holds her until she regains consciousness. It is worth noting that all of these parallels concern incidental details which do not form part of the narrative core of the story of the man with two wives, and were not therefore bound to appear in other versions of the tale. None is perhaps conclusive in itself, but the cumulative effect of such echoes does lend weight to the argument that *Eliduc* was Gautier's main source.

The relative chronology of the two works adds another dimension to the question. A firm *terminus ad quem* for Marie's *Lais* is either 1189 or 1183, depending on whether the 'nobles reis' to whom the work is dedicated is taken to be Henry II of England, or his son Henry au Cort Mantel, who was crowned during his father's lifetime and pre-deceased him. A number of critics have favoured a dating in the later 1160s for the *Lais*, which is consonant with a reference to their popularity in the *Vie de Seint Edmund le Rei* by Denis Piramus, which has been dated by its editor at around 1170. If Marie's work became as popular in court circles as Piramus claims, then Gautier might well have come in contact with her version of the story of Eliduc while working on *Eracle* for the court of Thibaut de Blois, before embarking on his second romance in the early 1170s. Recent work on *Partonopeus de Blois*, which was composed for the court of Blois, has identified a political subtext to the romance, which sets out to ridicule Henry II by subverting works of literature commissioned by him or associated with his court (see Penny Simons and Penny Eley, 'The Prologue to *Partonopeus de Blois*: text, context and subtext', *French Studies*, XLIX (1995), 1-16). Given that *Ille et Galeron* takes issue with the story of Eliduc in a number of ways, it is tempting to see in Gautier's work another reflection of the political and cultural rivalry between Henry and the house of Blois and their Capetian allies in the early years of the decade.

The balance of probability would therefore seem to be in favour of the view that Gautier knew Marie's *lai*, and that *Ille et Galeron* can usefully be approached as a response to *Eliduc*. Despite their similarities, it is clear that the two works represent fundamentally different conceptions of the story of the man with two wives. Hoepffner, Fourrier (pp. 285-86) and Renzi (1967) all saw *Ille et Galeron* as a moral reinterpretation of Marie's *lai*, explicitly designed to 'improve' on the original. The most obvious difference between the two works is that in Gautier's romance the hero's two relationships are arranged in series rather than in parallel. Ille is never guilty of being unfaithful to his wife either in thought or in deed: he agrees to marry Ganor because he believes that Galeron is dead; when she re-appears, he immediately gives up all claim to Ganor's hand, and to the empire which goes with it, and returns to Brittany with his one true love. Only after Galeron's retirement to a convent has effectively dissolved their marriage do his thoughts turn to Ganor, whom he is then able to marry without relying on others to resolve a moral and legal impasse.

The nature of the hero's relationships is also profoundly different from what we find in *Eliduc*. There, although we are told in the prologue that Eliduc and Guildeluec 's'entramerent leaument' (*Eliduc* l. 12), and although the hero never forgets his promise to remain faithful while he is away, Eliduc is powerless to resist the love which draws him to Guilliadun. A victim of the irrational force of passion, which is represented by Marie as an external force acting on individuals against their will, he is drawn into a web of conflicting loyalties which lead him to break faith with all the important figures in his life. The situation is saved only by the selflessness of Guildeluec, who sacrifices her own love for the hero in order to allow him to marry his *amie*. In the more rational world of *Ille et Galeron*, the hero's love for his wife remains constant throughout. The crisis in their relationship is brought about not by *Amor* but by an accident which intensifies the effect of an inherent flaw in Ille's personality. The resolution of the crisis in *Eliduc* depends on the supernatural, in the form of the weasel's magic herb, as much as on human intervention. In Gautier's romance, Ille is reunited with his wife as a result of undergoing a learning process which allows him to overcome his feelings of inferiority and appreciate the true nature of Galeron's love for him. When she retires from the world in fulfilment of a solemn vow, Ille's relationship with Ganor is free to develop without resulting in a conflict of loyalties. Moreover, unlike Eliduc, Ille is not overcome by passion for the second woman in his life: his love for Ganor has its roots in the pity she inspired in him in Rome, and grows organically from his compassion and his sense of obligation towards her.

The re-organisation of the central love-affairs also allows Gautier to expand the role of the first wife and so realise the potential of the contrasts between her and other characters which are only hinted at in *Eliduc*. Whereas Marie concentrates her attentions on the characterisation of the 'other woman' Guilliadun, Gautier gives a more balanced portrayal of both his heroines, and Galeron remains a central figure for four-fifths of the narrative. Her piety and total trust in her husband form an effective counterpoint both to Ille's self-doubt and to Ganor's very worldly reactions. Ganor herself also becomes a more interesting character than Guilliadun, whose portrayal was determined by the need to evoke audience sympathy for an innocent woman who has been deliberately deceived by the man she loves. Freed from the passive role of victim, Gautier's second heroine can play a more spirited part and add touches of humour to the narrative.

Gautier's desire to improve on his original also helps to explain why his version of the tale is presented as the story of Eliduc's son, rather than a straightforward re-telling of the life of Eliduc himself. If Marie's *lai* was as popular as Denis Piramus suggests, it might have been difficult to gain acceptance for a radically different history of the protagonist. Gautier's strategy seems therefore to have been one of outdoing his model rather than attempting to displace it. How much less effective it would have been to produce a rival Eliduc than to let the original hero continue to exist in the minds of the audience, and then to show him being outclassed by his own offspring! This strategy of *dépassement* may explain why the name Eliduc appears at such regular intervals throughout the romance (the first mention is in line 133; the last in line 6475), and why in 70% of cases it occurs in the formula *Ille, le fil Eliduc*. These constant reminders invite us to compare the careers of father and son, and to see how Ille succeeds where Eliduc had failed. Finding himself the object of a princess's affections in a distant land, Eliduc succumbed to her attractions and set in train a potentially fatal sequence of events. In a similar but more challenging situation, where the princess offers not only beauty but also supreme power, Ille is guided by a moral imperative, rather than by the destructive force of passion. At the critical moment outside St Peter's he is able to make the right choice between fidelity and empire.

The consequences of the re-modelling of Marie's *lai* are perhaps less fortunate in terms of the overall structure of the romance. *Eliduc* is marked by a gradual intensification of the drama from the moment the hero first decides to leave his homeland to the final resolution of his dilemma by the combined forces of magic and wifely devotion. This emotional crescendo is structured around Eliduc's two journeys from England to Brittany: the prospect of the first acts as a catalyst for the hero to commit himself irrevocably to eloping with Guilliadun; during the second she learns the truth about her lover and her apparent death then leads to the discovery of Eliduc's secret by Guildeluec. Gautier's decision to replace the eternal triangle by two successive relationships has the effect of shifting the centre of gravity of the story forwards, with the result that the hero's travels cease to have the same significance. By the time Ille makes his second journey to Rome, all the conflicts have been resolved, and all that remains to be told is the entirely predictable story of how he once more defeats the emperor of Constantinople and claims Ganor as his prize. For the modern reader, the final thousand lines of the romance may be something of an anti-climax compared with the ending of *Eliduc*.

Ille et Galeron and Andreas Capellanus

Another possible intertextual reference is to be found in the *De Amore* of Andreas Capellanus. The seventh chapter of Book II of Andreas's treatise contains a series of twenty-one judgements on matters of love attributed to important noblewomen of the day, such as the countess of Champagne and queen Alienor (Eleanor of Aquitaine). The fifteenth of these judgements concerns the case of a lover who suffers the loss of an eye (or some other part of the body) while fighting valiantly, and who is then spurned by his lady-love as being physically unattractive and unworthy of her. In her judgement, the countess of Narbonne condemns the woman's attitude on the grounds that an injury sustained in war is normally a sign of valour, and as such should inspire love rather than revulsion. The idea of a lover losing an eye in combat is not so remarkable that we need necessarily assume that Andreas was thinking of *Ille et Galeron* when he wrote this judgement (the *De Amore* has been dated at around 1185). As Fourrier argues (pp. 286-87), it is quite possible that cases such as this were widely debated in the courts of northern France, and that Gautier and Andreas both decided independently to include a popular topic in their works. However, the countess's judgement does bear a striking resemblance to the line of argument used by Galeron when she tries to convince Ille that her love for him has not been affected by his injury (ll. 1877-907). Moreover, the fact that the lady in question rejects her lover not only because he is disfigured, but also because she feels that he is no longer worthy of her, is an exact echo of Ille's fears, as expressed in ll. 1920-29 and 3680-87. The evidence does seem to point to the fact that Andreas was familiar with Gautier's work. Although Andreas's initial description of the lover's injury does not say in what context it occurred, the countess's judgement refers to 'the usual hazards of *war*', suggesting that it was the W version of *Ille* which he had in mind, in which the hero is injured in wartime, rather than at a tourney. This is entirely consistent with the views on the dating of the two versions which we have put forward above: by 1185 this revised version would have been in circulation, and, as the more recent of the two, might very well have been enjoying greater currency than its predecessor.

Literary Analysis

It would clearly be impossible to give a complete literary analysis of *Ille et Galeron* in the space available here. This section is therefore designed to give a brief overview of some of the more important questions of interpretation associated with this romance, and to suggest some lines of thought for those who may be approaching it for the first time. Fuller discussions of these and other literary issues can be found in a number of the studies listed in the Bibliography. Comments on structure and thematic content can also be found in many of the notes to the text.

One of the most striking features of the romance is its complete rejection of the *merveilleux*: supernatural elements, whether taken from Celtic mythology or the Christian tradition, are conspicuous by their absence. There is nothing equivalent in this work to the angelic visitations in some of the earlier *chansons de geste* or in Gautier's own *Eracle*, to the magic love-potion of the Tristan legend, or to the quasi-supernatural atmosphere of the *Joie de la Cort* episode in Chrétien's *Erec et Enide*. Much of the action of *Ille et Galeron* may be set in Brittany, but this is not the land of magic and mystery associated with Breton folk-tales: Gautier's Brittany is a thoroughly down-to-earth dukedom, where the hero faces only human enemies, and relies on his own human qualities to overcome them. The exclusion of elements of fantasy and the supernatural appears to stem from a deliberate *prise de position* in relation to the tradition of the *lais*. Near the start of the romance, as we have seen, Gautier commends his version of the story to his audience, and inveighs against tales which seem to bear little relation to reality (see above, p. xxxi). Criticism of other narratives is a standard element in the *romancier*'s 'pitch' to his audience, and often goes no further than contrasting the author's own 'true' version of a story with the corrupt and unreliable accounts put about by others (in the Prologue to *Erec et Enide*, for example, Chrétien de Troyes is content to claim that his *conte* is superior to the versions peddled at court by professional story-tellers, and will therefore outlast them). Gautier's comment on the fantastical nature of the *lais* is unusual, and reveals a fundamental difference of attitude towards the composition of fictional narratives.

In *Ille et Galeron*, rejection of fantasy and the supernatural goes hand-in-hand with a concern for realism which is reflected not only in the action and its physical surroundings, but also in the psychology of the protagonists. The geography of the romance is entirely realistic: all the action is set in familiar locations (Brittany, France and Italy), and the journeys between them reflect twelfth-century itineraries. Ille travels to Rome via Langres, which was a well-established stopping-point on the route down the Rhone valley to Italy. Galeron's fruitless search for Ille takes her on a credible clockwise tour of the countries of northern and central Europe. Battles take place in familiar landscapes of passes and open country, where woods provide cover for a surprise attack, or for a loyal knight to slip away from a band of traitors in search of help. The numbers of men involved are carefully matched to the likely resources of the parties concerned. Ille fights Hoel initially with the twelve companions he has brought from France, who join forces with twenty knights mustered by his uncles; later, when he has had time to rally support, he leads three hundred men out to meet Hoel's army of five hundred. In keeping with the status of the antagonists, and the stakes involved, the war in Italy brings much larger forces into play: after the death of the seneschal, Ille finds himself at the head of an army of ten thousand men, divided into ten companies, while his enemies field ten times that number, organised into thirty *escieles* (ll. 2490-525).

Ille et Galeron is also marked by a series of allusions to contemporary events. In addition to the references to Gautier's patrons, which have been discussed above, Fourrier identified a number of features of the romance which appear to reflect the historical reality of the later twelfth century (pp. 305-12). The two invasions of Italy by the emperor of Constantinople may well have been inspired by the territorial ambitions of the real-life Byzantine emperor Manuel Comnenus, who was engaged in a lengthy power-struggle with the Holy Roman Emperor Frederic Barbarossa from the 1150s onwards. Comnenus had occupied the Italian city of Ancona in 1151, and later allied himself with the Lombard League, who were hostile to Barbarossa. The latter had tried unsuccessfully to regain Ancona in 1167, and again in 1173, before embarking on his major Italian campaign in 1174. If *Ille et Galeron* was indeed being composed in the early 1170s, it provides an accurate reflection of the rivalry between the two emperors, which could have boiled over at any moment into open conflict on Italian soil. Moreover, we learn that Gautier's eastern emperor had married a count's daughter, Ganor's cousin, whom he had mistreated so badly that she died (ll. 5404-06). In 1146 Manuel had married the daughter of the count of Sulzbach, who was related by marriage to Barbarossa himself. Before long, Comnenus was involved in an open affair with one of his wife's nieces, and the unhappy empress died in 1160.

Another example of *vraisemblance* in the romance can be found in the central episode of Ille and Galeron's reunion on the day of the hero's planned marriage to Ganor. Becker observed (p. 134) that Galeron's proposal to withdraw to a convent, thereby leaving her husband free to marry the emperor's daughter, was at variance with ecclesiastical doctrine on the dissolution of marriage. According to canon law, if one spouse entered a religious foundation, after obtaining the full consent of the other, then his or her partner was not free to re-marry, but would be expected either to retire from the world as well, or to remain celibate. Rauhut later noted (pp. 167-68) that in practice re-marriages did sometimes take place in such circumstances, and concluded that Gautier had probably chosen to reflect the practice of his day (when some people did not know – or decided to ignore – official church teachings), rather than adhere to a doctrine which was to some extent theoretical. Fourrier gives several examples of twelfth-century noblemen who re-married after their wives entered convents, and suggests that they were acting in accordance with the older Merovingian law, which had included entry into a religious house, along with leprosy and adultery, as valid grounds for dissolution (pp. 299-300). Galeron's speech implies that it would have been entirely possible for Ille to give his consent to her proposal and then ask the pope to proceed to celebrate his wedding to Ganor. Even allowing for a certain degree of poetic licence in the time-scale envisaged, it is extremely unlikely that Gautier would have dared to associate so important a figure as the pope himself with a practice which was not widely tolerated. In this respect contemporary canon law appears to represent an ideal to which the devout could aspire, whereas Gautier portrays the everyday reality with which his audience were probably more familiar.

Rauhut also drew attention to an important aspect of Gautier's psychological realism, which he described as Ille's 'inferiority complex' (pp. 150-59). This is highlighted on a number of occasions in the first two-thirds of the narrative. When he falls in love with Galeron, the hero's thoughts turn immediately to the difference in rank between them. Despite the fact that he has become arguably the most powerful man in Brittany, and is trusted implicitly by Conain, who has made him his seneschal, Ille's reaction reveals that he is quite lacking in a sense of self-worth. The first words of his monologue are a statement of the impossibility of his being accepted by Galeron:

> Il pense en soi: «Ne li caut mie
> Qu'ele a tel home soit amie.» (1309-10)

He goes on to say that if the duke were to learn of his feelings, he would gain nothing but ill-will in return for his loyal service. Even when this fear is proved utterly groundless by Conain's proposal that Ille should marry his sister, the hero's feelings of inferiority still persist: far from being overjoyed, he declares that Galeron will never agree to have him, given that she has already refused the counts of Anjou and Poitiers, and the duke of Normandy (ll. 1503-06). Her prompt acceptance of Conain's plan proves him wrong again, and the reader might be forgiven for assuming that this would be the end of the matter: marriage signals the end of the hero's *enfances*, and presumably of his youthful insecurities as well. The fact that this is not so underlines Gautier's skill in characterisation: he continues to develop the initial portrait of the hero, and makes Ille's sense of inadequacy into the central dynamic of the intrigue.

After the wedding, Ille's inferiority complex remains latent until it is triggered once more by the loss of his eye. His immediate response to the injury is to hide it from his companions, and then to hide himself from Galeron, in order to avoid the anticipated trauma of being rejected by her. So convinced is he of his own lack of worth that even when Galeron seeks him out and reassures him, he cannot understand that a noblewoman of her rank could accept a disfigured husband and still love him for his intrinsic qualities. He accordingly flees to Rome, where he presents himself to the emperor as a man of no consequence, and is accepted as such. The whole cycle of his life is then repeated, as if the only way he can overcome his insecurity is to go through the same experiences again and learn from their outcome that he is indeed worthy of the love of an exceptional woman. In this respect, *Ille et Galeron* is structurally similar to Chrétien's *Erec et Enide* and to *Partonopeus de Blois*, both of which also present a 'flawed' hero who makes a serious error of judgement, and then has to put himself in a position to redeem it. Through sheer valour and tactical skill Ille rises from *soudeier* to seneschal, attracts the attentions of all the women of Rome, and is eventually accepted as a potential husband by no less a person than the emperor's daughter. His disfigurement makes no difference: he is still a fine-looking man, and Ganor loves him for this, for his valour, and for his modesty (ll. 3211-24 and 3311-26). By the time Ille explains to the pope why he could not initially agree to marry Ganor, he has discovered that, far from spurning him, Galeron left Brittany in search of him, and has not been heard of since. This is the final stage of his re-education: it becomes clear in the course of his conversation with the pope that he now realises that his judgement of Galeron was clouded by his fear of rejection (ll. 3680-99). When Galeron then reappears on the scene, Ille is finally able to accept her profession of love at face value: having learned the hard way to trust her and to trust himself, he returns to Brittany. In a delightfully ironic final touch, when Ille goes to take his leave of Ganor, he tries to console her by saying that he will not be a serious loss to her: after all, he is only the son of Eliduc. He is promptly put in his place by an indignant Ganor, who upbraids him roundly for implying that she attaches more importance to rank than to individual merit. Gautier rounds off the question of his hero's inferiority complex with a gleeful paradox: if an emperor's daughter is prepared to put worth before birth by marrying him, who is Ille to contradict her?

The same kind of psychological realism can be found in the portrayal of Ganor herself. Her reactions to major events in her life are entirely believable, and create a picture of a woman who may not always be sympathetic, but is certainly never two-dimensional. When the date is announced for her marriage to Ille, everyone in Rome criticises the emperor for not allowing people more time to assimilate the news and prepare for the celebrations. Ganor takes quite the opposite view: so impatient is she to be united with the man she loves that she feels nothing but resentment for those who are in favour of delaying the wedding (ll. 3970-79). Her response to Ille's decision to return to Brittany is equally true-to-life: she welcomes the fact that his departure will leave Rome at the mercy of its enemies, since then she will not be the only one who will have to die as a result of Galeron's reappearance (ll. 4594-625). Ganor's behaviour, unlike her rival's, does confirm the truth of popular sayings: her outburst here beautifully illustrates the fact that 'misery loves company' (see above, pp. xxvi-xxvii). Towards the end of the narrative, the vehemence of Ganor's reactions contributes to a rather more positive portrayal of the woman whom the hero is destined to marry. When she is abducted by the ten barons who intend to hand her over to the emperor of Constantinople, Ganor shows considerable spirit: knowing that she has nothing to lose, she denounces them as arrogant traitors, and hints at what their fate would be if Ille got wind of their treachery (ll. 6366-73). The traitors themselves are killed or put to flight when Ille comes to the rescue, but Ganor takes further punitive measures to re-impose her authority in Rome: she has all their strongholds destroyed and their followers banished in an act of exemplary justice.

The decisive role which Ganor plays in stamping out treason is emblematic of the way in which both she and Galeron are portrayed throughout the romance. As Wolfzettel (1988, 1990a) has shown, *Ille et Galeron* is characterised by the concept of feminine *aventure*: Gautier creates active heroines, whose independent adventures parallel – and even rival – those of the hero. After his injury, Ille makes a fairly straightforward journey to Rome to start a new life. Galeron, meanwhile, sets out on a long and arduous quest for him, which represents a symbolic tour of the known world. Once in Rome, Ille seeks employment as a hired soldier, but soon finds himself back in a position of power when he is chosen to replace the dead seneschal. Galeron, too, embarks upon a new career in Rome, but hers is spiritual rather than military: she takes humble lodgings and earns her keep as a seamstress while devoting her thoughts to God. When the opportunity to reclaim her former position as duchess presents itself, her first thought is to withdraw from the world altogether. Ganor, too, sets out on a quest which succeeds only after initial disappointment and great personal hardship. When her lands are threatened by invasion, she travels to Brittany in search of Ille, only to find that he has already left, apparently on a pilgrimage to Compostela. She then returns immediately to Rome, having spent only one day in Brittany before undertaking the long journey home (ll. 5570-71).

The parallels between the journeys undertaken by the three main protagonists are one aspect of a technique of *dédoublement* which forms the basic structure of the narrative. This structure was already present in Gautier's source, but he develops and enhances it with new elements which he did not find in *Eliduc*. Marie's *lai* is built around the hero's love for two women and his two journeys from Brittany to England and back. In *Ille et Galeron* there are two women, and two journeys to Rome, the only difference being that Ille does not return to Brittany

xl

after the second. As we have seen, the hero's travels are also mirrored in the journeys undertaken by Galeron and Ganor: Galeron duplicates his journeys from Brittany to Rome and back, while Ganor repeats the sequence Rome-Brittany-Rome. In addition, Ille's career in Rome is closely modelled on his initial exploits in Brittany. In both instances, the hero's prowess enables him to progress from modest beginnings to the position of seneschal, and then via marriage to the top of the social and political hierarchy (as duke of Brittany, and then emperor of Rome). In both cases his personal qualities win him the love of a close relative of the ruler, who is also heiress to his territory, and the progress of both relationships is interwoven with accounts of double victories over the same opponent (Hoel in Brittany, the emperor of Constantinople in Rome).

The portrayal of love in *Ille et Galeron* represents an amalgam of vernacular literary influences, including a deliberate *prise de position* with regard not only to *Eliduc* (see above, pp. xxxii-xxxiii), but also to concepts associated with the lyric poetry of the troubadours. Gautier is clearly acquainted with ideas about love popularised by the *romans d'antiquité*, particularly *Eneas*. Ille and Galeron both exhibit the reluctance to communicate their feelings which becomes something of a commonplace in twelfth-century romance, and both express their sufferings at the hands of a personified *Amor* in paired monologues marked by a certain rhetorical virtuosity (ll. 1309-72 and 1378-407). The way in which Gautier uses the term *fine amors* (or *amors fine*), on the other hand, reveals a rather more critical attitude towards literary tradition. This expression occurs five times in the romance: twice to describe women's feelings towards Ille (the *puceles* of Rome in l. 2989 and Ganor in l. 3419), once for Ille's feelings for Galeron (l. 4817), and twice in passages of narratorial commentary on the nature of love (ll. 3375 and 5327). It is worth noting that Gautier applies the term *fine amor* only to the love of a husband for his wife, or to the love of unmarried women for a man they hope to marry. The first of the two narratorial interventions in which the term appears is highly didactic in nature: the kind of fidelity which Ille demonstrated in Rome towards the absent Galeron is presented as the 'commandment' of *fine amor*:

> Illes si n'aime mie seus,
> Mais il n'en aime pas que l'une;
> K'amors n'a cose en soi commune,
> Mais que largece et cortoisie,
> Francise et jeu sans vilonie.
> C'est d'amors fine li commans,
> Que on truist çou en tos amans,
> Ne nus n'a çou entirement,
> Que il n'aime parfitement.   (3369-78)

The only love which merits the title of 'true' or 'refined' for Gautier is that which leads to, and thrives within marriage. Unlike Marie de France, who foregrounds a relationship between a married man and another woman, and unlike the troubadours, who celebrate an all-consuming love which is non-marital, if not necessarily adulterous, Gautier makes the centre of gravity of his romance the married couple, whose mutual affection eventually overcomes the forces which threaten to separate them.

Gautier reinforces his drama of marital devotion with a series of narratorial interventions on the subject of love. These bring into play a number of literary *topoi* which, like the proverbial expressions they ressemble, serve to validate the particular by reference to generally-accepted views. Ille and Galeron's monologues are preceded by a long diatribe against contemporary lovers, who are unwilling to wait for their rewards, and make worthless promises to deceive foolish women, who are criticised in turn for distributing their favours too widely and indiscriminately (ll. 1227-308). By making use of the *topos* that 'things aren't what they used to be' in love Gautier indicates that his narrative, which is set in the past, will provide an illustration of what love should be like, and so prepares the reader to accept Ille and Galeron as exemplars. The criticism of promiscuous men and women, who do not know what real love is, implies an ideal of indivisible love which leads us to expect that Eliduc's son will succeed in avoiding the mistakes of his father. Just as Gautier uses a *respit* to prove how exceptional his heroine is, so he also uses a commonplace contrastively to point up the exceptional nature of the love between his two main protagonists. When Ille has to go and take his leave of Ganor before returning to Brittany with his wife, the account of their interview is prefaced by sixteen lines of commentary on the power of love: when aided and abetted by a woman it can undo everything that the combined forces of religion, reason, justice and law can bring against them (ll. 4656-69). This *topos* sets up an expectation that perhaps Ille will not prove immune to Ganor's charms after all, and will be persuaded to abandon the woman to whom he is legally and morally bound. However, despite the best efforts of Ganor and *Amor*, and despite the terrible conflict he experiences between love for his wife and pity for the emperor's daughter, Ille holds firm, and the love of man and wife is seen to triumph over socially disruptive emotions.

Gautier also brings into play the so-called chivalry *topos*, the idea that love and prowess are interdependent, each inspiring and enhancing the other. This is illustrated at a number of points in the hero's development, the effects of his chivalric achievements being more and more clearly presented as his career progresses. To begin with, the *topos* is discreetly invoked when Gautier tells us of the 'mout grant joie' (l. 896) which Ille's initial exploits against Hoel inspire in the duke's sister Galeron. We then learn that he undertakes the fateful joust which costs him his eye 'por s'amie', for whose sake he dare not let a single opponent go unchallenged (ll. 1652-53; Ille's *amie* is, of course, now his wife). The relationship between love and chivalry is temporarily problematised, since the hero's response to the outcome of this joust nearly results in his losing Galeron, but the crisis only serves to open up a new theatre of action in which the *topos* can be shown to operate on a grander scale. During the course of the hero's career in Italy, the link between prowess and love is more clearly stated than before. When Ille takes over as seneschal, he is watched from the Roman stronghold by *puceles* and *dames* who are more interested in his exploits, and more concerned for his welfare, than for those of their brothers or husbands. After leading his troops to victory, he receives an unambiguous welcome from the womenfolk:

> Se il demorast .xv. jours,
> Ne fust pas sofraitex d'amors.　　　　(3057-58)

Ganor had paid little attention to Ille when he first arrrived at her father's court; now that he has proved his worth on the battlefield, she remembers his modest demeanour, and the combination of chivalry and *mesure* begins to attract her also. The more she hears of his achievements, the more she falls in love (ll. 3284-88). The chivalry *topos* is foregrounded even more explicitly in the monologue in which the hero reflects on the news from Brittany that Galeron is missing, presumed dead. There it is combined with the idea of the decline of social mores to form a lament for a lost world:

> «Chevalier gabent mais d'amors
> Et tornent tout a jouglerie;
> Si fu peruec cevalerie
> Par amors primes maintenue
> Et avoee et retenue,
> Et furent par amor espris
> D'aquerre honor et los et pris.»　　(3915-21)

Ille himself is destined to restore this golden age of chivalry, both by inspiring love through his actions and by undertaking deeds of prowess because of the love he feels, first for Galeron, and then for Ganor. When he becomes aware of his growing love for Ganor, Ille's thoughts turn immediately to action, and he determines to fight the emperor of Constantinople on her behalf (ll. 5673-80). Thus inspired, he makes short work of his old enemy, and his marriage to Ganor inaugurates a new empire, whose success is guaranteed by a return to the proper values of love and chivalry.

We cannot leave the question of chivalry without looking briefly at the battle scenes which are such a notable feature of the version of *Ille et Galeron* preserved in MS P. Over 2,100 lines out of a total of 6,616 in this edition (which includes 24 missing lines taken from W) are devoted to descriptions of warfare, first in Brittany, and then in Italy. Burgess takes issue with critics such as Fourrier and Lefèvre, who dismissed Gautier's battle scenes as little more than padding, devoid of any intrinsic interest. As he points out, they are in fact very carefully constructed, and form an integral part of the process of developing the hero's characterisation and the theme of personal merit (pp. 344-49) . Suspense is used to very good effect in the first battle in Brittany: Hoel's surprise attack on Ille's uncles makes us wonder whether Ille will arrive in time to help them; when he does arrive, the disparity between his forces and his opponents' maintains the sense of danger. The decisive confrontation between Ille and Hoel is skilfully delayed until after the hero has been to Conain's court, and both sides have mustered much larger armies, thereby providing a more dramatic backdrop for the combat. Ille's double victory over his old enemy establishes his credentials as a fighter and tactician, whose youth is no bar to his winning the seneschalcy and bringing peace and justice to Brittany. Likewise, the war in Italy provides an opportunity for Gautier to interweave dramatic cameos of individual combats with passages of direct speech which emphasise the hero's moral as well as his military superiority. To begin with, Ille asks the seneschal for some second-hand arms so that he can join the Roman army as it marches out to meet the forces of the emperor of Constantinople. His decisive taking of the first spoils then leads in to a conversation in which the seneschal attempts to discover the true identity of the mysterious poor knight. A second, and even more impressive, feat brings an urgent request for advice on tactics, which are successfully adopted. Next day, the death of the seneschal prompts the Romans to ask Ille to take his place; the course of the battle under his leadership is then described in detail, punctuated by his exhortations to his troops (ll. 2772-802) and the prayers of the watching Roman womenfolk (ll. 2946-65). By alternating descriptions of combats with dialogue and monologue, Gautier builds up a vivid counterpoint of action and reaction, through which the motif of Ille's steady rise in the estimation of his fellows runs like a unifying thread.

As Leon has noted (p.2), this foregrounding of the idea of personal merit is one of the most distinctive features of *Ille et Galeron*. The narrative is structured in such a way as to draw attention to the theme by reduplicating the process whereby the hero achieves success through his own efforts, and because of his own intrinsic qualities. At the beginning Ille has nothing: the son of a minor nobleman, exiled from his homeland, he is dependent on the king of France for his survival. As he grows up, his valour earns him a privileged position at the French court, where his modesty marks him out as an exemplar of *haute chevalerie*. When the king offers to reward his service with a gift of land, Ille refuses, choosing rather to return to his native land and win back his father's possessions. This is the first of two occasions on which Ille voluntarily foregoes the advantages his prowess has earned him, and begins to prove himself afresh. From being leader of a small band of foreign knights entering hostile territory, he then moves on to command a force of three hundred of his countrymen, before becoming seneschal, and ultimately duke, of Brittany. After his injury, in self-imposed exile, Ille presents himself to the Romans as 'uns pauvres hom' (l. 2167), who has never achieved even the status of a knight. Once again, he rises to the rank of seneschal, and thence to the highest position in the land.

Prowess is central to the hero's success, but it is not the whole story: throughout the romance we are reminded that Ille may be the supreme aggressor on the field of battle, but off it he is also a model of wisdom, courtesy, modesty, generosity, charity, and justice. These qualities are stressed at the very beginning of the work, when Ille's performance in tourneys is contrasted with his social behaviour:

> Si n'a el monde plus humain,
> Si franc, si douç, si debonaire
> Ne qui si voelle autrui bien faire
> Tres l'eure qu'il est desarmés.   (210-13)

They are highlighted again in Rome: after defeating the Greeks, Ille distinguishes himself for his hospitality (ll. 3269-70) and for feeding and clothing the poor, supporting orphans and obtaining justice for widows (ll. 3784-99).

Personal merit thus becomes a fundamental value in the conceptual world which Gautier creates in this romance. Its primacy over both wealth and rank is sanctioned by two marriages, both of which are actively sought by the hero's feudal superiors, and both of which see him displacing suitors of higher status than himself. In both cases, too, the woman involved vigorously defends her right to love on the basis of worth rather than birth. When trying to imagine how her brother would react if he knew that she wanted to marry Ille, Galeron's first thought is that he would be outraged, because of the difference in status between her and the seneschal. She then immediately presents the counter-argument:

> Lors se repense et dist: «Comment
> Te donroit il plus hautement?

Cis li a mis en pais sa tere
Et apaisie mainte guerre.»   (1399-402)

Here, recognition of personal worth is portrayed as an integral part of the ruler's duty of gratitude towards those who have served him well. Later, in Rome, Galeron herself recognises that Ille's exceptional qualities give him the right to marry the emperor's daughter, irrespective of his parentage (ll. 4084-88). The claims of individual merit are expressed even more forcefully by Ganor, in words which could serve as an epigraph for the whole romance:

«A cascun en son cuer demore
Por coi on l'aville u honore:
Ne li vient mie de plus long;
On ne li quiert autre tesmong.»   (4719-22)

The hero's irresistible rise to power also highlights an important political dimension in *Ille et Galeron*, which is entirely absent from Marie de France's *Eliduc*. In Marie's *lai* there is no progression: the social status of the male protagonist remains exactly the same at the end as it was at the beginning. By contrast, Gautier's romance is not simply an exploration of emotional conflicts, but also, as Castellani has shown, a story about the debasement of political power and its regeneration by a new type of leader (pp. 26-29). On four occasions the hero finds himself in a situation where the absence or failure of authority has led to a breakdown of social structures; on each occasion he becomes the agent by which the proper functioning of society is restored. He is exiled from Brittany as a boy because Conain is too weak to protect him against Hoel, who usurps the duke's authority and uses his military might to settle his own scores. Ille's victorious return allows those who had supported Hoel 'por soufraite de signeur' (l. 857) to ally themselves once more with a legitimate source of power; as a result, peace is restored, and the 'evil customs' (l. 1209) which are symptomatic of a dysfunctional society are abolished. Likewise, when Ille arrives in Rome, the empire is under attack because its ruler is too old and weak to provide effective leadership. The mockery to which Ille is subjected, both by the emperor and by members of his court, illustrates the degree to which Rome has neglected the fundamental values of *courtoisie*. By turning the tables on the *gabeors* through his prowess and courtliness, Ille opens the way for a renewal of those values and a restoration of the proper authority which they underpin. Moreover, he is shown to be an agent of renewal at the individual level as well as on the broader political scene: as seneschal of Rome his good example inspires people to reform their lives and abandon sin (ll. 3826-30).

The dynamics of power in *Ille et Galeron* are not unproblematic, however. In Gautier's story the hero is given conflicting political responsibilities, possibly as a way of compensating for the loss of emotional intensity which results from his love-affairs being placed in sequence rather than in parallel, as they were in *Eliduc*. Ille's success in Rome takes place against a background of turmoil in Brittany. His departure, which leads in turn to Galeron's abandoning her duchy in favour of a life of penitence, leaves a political vacuum which has disastrous consequences for the people of Brittany. The situation becomes even worse with the subsequent death of Conain. Ille himself is shown to be well aware of his role in the destruction of Brittany, and of the effects of the failure of proper authority:

> Illes entent et set mout bien
> Que il mesoirre d'une rien,
> C'est ce dont plus se desconforte:
> Set que Bretagne est tote morte
> Et que li dus Conains est mors,
> Et taut au foible li plus fors
> Canques bons sires doit tenser.   (4450-56)

Likewise, when he returns to his homeland as a *bon sire* to restore order, the people of Rome predict that his absence will lead to chaos and destruction. This prediction eventually comes true when the emperor of Constantinople takes advantage of the fact that the death of his counterpart has left Rome even more vulnerable than before, ruled by a woman without a husband. Ille's promise to return to help Ganor whenever he is needed sets up a potentially interesting tension between the claims of Brittany and those of Rome: how is the hero to fulfil his role as the symbol of order and stability in both communities if his absence from one always seems to bring political upheaval in its wake? However, this tension is never fully exploited by Gautier: at the end of the romance the hero's responsibilities towards Brittany are allowed to fade quietly from view as he succeeds Ganor's father as emperor in Rome. It is never made clear whether Ille's elder son is of an age to be installed as duke of Brittany, or indeed whether he and his siblings return to their homeland after visiting their father in Rome. In the end, though, Ille's accession to the throne brings the themes of individual merit and political renewal to such a satisfying conclusion that it is probably churlish to ask for every loose end to be tied up. As Wolfzettel (1990b, 1992) points out, Rome is not simply a wealthy city and the heart of an empire: it symbolises universal values, both temporal and spiritual. Ille's return as emperor represents the beginning of a new universal order, grounded in the values of faith, chivalry and charity which he embodies.

The Edition

The text of this edition is that of MS P, corrected where necessary by reference to W. There have been three previous editions of MS P, all of which are unsatisfactory for one reason or another. Those by Löseth and Foerster predate the discovery of MS W, and so are necessarily incomplete. Despite the fact that the discovery of W confirmed many of Löseth's emendations (Foerster's were shown to have been less judicious), his edition cannot be regarded as a suitable basis for critical study of the romance because of the way in which he 'regularised' the language of the MS. The usefulness of the recent edition by Lefèvre is also limited by the fact that the text was never fully corrected by the editor (whose untimely death led to the volume being published posthumously by colleagues). Although certain sections of Lefèvre's text are accurate and carefully transcribed, others contain numerous mistranscriptions, unconscious emendations and unacknowledged borrowings from W. I have identified some 190 errors and/or emendations which do not appear in the list of rejected readings, in addition to over 100 lines where readings from W are adopted in preference to P without sufficient justification. Moreover, Lefèvre's edition presents a hybrid text, which incorporates substantial extracts from W 'pour préciser le récit'. If, as I have argued, Gautier himself produced two versions of his romance – the original, represented by P, and a revised, shorter, version represented by W – there can be no justification for a modern editor to produce a third version, incorporating elements of both. The text of W is available in a good modern edition by Cowper; I have therefore chosen to present the text of P as it stands in the MS, with a minimum of alterations. Where P is obviously corrupt, I have corrected the text by reference to W, or to Löseth (primarily for those passages which do not figure in W), and occasionally Lefèvre. The rejected P readings, together with the source of the corrections, are indicated at the foot of each page of text. I have also made a very small number of my own emendations, where these appeared to be justified: these are discussed in the notes to the text. Where lines are clearly missing from P (i.e. where there is an incomplete couplet, an obvious non-sequitur, or where there is a reference in the immediate context to something which must have been present in the original), I have supplied from W the minimum number of lines necessary to create a coherent text. I have borrowed Lefèvre's convention of printing such lines in italics and numbering them 131a, 131b, etc. so as not to disrupt the numbering of the MS. If P makes sense as it stands, even if W may appear to make better sense, or to be more elegantly phrased, I have retained the P reading, on the grounds that the W reading may represent an authorial revision of the original text.

In other respects, I have adhered to normal editorial conventions: letters omitted in the MS are reinstated in brackets [ ], while superfluous characters are placed within parentheses ( ). The abbreviation *mlt* has been rendered throughout by *mout*; other abbreviations have been expanded in the normal way. Numerals, however, are retained where they appear in the MS. Word division is somewhat erratic in MS P; I have regularised it wherever the original text might be confusing for readers who are not familiar with the vagaries of scribal practice. For the same reason, I have corrected obvious case errors, including the omission of final *s* from feminine plural nouns. Effacement of pre-consonantal *s* meant that the scribe did not distinguish consistently between *dit* (present tense) and *dist* (simple past). Given that there is frequent tense switching throughout the text, I have corrected *dit* and *dist* only where all the other verbs in the immediate context are in the past or the present respectively, and a change of tense is highly unlikely to have been intended (e.g. l. 3335).

The Translation

Translating medieval texts is a hazardous enterprise. In the first place, translators face the problem of establishing exactly what the original text means, without the benefit of reference to native speakers. In the second, they have to decide how much or how little knowledge of medieval life and culture they can assume in their readers. I make no claims fully to have understood every phrase used in MS P of *Ille et Galeron*, but have tried in the notes to alert readers to potentially difficult passages, and to provide an explanation for my choice of translation where more than one version appears to be possible. The notes also provide a certain amount of background information, designed to help non-specialists understand such things as coinage, the divisions of the medieval day and the logistics of jousting. The translation itself attempts to remain reasonably close to the distinctive style and structures of the original without too great a sacrifice of readability. I have not, however, reproduced Gautier's habit (which he shares with most other *romanciers*) of shifting rapidly between the present, perfect and simple past tenses in passages of narrative. Instead, I have put the whole story into the past tense. Once or twice, this produced confusion as to whether an isolated past tense in a passage narrated in the present in the Old French should be rendered by the simple past or by the pluperfect in English, but I felt that an occasional uncertainty was preferable to the disconcerting effect that tense-switching in prose can have on modern readers.

Bibliography

Full details of all the critical works on *Ille et Galeron* referred to in the Introduction can be found here. Individual items by authors for whom more than one work is listed are identified in the text by the date of publication, e.g. Renzi (1964); where two items have the same date of publication, the letter *a* after the date indicates the first of the two items listed in the bibliography, and the letter *b* the second.

Editions

Oeuvres de Gautier d'Arras, edited by E. Löseth, 2 vols, II, *Ille et Galeron*, Bibliothèque française du moyen âge (Paris: Bouillon, 1890).

Ille und Galeron von Walter von Arras, edited by Wendelin Foerster, Romanische Bibliothek, 7 (Halle: Niemeyer, 1891).

Ille et Galeron par Gautier d'Arras, edited by Frederick A. G. Cowper, SATF (Paris: Picard, 1956).

Gautier d'Arras, *Ille et Galeron*, edited by Yves Lefèvre, CFMA, 109 (Paris: Champion, 1988).

Translations

Gythiel, Anthony P., '*Ille et Galeron* and *Eracle*: two twelfth-century French romances, translated with an introduction', unpublished Ph.D. thesis, University of Detroit, 1971.

Ray, Ashton Laurent, 'A Translation and Criticism of *Ille et Galeron* by Gautier d'Arras', unpublished Ph.D. thesis, University of South Carolina, 1974.

Gautier d'Arras, *Ille et Galeron*, traduit en français moderne par Jean-Claude Delclos et Michel Quereuil, Traductions des CFMA, 51 (Paris: Champion, 1993).

Studies

van Acker, G., 'Gautier d'Arras, le plus ancien trouvère du nord de la France', *Revue du Nord*, XLIII (1967), 273-79.

Batany, Jean, '"Home and Rome", a Device in Epic and Romance: *Le Couronnement de Louis* and *Ille et Galeron*', *Yale French Studies*, LI (1975), 42-60.

Becker, Philipp August, 'Gautier d'Arras', in *Der altfranzösische Roman*, edited by

Erich Köhler (Darmstadt: Wissenschaftliche Buchgesellschaft, 1978), pp. 112-41 (reprinted from 'Von den Erzählern neben und nach Chrestien de Troyes', *Zeitschrift für romanische Philologie*, LV (1935), 269-92).

Beckmann, Gustav Adolf, 'Der Tristandichter Thomas und Gautier d'Arras', *Romanistisches Jahrbuch*, XIV (1963), 87-104.

Burgess, Glyn S., 'The Theme of Chivalry in *Ille et Galeron*', *Medieovo romanzo*, XIV (1989), 339-62.

Calin, William C., 'On the Chronology of Gautier d'Arras', *Modern Language Quarterly*, XX (1959), 181-96.

Castellani, Marie-Madeleine, 'La cour et le pouvoir dans les romans de Gautier d'Arras', *Bien dire et bien aprandre*, VIII (1990), 19-34.

Cowper, Frederick A.G., 'The New Manuscript of *Ille et Galeron*', *Modern Philology*, XVIII (1920-21), 601-08.

— 'The Sources of *Ille et Galeron*', *Modern Philology*, XX (1922-23), 35-44.

— 'Gautier d'Arras and Provins', *Romanic Review*, XXII (1931), 291-300.

— 'More Data on Gautier d'Arras', *PMLA*, LXIV (1949), 302-16.

— 'Supplementary Material on Gautier d'Arras', *Bibliographical Bulletin of the International Arthurian Association*, VI (1954), 110.

— 'Origins and Peregrinations of the Laval-Middleton manuscript', *Nottingham Medieval Studies*, III (1959), 3-18.

— 'Chronology of Chrétien de Troyes and Gautier d'Arras', *Bibliographical Bulletin of the International Arthurian Association*, XII (1960), 137.

Delbouille, Maurice, 'A propos des rimes familières à Chrétien de Troyes et à Gautier d'Arras (signification de la fréquence relative des "rimes répétées")', *Etudes de langue et de littérature du Moyen Age offertes à Félix Lecoy* (Paris: Champion, 1973), 55-65.

Eley, Penny, 'Patterns of Faith and Doubt: Gautier d'Arras's *Eracle* and *Ille et Galeron*', *French Studies*, XLIV (1989), 257-70.

Fourrier, Anthime, *Le courant réaliste dans le roman courtois en France au Moyen Age*, I (Paris: Nizet, 1960), especially pp. 179-313.

Greenwood, J.M., 'The Sources of *Ille et Galeron*', unpublished M.A. thesis, University of Manchester, 1956.

Haidu, Peter, 'Narrativity and Language in Some XIIth Century Romances', *Yale French Studies*, LI (1974), 132-46.

Heimer, Helge W., 'Etude sur la langue de Gautier d'Arras', doctoral dissertation, Lund, 1921.

Heinermann, Theodor, 'Zur Zeitbestimmung der Werke Gautiers von Arras und zu seiner Stellung zu Chrétien de Troyes', *Zeitschrift für französische Sprache und*

Literatur, LIX (1935), 237-45.

Hoeppfner, Ernest, 'Le roman d'*Ille et Galeron* et le lai d'*Eliduc*', in *Studies in French Language and Medieval Literature presented to Mildred K. Pope* (Manchester: Manchester University Press, 1939), pp. 125-44.

Hüppe, Wilhelm, 'Der Sprachstil Gautiers von Arras', doctoral dissertation, Westfälische Wilhelmsuniversität Münster, Bochum, 1937.

Lefèvre, Yves, Guy Raynaud de Lage & Robert Anderson, 'Autres romans du XIIe siècle b)', in *Grundriss der romanischen Literaturen des Mittelalters, IV.1: Le Roman jusqu'à la fin du XIIIe siècle*, edited by J. Frappier & R. R. Grimm (Heidelberg: Winter, 1978), pp. 269-74.

Leon, Chiara, 'Chrétien de Troyes, Gautier d'Arras et les débuts de roman', unpublished Ph.D. thesis, Brown University, 1981.

Lot, Ferdinand, 'Une source historique d'*Ille et Galeron*', *Romania*, XXV (1896), 585-88.

Matzke, John E., 'The Source and Composition of *Ille et Galeron*', *Modern Philology*, IV (1906-1907), 471-88.

— 'The Lay of Eliduc and the Legend of the Husband with Two Wives', *Modern Philology*, V (1907-1908), 211-39.

Nightingale, Phyllis O., 'Contemporary Life as Portrayed in the Works of Gautier d'Arras', unpublished M.A. thesis, University of London, 1953.

Nykrog, Per, 'Two Creators of Narrative Form in Twelfth Century France: Gautier d'Arras - Chrétien de Troyes', *Speculum*, XLVIII (1973), 258-76.

Offord, M.H., 'Etude comparative du vocabulaire de *Cligés* de Chrétien de Troyes et d'*Ille et Galeron* de Gautier d'Arras', *Cahiers de Lexicologie*, XXXIV (1979), 36-52.

Payen, Jean-Charles, 'Compte rendu de Lorenzo Renzi, *Tradizione cortese et realismo in Gautier d'Arras*', *Le Moyen Age*, LXXIV (1968), 344-49.

Pierreville, Corinne, 'Le couple et le double dans les romans de Gautier d'Arras', in *Arras au Moyen Age: histoire et littérature*, edited by Marie-Madeleine Castellani (Arras: Artois Presses Unversité, 1994), pp. 97-109.

Rauhut, Franz, 'Das Psychologische in den Romanen Gautiers von Arras', in *Der altfranzösische Roman*, edited by Erich Köhler (Darmstadt: Wissenschaftliche Buchgesellschaft, 1978), pp. 142-69 (reprinted from *Wissenschaftliche Zeitschrift der Friedrich-Schiller Universität Jena*, V (1955-56), 343-52).

Renzi, Lorenzo, '"Amore" in Gautier d'Arras', *Mélanges Balduino Bianchi* (Padua: CEDAM, 1962), pp. 5-7.

— *Tradizione cortese e realismo in Gautier d'Arras* (Padua: CEDAM, 1964).

— 'Le décor celtisant dans *Ille et Galeron*', *Cahiers de civilisation médiévale*, X (1967), 39-44.

Rychner, Jean, 'Compte rendu de Lorenzo Renzi, *Tradizione cortese et realismo in Gautier d'Arras'*, *Cahiers de civilisation médiévale*, IX (1966), 249-51.

Schnell, Rüdiger, 'Von der kanonistischen zur höfischen Ehekasuistik. Gautiers d'Arras *Ille et Galeron'*, *Zeitschrift für romanische Philologie*, XCVIII (1982), 257-95.

Schulze-Busacker, E., 'Proverbes et expressions proverbiales chez Chrétien de Troyes, Gautier d'Arras et Hue de Rotelande', *Incidences*, V (1981), 7-16.

— *Proverbes et expressions proverbiales dans la littérature narrative du moyen âge français*, Nouvelle Bibliothèque du Moyen Age, 9 (Geneva & Paris: Slatkine, 1985), especially pp. 64-75.

Sheldon, E.S., 'On the Date of *Ille et Galeron'*, *Modern Philology*, XVII (1919-20), 383-92.

Spensley, R.M., 'The Meaning of Ille's "desmesure"', *Romanische Forschungen*, LXXXIV (1972), 585-87.

Stevenson, William M., 'Der Einfluss des Gautier d'Arras auf die altfranzösischen Kunstepos, insbesondere auf den Abenteuerroman', doctoral dissertation, Georg-August Universität Göttingen, 1910.

Warren, F.M., 'Some Features of Style in Early French Narrative Poetry', *Modern Philology*, III (1905-06), 179-209 and 513-39; IV (1906-07), 655-75.

Wolfzettel, Friedrich, 'Wahrheit der Geschichte und Wahrheit der Frau: *honor de feme* und weibliche *aventure* im altfranzösischen Roman', *Zeitschrift für romanische Philologie*, CIV (1988), 197-217.

— 'La découverte de la femme dans les romans de Gautier d'Arras', *Bien dire et bien aprandre*, VIII (1990), 35-54.

— 'La recherche de l'universel. Pour une nouvelle lecture des romans de Gautier d'Arras', *Cahiers de civilisation médiévale*, XXXIII (1990), 114-31.

— 'Rom und die Anfänge des altfranzösischen Romans. Liebe, Religion und Politik bei Gautier d'Arras' in *Rom im hohen Mittelalter. Studien zu den Romvorstellung und zur Rompolitik vom 10. bis zum 12. Jahrhundert*, edited by Bernhard Schimmelpfennig & Ludwig Schmugge (Sigmaringen: Thorbecke, 1992), pp. 139-63.

Wilmotte, Maurice, *L'évolution du roman français aux environs de 1150* (Paris: Bouillon, 1903).

— 'Problèmes de chronologie littéraire', *Le Moyen Age*, XL (1940), 99-114.

Chi commence d'Ille et de Galeron[1]

Aïe Dius, Sains Esperis!
K'a le millor empererris
Qui onkes fust, si com je pens,
Otroi mon service et mon sens.
5 Tel me convient: atempreüre
Voel metre en ceste troveüre
Et trover atempreement,
Mais que de loer seulement
Celi qui a honour enclose.
10 Çou est la letre, mes la glose
Puet on atorner faussement
Sor cui c'on veut; mes longement

15 Ne se tient nule doreüre
A envers d'une laveüre.
Por Diu, que monte ne que vaut?
Ne sai por coi nus se travaut
Por cose qui fausse en la fin;
Mais la ou Dix mist tant de fin
Com en l'empererris de Rome
20 Doivent entendre angele et home
Et proier Diu et jour et nuit
Qu'ele n'ait rien qui li anuit.
    Gautiers ichi endroit semont
    Toutes les dames de ce mont

Here begins the story of Ille and Galeron[1]

May God and the Holy Ghost help me! For I am dedicating my service and my wit to the empress who, to my mind, is the best who ever lived. As such, she is a fitting choice for me: I intend to make this a moderate composition and compose with moderation, with the one exception of praising the lady who has made honour her own. That is the text, but it may be glossed falsely in favour of whomsoever you wish; but no gilding lasts for long without coming off in the wash. In God's name, what is it worth, what value does it have? I do not understand why anyone should put himself to great trouble for something which may prove false in the end; but angels and men should turn their thoughts to the lady whom God endowed with so much excellence – that is the empress of Rome – and pray to God night and day that no harm may come to her.

Here and now Gautier calls upon all the noblewomen of this world

---

[1] In P the hero's name is usually abbreviated to a single capital letter. When given in full, it is spelt either with an I (e.g. l. 1596), or with a Y (e.g. l. 1650); the first spelling has been adopted for both text and translation. The abbreviated form has been expanded throughout, with flexional s being added where appropriate.

25 K'eles aient de lui envie:
Example pregnent a sa vie.
Bien i doivent prendre examplaire,
Car en li n'a rien a desplaire
N'en son sage contenement
30 Ne en son bel maintenement
N'en son savoir n'en sa proece
N'en sa bonté n'en sa largece.
Tant mainte dame ai ja trovee
Qui de grans biens est esprovee;
35 Moi ne caut, car n'i a celi
Qui s'aparaut de rien a li,
Ne que li coevres a fin or.
D'Onor a garni son tresor,
Et Cortoisie et Porveance
40 L'ont consillie tres enfance.
Tant li a Sens mis en l'orelle
K'a ces .ii. dames se conselle:
Adés le gaite Cortoisie
Qu'ele ne face vilonie;
45 Et Porveance li est prés,
Par cui consel ele oevre adés.
Par Sapience, sa compaigne,
Agencist le cuer d'Alemagne,
Qu'il est trestous entalentés
50 De faire adiés ses volentés.
Ele ne veut se tout bien non,
Et trestuit le servent par non;
Tos li avoirs a lui s'adrece
Et ele en paist sa grant largece.

55 La dame est mout senee et sage
Et ce li vient bien de parage,
Car de Viane furent né
Del siecle tout li plus sené,
Li plus jentil, li plus haut home.
60 Apostole ont esté de Rome,
Si ont esté empereür
Et roi, ce sevent li pluiseur,
De maint roiame, et d'outremer
Dont Dix se fist ja roi clamer.[1]
65 Mout furent haut, mes la lignie
Par cesti n'est pas engignie,
Car de si haute signorie
N'est dame, quel ke nus en die.
Rome le vit ja coroner,[2]
70 Qui nos en puet tesmong doner.
Rome est de grant antiquité,
Et ki dame est de la chité
Ne puet avoir si grant hautece,
Car Rome est de si grant noblece;
75 Mais ele, qui s'i corona,
Au jour plus d'oneur li dona
Que Rome ne li pot doner
De le corone abandoner.
Mout ama Dix honor de feme
80 Quant nestre fist si bele geme,
Se por ce non que lor vallance
Pert mains et mains a d'aparance
Par l'honeur qu'en cesti s'aüne;
Car du solel palist la lune,

54 grans]Lö   82 peu mains]Lö   83 Par honeur]Lö

2

to feel envious of her: let them take her life as a model. They would do well to model themselves on her, for there is nothing displeasing about her, either in her judicious conduct or in her fine demeanour, in her knowledge or her worth, in her goodness or her generosity. I have already encountered many a lady of great and proven virtues; it makes no difference to me, for there is none who in any way compares with her, any more than copper compares with pure gold. She has set Honour to guard her treasure, and Courtliness and Prudence have been her counsellors since childhood. Good Judgement has had her ear for so long that she takes counsel from these two ladies: Courtliness always keeps a watch on her, so that she may not do anything uncourtly, and Prudence, whose advice always guides her actions, is never far from her side. (47) Through her companion Wisdom she won the heart of Germany, inspiring in it a great eagerness to carry out her every wish. Nothing she wants is other than wholly good, and everyone serves her as they should; all wealth gravitates towards her, and she uses it to feed her great generosity. There is no doubt that this lady inherits her great good sense and her wisdom from her noble family; for the very wisest, noblest and most eminent men in the world were born into the house of Vienne. They have been popes in Rome, and emperors and kings, as many people know, of many realms, including the Holy Land, of which God once had Himself proclaimed king.[1] (65) They were very eminent men, yet this lady is no disgrace to the lineage, for there is no other lady of such high nobility, whatever anyone may say. For this, we have the testimony of Rome, which in recent years[2] witnessed her coronation. Rome is of great antiquity, and whoever is lady of the city cannot equal its eminence, so great is Rome's nobility; but this lady, who was crowned there, bestowed more honour on Rome that day than Rome could bestow on her by yielding the crown to her. God showed great love for woman's honour when he brought so fine a gem into being, except in so far as other women's worth is less apparent and less in evidence because of the honour which is concentrated in her; for the moon pales before the sun,

---

[1] The empress Beatrice was the daughter and heiress of Count Renaud III of Burgundy, whose domain was also known as the *regnum Viennense* or kingdom of Vienne. Beatrice was related to the popes Calixtus II and Leo IX, to the Holy Roman Emperors Conrad, Henry III, Henry IV and Henry V, and to Godefroy de Bouillon, who was elected to be the first ruler of the Latin kingdom of Jerusalem at the end of the 1st Crusade (1096-99). Godefroy actually refused the title of king, but his brother Baldwin, who succeeded him in 1100, was crowned, so Gautier's reference is correct.

[2] See Introduction, pp. xx-xxi.

85 De la lune palist l'estole,
Del cler jor palist la candoile,
Et li argens de l'or requit;
Et si est voirs si com je quit.
Mout fu a grant honor voee
90 Rome a cel jour que fu doee
Et [de] la dame et de son per.[1]
Rome est et ert tous jors nonper:
Si est et ert l'empererris
De dames par nies uns affis.[2]
95 Et dient pluisor par envie
Que ciex Gautiers n'esgarde mie
Le pooir que les autres ont,
Qui petis est, et petit font.
Si fas; mes s'ele ert castelaine,
100 Si seroit envers li vilaine
Le plus cortoise et le plus sage
Que j'onques vi en mon eage.
Ele a pooir a grant plenté,
Mais ele a plus de volenté;
105 Plus puet que nule que on truist,
Et si veut plus qu'ele ne puist.
Por grant pooir et por honeur
Est vis que largece ait meneur;
Mais se largece est si tres grans
110 Que ses pooirs est mains parans.
Mout par se set bel contenir:
Devant li pueent tot venir,
Mais naient si qu'il s'i apuient
N'ele sor ex; aillors s'estuient,
115 As autres aillent consillier,
Parler, jangler et orillier.

Ele preste mout bien s'orelle
117a *Tant come Honors loe et conselle,*
C'autre querele ne reqeut;
De lonc paraut, qui parler velt.
120 Riens ne li vient en volenté
Qui soit contre sa dignité;
Sa volenté rien ne li done
Qui soit encontre la corone.
Ice tesmoignent de sa vie
125 Trestot, fors solement Envie,
Qui a honie se tendroit
S'ele perdoit en li son droit,
Qu'ele art de maltalent et d'ire
Quant ele ot d'ome nul bien dire;
130 Dont est bien drois que de doel fonde
Por la millor de tout le monde.
131a *Servir le voel si com jo sai,*
131b *Car a s'onor voel faire .i. lai*
De Galeron, seror le duc,
Et d'Ille le fil Eliduc.
Or m'en puisse Dix avancier![3]
135 Saciés que .ii. Bretagnes sont
Et gens diverses i estont:
Li Englois sont en le grignor,
Mais li Normant en sont signor;
En la menor sont li Breton.
140 Uns dus l'ot ja; Conains ot non
Et Galerons sa suer estoit.
La bele mout bel se vestoit;
Ce convenoit a se faiture,
Car mout ert bele creature:

---

90 A Rome au jour]Lö   97 font]Lö   134 inserted after 131   140 Corains]W

4

the star pales before the moon, the candle pales before full daylight, and silver before pure gold; and this is the truth as I see it. Rome was destined for great honour on the day when she was endowed with the lady and with her match.[1] Rome is and always will be without equal: so too the empress is and will be Rome's unchallenged counterpart among noblewomen.[2] Many people say out of envy that this man Gautier takes no account of others who enjoy less power and so achieve less. I do; but even if she were only a chatelaine, the wisest and most courtly lady I ever saw in my life would be a peasant in comparison with her. She enjoys a great deal of power, but her desire to do good is more powerful still; she is able to do more than any lady you might come across, and yet she wants to do more than she is able to. (107) On account of her great power and her honour, it may seem that her generosity is less impressive; but her generosity is so outstanding that it eclipses her power. She is fully aware of how to conduct herself properly: everyone may have an audience with her, on condition that they are not too familiar with her nor she with them; such people can find themselves a niche elsewhere – let them go and do their whispering, their prattling, their gossiping and their ear-wagging with others. She lends a very willing ear *as long as Honour approves and advises her to,* but does not entertain other suits; whoever wishes to speak with her must keep his distance. She does not entertain any wish which is inconsistent with her position; no wish of hers leads to anything detrimental to the crown. (124) Everyone bears witness to this in relation to the way she lives, with the one exception of Envy, who would consider it a disgrace if, in this case, she were to forfeit her right to burn with resentment and anger whenever she hears anything good said of someone; it is right and proper, therefore, that she should break down in despair on account of the most virtuous lady in the whole world. *I wish to serve her as I know best, for I intend to compose a lay in her honour* about Galeron, the duke's sister, and Ille, the son of Eliduc. Now may God speed me on my way![3]

Let me tell you that there are two countries called Britain, inhabited by different peoples: the English live in Great Britain, but it is ruled by the Normans; the Bretons live in Little Britain, or Brittany. Once upon a time it was ruled by a duke called Conain, and Galeron was his sister. She was a beauty who used to dress most beautifully, in keeping with her looks, for she was a very beautiful woman:

---

[1] *Son per* could refer either to Beatrice (a fitting match for Rome) or to the emperor (a fitting match for Beatrice).

[2] I take *affis* to mean 'challenge' rather than 'insult' (see Lefèvre's note, p.231), giving 'without a single challenge', hence 'unchallenged'.

[3] Incomplete couplet. In W the prologue ends with the previous couplet.

145 Mout plot a tote rien vivant.
Li dus n'ot ainc feme n'enfant.
Al tans que Bretaigne ot li dus
Morut li pere Ille, Elidus,
Vassax et durement vallans;
150 Illes n'ot adont que .x. ans.
Por le pere, qui si fu preus,
Le het Oiaus et si neveu;
De totes pars li corent seure,
Si l'ont destruit en mout poi d'eure:
155 Ille escillierent li baron.
Onques del frere Galeron,
Del foible duc, ne fu tensés,[1]
Et li varlés s'est porpensés
Qu'il en ira au roi de France.
160 Cele part vait sans demorance;
Plus tost que puet i est venus,
Et ricement fu retenus.
Li rois l'onore et sel cierist:
Le pere ama, se li merist
165 Son grant traval et son service.
Et qant eages le devise
Que li vallés soit chevaliers,
Li rois l'adoube volentiers,
Et bien et bel, tot por s'amor,
170 En adouba .xv. le jour.
Ensanle vont a la quintaine;
Illes i brise se vintaine
De grosses lances bien ovrees,
Et plus, ses eüst recovrees.

175 Il point amont, il point aval,
Et si avient si au cheval,
Ce sanle qu'il nasquist a tout.
Encor le troveront estout
Cil qui le vaurent escillier.
180 Por çou ne doit nus avillier
Poulain velu de novel né
Ne vallet petit depané:
Tel les ont eüs en despit,
Puis lor sovint de cel respit.[2]
185 Illes cuide mout bien desdire
Cex qui le soloient despire.
Illes est mout de rice atour:
Mout par li vait Voidie entor
Por lui ensignier et estruire
190 Comment il puist tous cex destruire
Qui l'ont destruit et dekacié.
Dedens .iii. ans a porkacié
Honor et pris et vasselage;
.II. compaignons de son eage
195 A retenus ensanle od soi.
Il n'ot parler de nul tornoi
Que il n'i aille son pris querre,
Et cerke por ce mainte tere,
Et tient li chevaliers nouviaus
200 Hostex mout rices et mout biax.
Et qant se vait esbanoier
La fors as cans por tornoier,
En tot le plus espés s'eslesse,
Ne mes cascuns le camp li lesse;

172 i brise a se v.]Lö   177 tous]Lö   183 Tes]W

6

every living soul found her very attractive. The duke never married nor had any children. During the time when this duke ruled Brittany, Ille's father Eliduc, a man of courage and remarkable valour, died; Ille was only ten years old at the time. Hoel and his nephews hated Ille on account of his father, who had been such a gallant man. These barons attacked Ille from all sides, overcame him in a very short time, and banished him from his lands. Galeron's brother the duke was weak,[1] and failed to come to his defence, so the boy resolved that he would go to the King of France. He headed in that direction without delay, arrived at the court as soon as he could, and was given a splendid reception. The king honoured him and held him dear: he had loved his father, and now Ille was rewarded for his father's great efforts and his service. (166) And when the boy was of an age to become a knight, the king gladly dubbed him; and out of affection for Ille he actually dubbed fifteen young men that day. They went off to joust at the quintain together, and there Ille broke his score of sturdy, well-made lances, and would have broken more if he could have come by them. He spurred his mount up and down, and looked so good on horseback that it seemed as if he had been born in the saddle. Those who wished to banish him would yet find him a fearless opponent. This is why no-one should under-estimate a new-born foal with its shaggy coat or a humble boy in rags: some people who have looked down on them have had cause to remember this saying later on.[2] (185) Ille certainly planned to give the lie to those who used to look down on him. He was splendidly provided for: Shrewdness was in constant attendance, to teach and instruct him how to defeat all those who had defeated and exiled him. Within three years he had acquired honour and renown and valour; he chose two young men of his own age to be his companions-at-arms. He never heard about a tourney without attending it, to seek renown; he travelled the length and breadth of many a land in this pursuit, and this newly-fledged knight excelled in splendid hospitality. When he took the field to enjoy the sport of the tourney, he would ride headlong into the thick of it, only everyone would leave the field to him;

---

[1] Gautier would seem to be thinking here of Conain IV, Duke of Brittany from 1148 until 1166, who proved incapable of dealing with his rebellious vassals, and eventually abdicated in favour of Henry II of England. The duchy later passed to Henry's third son, Geoffrey Plantagenet. During the 1150s, Conan had found himself in conflict with his uncle Hoel, Count of Nantes.
[2] An allusion to the action of *Eracle*, in which the boy hero is asked to prove his God-given powers of discernment by identifying the most powerful stone, the best horse, and the most suitable wife for the emperor. His choice of horse is a young

205 N'est onques si espés li rens
Qu'il n'aclarit en poi de tens.
Mout criement durement son estre,
Que nus n'en puet aler en destre
Pour qu'il soit ferus de sa main.
210 Si n'a el monde plus humain,
Si franc, si douç, si deboinaire
Ne qui si voelle autrui bien faire
Tres l'eure qu'il est desarmés;
Et par çou est il tant amés
215 Qu'il est as armes chevaliers
Et a l'ostel li mains parliers
Qui onques en ceval montast.
Ne cuidiés mie qu'il contast
Cose qui li fust avenue:
220 Parole n'en ert ja tenue
N'endroit de lui n'endroit d'autrui
Qui le vausist laissier por lui.
Ne melloit nule janglerie
A se haute chevalerie,
225 Car il nel voloit mie vendre;
Onques nul jor n'i vaut entendre.
Cevalerie que on vent
Par jangler menu et sovent
Ne puet au lonc a bien venir,
230 Car nul n'en daigne sovenir.
S'Illes eüst esté janglere,
Or ne fust nus hom nés de mere
Qui en bien le ramenteüst
Por vasselage k'il eüst,

235 Que cil qui jangle nen a song
C'on le retraie en bien au long,
Ou il cuide mervelles dire
Quant il fait cex d'entor lui rire.
On rit sovent d'un jogleor
240 Et d'un chevalier jangleour.
Illes n'est mie foursenés,
Car il n'est hom de mere nes,
Tant par i sace entente metre,
Quil voie de rien entremetre
245 Qui n'apartiegne a rice ovragne;
Ne il n'est riens qui li sofraigne.
Ainc de bien faire ne se fainst;
Onques a nul jor ne se plainst
Cevalerie de son cors.
250 Bien torna le plus bel defors[1]
Nature au jor k'ele le fist.
Ne sai ou el le forme prist:
S'il eüst biauté a devise,
Ne peüst estre en nule guise
255 Qu'il n'eüst ançois mains que plus.
Or est Illes bien el desus
Des que il est et preus et biax
Et tos jors plus et plus noviax.
    Kuel que il erroit en enfance,
260 Ses repairiers estoit en France.
Ne sot mie aler en Bretaigne,
Car cil qui ocist et mehaigne,
Vers cui on ne se puet fier,
Fait bien tous jors a eskiver.

208 Que mais]W   223 nul ingleerie]Lö (W joglerie)

8

no matter how thick the press might be, it would quickly thin out. His presence made them heartily afraid, because no-one could slip away without receiving a blow from him. And yet no-one on earth could be more sympathetic or so open, so gentle, so good-natured or so eager to do good to others, when once he had disarmed; he was so well liked because on the field he was a true knight, and off it the least boastful who ever rode a horse. Do not imagine that he would tell stories about what had happened to him: it would never be discussed, either by himself or by anyone else who was prepared to keep quiet for his sake. He did not adulterate his noble chivalry with bragging, for he did not wish to compromise it; he never had any intention of doing that. (227) Chivalry which is compromised by constant bragging can come to no good in the long run, for no-one thinks fit to remember it. If Ille had been a braggart, no man alive would have good memories of him now, however courageous he had been, because a braggart does not care whether people speak favourably of him in the long run, or else he imagines that he is telling a wonderful tale when in fact he is making himself a laughing-stock. People frequently laugh at jongleurs and at boastful knights. Ille was certainly in his right mind, for however hard he might try, no man alive could find him engaging in anything which was not connected with some noble undertaking, and there was nothing lacking in him. (247) He was never slow to do good; chivalry never once had cause to complain about him. Nature really put on her Sunday best[1] the day she created him. I do not know where she found the mould for Ille: if he had had unlimited good looks, it would still have been quite impossible for him not to have had more as time went on. Now Ille was certainly in a strong position, once courage and good looks were both his, and grew more and more impressive day by day.

However much he travelled during his adolescence, Ille would always return to France. He was unable to go to Brittany, for it is always a good idea to keep well away from a man who kills and maims people, and whom you cannot trust.

---

colt, which outruns the emperor's finest stallion, but dies after the contest because it was raced too soon, against the advice of the *vallet* Eracle.

[1] A reference to the custom of wearing robes with fur or silk linings 'inside out', i.e. with the most splendid part on view. The translation attempts to retain something of the imagery.

265 Illes ses anemis esqive,
Que il n'i quiert ne pais ne trive.
Mais qant Dix l'a issi monté
Com je vous ai ichi conté,
Li rois de France l'araisone
270 Et mout loial conseil li done:
«Biaus dous amis, ce dist li rois,
Mout par fu prex, dous et cortois
Tes pere en ceste mortel vie,
Et tu ne le fourlignes mie.
275 Je l'amai mout de bone foi.
Li biens ne faut mie endroit toi:
Servi m'as bien et volentiers
Des puis que tu fus chevaliers.
Ta garnison voel asseoir
280 De canques tu pues sorveoir
De bos, de prés et de rivieres;
S'i a .vi. liues bien pleneres.
Je t'en ravés; tien, pren le chi!
— Biax sire ciers, vostre merchi
285 De l'ofre que vos m'avés fait;
Mais chi aroit estrange plait
Se j'en tel guise m'abessoie,
Car se je mon païs lessoie
Por vivre en l'autrui a repos,
290 M'onor metroie ariere dos.
N'est dignes d'avoir autrui terre
Qui la soie laisse a conquerre
Par malvestié et par perece.
Mix voel esprover ma proece

295 Ou vivre u morir a honeur
Que on me claint a tort signeur:
N'ai song de tere ou je n'ai droit.
Mais qui le moie me rendroit
Salve m'onor, je le prendroie;
300 Biax sire ciers, je n'atendroie
.XV. jours mais por nule rien.
Mais or faites aumosne et bien:
Si me balliés de vostre gent,
Et si me carciés tant d'argent
305 Que j'en puisse aler en Bretaigne
A un preudome qui me taigne[1]
Et me retiegne et soit amis
Contre mes mortex anemis.
Et se j'en venoie au desus
310 Et g'ere rices rois, u plus,
Trestos mes pooirs seroit vostres,
Et tuit li François et li nostre
Le vos atorneront a bien.
— Amis, et des miens et del mien
315 Pues auques de ton plesir faire.
— Sire, or est mestiers qu'il i paire,
Que raler m'en voel en ma tere.»
Li rois li fist esranment querre
.X. chevaliers de grant vaillance;
320 L'argent li baille et le balance,
Et cil en a .m. mars pesés.[2]
Or est li ars si entesés
Qu'il n'i ert ja mais destendus,
Ançois sera mout cier vendus

10

Ille kept well away from his enemies, not looking for peace or a truce from them. But when God had raised him to the position which I have described for you, the King of France addressed him and made him a very honourable proposal: 'Fair gentle friend,' the king said to him, 'Your father was a man of great bravery, gentleness and courtliness in this earthly life, and you surely take after him. I had a deep and true affection for him. Virtue is not lacking in you: you have served me well and willingly ever since you became a knight. I intend to set you up as lord of all you can see from here – six full leagues of woods, fields and rivers. I invest you with it; here, accept it from me!' – (284) 'Fair dear lord, I am grateful for the offer which you have made me; however, this would be a curious business if I were to abase myself in this way, for if I were to abandon my country to live an easy life in another man's, I would be turning my back on honour. A man who neglects to win back his own land through cowardice and indolence is not worthy to rule someone else's. I prefer to put my prowess to the test, to live or die with honour than be proclaimed lord without deserving it: I do not care for land to which I have no title. However, if someone were to give me back my land without prejudice to my honour, I would take it; fair dear lord, nothing could make me wait a fortnight longer. But now, put your charity and goodness into action: give me some of your men and grant me enough silver to go to Brittany to a gallant man who will take me into his service[1] and be my ally against my mortal enemies. (309) And if I were to get the better of them and became a mighty king, or better, the whole of my domain would be yours, and your position would be enhanced in the eyes of all the French and our people.' – 'My friend, you may do as you please both with my men and with my silver.' – 'My lord, now is the time to put your generosity into action, because I wish to go back to my own country.' The king swiftly had ten very valiant knights selected for him; he gave him the silver and the scales, and Ille weighed out a thousand marks from it.[2] Now the bow was bent so far that it would never be released until the full price had been paid

---

[1] An alternative form of the subjunctive of *tenir*, used here as a synonym of *retenir*.
[2] The mark was originally a measure of weight, equivalent to eight ounces (244.5 grams), rather than a coin. Gold and silver were normally measured in marks.

325 A tel qui nul regart n'en a.
Illes et cil k'il en mena
Prenent atant del roi congié.
Mout pueent avoir grief songié
Li dui chevalier dont je dis[1]
330 Et leur sire aussi e li dis
Qui vont o li de par le roi.
Mout par sont rice lor conroi.
   Tant ont lor droit chemin tenu
Qu'il sont en Bretaigne venu;
335 En mout grant peril se sont mis.
Illes avoit .ii. bons amis;
Mandé lor a que contre lui
Vegnent au pont de piere andui.
Cist ont le cose bien seüe
340 Par une ensegne conneüe
Qu'il ont trové[e] el parcemin.
Andoi se metent al chemin;
Si ont .xx. chevaliers armés,
Dont Illes est mout bien amés.
345 Mais li caitif qui a lui vont
Et li François qui o lui sont
Ne sevent mie la mervelle
C'on lor engigne et aparelle:
Uns pautoniers les a vendus,
350 Qui ne fu pas mesentendus,
Qu'il .c. se corent adouber.
Hoiaus s'escrie come ber:
«Signor, ne soiés esclenquier!
353a Pensés del gloton detrenchier!»
Cados et cil qui ert ses niés[2]

355 Jurent que siens en est li ciés
Et qu'il i rendront mort ou vif.[3]
Atant se montent par estrif;
A grant bruit issent de la vile.
E Dix, car fuissent or .ii. mile
360 Li François qui sont od celui
Et li secors qui vient vers lui!
Ja nos metroient au desous
Les orgillex et les estous;
Ille cuident trencier en pieces
365 Et metre a duel nevex et nieces,
Que .vii. ans a nel virent mais.
Li cent, qui vienent a eslais,
Gardent a destre un poi amont;
Les .xx. coisirent sor le pont:
370 Illoec atendent lor neveu,
Ille, le bon, le bel, le preu.
Mout l'i ont longes atendu;
Or cuident bien estre vendu,
Quant tant demore lor amis
375 Et voient de lor anemis
Com il vienent vers eus a kace.
Li plus hardis ne set qu'il face
Ne en quel guise se contiegne(nt).
Nus d'eus n'est seürs qu'il i viegne;
380 N'ont de sen venir esperance,
N'il n'ont que sol en Diu fiance;
Ne nus d'aus tos fuïr ne dagne.
Neporqant raisons lor ensagne
S'il pueent fuïr, qu'il s'en fuient,

---

336 des]W   345 o lui vont   356 il i venront]Lf

12

by someone who at present suspected nothing. Then Ille and the men he took with him took their leave of the king. Well might they have had nightmares, the two knights of whom I am speaking,[1] as well as their leader and the ten men the king sent with him. Their arms were very splendid indeed.

They followed a direct road until they arrived in Brittany; they were putting themselves in very great danger. Ille had two close kinsmen: he sent for them both to come and meet him at the stone bridge. They knew that the message was genuine by means of a sign which was known to them and which they found in the letter. The two of them set out; and with them were twenty armed knights who had great affection for Ille. (345) However, these unfortunate men who were riding to meet him and the French knights who were with him knew nothing of the terrible surprise which was being devised and prepared for them: they had been betrayed by a scoundrel, whose words did not fall on deaf ears, because a hundred men rushed to arm themselves. Hoel cried out like the brave warrior he was: 'My lords, don't do things by halves! *Put your minds to hacking the wretch to pieces!*' Cador the brave and the man who was Hoel's nephew[2] each swore that Ille's head was his, and that they would deliver him to Hoel[3] dead or alive. Then each tried to be first into the saddle, and they caused a great commotion as they rode out of the town. Oh God, if only the Frenchmen with Ille and the reinforcements coming to join him had numbered two thousand! They would soon have got the better of those arrogant and foolhardy men for us; they were planning to hack Ille to pieces and make mourners of the nephews and nieces who had never laid eyes on him in seven years. (367) The hundred men, who were riding flat out, looked slightly uphill to their right and noticed the group of twenty on the bridge, where they were waiting for their nephew, Ille, the virtuous, the handsome, the brave. They had been waiting for him for a long time; now they really believed that they had been betrayed, since their kinsman was taking so long to arrive and their enemies were bearing down on them so swiftly. Even the boldest of them did not know what to do or how to conduct himself. None of them was confident that Ille would arrive; they held out no hope of his arriving, and placed their trust in God alone; not one out of all of them deigned to flee. Nevertheless, common sense told them to flee, if they could,

---

[1] These are Ille's companions-at-arms (l. 194), who accompany him to Brittany. It would not be surprising if they had bad dreams, given the dangers which lie ahead.
[2] W names this second man as Ris. Lines 152 and 531 make it clear that *ses* here refers to Hoel: Cador and Ris are cousins, and both are nephews of Hoel.
[3] *Qu'il i* is a Picard graphy for *qu'il li*. The text of P makes little sense here. *Rendront > vendront > venront* is a plausible sequence of scribal errors.

385 Car la ou .c. a .xx. s'apuient
 Si tornent a desconfiture
 Se trop n'ont grant bone aventure.
 Il sevent bien que ço est voirs
 Et del fuïr seroit savoirs,
390 Et neporqant fuïr ne voelent,
 N'onques vilener il ne suelent;
 Or sont il huimés a bandon.
 Li .c. lor vienent de randon:
 Al parvenir baissent les lances,
395 El sanc tagnent lor connaissances,
 De tos sens les ont acoellis,
 Et cil les ont si recoellis
 Que il n'i doivent avoir blasme.
 Mains en muert et mains en i pasme.
400 Li .xx. chevalier bien se tinrent,
 Mes que li .c. qui sor ex vinrent
 Lor i firent trop grant moleste,
 Car la ou .xx. vers .c. areste¹
 Trop est la mesqueance griés:
405 De .ii. a .x. est grans mesciés,
 De .iiii a .xx., d'uit a .xl.
 De .xii. a mescief a .lx..
 Ainc n'i ot jouste devisee
 Ne rien qui tornast a risee,
410 Mes de grant doel i a matire,
 Qu'il s'entreocient a martire.
 Lor lances brisent li pluiseur;
 Espargnant vont li .xx. les leur:
 Effondrent les escus valtis,
415 Et des haubers fors et treslis

 Rompent les malles et les las;
 En sanc espandre est lor solas.
 Mais trop sont poi de gent assés
 Et cil les ont forment lassés,
420 Si que d'angoisse tuit tressuent;
 Li .c. par force les remuent,
421a *Si les commencent a cachier.*
 La oïssiés fer et acier
 Plus d'une liue retentir;
 Ces haubers rompre [et] desmentir
425 I veïssiés espessement.
 Et cil s'en vont sereement:
 Bien sevent qu'il ne lairont mie
 Nul autre ghage que la vie
 Se il sont pris a le tençon.
430 Trop criement ceste raençon:
 Por çou se tienent plus seré.
 Mout a envers eus meserré
 Illes et cil qui o lui vienent!
 A mout grant paine mes se tienent
435 Li .xx. chevalier dont j'ai dit:
 A poi ne sont tuit desconfit,
 Ne se pueent mes preu tenir.
 Gardent et voient cex venir:
 Joie ont, ainc mes n'orent si grant.
440 Illes s'en vait esmervillant
 De cele kace que il voit;
 Mervelle soi quels gens c'estoit.
 Les armes coisist et conoist;
 Ne laira mie qu'il n'i voist.

---

395 tienent]W   422 veissies]W   443 Les a. saisist]W

14

for where a hundred men set upon twenty, the twenty are likely to be defeated, unless they have extremely good fortune. They were well aware that this is so, and that it would make sense to flee, and nonetheless they had no intention of fleeing, and acting dishonourably was never their way; from this point on they had nothing to lose. The hundred men came at them at full gallop: as they joined battle, they lowered their lances and dyed their pennons in blood; they attacked them on all sides and the others gave them the kind of reception for which no blame could attach to them. Many a man died and many a man fell unconscious there as a result.

The twenty knights held their own well, yet the hundred men bearing down on them inflicted very serious casualties on them, for when a score of men take on a hundred,[1] they are in a very unfavourable position: two against ten are at a great disadvantage, as are four against twenty and eight against forty; twelve are at a disadvantage against sixty. (408) This was never an equal combat, and it was no laughing matter; rather, there was cause for great sorrow, as they met an agonising death at one another's hands. The majority of Hoel's men broke their lances; the twenty men were more careful with theirs: they smashed the convex shields and tore apart the links and laces of the strong triple-mailed hauberks; they took their delight in shedding blood. However, they were far too small a force, and the others had taxed them to the limit, so that they were bathed in sweat from their exertions; the hundred men put them forcibly to flight, *and began to give chase.* You could have heard the clash of iron and steel from more than a league away; you could have seen hauberks being torn and ripped apart thick and fast. (426) The twenty men closed ranks as they retreated: they were well aware that the only surety they would leave behind would be their lives, if they were taken prisoner in the fighting. They were very much afraid of this kind of ransom, and so they kept closer together. Ille and those who were with him had let them down badly! The twenty knights of whom I have been speaking were having very great difficulty in holding their own now: they were close to total defeat, and could not hold out much longer. They looked up and saw Ille's men approaching: they were more overjoyed than they had ever been before. Ille was astonished at the hot pursuit he could see, and wondered who the men were. He made out the coats of arms, and when he recognised them nothing could stop him from going to the rescue.

---

[1] The singular verb indicates that *vint* is being used as singular noun, rather than a cardinal number, hence my translation.

445 Met pié a tere isnelement,
Et li François tot ensement.
«Signor, dist il, traï nos somes
Sans nos escuiers et nos homes:
Por amor Diu, armés vos tost!
450 .XIII. home valent tot .i. ost
Por que li .xiii. soient tuit
Itex com je vos croi et quit.
Grant gent malvese sanle l'ombre
Qui honist le place et encombre;
455 On fait plus par poi gent sovent
Que on ne face par grant gent.
– Sire, cor fuissiens nos en France,
Ce pleüst Diu et sa poissance!
Mes puis que la cose est ensi,
....1
460 Si mostre cascuns sa proece,
Car n'avons autre forterece
Mais que proece et hardement.»
Armé se sont isnelement.
    Al pié du pont, el fons du val
465 Monte cascuns sor son cheval,
Saisist l'escu et prent l'espié.
Ançois qu'il soient mis a pié,
Le comperront espoir tel gent
Que por lor pois de fin argent
470 N'i vauroient estre meü.
Li cent ont coisi et veü
Le secors qui lor croist et vient:
Bien lor ramenbre et lor sovient
Qu'il onques mais n'orent paour

475 Qu'il n'aient or .c. tans grignor.
Mout s'esmaient de ce qu'il voient,
Et cuident bien que grans gens soient
Por ce qu'il vienent si rengié.
Dient entr'aus: «Or est vengié
480 Ce que nos avons trop couru:
Icist seront ja secouru.»
Atant retornent tot irié.
Ne mais li .xx. sont or mout lié;
Mout par lor plaist et atalente.
485 Illes ot compaignie gente
Que il amaine od lui de France.
Petit prisent mes nul sofrance:
Il voient que li fiex leur frere
Porte les armes a son pere,
490 Tout ausi faites connissances.
Retornent les fers de lor lances
Et moustrent a leur anemis
Hardies cieres et fiers vis.
As .xiii. poignent li .lx.,
495 As .xx. retornent li .xl.,
Et cil lor vienent a eslés.
Ains que li jeus remagne mes,
Ert li plus liés tous irascus,
Qu'il s'entrefierent es escus,
500 Et s'entreportent a la terre
Tel qui cier comperront la guerre.
Assés i a des abatus
Et des navrés et des batus.
Chevaliers qui sa lance a fraite

455 par grant gent]Lö

16

He swiftly dismounted, and the French did the same. 'My lords,' he said, 'We have been betrayed, and we are without our squires and our men: for the love of God, arm yourselves quickly! Thirteen men are worth a whole army, provided that the thirteen are all the sort of men I think and believe you to be. A large force of cowards is like a shadow which soils and leaves a stain upon the ground; more can often be achieved with a small force than with a large one.' – 'My lord, would that it had pleased God and His might for us to be in France now! But since this is how things are ....[1] Let each man display his prowess, for prowess and daring are our only fortress.' They swiftly armed themselves.

(464) At the foot of the bridge, deep in the valley, each man mounted his horse, grasped his shield and took up his lance. Before they were forced off their mounts again, a group of men who would not have wished to set out for their weight in pure silver were likely to pay dearly for it. The hundred men noticed and saw that help was arriving to swell their opponents' numbers: they recollected and recalled that if they had ever known fear before, what they felt now was a hundred times more intense. They were very frightened by what they saw, and believed that they were a large force because they were approaching in such close formation. They said to one another: 'Now the quarry we have pursued too far is avenged: help is at hand for them.' Whereupon they turned back, in total dismay. Now the twenty men were the only ones to be glad; it gave them enormous pleasure and satisfaction. Ille had a noble company which he brought with him from France. Any suffering meant little to them now: they could see that their brother's son was bearing his father's coat of arms, with exactly the same devices. They pointed their lances in the opposite direction and displayed bold faces and fierce expressions to their enemies. Sixty of Hoel's men rode at Ille's thirteen, while the other forty turned back towards the twenty men, who came at them full tilt. Before this sport came to an end, the gladdest man amongst them would be filled with bitter dismay, because they were striking one another's shields, and men who would pay dearly for the war were knocking one another to the ground. There were large numbers of dead and wounded and vanquished. Any knight who had broken his lance

---

[1] Line missing. This passage does not figure in W.

505 S'a demanois l'espee traite.
Commencié ont estor mortel;
De tant de gent ne vit nus tel.
N'est mie tornois a escar,
Qu'il s'entrefierent en la car:
510 Mout par est durs li capleïs.
Tant dure entr'aus li fereïs
N'i a remés de .xx. que .xiii.
Ne de .xl. mais ke .xvi.
Qui puissent aidier gaires preu
515 Ne vengier cousin ne neveu.
Mais or laissiés dont covenir!
As .lx. voel revenir,
Qui vers le pont en sont alé.
Ne l'ont pas bien adevalé
520 Li François qui sont o celui,
Quant li troi .xx. vinrent sor lui.
Ris li a dit: «Mar i entras,
Mar me vis et mar m'encontras!
Mout recevront males saudees
525 Les gens que tu as amenees.
Sont il ça venu por conquerre
Nostre païs et nostre terre?
Com mar te virent né de mere!
Cist comperront l'orgoel ton pere.
530 Juré l'avons et fiancié,
Cados, li fix mon oncle, et gié,
Que nos par force te prendrons
Et a mon oncle te rendrons,
Qui mout te het et mout t'a vil:

535 Por voir te di q'ensi ert il.
– Non ert, se Dix me velt secorre.»
Atant lessent les cevax corre;
Vistement vienent au besong.
Ja la tere ne m'ert pas long,
540 Que n'en puisse l'un entercier!
Ou il feront escu percier,
Ou haubers i desmentira,
Si que li cors s'en sentira.
Ris, qui ne quiert trive ne pais,
545 Fiert sor celui de plains eslais
En son escu paint a lion
C'amont en volent li tronçon.
Et cil l'ataint par grant vertu,
L'auberc li fausse sos l'escu:
550 Ne li vint pas devers senestre,
Car droit en le mamele destre
L'a si feru a l'encontrer
Que fer et fust i fist entrer;
De plains eslais le porte a terre.
555 Mout par avive bien la guerre!
Bruns d'Orliens va ferir Cador
Desor la boucle de fin or;
Perce l'escu et l'entresaigne
Parmi l'auberc el cors li baigne:
560 Mort le trebuce del destrier.
Li dui cheval vont estraier.
Huimais n'i a ne jeu ne ris
Des que mors est Cador, et Ris,
Qui hui jurerent par estrif

520-523 couplets inverted]W   548 le tient]W   549 sor]W

18

immediately drew his sword. They had begun a mortal combat, the like of which, involving such numbers of men, has never been seen. This was no mock tourney, for they were striking one another in the living flesh: the hand-to-hand fighting was very fierce. The exchange of blows between them went on so long that only thirteen of the twenty and sixteen of the forty remained in a state to be of very much help to cousin or nephew, or to avenge them. But now leave them to decide it! I wish to return to the sixty who had gone off towards the bridge. The Frenchmen who were with Ille had not quite ridden down off the bridge when the three score came at him. Ris said to him: 'It was an unlucky day for you when you set foot on this bridge, an unlucky day when you saw me and an unlucky day when you encountered me! The men you have brought here will get their pay in very unpleasant coin. (526) Have they come here to conquer our country and our land? How unlucky for them that you were ever born of woman! These men will pay for your father's arrogance. Cador, my uncle's son, and I have sworn and pledged that we will take you by force and deliver you up to my uncle, who hates you bitterly and holds you in great contempt: I assure you that this is how it will be.' – 'It will not, if God will come to my aid.' At this, they gave the horses their heads and rushed eagerly into combat. They would never be too far away for me not to be able to recognise one of them! Either they would pierce a shield, or a hauberk would be torn apart and the body inside would feel the blow. (544) Ris, who was not looking for a truce or peace, struck his opponent's shield, which had a lion painted on it, at full tilt, so that the splinters flew up into the air. And Ille dealt him such a powerful blow that he damaged his hauberk behind the shield: he did not aim towards the left, for when they met he struck him so hard that he thrust the lance-head and the shaft into the right side of his breast; he knocked him to the ground at full tilt. He certainly succeeded in livening up the war! Brun of Orleans went to strike Cador on the pure gold boss of his shield; he pierced the shield and plunged his ensign through the hauberk into his body: he hurled him down dead off his charger. The two horses ran loose. From this point on things became deadly serious, now that Cador and Ris were dead, who had vied with each other that same day in swearing

565 Qu'Ille tenroient mort ou vif.
    Hoiaus, li fors, li fel, li fiers,
    Les pot tenir a mençoniers.
        As François est huimés trop tart
    Que cascuns poigne cele part.
570 La tere estormist tote et tranle
    Del poindre qu'il ont pris ensanle.
    Quant vint as lances abaissier,
    Escus i veïssiés plaissier,
    Fendre, percier et estroer,
575 Ces poitraus rompre et desnoer.
    Hoiax est chevaliers mout preus
    Et voit illuec mors ses neveus.
    A Brun s'eslesse et sel requiert;
    Par mout grant maltalent le fiert
580 Et de tant com le hanste dure
    L'abat jus a le tere pure.
    Biax sire Dix, quel deus sera
    Se Bruns remaint a cex de la:
    Nel garira tous l'ors del monde
585 Que li fel provos nel confonde.¹
    Or le gart Dix, li fix Marie,
    Qui mainte gent ara garie!
    Quant ce coisissent li Breton,
    Cele part vont a esperon,
590 Mais Bruns est tost en piés salis
    Com chevaliers amanevis.
    L'espee a traite et fiert a destre
    Et puis reguencist a senestre;
    Menuement les va ferant.

595 Leus qui sa proie va querant
    N'ocist plus menu ne estranle
    Toutes les bestes qu'il enangle
    Que Bruns les ocist et mehagne;
    El sanc des chevaliers se baigne.
600 Lors commence uns estors si fors
    Ja i sera u pris u mors,
    Se Damedix n'en a merci.
    «Biaus Dix, dist il, se je muir chi,
    A com mal port sont arivé
605 Tuit cil qui sont de moi privé!
    Ne mais, se Dix me velt conduire,
    Cier me vendrai ains que je muire.»
    Lores i ot des cols donés:
    C'est li lions avironés
610 Qui fiert cestui et fiert celui,
    Et ki n'espargne a cop nului.
    S'Ector i fust, ne se tenist²
    Que ses compains ne devenist:
    Ne li fausist toute sa vie
615 Ne d'amor ne de compagnie.
    Trop par li sont li François lonc,
    Mais bien l'ont fait a ce besong:
    Mout par ont soustenu grief fes;
    Ochis i ont des lor adiés,
620 Mout par i ont entente eüe.
    Mais qant la cose est conneüe,
    Que Bruns d'Orliens est entrepris,
    D'ire et de maltalent espris
    poig[n]ent ensanle cele part,

20

that they would take Ille dead or alive. Hoel the vigorous, the villainous, the violent could consider them liars.

Now none of the French could charge quickly enough in that direction. The ground shuddered and trembled all around under the force of their combined charge. When it came to lowering their lances, you would have seen shields being buckled, split open, pierced and holed, and horses' breast-straps breaking and coming apart there. Hoel was a knight of great courage, and he saw his nephews lying dead on that field. He rode headlong at Brun and attacked him; in a towering rage, he struck him and hurled him down onto the bare earth a full lance's length away. Dear Lord God, what a tragedy it would be if Brun remained in the hands of the enemy: all the gold in the world would not save him from being put to death by that cruel judge.[1] (586) Now may God defend him, the son of Mary, who must have saved many a person's life! When the Bretons noticed this, they spurred their horses in Brun's direction, but he leapt quickly to his feet, like the skilful knight he was. He drew his sword and struck out to his right, and then swung round to his left; he was raining blows down on them. A wolf in search of prey does not kill or throttle all the animals it corners with more speed than Brun was killing and maiming them; he bathed in the knights' blood. Then there began such a fierce combat that he would soon be either captured or killed if God did not have mercy on him. 'Dear God,' he said, 'If I die here, what dire straits all those who are close to me will find themselves in! (606) Only, if God will be my guide, I will make them pay dearly before I die.' Then blows were dealt in earnest: he was like a lion at bay, which lashes out right and left, and which spares no-one its blows. If Hector[2] had been there, he could not have resisted becoming Brun's companion-at-arms: his love and companionship would not have failed him as long as he lived. The French were a very long way away from him, but they had fought well in this battle: they had withstood a very severe onslaught; they had killed some of their opponents straight away, and had been concentrating very hard on this. However, when it became known that Brun of Orleans was surrounded, they were fired with anger and rage and all charged together in his direction,

---

1 Delclos and Quereuil take *provos* to be a copying error for *provés* and suggest that this phrase should be translated 'le traître patenté'. The image of Hoel as an evil provost attempting to mete out justice to the man who has just killed his nephew seems, however, to be entirely appropriate in this context.

2 For Gautier's audience, Hector was one of the archetypal warrior heroes of antiquity. His exploits had recently been celebrated in Benoît de Sainte-Maure's *Roman de Troie* (c. 1165).

21

625 Et font des Bretons el essart
Ja mes n'ert jors qu'il ne s'en plagnent:
Mout en ocient et mehaignent.
Estous de Lengres ert mout fiers
Et si estoit bons chevaliers,
630 Ainc nen ama cri de garçons;
As .ii. fait vuidier les arçons.
A cex rescorre ot mout grant bruit,
Et li François entendent tuit
Que Bruns d'Orliens rot son cheval.
635 Estous s'eslaisse a un vasal
Qui l'en menoit, et tant li fait
Que malgré sien aler l'en laist.
Or l'a rendu a Brun, le preu,
Qui tost i monte et fist un veu
640 Qu'il nen ert ja mes sans contraire[1]
Desi c'on sace qu'il set faire:
De ce s'afice durement.
S'espee sace isnelement;
Uns vallés de sa connissance
645 Li a lués mis el poig le lance.
Le ceval broce, point vers eus,
De plains eslais se fiert entr'ex.
A un s'adrece, si l'ataint,
Si l'a par tel aïr empaint
650 Qu'il li esfondre endroit le pis
L'escu u paroit li vernis.
Del hauberc n'ert si fors la malle
Que contre son espié li valle:
Plaine se lance jus l'envoie,

655 Si qu'il ciet mors les une voie.
Illes nes espargne de rien:
Onques mais hom nel fist si bien,
Et, qui le verté vous en dist,
Tote la moitié qu'il i fist
660 Ne voel or conter ne ne puis.[2]
Mes a un poindre qu'il fist puis
Nos mist par tere li vassaus
.II. chevaliers bons et loiaus:
Çou esbaudi plus les François
665 Que riens qu'il eüst fait ançois.
Lors les ont pris a envaïr
Par grant vertu et par aïr,
Et fierent plus menuement
Que nois ne vole par grant vent.
670 En Hoel a bon chevalier,
Hardi et combatant et fier;
En lui n'a autre mesproison
Mais que trop aime traïson.
Ses escus ert a lionchiax,
675 Et il estoit mervelles biaus;
Ses armes valent un tresor,
Et siet desor un ceval sor.
Ille het mout de fine mort;[3]
S'il le het, il n'a mie tort;[4]
680 Li uns velt l'autre damagier,
Si s'entretuent de legier.
Cascuns par fiere contenance
Point le ceval, baisse la lance.
Hoiaus feri le cop premier,

658-659 inverted   682 por faire]W

22

and felled so many of the Bretons that there would never come a day when they did not lament it: they killed and maimed a large number of them. Estout de Langres was a very aggressive and able knight who had no love for bleating cowards; he knocked two of them from the saddle. There was a great commotion over rescuing these two, and the French were all intent on getting Brun of Orleans' horse back for him. Estout rode headlong at a knight who was leading the horse away, and dealt him such a blow that he let it go, in spite of himself. Then he gave it back to Brun the brave, who mounted quickly and made a vow that he would never rest easy again[1] until he had shown them what he was capable of: this was his uncompromising pledge. He swiftly went to draw his sword; a young man whom he knew immediately placed a lance in his hand. (646) He put the spurs to his horse, charged towards them, and plunged into their midst at full tilt. He made for one of them, struck him, and gave him such a violent thrust that he shattered the shield, with its covering of varnish, close to his chest. The mail of his hauberk was not strong enough to protect him against Brun's lance: he sent him toppling down with the full force of his lance, so that he fell dead at the side of a track. Ille gave them no quarter at all: no man ever fought so well, and, if the truth be told, I will not – indeed I cannot – describe even the half of it now.[2] However, during one charge he made subsequently, this young hero unhorsed two able and loyal knights for us. This heartened the French more than anything he had done before. (666) Then they began to assail them with great force and violence, and rained blows down upon them thicker than snow blown by a strong wind. Hoel was an able knight, daring and pugnacious and aggressive; there was no defect in him, except that he was too fond of treachery. His shield bore a device of lioncels, and he himself was exceptionally handsome; his arms were worth a fortune, and he sat astride a chestnut horse. He had a mortal hatred for Ille,[3] and was quite justified in hating him;[4] each of them wanted to do the other harm, and it was not hard for them to kill one another. With fierce demeanour each spurred his horse and lowered his lance. Hoel struck the first blow,

---

1 *Contraire* could mean either 'opponent' or 'vexation'; I have opted for the latter.
2 Lines 656-660 are problematic as they stand; inverting ll. 658 and 659 produces a much more coherent line of thought, although it is still necessary to read *dist* in l. 658 as *deïst*, as suggested by Foerster.
3 A play on *fin'amor*, which it is impossible to preserve in translation.
4 W's 'S'Illes het lui, n'a mie tort' involves an awkward change of subject, and reads like an attempt to avoid justifying the actions of the villain of the piece. Hoel is, however, entirely justified in hating the man who has just killed his nephew.

685 Que de le hanste de pumier,
Dont il cuida Ille afoler,
En fait amont les trous voler.
Icil l'ataint de tel vertu
Que il li perce son escu,
690 L'auberc li ront et li desment
Et si l'enpaint si durement
N'i a çaingle ne voist en .ii.;
Cil ciet a tere tous hontex.
Illes un petit le navra:
695 Cui caut? ja mal ne li fera.
Et neporqant si s'en esmaie,
Cuide que grande soit la plaie,
Mors en cuide estre et malballis;
Por qant s'est il en piés salis.
700 Illes le prent a embracier
Et le ventalle deslacier:
Ja li fesist un geu malvés,
Quant ses gens vienent a eslés.
De totes pars l'ont entrepris:
705 Mervelle est qu'il n'est mors u pris.
Illes atant aler l'en laist,
A ceval outre lui s'en vait.¹
Au kaïr durement se blece,
Et neporqant tost se redrece;
710 Por sa gent a vergoigne et honte:
Vient au ceval et tost remonte.
Grant paor ont si home eüe
De sa plaie, qant l'ont veüe:
Maint i deslace sa ventaille,

715 Trait ses cevex, tire et detalle;
Cuident qu'il soit navrés a mort.
«Signor, dist il, vos avés tort:
Laissiés a faire vostre duel!
– Biax sire ciers, a nostre voel
720 N'i serés plus. Garissiés vous,
Et si faites escu de nous.
Ce est diables empenés
Qui si nos a hui tous penés:
Vers lui ne puet nus arester.
725 – Signor, laissiés tot ço ester,
Et si le suiés a enchaus!
Dementres que li fers est caus,
Le doit on batre, qu'il ne monte,²
Et vengier esranment sa honte;
730 Çou est del miex, si com moi sanle.»
Lor poindre ont pris trestot ensanle.
Illes le soie gent ralie
A se vois haute qu'il escrie,
Et il i vienent a eslais.
735 De si fait caple n'orés mais,
De tant de gent si fet martire.
Atant i fierent tout a tire;
Dolor i a a grant fuison:
Sans mire i donent tel puison
740 Tot par aillors que par la bouce,
Que mors proçaine as cuers les touce.
Illes les plaisse, Illes les fiert,
Illes les destruist et requiert,
Illes lor perce lor escus,

24

and caused splinters to fly into the air from the apple-wood shaft with which he planned to slay Ille. Ille struck him with such force that he pierced his shield, ripped his hauberk and tore it apart, and so violent was his thrust that every strap on the harness snapped in two; Hoel fell to the ground, covered in shame. Ille had injured him slightly, but what matter? It would never cause him any pain. Nevertheless, he was frightened by it, imagining that the wound was serious, imagining that it meant death and destruction for him; nevertheless, he leapt to his feet. Ille went to grab hold of him and unlace his ventail: he would soon have played a fatal trick on him, when Hoel's men came rushing up. They surrounded Ille on all sides: it was a wonder that he was not killed or taken prisoner. (706) At this, Ille let go of Hoel and rode away past him.[1] Hoel injured himself badly as he fell; nevertheless, he quickly got up again. He was humiliated and ashamed for his men's sake; he went to his horse and quickly remounted. His men had been terrified when they saw his injury: many a man unlaced his ventail, pulled out his hair, tugged at it and tore it out; they believed that he was fatally wounded. 'My lords,' he said, 'You are mistaken: leave off your grieving!' – 'Fair dear lord, if we have our way, you will take no further part in this. Make for safety, and use us as your shield. This is a winged devil who has so tormented us all today; no-one can hold his ground against him.' – (725) 'My lords, leave all this be, and go chase after him! One should strike while the iron is hot, lest it get the better of you,[2] and avenge a humiliation promptly; this is the best course, so it seems to me.' They all made a charge together. Ille cried out at the top of his voice to rally his men, and they came rushing up. You will never hear tell of such a mêlée, of such slaughter involving this number of men. Then blows were struck in swift succession; there was no shortage of suffering: without the help of a doctor they administered such strong potions, by routes quite other than the mouth, that they soon felt death's icy fingers on their hearts. It was Ille who bent them double, Ille who struck them, Ille who slaughtered them and attacked them, Ille who pierced their shields,

---

[1] Foerster posited a lacuna after l. 707. There is, however, no obvious gap in the sequence of events: Ille has unhorsed Hoel, who then leaps to his feet to defend himself. Ille, still mounted, grabs hold of him, presumably lifting him off the ground, but lets go once Hoel's men gallop up. Hoel falls heavily to the ground and injures himself (l. 708).

[2] I follow Lefèvre (p. 234) in taking the verb *monte* as a subjunctive. The interpretation proposed by Delclos and Quereuil ('on doit battre le fer tant qu'il est chaud, car [si on ne le bat pas tant qu'il est chaud] cela ne sert à rien') presupposes a degree of ellipsis which would be unusual, even for Gautier.

745 Illes les fait tous irascus,
Illes lor fausse lor haubers,
Illes les fait chocier envers.
Il i fist plus, en mains de tens
Que je ne di, si com je pens,
750 C'uns clers n'escriroit en un jor
Par grant loisir et par laissor;
Car nus ne fait si volentiers
Com cil a cui il est mestiers,
Et il est tex en tous besoins
755 Que nus nel vaut ne prés ne lons.
Ponçon encontre et Ponces lui,
Si s'entrefierent ambedui
C'amont en volent li tronçon.
Cil trait l'espee et fiert Ponçon
760 Si que li cols fu bien parans,
Que hiaumes ne li fu garans
Ne la coife, tant fust eslite,
Que il ne claint la guerre cuite:
Od le plus trencant de l'espee
765 Li a le cervele entamee.
A terre ciet, Marciax le voit,
Qui ses cousins germains estoit.
A lui en vient l'espee traite,
Si l'a si feru de retraite
770 Que, se l'espee ne glaçast,
Ja mes a prestre ne parlast.
Mout le cuide bien afoler:
Del cercle d'or li fist voler
Une partie contre val,

775 Mes, merci Diu, ne li fist mal
Qu'en perdist rien de son voloir;
S'il li a fait le cief doloir,
Il le ferra sans manecier.
De l'espee trencant d'acier
780 Li a assise une colee
Qui dusq'es dens li est coulee:
Mort le trebuce voiant tous.
Illes s'eslaisse as plus estous,
Ou il voit que la presse est graindre.
785 Hoiax n'i ose plus remaindre:
Vit son grant doel et son damage,
K'Illes a mort de son parage
Bien au montant de .xviii..
N'a mie tort se il s'en fuit,
790 Que trait se sont si home arriere;
Tornent les dos, la kace est fiere.
Li un, puis que li autre fuient,
N'ont aresté; un tertre puient.
Li .xx. les sivent mout de prés,[1]
795 Qui d'aus vengier sont mout engrés.
D'ambe .ii. pars est grans la kace,
Coverte en est de sanc li trace;
La kace est mout desmesuree:
.II. liues plaines a duree.
800 Des fuians est mout grans la perte:
Trop grant angoisse i ont soferte.
Seré se tienent et estroit
Entrués qu'il vienent al destroit
U li cris de la tere ert leur.[2]

750 uns clers]W   757 Ambedui   773 Le cercle   800 De fuians]W

Ille who filled them with bitter dismay, Ille who cut through their hauberks, Ille who knocked them backwards from their saddles. In less time than it takes me to describe it, he achieved more, or so I think, than a clerk who was quite undisturbed and at his ease could write down in a day; for no-one fights with such a willing heart as the man who is driven by necessity, and he was the sort of man that no-one, near or far, could match in any kind of emergency. He came face to face with Ponçon, and Ponçon with him, and they both struck each other so hard that the splinters flew up into the air. Ille drew his sword and struck Ponçon a blow which was clear for all to see, for neither the helmet nor the coif, however excellent it might have been, could safeguard him from having to renounce his part in the war: Ille had sliced into his brain with the sharpest part of his sword. (766) He fell to the ground, in full view of Marcel, who was his first cousin. He came at Ille with drawn sword, and struck him so hard in return that if the sword had not been deflected he would never have gone to confession again. He certainly planned to slay him: he sent one section of his golden cerclet flying to the ground, but, thank God, he did not injure Ille enough for him to lose any of his determination; if Marcel had given him a headache, he would strike him without stopping to utter threats. With his sharp steel sword he fetched him a blow which sank right down to his teeth: he hurled him down dead in full view of everyone. Ille rode headlong at the boldest of them, where he saw that the press was thickest. (785) Hoel did not dare remain there any longer: he could see the great tragedy and the losses he had suffered, for in total Ille had killed a good eighteen members of his family. He was quite justified in fleeing, for his men had retreated; they turned and fled, with the French in hot pursuit.

Since Hoel's men were fleeing, the other Bretons did not hold their ground; they rode up a hill. Hard on their heels followed the twenty men,[1] who were fiercely determined to have their revenge. There was hot pursuit in both directions, and their tracks were covered in blood; the pursuit was fierce in the extreme: it lasted for two full leagues. Those fleeing suffered very heavy losses: they endured terrible agonies out there. They kept in a close and tight formation until they came to the defile at the boundary of their territory.[2]

---

[1] These are the twenty men led by Ille's uncles, and not, as Delclos and Quereuil maintain, their opponents. There may be a certain poetic licence here: in l. 512 seven of them are described as being barely in a fit state to fight.

[2] The expression *cris de la tere* is listed as obscure by Tobler-Lommatzsch, but perhaps indicates the point beyond which Hoel has the power to summon the inhabitants to pursue Ille and his men.

805 La passent outre a grant doleur;
La les ont François abatus,
Navrés et mors et confondus.
La haie ert grans: n'i passent mie,
Car il torneroit a folie.
810 Or n'i a que del retorner,
Qu'il fait illoec mal sejorner:
El repairier se sont tot mis.
Illes en vient a ses amis:
Sovent se sont entrebaisié.
815 Tost sont lor hiaume deslacié;
Cascuns sa ventalle deslace:
Icil le baise et cil l'embrace.
Mervelles ont grant joie eüe
Por sa proece c'ont veüe:
820 Por sa proece et sa valeur
Oublient tote la doleur
Qu'il ont soferte tote jour,
Ou il estuet mout de sejour.
Les François ont mout conjoïs,
825 De bon cuer veüs et oïs.
Trestot ensanle s'entrebaisent,
As ostex vont et si s'aaisent.
Castiax ont bons et prés de gent,¹
Si ont assés or et argent,
830 Ne crieme n'ont de nul assaut
Fors sol de Diu, qui est en haut.
Puis qu'Illes issi de la terre,
Se sont fermé contre la guerre.
Illes li preus, li jens, li biax,
835 En son demaine a dos castiax,

Et dos li ot par tere mis
Hoiaus li fel, ses anemis,
Et s'en i avoit encore un
Qu'il et Hoiax orent commun,
840 Por cui la guerre commença,
C'onkes de .vii. ans en ença
N'en ot le montant d'un denier:
Tort li a fait grant et plenier.²
Li mires qui les navrés saine
845 Les a garis en le quinsaine.
Cil de la ront garis les lor,
Qu'il n'en ont ne mal ne dolor,
Fors seulement li .xviii.
Qui furent mort par mal conduit.
850 Tuit cil du païs joie en ont
Fors cil qui du parage sont
851a *Hoiel u il n'ot point de bien;*
851b *Ne mais cascuns aime le sien:*
Mix aiment lor felon parent
C'un bien preudome d'autre gent.
Tot voelent Hoel grant damage
855 Fors cil qui sont de son parage.
Et cil du païs, li pluiseur,
Qui por soufraite de signeur
S'estoient a Hoel torné,
Sont a cestui tot retorné.
860 Maint prodome ot en cele terre
Que cil avoit destruit par guerre,
Qui tuit ensanle a cesti vienent
Et de le guerre a lui se tienent;
A lui se tienent tot de bout

835 des]Lö   853 De bien]W

28

There great pain was inflicted on them as they rode through; there they were struck down, wounded, killed and overcome by the French. The hedge was high: the French did not cross it, for this would have proved to be madness. Now there was nothing to do but turn back, as this was certainly not a good place to tarry for any length of time: they all began to make their way back. Ille went up to his kinsmen: they kissed one another time and again. Soon their helmets were unlaced, and each man unlaced his ventail: one of them kissed Ille and the other embraced him. They had been mightily overjoyed at his prowess, which they had witnessed: on account of his prowess and his valour they forgot all about the pain which they had suffered all day long, and which called for a long period of recovery. They greeted the French joyfully, delighted to see them and hear what they had to say. (826) All together, they kissed one another, then went to their lodgings and rested. They had good castles which were not in isolated positions,[1] and plenty of gold and silver, and they had no reason to fear any assault except from God, who dwells on high. Since Ille had left the country, they had built fortifications in readiness for a war. Ille the brave, the noble, the handsome, had two castles in his domain, and his enemy, the villainous Hoel, had demolished two more, and there was yet another which he and Hoel held in common, which was Ille's reason for declaring war, for he had not received so much as a denier's worth of revenue from it for the previous seven years: Hoel had committed a serious and significant offence against him.[2] The doctor who was tending the wounded cured them within a fortnight. (846) The other side also cured their wounded, so that they felt no pain or discomfort as a result – except for the eighteen men who had died under Hoel's evil leadership. Everyone in the country rejoiced at their deaths, except for those who were related to *Hoel; even though he was thoroughly evil, everyone still loves his own* kin: they prefer their villainous relative to a truly gallant man from another house. Everyone wished Hoel great harm, except for those who were related to him. Moreover, the majority of Ille's countrymen, who had gone over to Hoel for want of a leader, went back over to Ille. There were many gallant men in that land, whom Hoel had ruined by war, who all came as one to Ille, and came over to his side in the war. They came over to his side at a stroke

---

[1] W's 'bone gent' is clearly the *lectio facilior*. *Prés* is less common as a preposition than as an adverb in Old French, but is not by any means unknown in this kind of context. The phrase *lonc de gent* is used in l. 1373.

[2] Gautier is at pains to point out that Ille has the law on his side in the war with Hoel. Hoel's withholding of Ille's share of the revenue from their joint possession provides the legal justification Ille needs to pursue matters further. The denier was

29

865 Et ont lessié celui du tout:
    Hoiax pert mout de son revel.
    Al duc Conain en fu mout bel
    Qu'il en a tel novele oïe.
    Sa suer s'en est mout esjoïe,
870 La prex, la bele, la plus sage
    Qui onques fust de nul parage;
    Ainc Galerons n'oï novele
    Qui tant li fust amee et bele.
    Al tans k'Illes enfes estoit
875 A la cort mostrer ne s'osoit,
    Por Hoel, le felon prové,
    Car s'il l'eüst a cort trové,
    Ja por le duc ne remansist
    Que il enfin ne l'ocesist;
880 Mais des ore, se lui est buen,
    I ira il tot maugré suen.
    A trois cens chevaliers i muet;
    Sagement vait, ce li estuet.
    Illes n'est mie a escarnir:
885 D'armes les fist mout bien garnir,
    Et les chevax fist traire en destre.¹
    Illes est preus et de bel estre,
    Le cuer a mout de joie plain.
    A la cort vint al duc Conain
890 Qui a grant joie les reçoit,
    Et tant li dist qu'il s'aperçoit
    Que lui est bel de la victore
    Et de l'oneur et de la glore
    Que Damedix li a donee.

895 Et Galerons, la bele nee,
    A mout grant joie de celui.
    Puis torna mout a grant anui
    A amedos cele acointance.
    Lor grant bialté et lor vallance,
900 Lor cortoisie et lor proece
    Les misent puis en tel destrece!
    Ice k'ele est cortoise et bele
    Plus que ne soit el mont pucele
    Fait celui a s'amor entendre
905 Et si tres haute amor emprendre.
    Et tout içou ra en celui,
    Et ce fait cele entendre a lui.
    Frans est et dous et debonaire,
    Mais n'est pas de si haut afaire
910 Com Galerons de la moitié.
    Or ont andoi si esploitié,
    Amors les a bien pris a las.
    Com avroit il de li soulas,
    N'ele, qui est li suer au duc,
915 Com avroit le fil Eliduc?
    Mais de ces .ii. ai tant apris
    Qu'il ne sont mie si soupris
    Que .c. [t]ans encor plus ne soient.
    Auques lor plest qu'il s'entrevoien'
920 Sil font encor com de lor gré,
    Car en amor a maint degré:
    Al commencier est debonaire,
    Le gent blandist por mix atraire,
    Et puis, qant il est ore et leus,

874 Au jour]W   901 misent tos]W

30

and abandoned Hoel completely: much of Hoel's good cheer was deserting him. It gave Duke Conain great pleasure to hear such news of Ille. His sister who was virtuous and beautiful, the wisest young woman who ever belonged to any noble family, took great delight in it; Galeron had never before heard news which she found as sweet and agreeable as this.

During the time when Ille was a boy, he did not dare to show himself at Conain's court, on account of Hoel, the proven villain, for if Hoel had found him at court, the duke's presence could never have prevented him from killing Ille eventually; but from now on he would go to court in spite of Hoel, if he felt like it. He set out for the court with three hundred knights, and travelled prudently, as well he might. Ille was not someone to be taken lightly: he had them well provided with arms and had the war-horses led along beside them.[1] (887) Ille was brave and knew how to conduct himself; his heart was full of joy. He came to the court of Duke Conain, who gave him a very joyful reception, and said enough to Ille for him to realise that the duke was pleased at the victory and the honour and glory which God had bestowed on him. And Galeron, the beautiful creature, was overjoyed at meeting Ille. This meeting later became a source of great distress to both of them. Their great beauty and their virtue, their courtliness and their worth later occasioned them such anguish! The fact that she was more courtly and more beautiful than any other maiden in the world made him aspire to her love and embark upon a love so far *love* above him. (906) And the fact that he had exactly the same qualities made her turn *overcomes* her every thought to him. He was so open and gentle and good-natured, but he was *reason* of nowhere near as high rank as Galeron. Now both of them had progressed so far that Love had well and truly ensnared them. How could Ille receive solace from her, and how could she, the duke's sister, accept the son of Eliduc? However, I have learnt enough about these two to know that however smitten they might be now, they would be a hundred times more smitten later on. They took some pleasure in seeing each other, and still did so as if of their own accord, for there are many stages in love: to begin with, it is good-natured, and flatters people, the better to draw them in, and then, when the time and place are right,

---

a small silver coin, worth one twelfth of a *sou*, and was roughly equivalent to an old penny.

[1] Ille is guarding against a surprise attack by having his men well equipped and keeping the war-horses close at hand: the expression *traire en destre* refers to a horse being led along, normally by a squire who holds its reins in his right hand. There are several episodes in the text which highlight Ille's qualities as a strategist (see ll. 2281-304, 4911-14 and 5707-826).

925 Reset bien mostrer de ses jeus.
Cist n'en ont pas encor grant cure:
Bien lor ira s'il suit l'ordure;[1]
Mes s'autrement n'alast l'amors,
Li lais ne fust pas si en cours
930 Nel prisaissent tot li baron.
Grant cose est d'Ille a Galeron:[2]
N'i a fantome ne alonge,
Ne ja n'i troverés mençonge.
Tex lais i a, qui les entent,
935 Se li sanlent tot ensement
Com s'eüst dormi et songié.
Illes s'en lieve et prent congié:
«Pucele, fait il, Dix vos saut!
Cil Damedix qui maint en haut
940 Me doinst encore liu et aise
De faire cose qui vos plaise.
– Amis, et Diex vos beneïe
Et il confonde et maleïe
Tote la gent qui mal vos voelent
945 Et vostre mal porkacier suelent,
Et il me doinst le jour savoir
Que je leur voie honte avoir.»
Uns gars pusnais qu'iluec estoit
L'a tout oï; monte a esploit,
950 Rogelion le va retraire,
Qui mout est fel et deputaire.
Il volt que ceste fust s'amie,
Mais ele ne l'adaigne mie.
Rogelions ert niés Hoel,

955 Et si estoit freres Marcel,
Cui Illes dona la colee
Au departir de le merlee,
Que n'i estut mais referir.
Or li cuide cil bien merir
960 La mort son frere, dont se deut,
Et qu'om en cort si bel l'aqeut.[3]
Tes gens ne fu pieça veüe
Com li traître a esmeüe.
A son oncle vient a emblee,
965 Qui ra mout grant gent asanlee.
Illes est issus de la cambre,
Entre el palais pavé de lanbre:
Au duc Conain en est venus,
Ses hom liges est devenus,
970 S'en a sa tere receüe
Si com ses pere l'ot eüe,
Por que la puisse reconquerre
Et a cief traire cele guerre.
Congié a pris mout bonement;
975 De cort se part mout lïement
A tout ses .iii. .c. chevaliers.
.II. jors cevalcent tos entiers;
Al tierç se sont mis a le voie,
Demenant grant feste et grant joie,
980 Si ont en une tere esré,
Mais ains qu'il aient mout alé,
Lors est venus uns mes devant
Qui nes vait mie dechevant.
«Signor, fait il, armés vos tost!

---

925 Ne set]Lö   952 Il voit]W   955 Martel]Lö (W Marciel)   961 Et qu'en sa cort
976 .ii. .c.]Lö

32

it is well able to display some of its other tricks. These two were not very concerned about this yet: things would go well for them if love followed the proper sequence;[1] but if their love had not taken another direction, this lay would not be so popular or so highly esteemed by all noblemen. The story of Ille and Galeron is no trifling matter:[2] it is not padded out with fantasies, and you will find no fabrications in it. Some lays, when you hear them, make you think for all the world that you have been asleep and dreamt them. Ille stood up and took his leave: 'Maiden,' he said, 'God save you! May God who dwells on high yet grant me the occasion and the opportunity to do something which gives you pleasure.' – 'My friend, may God bless you, too, and confound and curse all those people who wish you harm and make a habit of pursuing your downfall, and may He grant that I live to see the day when I see them dishonoured.'/ (948) A low-born scoundrel who was in the chamber had heard all this; he hastily mounted and went to relate it to Rogelion, a very villainous and evil-natured man. He had wished to have Galeron for his own, but she did not think him worthy of her. Rogelion was Hoel's nephew, and the brother of Marcel, who received the blow from Ille, as the mêlée was breaking up, which meant that he never had to strike him again. Now he planned to pay Ille back in kind for the death of his brother, for which he grieved, and for the fact that Ille received such a warm welcome at court.[3] A force such as this traitor mobilised had not been seen for a long time. He came surreptitiously to his uncle, who had also assembled a very large force. (966) Ille left the chamber, and entered the palace, with its floor of polished wood: he came before Duke Conain, and became his liegeman, and was invested with his domain by the duke, just as his father had held it, so that he could win it back legitimately, and bring this war to a successful conclusion. He took his leave very courteously; then he left the court in high spirits, taking his three hundred knights with him. They rode for two whole days; on the third day they set out again, with great merry-making and great joy, and travelled into an area of open land, but before they had gone very far, they were met by a messenger, who was not about to play them false. 'My lords,' he said, 'Arm yourselves quickly!

---

[1] This refers to the stages of love: if all goes according to the normal sequence, Ille and Galeron's love will prosper; as it turns out, love will not respect the proper order of events, and they will become estranged. *Ordure* is listed in *AND* as a variant of *ordre*.

[2] See Introduction, pp. xxx-xxxi.

[3] There is a possible lacuna here. P's reading would make sense if l. 961 were followed by a couplet expressing the idea '[was welcomed at his court] by Duke

985 Hoiax vos vient a tote s'ost,
A .v. cens chevaliers armés.
Ensi com vos vos cors amés,
Garnissiés vos, qu'il vienent chi.
Se Damedix n'en a merchi
990 Et proece ne nos desfent,
Mort estes tuit communement.
Chi vient li sire des felons,
Chi vient ses niés Rogelions,
Qui ainc ne firent se mal non
995 Et trecerie et traïson,
Et ains que soit li jours passés,
En cuident il bien faire assés.»
Ceste novele est espandue,
Et qant il l'ont tuit entendue
1000 Des palefrois tantost descendent
Et ces armes par tere estendent;
Nen i a nul qui tant soit fiers
De tous les .iii. .c. chevaliers
K'Illes n'ait plus grant vasselage
1005 Et plus de cuer et de corage.
Il s'arme au plus tost que il puet:
Tes armes a com lui estuet.
Monte el ceval par son estrier,
Saisist l'escu et prent l'espié;
1010 N'a song de faire malvés plait.
Des .iii. .c. trois batalles fait:
L'une en a son oncle livree,
L'autre a son neveu commandee.
Li François de sa compaignie
1015 Sont en celui qu'il maine et guie,

Çou est en tote la premiere,
Qui a plaissier n'ert pas legiere.
«Biax niés, fait il, n'i ait desroi:
Belement venés aprés moi,
1020 Et vous biax oncles, demorés
Et au besong me secorés.»
Illes li prex atant s'en part,
Enbruns sos l'elme, a un regart
Durement fier(s) et orgillous.
1025 Ses anemis ne vient pas sous:
A .v. cens chevaliers li sourt.
Il nen a pas el mon[t] tant sort
Qui bien n'oïst a l'assanler
1028a *La tiere bondir et tranbler.*
Al parvenir les lances baissent
1030 Et les escus fendent et plaissent,
Ces haubers rompent et desmallent;
Cist se desfendent, cist assalent.
Li nostre et cil sont tot commun,
.X. contre .ii. et .v. contre .i..
1035 Illes n'en a ke cent od lui,
S'en a bien .v. cens o celui,
Hardi et plain de grant vallance.
Illes i fiert tant de sa lance
Que ce n'est se mervelle non;
1040 Si fait Hoiax au cuer felon.
Ne s'entrecontrent cele fois
Que cascuns d'eus ne soit destrois.
Li estors est mout fors et fiers
Des .c. as .v. cens chevaliers:

987 armés]W   999 il ont]W   1011 De]W   1015 Dont]W   1017 plaisir]W
1023 sor l'elme]W   1033 u cil]Lö

Hoel is coming to meet you with his whole army, with five hundred armed knights. As you value your lives, put on your armour, for they are coming this way. If God does not have mercy on us, and prowess does not defend us, you are dead men, every last one of you. Here comes the lord of the villains, here comes his nephew Rogelion, two men who never did anything but evil and treachery and treason; and before the day is out, they surely plan to do a great deal more.' This news spread rapidly, and when all of them had heard it, they quickly dismounted from their palfreys and laid their arms out on the ground; and none of the whole three hundred knights was so bold but that Ille's valour and heart and courage were greater than his. (1006) He armed himself as quickly as he could: his arms were such as were befitting for him. He mounted his horse using the stirrup, grasped his shield and took up his lance; he was not worried about giving a poor account of himself. He divided the three hundred men into three companies: one he handed over to his uncle, and entrusted the other to his nephew. The French knights who accompanied him were in the company of which he was leader and commander: that is, the first in line, which would not be easy to overpower. 'Fair nephew,' he said, 'Let there be no confusion in the ranks: come quietly along behind me, and you, fair uncle, stay behind and come to my rescue if I need you.' At this, Ille the brave rode off, grim-faced beneath his helmet, with a look of great aggression and pride in his eye. (1025) His enemy did not come alone: he launched his attack on Ille with five hundred knights. No-one on earth is so deaf that he could not have heard *the ground ring and shudder* as they joined battle. As they closed with one another they lowered their lances and split and buckled their shields, tore and ripped open their hauberks; some defended, some attacked. Our side and the enemy all mingled together, ten men against two and five against one. Ille had only one hundred men with him, and Hoel had a good five hundred bold and extremely valiant men with him. Ille struck them so many blows with his lance that it was nothing short of marvellous; black-hearted Hoel did the same. They did not engage each other at this stage, in case both of them suffered. The battle between the hundred and the five hundred knights raged very fiercely:

Conain and his lovely sister Galeron'. W's 'Grant duel a son cuer en akiolt' may represent a scribal emendation of an original from which a couplet is missing.

1045 De tant ne fu ainc tex veüs.
Li .v. cent nes ont remeüs,
Les .c. chevaliers, de la place;
Mortex eüst esté la kace,
Ne fust la flors des chevaliers.
1050 Por çou vaut il estre as premiers,
Car, qui fait bien premierement
C'est avantages durement[1]
....
....
Ses anemis au premier tor,
Plus en est cremus tot le jor,
1055 Et cil en to[l]t le jor mains fier
Que l'on estoutoie au premier.
Mes cist sostienent trop grié fais.
Li doi cent vienent a eslais,
Dont Illes fist les .ii. batalles,
1060 Si ont lacies les ventalles,
Les lances sor les feutre[s] mises.
Sempres feront tex ademises
Qui mout feront a redouter.
Signor, plest vos a escoter?
1065 Es .ii. batalles dont je di
Sont li chevalier plus hardi
Que tigre u lion u lupart.
Li .c. lor vienent d'une part,
Et d'autre part li autre cent,
1070 Plus tost que quariax ne destent;
Tant com ceval pueent aler
Se vont lores entredoner.
Li vassal sont hardi et fier,

Et les anstes sont de pumier,[2]
1075 Et li fer agu et trencant,
Et li cop vertuex et grant;
S'i veïssiés tant escu fendre,
Et tant hauberc rompre et estendre
Et demallier et desconfire;
1080 N'est se mervelle non a dire.
Rogeslions au cuer felon
N'i fait le jor se tot mal non.
A .v. cens chevaliers i est
Qui trestot sont garni et prest
1085 D'Ille et des suens adamagier.
Tel i vont autrui ostagier
Qui i laisse[nt] le vie en ghage;
Ainc n'i ot parlé d'autre ostage.
Rogeslions soit li maudis!
1090 Il seus les a tous esbaudis.
Mout par i a hardi vassal:
Se plus n'i eüst fait de mal
Fors seulement ce qu'il i fait,
Assés i eüst honte et lait.
1095 Ille nos cuide desconfire
Et le nos cuide bien ochire,
Par ce que il le puisse aerdre,
Car por lui cuide honor perdre,
Qu'il onques n'ot ne ja n'avra.
1100 De Marcel que a mort navra
Le rehet mout estrangement,
Et cil ne l'aime de noient.
Tant vont li chevalier menbré
Que il se sont entrecontré.

1056 que l'en]W   1065 Ces]W (As)   1078 tant escu]W (obierc)
1093 il li fait]Lö   1100 qui amor navra]Lö

36

such a fierce battle was never seen between such numbers. The five hundred did not force the one hundred knights to give ground; there would have been a deadly pursuit if it had not been for Ille, the flower of knighthood. This is why he wanted to be in the front line, because for the man who fights well at the outset it is considerably to his advantage[1].................... on his enemies in the first encounter is more greatly feared by them for the rest of the day, while the man who has damage inflicted on him early on is less aggressive for the rest of the day. However, Ille's men were having too severe a punishment inflicted on them. The two hundred men whom Ille had allocated to the other two companies came galloping up with ventails laced and lances couched. They would soon be launching the sort of attacks which would inspire terror in the enemy. My lords, would you like to hear on? (1065) The knights in the two companies I am telling you about were fiercer than tigers or lions or leopards. One hundred came at them from one direction, and the other hundred from the other direction, swifter than the bolt flies from a crossbow; then they went to strike one another as fast as their horses could go. These were bold and aggressive knights, and the shafts of their lances were made of apple-wood,[2] and their iron lance-heads were pointed and sharp, and their blows were mighty and powerful; you would have seen countless shields being split open, and countless hauberks being torn and stretched to breaking-point, being ripped apart and destroyed; it was nothing short of marvellous to describe. Black-hearted Rogelion did nothing but the most evil of deeds that day. He was accompanied by five hundred knights who were all armed and ready to inflict damage on Ille and his men. (1086) Some men who went in to take others hostage left their own lives behind as surety; no other kind of hostage was mentioned there. A curse on Rogelion! His presence alone gave all his men new heart. He was an extremely daring knight: if no more harm had been done there than simply what he did, there would have been insult and injury enough. He planned to destroy our hero Ille and surely planned to kill him, provided that he could catch hold of him, for he imagined that on account of Ille he was losing honour, which never was and never would be his. He also hated Ille vehemently because of Marcel, who had been fatally wounded by Ille, and Ille certainly had no love for Rogelion. These celebrated knights fought on until they encountered each other.

---

[1] Löseth posits a lacuna after l. 1052; W's 'et estoltie durement' reads like a scribe's attempt to fill an equivalent gap in his original.

[2] The shafts of lances were commonly made of ash, a tough fibrous wood which is still widely used for handles of tools, etc. Apple wood has much the same physical

1105 Li chevalier sont mout tres bel
Et li ceval forment isnel,
Et li vassal bien les eslaissent;
Au parvenir les lances baissent
Et s'entrevienent par vertu.
1110 Et cil fiert Ille en son escu,
Isnelement sa lance froisse.
Illes le fiert par grant angoisse,
Car il l'ataint a descovert:
Le costé li a entrovert.
1115 Je vos di bien sans nul cuidier
Qu'il li fist la sele vuidier.
A tere ciet d'eus tous li pire;
S'il ja garist, c'ert par bon mire.
Sor une coute si l'emportent
1120 Icil qui mout se desconfortent.
    Grant sont li cri, grant sont li plor,
Mais onques por ce n'a retour
Que li estors ne soit pleniers.
Nus ne s'i prise .ii. deniers
1125 Se il n'i mostre sa vallance
Od l'espeë et o la lance.
Por la plaie Rogelion
En prenent tel religion
Dont maint ami pert mainte drue;
1130 Abatent les sor l'erbe drue
Navrés et mors et malballis.
Illes i est mout assalis:
Ce jor i suefre mout grant paine.
Le doel que Hoiax i demaine

1135 Ne puet nus dire ne conter;
Li maus en commence a monter.
Hoiax cerke les rens entor:
Ille vait querant en l'estour,
Une eure la, une eure chi,
1140 Tot sans pitié et sans merchi;
Cil revait ensi lui querant.
Tant vont le place requerant
Qu'il s'entrevienent en un val.
Mout sont andoi bon a ceval:
1145 Li quels que soit, sa mort i quiert.
Hoiax de plains eslais le fiert,
Que mout le cuida bien confondre:
L'escu li perce et li esfondre;
Petit en faut qu'il ne l'afole,
1150 Mes que la lance en pieces vole.
Illes, ki mie ne se faint,
Hoël en tel endroit ataint
Que l'auberc desront et desmalle
Et qu'il li perce la ventaille;
1155 Par son la crupe du ceval
En porte a tere le vassal.
En fuies tornent li plus haut;
Desconfit sont, autant se valt.
Tant en ocient a le kace,
1160 N'est hon el mont qui conte en face
Ne qui en sace a cief venir;
De pesme jour puet sovenir
Celui qui prison ne se rent.
Les uns ocist, les autres prent

38

The two knights cut very handsome figures and their horses were extremely swift, and the two men spurred them on well; as they joined battle they lowered their lances and encountered each other with force. And Rogelion struck Ille on his shield and immediately shattered his lance. Ille struck him an agonising blow, for he caught him unprotected: he sliced open his flank. I can tell you, and I am not imagining this, that he knocked him from the saddle. It was quite the worse of the two who fell to the ground; it would take a good doctor if he were ever to recover. He was carried off on a litter by his men, who were in a state of great distress.

There was great weeping, there was great wailing, but this did not prevent there being a pitched battle. No-one thought he was worth tuppence if he did not demonstrate his valour with sword and lance. (1127) In return for the wounding of Rogelion they imposed on their enemies a penance which meant that many a lady lost her lover; they struck them down wounded and dead and maimed on the thick grass. Ille was under fierce attack: he underwent a great ordeal out there that day. The grief that Hoel displayed out there defied description and narration; the danger began to intensify because of it. Hoel searched the ranks all around: he went looking for Ille in the mêlée, now here, now there, as pitiless and merciless as can be; Ille, likewise, went looking for him. They went searching the field until they encountered each other in a valley. Both of them were very good horseman: one of them, whichever it might be, was riding to his death. (1146) Hoel struck Ille at full tilt, having made up his mind to destroy him: he pierced his shield and broke it apart; he came very close to killing him, except that the lance flew into pieces. Ille, who was certainly not half-hearted, landed Hoel such a blow that he tore and ripped open his hauberk and pierced his ventail; he hurled his man to the ground straight over the horse's cruppers. The most senior of Hoel's men turned and fled; they were as good as defeated. Ille's men killed so many as they gave chase that no man on earth could have kept a count of them or have proved himself equal to the task; anyone who did not give himself up would remember this as the cruellest of days. Some were killed, and others taken prisoner

---

characteristics as ash. Apple trees were also reputed to have magical powers: the implication may be that a shaft made of apple-wood would help to protect its owner.

1165 Illes, qui cuer a de baron;
     Tous cex du linage felon
     Ra a le kace ocis et mors
     Et pris les autres par effors.
     Rogelion, ocis l'eüst
1170 Mout volentiers, se il peüst,
     Mes mout sont lonc de grant maniere
     Cil qui l'en portent en litiere.
     Et cil ki pris sont en l'estor
     Ont Ille rendu mainte tor
1175 Et maint palés et maint dongon;
     Tuit sont en sa subjection.
       Trestot s'asanle li barnages,
     Si en prent Illes les homages,
     Sauve le feüté le duc.
1180 Or est Hoiax pris au trebuc,
     Que canques fel vait decevant
     Li vient en le fin par devant.
     Or est Illes sire clamés,
     Or est il durement amés;
1185 Bien a deservi qu'il soit sire.
     Et qant li dus Conain[s] l'ot dire,
     Mout en a grant joie a[n] son cuer,
     Et Galerons, sa bele suer,
     En a tel joie qant el l'ot
1190 Que onques mais si grant nen ot.
     Li dus Conains a lui le mande:
     Tote Bretaigne li commande,
     Qu'il en soit sire et senescaus,
     Que cambrelens ne mariscax

1195 Ne nus hom de sa region
     Ne face rien se par lui non.
     Il meïsmes del tot s'i met,
     Que il sor lui ne s'entremet
     De rien dont on le mete en plait.
1200 Tot ce k'Illes veut faire est fait;
     Nus ne li ose estre a contraire.
     Illes est mout de bel afaire
     Et preus et sages et senés;
     Del duc servir est mout penés.
1205 Tote Bretagne la petite
     Li met en pais et li aquite;
     Les tors abaisse et fait les drois
     Et en justice est fors et rois:
     Mainte male costume abaisse.¹
1210 Mais il, qui les orgillex plaisse,
     Est durement bleciés d'amor:
     Ses maus ne fine nuit ne jor.
     Por celi est en grant bataille
     Qui por s'amor paine et travalle;
1215 Andoi en sont a cier escot,
     Mais l'uns de l'autre ne set mot.
     Ne Illes nel set de celi,
     Ne Galerons que cil aint li,
     Car cele est si tres haute cose
1220 Que cil descouvrir ne li ose,
     N'ele ne li descoverroit
     Premierement por rien qui soit,
     Qu'il n'afiert pas que feme die
     «Je voel devenir vostre amie»,

1165 de felon]W   1172 porte]Lö   1189 ele ot]W   1196 por lui]W

by Ille, who had the heart of a noble warrior; he also killed and slew in the chase all those who belonged to Hoel's villainous family, and took the others prisoner by force. He would very gladly have killed Rogelion, if he could have, but the men who were bearing him away on a litter were a very long way off indeed. Those who were taken prisoner in the battle also surrendered many a tower and many a palace and many a keep to Ille; they all submitted to his authority.

The whole assembly of barons gathered, and Ille received their homage, without prejudice to their fealty to the duke. Now it was Hoel who was caught in the trap, because whatever treachery a villain commits catches up with him in the end. Now Ille was proclaimed lord, now he was held in very great affection; he had thoroughly deserved to be lord. (1186) And when Duke Conain heard about it, he rejoiced greatly in his heart, and when she heard the news his beautiful sister Galeron was more overjoyed than she had ever been before. Duke Conain sent for Ille: he commanded the whole of Brittany to him, making him its lord and seneschal, so that no action could be taken by chamberlain or marshal or any man in Conain's territory, except through him. Ille himself put all his energies into ensuring that nothing for which the duke gave him responsibility would give cause for complaint. Everything Ille wanted to do was done; no-one dared to oppose him. Ille conducted himself admirably, and he was a man of courage, wisdom and good sense; he strove hard to serve the duke. (1205) He restored peace to the whole of Brittany for him and brought it back under his control; he demolished his enemies' towers and dispensed justice and was strong and firm in his judgements: he abolished many an evil custom.[1] However, the man who subdued the arrogant was himself seriously wounded by love: his suffering continued night and day. He was being hard pressed on account of a woman who was suffering and struggling for love of him; both of them were being made to pay a heavy price, but neither knew a thing about the other's situation. Ille did not know that she loved him, nor did Galeron know that he loved her, for she was of such elevated rank that he did not dare reveal his love to her, and she would not reveal her love to him first for anything in the world, because it is not fitting for a woman to say 'I want to be your love',

---

[1] Gautier observes the romance convention which casts the hero in the role of abolisher of evil customs, but without making the ending of an evil custom into a separate episode, as Chrétien de Troyes does in *Erec et Enide* or *Yvain*.

1225 Por c'on ne l'ait ançois requise
Et mout esté en son service.
Ne li bas home ne li haut
N'estoient mie lors si baut
Com il sont ore la moitié:
1230 Or cuide il avoir esploitié
Ains qu'il ait fait le quarantaine,
Car s'on n'esploite en la semaine,
Ja n'i querra on puis venir.
On ne voit mais lonc plet tenir:
1235 Nus hom n'est mais coars del dire,
Car se ce vient a l'escondire,
Aillors revait querre autretel;
S'il a son bon, il ne quiert el.
Amors n'est pas de tel manere,
1240 Qu'el ne volt pas que nus i quiere
Riens outre ce qu'il i dessert;
Mes son service nus n'i pert,
Por que il soit de bone atente:
Amors ne taut nului sa rente.
1245 Cil qui tant set plaindre et proier
Ne fait el k'amour desvoier
Com li popelicans la loi,
Qui les homes maine a besloi,
Qui se consire(nt) de la car
1250 Por les gens mener a escar.
Ce fait, et promet plus a faire,
Por nous et por la loi desfaire:
Ensi l'ont commencié pieça.¹
Autresi font cist par deça

1255 Qui se plaignent et mal nen ont,
Et mout prometent et poi font.
Sovent en sont les durfeües
Par ces promesses deceües.
De legier croit, tost est gabee
1260 Cele qui a folie bee,
Mes pluisors qui de ce n'ont cure
Ont por promesses grant rancure,
Croient por ce que trop sont simples:
Sovent en mollent puis lor gimple[s],
1265 Qu'eles en plorent caudes lermes.
Sire Dix, venra ja li termes
Que tel amant soient destruit?
Cui chaut? Ja voit on par le fruit
Quels est de l'arbre li raïs.
1270 Bien gart cascuns ne soit traïs,
Cascune que ne soit traïe!
La sage a tos jors bone aïe,
Car Sapience est sa compagne,
Que nus hom ne li face engaigne,
1275 Et bien li mostre apertement
Se nus l'aime parfaitement.
Fole ne connoist son anui,
N'ele ne set amer nului,
Ne nus ne doit a li entendre,
1280 Ne por s'amor grant paine rendre,
Qu'en fol n'en fole nen a rien
De bone amor ne d'autre bien,
Car Amors est sans vilonie,
Et fol et fole nel sont mie.

· 1228 n'e. pas livre si haut]W (balt)   1232 s'on esploite]W   1233 pora]W
1238 il requiert el]W   1240 ne voit pas]W(violt)   1247 n'a loi]W   1264 plus]W
1268 Qui]W   1272 Li sage]W

if a man has not previously asked for her love and spent a long time in her service. Neither men of low nor men of high estate were half so full of themselves then as they are now: nowadays a man plans to have had his way before he has put in forty days' service, for if he does not have his way within the week, he will make no attempt to approach her again. You no longer see men engaging in long courtships: no-one is backward in coming forward any longer, for if he ends up being rejected, he simply goes after the same thing elsewhere; if he gets what he wants, that is all he is after. Love is not like this, because she does not wish a man to ask anything of a woman beyond what he deserves from her; but no-one's love-service is wasted, provided that he is patient: Love does not deny anyone the return on his investment. (1245) The man who is forever bemoaning his lot and making demands is simply subverting love, just as the true faith is subverted by the heretic who leads men astray, who abstains from flesh and the pleasures of the flesh in order to make a laughing-stock of people. This is what he does, and he promises to do more, in order to bring us and the true faith to ruin: the heretics embarked on this some time ago.[1] The same is being done by these people over here who bemoan their lot when they are not suffering, and promise much and deliver little. Hapless women are often deceived by these promises. A woman who is prone to folly readily believes and is easily made a fool of, but many women who have no inclination for folly experience great sorrow on account of promises, believing in them because they are so naïve: later on, their wimples are often wet with the bitter tears they weep because of them. Lord God, will the time ever come when such lovers are done away with? What matter? One can always tell by the fruit what the root of the tree is like. (1270) Let every man take good care not to be deceived, let every woman do likewise! The wise woman always has good help at hand, for her companion is Wisdom, who is there so that no man may practise deception upon her, and shows her quite clearly whether a man's love for her is true. A foolish woman does not recognise what is bad for her, nor does she know how to love a man, nor should any man aspire to her love, or go to great pains to win it, for neither foolish men nor foolish women have anything of true love or other virtues in them, for Love is devoid of baseness, and foolish men and foolish women are not.

---

[1] By Gautier's day the Cathar heresy, a form of Manichean dualism which had originated in the Balkans in the 10th century, was known throughout France and was perceived as a serious threat by the orthodox church. The *perfecti*, or Cathar priesthood, were rigorously ascetic, and abstained from eating meat and having sexual intercourse. Likening insincere lovers to heretics is an interesting extension of the idea of love as a religion, which is common in romance and lyric poetry.

43

1285 Ne cuidiés ja que garçonier
　　　Soient ja d'amor parçonier,
　　　Ne ja nc scront parçonieres
　　　Celes qui en sont garçonieres,
　　　Que tote gent lor sont commun,
1290 Ensi li blanc come li brun,[1]
　　　Et aiment ausi tost o ains
　　　Les plus sos et tous les plus fains
　　　Com ceus qui ont en lor baillie
　　　Proece, sens et cortoisie.
1295 Icestes qui ce faire suelent
　　　Heent si tost com eles voelent,
　　　K'Amours ne les puet assegier;[2]
　　　Por ce si heent de legier:
　　　Qui ainc n'ama, de legier het.
1300 Cele qui plus faindre se set
　　　Et cil qui plus de ciere en font
　　　Sont cil qui mains soupris en sont,
　　　Car s'il amoient tant ne quant,
　　　Il ne feroient ja sanlant;
1305 Ains souferroient lor anui
　　　Si faitement com font cist dui,
　　　Qui se lairoient ains desfaire
　　　Que nus hom seüst lor afaire.
　　　Il pense en soi: «Ne li caut mie
1310 Qu'ele a tel home soit amie,
　　　N'a moi que soie ses amis.
　　　Mout ai en fol liu mon cuer mis,
　　　Car se li dus s'apercevoit
　　　De sa seror que je covoit,

1315 Trestot mon service en perdroie,
　　　Et d'autre part rien n'en aroie
　　　Se mal gré non: ne sai que faire.
　　　Assés est fel et de mal aire
　　　Qui tel destorbier melle et muet
1320 Que il puis abaissier ne puet,
　　　Mes maint le font, ne sai por coi.
　　　Issi a fait Amors de moi,
　　　Qui por celi me fait villier
　　　Dont nus ne me puet consillier;
1325 Ne nul conseil sossiel ne truis
　　　Fors en ce que j'avoir ne puis.
　　　Amors maint vallant home esprent
　　　De ce dont talens ne li prent,
　　　Ne n'en poroit a cief venir
1330 Ne k'empereres devenir;
　　　Et s'il en ert a cief venus,
　　　Si en seroit por fol tenus,
　　　Por c'on le peüst aperçoivre.
　　　Puet ele donques mix deçoivre
1335 Et puet ele dont mix traïr?
　　　Mix me venroit celi haïr
　　　Qui de moi nuire est costumiere,
　　　Que li amer en tel maniere;
　　　Mais haïr ne le doi je mie,
1340 Ne voloir qu'ele soit m'amie,
　　　Ne li amer en tel endroit,
　　　Ne de noient haïr par droit.
　　　Las! s'a çou tenir me pooie,
　　　N'aroie mal; garis seroie.

1302 plus soupris]Lö　1317 maugre]Lö　1319 Que]Lö

44

Do not imagine that men of easy virtue could ever have a share in love, and love will never be shared by women of easy virtue, for they are intimate with all sorts of men, the fair as well as the dark,[1] and they would just as soon, or sooner, love the most stupid of men and the greatest cowards as those who are possessed of courage, good sense and courtliness. Women who normally behave in this way are able to hate a man as soon as the fancy takes them, because Love cannot lay siege to them;[2] this is why they can hate so easily: a person who never loved finds it easy to hate. (1300) The woman who is best at faking love and the men who put it on the most are the ones least affected by it, for if they loved at all, they would never make out that they did; rather, they would suffer their distress in silence, just as these two did, who would have let themselves be put to death before anyone learned of their situation. Ille thought to himself: 'She has no interest in being loved by a man like me, nor is it in my interests to be loved by her. I have set my heart on a very foolish thing, for if the duke were to realise that I desired his sister, all my service would be wasted, and, what's more, I would have nothing but ill-will in return: I do not know what to do. Anyone who stirs up and provokes trouble which he cannot then overcome is pretty much of an evil-natured villain, but many people do it, I do not know why. This is what Love has done with me, forcing me to dishonour myself on account of a woman no-one can help me to attain; I can find no earthly help except in what I cannot have. (1327) Love fires many a valiant man with passion for a woman he does not wish to love, and whom he could no more make his own than he could become emperor; what's more, if he did make her his own, people would only have to become aware of it for him to be taken for a fool. Can there be a better way for Love to deceive people, a better way for her to betray them? It would be better for me to hate this woman who is in the habit of hurting me, than to love her the way I do; but I must neither hate her nor want her to be my love; the right thing to do is neither to love her in this fashion nor in any way hate her. Alas! if I could keep to this, I would feel no pain: I would be cured.

---

1 W has 'Ensi li bai come li brun', which makes a nonsense of the rhetorical figure of *distributio*: a bay horse *is* brown.

2 Gautier here anticipates the siege imagery of ll. 5612-31, where Ille's growing love for Ganor is represented as a knight besieging the citadel occupied by his feelings for Galeron. Lines 1329-30 also look forward to a later stage in the narrative: Ille will, of course, marry the woman he has fallen in love with, and ultimately become emperor. What is impossible for most men is achieved by the hero.

1345 Mais ne sui pas del tot a moi,
Et cil qui mie n'est a soi
N'oevre pas tot si com il veut,
Ains fait sovent dont mout se delt.
E las! caitis, com je me duel!
1350 Je faç tot el que je ne voel.
Amors, qui m'ocit et enserre,
Devroit on le mesfait requerre,
Qu'ele m'a mis en ceste brice;
Mais de tot ce que font li rice,
1355 Li roi, li conte, li haut home
Sostienent li caitif la some:
Li rice tencent, mes l'estrif
Comperent sovent li caitif.
Espoir Amors n'est pas haitie,
1360 K'aucuns l'a malement traïe.
Or si me vent autrui mesfait[1]
Tot ausi com li dervés fait,
Qui ja ne toucera celui
Qui feru l'a, ains fiert autrui.
1365 Grant pieç'a que jou ai apris
Que haute amors met home en pris,
Mais de cesti n'aroie cure,
Qu'el est trop haute a desmesure.
E las! por coi m'en sui je plains?
1370 Et ne poroit pas estre estains
Li max qui si me trait et tire
Se par mort non u par martire?»
Si se plaint Illes lonc de gent,
Et Galerons o le cors jent

1375 N'est de rien nule plus a aise,
Qu'ele n'a cose qui li plaise.
Belement dist et en recoi:
«Biax sire Dix, qu'ert il de moi?
Com je par sui maleüreuse
1380 Quant de celui sui sofraiteuse
Qui devroit estre sofraitex,
De mon jent cors le covoitex;
Et bien me devroit covoitier
Se il i cuidoit esploitier.
1385 Amors me fait a celui tendre
Qui d'amor n'ose a moi entendre.
A grant soufraite me deduis
De la cose que j'avoir puis;
La cose que je plus desir
1390 Puis bien avoir, si m'en consir.
Mais qu'en diroit li fix mon pere
Se je disoie: «Biax dous frere,
Car me donés Ille a mari.»?
A! com se tenroit a gari!
1395 Amee m'a tant comme soi,
Si laisse por amor de moi
Qu'il ne prent feme a mariage,
Qu'il veut que j'aie l'iretage.»
Lors se repense et dist: «Comment
1400 Te donroit il plus hautement?
Cis li a mis en pais sa tere
Et apaisie mainte guerre.
Sire Dix, qu'en dira li dus?
S'il ne le veut, je n'en sai plus,

1351 ocist]Lö   1361 Or si muevent   1368 Quil]Lö (ele)

46

But I am not altogether my own man, and anyone who is not his own man does not act entirely as he wishes; instead, he often does things which make him very unhappy. Alas, poor wretch, how unhappy I am! What I am doing is quite the opposite of what I want. It is Love, who has me in her deadly clutches, who should be held reponsible for this crime, because she is the one who has put me in this predicament; but the poor have to bear the brunt of everything the rich – the kings, the counts, the high-ranking men – do: the rich may quarrel, but it is the poor who often pay for the dispute. Maybe Love is out of sorts because she has been cruelly betrayed by someone. So now she is making me pay for someone else's misdeed,[1] just like the madman who will never touch the person who has struck him, but strikes someone else instead. (1365) It is a long time since I learned that a noble love enhances a man's reputation; but I should not concern myself with this love, because it is too noble for me, by a long way. Alas! why have I been lamenting over it? And would death or martyrdom be the only way to quench this fever which is tormenting me so?' So Ille lamented, away from everyone, and the beautiful Galeron was certainly in no more enjoyable a situation than him, for nothing she had gave her any pleasure. Quietly and in secret she said to herself: 'Dear Lord God, what will become of me? How dreadfully unfortunate I am, to be yearning for someone who should be yearning for me, desiring my beautiful body; and desire me he would, if he thought he could succeed in it. (1385) Love is fixing my hopes on someone who dare not entertain thoughts of love for me. This deep yearning is all the enjoyment I derive from something which I can have; I can surely have the thing I most desire, yet I am doing without it. But what would my father's son say if I were to say: "Fair gentle brother, give me Ille in marriage"? Ah! he would indeed think himself lucky! He has loved me like himself, and he refuses to take a wife out of love for me, because he wants the inheritance to come to me.' Then she thought again and said: 'How could he give you to a nobler man? Ille has restored peace to his country and put an end to many a conflict for him. Lord God, what will the duke say? All I know is that if he does not agree,

---

1 W has 'Or se muet et autrui mesfait', which is less satisfactory than the emendation proposed here, and reads like a scribe's attempt to make sense of a MS which also had the reading *muevent*.

folio 299^r a

1405 Mais tot le siecle guerpirai
      Et por amor Diu m'en irai
      En l'abeïe de nounains.»[1]
      Un jour avint que dus Conains
      Monta por soi esbanoier.
1410 De cex quil suelent gerroier
      Se prist li dus a porpenser
      K'ainc ne se pot vers ex tenser;
      Ore n'a il un seul voisin
      K'Illes n'ait fait a lui aclin:
1415 Tous les a mis desous ses piés,
      S'en est li dus joians et liés.
      Or li vaurra gerredoner,
      Sa seror li vaura doner:
      Miex ne le puet il marïer,
1420 Que se nus le veut tarïer
      Et guerroier et assalir,
      Cil ne li pora pas falir;
      Prés li sera s'il a besong.
      Mes d'une cose est il en song,
1425 Que Galerons ne voelle mie
      Estre sa feme ne s'amie;
      Mais trop li tarde et li demeure.[2]
      Qant li dus voit le terme et l'eure,
      Si l'aparole en tel maniere:
1430 «Entendés moi, suer doce ciere.
      Par icel Diu qui maint sor nous,
      Je n'aim riens nule plus de vous.
      Por ce me plairoit, bele nee,
      Que vous fuissiés bien assenee

1435 En mon vivant a tel signeur
      Que vous i eüssiés houneur
      Et ki ma tere maintenist,
      Quel que de moi puis avenist.
      – De qui volés vos dire, sire?
1440 – Bele sage, je n'ose dire.
      Je vous dirai assés de cui;
      Sel saverés encor encui.
      – Trestot en soiés, sire, quites.
      Gardés que ja rien ne m'en dites
1445 Que ne soit prex a maintenir,
      Ne dont ne puisse a cief venir,
      Car je vauroie mix estre arse
      Et fust a vant la pourre esparse
      Que jel feïsse contre cuer.
1450 – Est il dont nus hom, doce suer,
      Qui soit a vostre volenté?
      – Sire, se Dix me doinst santé,
      Oïl, car un tel home sai.
      Ja nul n'en arai se lui n'ai.
1455 – Suer, qui est il? Només le moi!
      – Sire, par le foi que vous doi,
      Içou est vostre senescaus.
      S'il estoit tos nus et descaus,
      Si me plairoit il mix, biaus sire,
1460 Que l'emperere a tout l'empire.
      – Suer, n'avés mie mescoisi,
      Et Damedex m'aït ensi
      Com c'est li hom qui plus me plaist,
      Que de tos ses bienfais se taist

1426 Estre sa seror]W

48

I shall renounce this world altogether and retire into the nunnery for the love of God.'[1] One day, Duke Conain happened to go riding to amuse himself. The duke began to think about those who used to make war on him, and the fact that he could never defend himself against them; now he did not have a single neighbour whom Ille had not made subject to his authority: they had all been brought to heel, and he rejoiced and was glad of it. Now he intended to reward Ille; it was his intention to give him his sister's hand: he could not arrange a better marriage for her, since if anyone wanted to harm him, make war on him or attack him, Ille could not fail him; he would be close at hand if the duke needed him. (1424) However, one thing was worrying Conain: namely, that Galeron might not want to be Ille's wife or his love; but, for her, that day could not come soon or swiftly enough.[2] When the duke saw the right time and the opportunity, this is how he spoke to her: 'Listen to me, sweet sister of mine. By the God who dwells above us, there is no-one I love more than you. For this reason, lovely girl, I would like proper provision to be made for you during my lifetime with a husband who would bring you honour and preserve my dukedom, whatever might happen to me subsequently.' – 'Whom do you mean, my lord?' – 'Wise and beautiful girl, I dare not tell you. I shall tell you a good deal about him; you will know who it is before the day is out.' – 'You are not under any obligation to, my lord. (1444) Be careful not to tell me anything about him which it would be dishonourable for me to endorse, or which I would not be able to come to terms with, for I would rather be burned alive and have my ashes scattered to the winds than be a reluctant bride.' – 'Is there a man, then, who meets with your approval, sweet sister?' – 'My lord, as God may grant me health, yes, I do know of one such man. I shall never have any man if I do not have him.' – 'Sister, who is he? Tell me his name!' – 'My lord, by the loyalty I owe you, it is your seneschal. Even if he were naked and barefoot, I would like him better, my lord, than the emperor with all his empire.' – 'Sister, you have not made a bad choice at all, and, so help me God, he is the man I like the best, because he keeps quiet about all his good deeds

---

[1] This resolution forms the first stage in the process of preparing the audience for Galeron's eventual retirement to a convent after the birth of her third child (ll. 5304-10).

[2] *Li* is ambiguous here: it could also be taken as referring to Conain himself ('but for the duke, the day could not come soon or swiftly enough'). I prefer to see this line as a narratorial reminder of Galeron's true feelings.

1465 Et de le moitié qu'il fait seus
Esrageroit uns orgillex.
Rendue m'a en pais ma terre.
– Se je le vos osaisse querre,
Pieça gel vous eüsse quis.

1470 – Ore m'avés del tout conquis;
Ainc mais de rien ne fui si liés.»
Et Galerons li vait as piés;
Li dus Conains l'en lieve amont,
Qui de grant joie le semont.

1475 Li dus Conains a Ille vient:
«Amis, fait il, bien me sovient
Que m'avés ricement servi.
Bien soit de l'eure que vous vi!
Or vos ert tot guerredoné.

1480 – Sire, vos m'avés tant doné!
– Encor vos ferai plus d'oneur,
Car je vous donrai ma sereur
Par mains d'evesques et d'abés.
– Sire, por Diu, ne me gabés,

1485 K'ainc nel desservi a nul jour.
– Amis, se Dix me doinst honor,
N'ai de vos gaber nule envie,
Car je vous donrai en ma vie
Assés de canques tere carge,

1490 Et .iiii. castiax en la marce,
Et plaine tere avrés adiés,
Et trestot aprés men decés,
Et ma seror qui tant est bele,
De cui li quens d'Angau m'apele,

1495 Et cil de Poitiers, qui m'en prie,
Et li bons dus de Normendie.
Ele nen a de nul d'aus cure;
Si m'en portent tot .iii. rancure,
Que je ne lo(i)r dong ma sereur.»

1500 Cil en va as piés son signeur;
Li dus l'en lieve isnelement,
Et cil li dist mout belement:
«Sire, vos m'avés mout offert,
Mais il n'ert ja espoir sofert

1505 Endroit de li k'ele me pregne,
Des qu'ele nul de cex n'adaigne.
– Amis, s'a li en voel plaidier,
Je vos i porai bien aidier,
Mais j'en voel estre bien loés[1]

1510 – Sire, se faire le poés,
Nel vos porai guerr(r)edoner.
Vendre me poés et doner,
Mais tout ice monte a petit.»
Et li dus Conains en sorrit.

1515 Li dus tramet por la pucele
Et se li dist: «Amie biele,
Je vos aim mout de bone foi.
Car prenés por l'amor de moi
Ille a mari, car entresait

1520 Voel et commanc que il vos ait.
– Biax sire, qant? – Hui en ce jour.
– Et je l'otroi por vostre amour.»
A le court ot un arcevesque
Et un abé et un evesque,

488 en maie]W   1506 nus]W   1509 luies]W

50

when an arrogant man would rant and rave about half of what Ille achieves alone. He has restored my dukedom to me free of conflict.' – 'If I had dared to ask you for him, I would have asked you long before now.' – 'Now you have completely won me over: I was never so glad about anything before.' Then Galeron threw herself at his feet; Duke Conain, who held out the prospect of great joy to her, raised her up. Duke Conain came to Ille: 'My friend,' he said, 'I am very mindful that you have given me splendid service. Blessed be the day when I first saw you! Now you will be rewarded for everything.' – 'My lord, you have already given me so much!' – 'I shall do you an even greater honour, for I shall give you my sister, and bishops and abbots will celebrate your marriage.' – 'My lord, for God's sake, do not make fun of me, for I never deserved it at any time.' – (1486) 'My friend, as God may grant me honour, I have no desire to make fun of you, for while I am alive I shall give you an abundance of everything the earth produces, and four castles in the marches, and open land will be yours straight away, and after my death everything will be yours, as well as my sister, who is so beautiful that the Count of Anjou keeps asking me for her hand, and the Count of Poitiers keeps begging me for it, as does the good Duke of Normandy. She is not interested in any of them, and all three of them bear a grudge against me for not giving them my sister.' Ille fell at his lord's feet; the duke immediately raised him up, and Ille said to him, very courteously: 'My lord, you have offered me a great deal; but, for her part, she is unlikely to be content to marry me, since she does think any of these men worthy of her.' – (1507) 'My friend, if I am willing to plead your case with her, I shall certainly be able to further your cause, but I expect to be well rewarded for it.'[1] – 'My lord, if you can do it, I shall not be able to repay you. You may sell me and give me away, but all this does not amount to very much.' Then Duke Conain smiled at this. The duke sent for the noble maiden and said to her : 'Fair friend, I love you dearly, in good faith. Now, for love of me, take Ille as your husband, for it is my wish and my command that he should marry you straight away.' – 'When, fair lord?' – 'This very day.' – 'And I agree, for love of you.' There was an archbishop at court, and an abbot and a bishop,

---

[1] Although the graphy *loés* is required for the rhyme, this is clearly *luer/luier/loer* = 'to hire, to pay' not *loer* = 'to praise'. Ille's reply continues the motif of payment and reward.

1525 Si ont la pucele espousee.
Illes, ki mout l'a goulousee,
Et Galerons ne font c'un lit,
Et ont tel joie et tel delit
Que nus hom nel poroit conter.
1530 Or commence joie a monter,
K'ainc tant n'ot hom en une nuis.
Puis orent entr'aus mains anuis
Et mainte grant mesaventure.
Tele est Amors et sa nature:
1535 Nus ne le maintient longement
Qu'il n'ait entremesleement
Assés de tel misture en lui:
Une eure joie et l'autre anui.
Qant li conte oent la novele
1540 Et d'Ille et de la damoisele,
L'uns mande l'autre par mesage
Qu'il face assanler son barnage
Et viegne vengier cele honte.
Vient i et li dus et li conte,
1545 Et cascuns d'aus a tel pooir
Com il puet sossiel plus avoir.
Ne vienent pas si a emblee
K'Illes n'ait faite s'assanlee
Ançois que viegnent en Bretagne:
1550 Il n'est nus hom c'a lui ataigne
Qui la ne viegne a son effors.
Par uns destrois doutés et fors
Convient passer les Poitevins,
Les Normans et les Angevins.

1555 Tant oirrent seré et estroit
Qu'il sont venu a cel destroit;
Prés de la haie se logierent.
Nuis fu qant illec herbergierent,
Et a l'endemain passeront,
1560 Ce dient tuit, mes non feront:
Ne cuic pas k'Illes lor consente,
Que livrer lor cuide autre entente.
Illes, li preus, li bien apris,
Les a ains l'ajorner soupris,
1565 Et prent le duc et les .ii. contes.
Li autre ont assés lais et hontes,
Malaventure et mesproison,
Des que li prince sont prison.
Qui qu'en ait joie ne moleste,
1570 La suer au duc en fist tel feste,
La dame n'ara mais tel joie:
Mout li demeure qu'el le voie.
D'Ille, le preu, le bel, le jent,
Parolent en bien toute gent,
1575 Car il n'est nus qui tant soit sire
De cui on puisse tel bien dire.
En lui nen a riens a blasmer,
Qu'il aime canqu'il doit amer,
Et mostre a l'ome cui il het
1580 Confaitement haïr le set.
Or est la suer au duc mout lie,
Qui a esté contraliie
De gent malvaise et anïeuse,
De pesme et de contralïeuse.

1533 grans]W   1536 entre mes liement]W   1537 mistere   1556 tel destroit]Lö
1558 qant Ille]Lf

and they celebrated the maiden's marriage. Ille, who had longed for her so much, shared one bed with Galeron, and they experienced such joy and such delight that it defies description. Now joy was in the ascendant, for no man ever experienced so much in one night. Later, the two of them experienced much grief and many a great misfortune. Such is love, such is its nature: no-one keeps it for long without such mixed emotions frequently intermingling within him: joy one moment and grief the next. When the counts heard the news about Ille and the damsel, one sent a messenger to the other, urging him to muster his troops and come to avenge this insult. (1544) Both the duke and the counts arrived, and each of them had the largest force that he could possibly bring. Their advance was not secret enough to prevent Ille from mustering his troops before they entered Brittany. Every man who was in any way related to Ille came there to join his forces. The Poitevins, the Normans and the Angevins had to pass through a formidable defile. They travelled in a close and tight formation until they came to this defile, and camped near the hedge. It was night-time when they made camp there, and they all said that they would pass through the defile next morning; but they would not. I do not believe that Ille would allow them to; he had a different plan in mind for them. Ille the brave, the accomplished, made a surprise attack on them before daybreak, and took the duke and the two counts prisoner. (1566) The others suffered considerable damage and disgrace, misfortune and humiliation, when once the princes were prisoners. Whoever else may have been joyful or despondent at the news, the duke's sister was so elated that this lady would never know such joy again: she was very impatient to see Ille. Everyone spoke well of Ille the brave, the handsome, the noble, for there was no-one in a position of such authority about whom so much good could be said. There was nothing blameworthy about him, for he loved whoever deserved his love, and showed the men he hated just how capable he was of hating them.

Now the duke's sister, who had been defied by evil-minded trouble-makers, wicked and defiant men, was very happy.

1585 Illes, li preus, li afaitiés,
Est durement fors et haitiés:
Il est amontés par proece,
Par cortoisie et par largece.
Por çou les tient il en cierté,
1590 Et mains lor mostre de fierté
Qu'il ne fist ains qu'il l'eüst pris:[1]
Ne puet pas estre de grant pris
K'a celui faire honte bé(e)[2]
Qui l'a haucié et amonté(e).
1595 Diex! qui veïst et qui oïst
Com Illes, li preus, s'esgoïst!
Sa joie croist et renovele
Por amor a le demoisele,
Car il nen a el mont celi
1600 Qui de biauté se pregne a li;
Trestos li mons le loe et prise,
Car on ne set si bien aprise.
Por çou est Illes plus en grant
D'estre tous jors a son commant,
1605 A son voloir, a son plaisir.
Illes n'ot onkes jour loisir
De dire a nului vilonie,
Ne ramprosne ne felonie:
N'ert mie vilains chevaliers,
1610 N'aprés les armes malparliers.
Chevaliers n'ert lors si Rollans,
Si Oliviers, si Agoulans,[3]
S'il fust enteciés de tel visse,
Qu'on [ne] le tenist mout a nice.

1615 Bien sai que du diable est plains
Qui por sa proece est vilains.
Vilenie vient de vil leu,
Et cortoisie vient de Diu,
Et qui de par Diu prex devient,
1620 Cortoisie aime et se s'i tient.
Or a Illes tout a son cois
Por çou qu'il est preus et cortois.
Tos jors estoit amis entiers:
Mout le veoit on volentiers
1625 Quant il aloit esbanoier.
Un jour ert alés tornoier,
Si com il ot fait mainte fois.
Mout par ert rices li tornois,
Qu'il i ot trois mil chevaliers
1630 Hardis et corajous et fiers,
Et s'en i ot de mout estous,
Et Illes les i venqui tous.
Ensi fu li afaires pris
K'Illes ot d'ans .ii. pars le pris:
1635 Ne li remaint lance a brisier.
La riens qui mains fait a prisier
Et puet avoir mains de duree,
C'est cose trop desmesuree;
Ne mais ce que avenir doit
1640 Ne puet nus tolir qu'il ne soit,
Soit de noier, ocire u ardre.
Si com li tornois dut espardre,
Illes, li preus, ki s'en venoit,
Vit une lance c'uns tenoit,

1603 en grans]Lö

54

Ille the brave, the well-bred, was in an extremely strong and healthy situation: courage, courtliness and generosity had brought him his success. This is why he treated the princes with affection and displayed less hostility towards them than he did before he had taken them prisoner:[1] no-one deserves to be held in great esteem who seeks to inflict dishonour[2] on the man who has enhanced his reputation and success. God! If you had seen and heard how Ille the brave rejoiced! His joy increased and redoubled because of his love for the damsel, for there was no woman in the world who could rival her beauty: she was praised and esteemed by everyone, because she was the most accomplished woman they knew. This is why Ille was all the more eager to be always at her command, to do her wishes and her pleasure. (1606) Ille never had occasion to make uncourtly, insulting or malicious remarks to anyone: as a knight he was free from baseness, and not one for backbiting when he had left the field. At that time, any knight, however much of a Roland or an Oliver or an Agolant he might be,[3] would have been considered a proper simpleton if he had been tainted with such a vice. I know for a fact that a man who is guilty of baseness on account of his own prowess is possessed by the devil. Baseness comes from a base source, and courtliness comes from God, and a man whom God enables to become a hero loves courtliness and holds fast to it. Now Ille had everything as he wanted it, because prowess and courtliness were his. He was an unfailingly loyal friend: people were very glad to see him when he went out in search of sport. (1626) One day he had gone to take part in a tourney, as he had done many times before. It was an extremely splendid tourney, attended by three thousand bold, courageous and aggressive knights; there were some very daring fighters there, and Ille won the day against all of them. As events turned out, Ille was proclaimed champion by both sides: he had no lances left to break. The least praiseworthy thing there is, and potentially the shortest-lived, is something that exceeds the bounds of moderation; only no-one can prevent what must be from happening, be it death by water, by the sword or by fire. Just as the tourney was due to break up, Ille the brave, who was leaving it, saw someone holding a lance,

---

1 The sense requires the plural pronoun *les*, which would give a line of 9 syllables. The majority of lines in P which appear to be hypermetrical (e.g. ll. 530, 555, 622, 634, 2531) include a word containing *ié*, which could be pronounced as either one syllable or two.

2 *Ke* (*que*) for *ki* (*qui*); a Picard trait.

3 Three of the most famous heroes of the *chansons de geste*: the Christian knights Roland and Oliver appear in *La Chanson de Roland*, as well as in a number of later epics of the *cycle du roi*, while the Saracen Agolant is one of the protagonists of *La*

1645 Si le toli a l'escuier
Por jouster a un chevalier
Qui la tout droit estoit venus;
Galopant va les saus menus.
Et Illes se porpense en soi
1650 Qu'il ot tot vencu le tornoi
Et ke cis seus n'en ira mie
Qu'il n'ait le joste; por s'amie
Ne l'osa ne nel vaut laissier.
Le ceval prist a eslaissier,
1655 Point vers celui et cil vers lui,
Si s'entrevienent ambedui.
Mais icil qui vient devers destre¹
L'ataint tot droit en l'oel senestre.
Qant il sot que il l'ot perdu,
1660 Onques hom si dolans ne fu.
ses compagnons ensi deçut
Que nus le cose n'aperçut.
A son desarmer home n'ot
Ne mes c'un clerc qui mout l'amot,
1665 Cui ses pere fist mout grans biens,
Et si estoit bons surgiiens.
Ses compaignons fist atorner
Et en lor païs retorner:
Mostré lor a que il se deut
1670 Et k'a privé sejorner veut.
A un sien manoir se torna,
Et longement i sejorna;
Biax ert li bos et jens li lex,
A ués malade mout soutiex.

1675 En une cambre l'ont koucié,
Mais puis n'i a nus hom toucié
Ne mes li clers tant solement,
Qui set trestot son esrement.
Li clers set auques la verté,
1680 Mais Illes a double enfierté:
L'une est de l'oel que il n'a mie,
L'autre de ce qu'il crient s'amie,
Qui suer est au duc de Bretagne,
Et crient mais qu'ele ne l'adagne
1685 Et k'ele l'ait mais en despit;
Si se crient mout de ce respit:
«Tant as, tant vax, et je tant t'aim.»
«Las! fait il, com fui pris a l'aim
Quant Dix a fait de moi martir
1690 Et se vaurra de moi partir
Cele dont partir ne me puis!
E las! por coi vesqui je puis
Que cis tormens me corut seure?
Maleoit soit le jour et l'eure
1695 Que je ne sui esranment mors,
Car ce m'eüst esté confors,
Si me plainsist ma dolce amie,
Qui ore sera m'anemie.
Entrués que je .ii. iex avoie
1700 Ere petis et poi savoie
Por avoir le seror au duc:
Ains ot poi li fix Eliduc;
Or a il mains de la moitié.
E las! com ai mal esploitié!

1665 Qui]W   1671 satorna]W   1674 Avoec]Lö   1692 nasqui]W
1700 Et repetis]Lö

and took it from the squire to go and joust with a knight who had ridden up to that very spot and was cantering by. Ille thought to himself that he had been the winner of the entire tourney, and that this one knight would not leave without giving him a joust; for the sake of the woman he loved he neither dared nor wished to forego it. He began to spur his horse on and charged at the knight, who charged at him, and the two of them came at each other. However, the knight, who was aiming to the right,[1] struck Ille full in the left eye. When Ille realised that he had lost his eye, he was more grief-stricken than any man had ever been before. He managed to deceive his companions in such a way that none of them noticed the injury. No men were present when he disarmed, except for a clerk who loved him dearly, to whom Ille's father had been extremely generous, and he was a good surgeon. (1667) Ille had equipment given to his companions and sent them back to their own country: he let them know that he was in pain and that he wanted to recover in private. He took himself off to one of his manors and spent a long time there recovering; it was an attractive place, with fine woodland, very appropriate to a sick man's needs. He was put to bed in a chamber, but after that no-one touched him, with the one exception of the clerk, who knew all about his situation. The clerk knew something of the truth, but in fact Ille was suffering from a double infirmity: one was due to the loss of his eye, the other to his fear of the woman he loved, who was the duke of Brittany's sister; he was afraid that she would no longer think him worthy of her, and that she would despise him from then on, and he was very much afraid on account of this proverb: 'What you have is what you are worth and what I love you for.' (1688) 'Alas!' he said, 'I have been caught hook, line and sinker, since God has made a martyr of me, and the woman I cannot be parted from will want to be parted from me. Alas! why did I go on living after this torment inflicted itself on me? Cursed be the day and the hour when I did not die straight away, for death would have been a comfort to me, and my sweet friend, who is now going to be my foe, would have wept for me. Even when I had two eyes, I was an insignificant and ignorant man to be the husband of the duke's sister. The son of Eliduc had little enough before; now he is poorer by half. Alas! how badly things have gone for me!

Chanson d'Aspremont, a later 12th-century text from the same cycle. The mention of Agolant here suggests that the story of *Aspremont* was known in some form before the probable date of composition of the extant version (c. 1190).
[1] Seen from the knight's point of view, Ille is approaching on his left, but the knight is aiming towards the right-hand side (as he sees it) of his opponent's body. For discussion of the motif of the lover who loses an eye in combat, see the Introduction, pp. xxxiv-xxxv.

1705 Com or m'a mis Dix en oubli,
Qu'ensanle ai perdu moi et li!
De Diu sont sacré et cnoint
Cil qui muerent en lor bon point,
Car tos li mons les plaint et pleure.
1710 E las! ja vic je ja tel eure,
Se je morusse a droit n'a tort,
Que Diex fust blasmés de ma mort.
Las! ques peciés m'a encombré?
Cele ki m'a tos jors amé
1715 Et haï canque me vaut nuire
Valra ma mort et que je muire,
Por k'ele sace m'aventure;
Mais ja la douce creature,
Se Diu plaist, le voir n'en savra.
1720 Diex! com m'a mort qui me navra,
Quant ne me pot el cuer ferir.»
Au tierç jor, droit a l'enserir,
Vint la novele a Galeron.
S'ele ot grant doel de son baron,
1725 Ne s'en doit nus hom mervillier.
Ne se set mie consillier,
Que nus hom ne li set a dire:
«Si faite plaie a vostre sire.»
Il n'estoit compains qu'il eüst
1730 Qui vraie novele en seüst.
Aler i veut, si le verra;
Mais, s'il puet, ja n'i enterra.
La dame muet vers son ami,
N'i met que .ii. jours et demie;
1735 S'i a bien voie a .iiii. jours,

Mais lonc cemin acorce amors.
Del palefroi est descendue
Et voit le cambre portendue.
Entrer i veut, ce fu noiens:
1740 Li cambrelens qui est laiens
Li a mout bien l'uis escondit,
Et en aprés se li ont dit:
«Bele dame, por Diu, merci!
Vos n'avés or que faire chi.
1745 Por Diu, ne vos en coreciés,
Car vos amis est mout bleciés
Et navrés par mesaventure;
Si est ses maus de tel nature
Que il li feroit double anui
1750 Se feme venoit devant lui.
– Certes, signor, ce poise moi;
Irie sui qant je nel voi.»
En un liu coiement s'en vait,
Plore, sospire, grant doel fait:
1754a *A bien petit que ne se tue.*
1754b *D'uns dras a home s'est vestue,*1
1755 Entre les cambrelens se met
Et des afaires s'entremet.
A l'avesprer en le cambre entre.
Mout li tressaut li cuers el ventre:
Crient ke peciés ne le deçoive
1760 Et c'on sa voidie aperçoive.
    Or est Illes mout angoissex
Et mout iriés et coreceus:
Tel doel n'ot hom ne ainc ne puis,
Qant a celi escondi l'uis

1714 Celi]W 1729 qui eust]W 1736 Mais lor]W 1763 home ainc]W

58

How God has forgotten me now, since I have lost myself and her at one go! Those who die a timely death are blessed and anointed by God, for everyone cries and weeps for them. Alas! in the past, I once knew a time when people would have reproached God for my death, whether I deserved to die or not. Alas! what sin have I been burdened with? The woman who has always loved me and hated anyone who wished to harm me will wish for my death and want me dead, if she learns of my accident; but, please God, the sweet creature will never know the truth about it. God! what a mortal blow he dealt me, that man who wounded me, when he did not manage to strike me in the heart.'/ On the third day, just as evening was falling, the news reached Galeron. No-one should be surprised if she was heart-broken about her husband. (1726) She did not know what to do for the best, since no-one was able to tell her: 'This is the sort of wound your husband has.' Not one of his companions knew the truth about what had happened to him. Galeron intended to go to where Ille was and see him; but she would never enter the chamber if he could do anything about it. The lady set out to see the man she loved, and only took two-and-a-half days to get there; it was a good four days' journey, but love makes a long road shorter. She dismounted from her palfrey and saw the curtained chamber. She wanted to go inside, but she had no chance to: the chamberlain who was indoors firmly barred her from the door, and afterwards the attendants said to her: 'Fair lady, have mercy, for God's sake! You are not needed here now. (1745) For God's sake, do not be angry, for the man you love has had the misfortune to be seriously hurt and wounded; and his injury is such that it would cause him double the distress if a woman were to come into his presence.' – 'Indeed, this grieves me, my lords; I am bitterly dismayed at not being able to see him.' She went off quietly into a corner, where she wept and sighed and gave vent to her grief: *it would not have taken very much for her to kill herself. Then she dressed up in a set of man's clothes,*[1] and mingled with the chamberlains, seeing to the household duties. At nightfall she went into the chamber. Her heart was pounding in her breast: she was afraid that sin might waylay her, and that someone might notice her ruse.

At this point Ille was in a state of great anguish, of bitter distress and frustration: he was more heart-broken than any man has been, before or since, because he had barred from the door the woman

---

[1] It is clear from ll. 1824-28 that Galeron is dressed as a man, so this couplet must have been included in the original version of the poem.

1765 Que il aime autant comme soi.
Entre le lit et le paroi(t)
S'est la dolante atapinee
Dedens le cambre encortinee;
Mucie s'est sous la cortine.

1770 L'uis ont gardé par aatine;
Cui caut, que deceü en sont
Trestot cil qui en garde l'ont?
Andui ont tel doel et tel ire
Que nus nel puet conter ne dire.

1775 «Aï, fait il, ma doce suer,
Com je par ai en moi dur cuer
Quant je sui chi et vos la fors!
Bele, se vos n'avés mon cors,
Mes cuers est vostres nuit et jor.

1780 Las! com je muir por vostre amor!
Grans est li max qui me tormente
Et l'amors graindre ou j'ai m'entente.
De l'amour ere a cief venus,
Mais or sui de tel mal tenus

1785 Qui de l'amor m'eslongera,
Car ja mais ne m'adaignera
Cele qui n'adaigna por moi
Conte ne duc ne fil(le) a roi.»¹
Si se demente tote nuit,

1790 Et cuidiés vos que il n'anuit
A la bele qui autant l'aime
Com il meïsmes, qui s'en claime?
Illoeques gist, mes n'est si ose
K'ele li die aucune chose;

1795 S'ele osast viax plorer ne plaindre
Si en peüst son duel refraindre.
Mout saroit volentiers la bele
De son ami vraie novele
Dont il est issi estormis.

1800 Sor l'ajorner s'est endormis
Li ber, qui tant a travellié,
Et cele a dusc'al jor villié,
Et voit celui qui d'un cendé
A lasquement son cief bendé.

1805 Li bendiax ert keüs aval,
Et cele esgarde son grant mal.
Un petitet en sus se trait,
Et son grant dol sovent retrait
Et plaint illueques son signor:

1810 Doel ot, onques mais n'ot grignor,
Et s'ele un petit demorast
Qu'ele son grant dol ne plorast,
Ses cuers li fust partis en .ii..
Atant si pleure; ses espeus,

1815 Qu'ilueques langist et perist,
Entent le cri, si s'esperist,
Et si s'a mout esmervillié
Qui l'a en plorant esvillié:
Ne cuide qu'il i ait nului

1820 Que seulement son clerc et lui.
Quant son bendel a ratorné,
Vers l'esponde a son cief torné
Et voit illoec ester s'amie;
Ne mais il ne le connoist mie,

1765 Com il]Lö 1782 atente]W 1808 En son]W

can mean to know + to recognise.

∴ could mean like didn't know her, know her well enough to know she doesn't care.

60

he loved as much as himself. His disconsolate wife crept between the bed and the wall in the curtained chamber and hid herself behind the curtain. The attendants guarded the door assiduously; what did it matter, when all those who were meant to be guarding it had been fooled? Both of them were so heart-broken and so upset that it defied narration or description. 'Ah!' he said, 'Sweet sister of mine, I must have a heart of stone to be lying in here while you are there outside! Fair lady, if my body is not with you, my heart is yours night and day. Alas! how I am dying for your love! Great is the affliction which torments me, and greater still is the love which fills my thoughts. (1783) I had made that love my own, but now I am in the grip of an affliction which will divorce me from love, for the woman who spurned a count and a duke and a king's son for my sake will spurn me from now on.'[1] So he lamented all night long, and do you imagine that this did not distress the fair lady who loved the man who was accusing her as he loved himself? She lay there, but did not dare to say anything to him; if she had dared at least to cry or to weep, it would have enabled her to alleviate her sorrow. The lady would very gladly have learned the truth about what it was that was making the man she loved so agitated. Just before dawn sleep came to the noble lord who had suffered so much, and Galeron stayed awake until daylight came, when she saw that Ille's head was loosely bandaged with a piece of silken cloth. (1805) The bandage had slipped down, and she could see his great misfortune. She withdrew a short distance and rehearsed her grief time and again, and wept for her husband: she felt greater sorrow than she had ever felt before, and if she had put off giving vent to her grief in tears for even a short while, her heart would have broken in two. And so she wept at that point; her husband, who lay there ill and weak, heard the crying, roused, and wondered in amazement whose weeping had woken him: he did not believe that there was anyone there apart from just his clerk and himself. When he had replaced his bandage, he turned his head towards the side of the bed and saw the woman he loved standing there; only he did not recognise her

---

1 In ll. 1494-96 the suitors are identified as the Count of Anjou, the Count of Poitiers and the Duke of Normandy. The use of the phrase *fil a roi* here to describe the second count suggests an allusion to the three sons of Henry II of England, who took over control of their father's continental territories (which included the counties of Anjou and Poitiers and the duchy of Normandy) from early 1169 onwards.

1825 Ains cuide que ce soit uns hom,
Car de ses piés dessi en son
Ne puet sor lui rien aperçoivre
Qui ne le puist mout bien deçoivre.
«Di va, dist il, que fais tu chi?
1830 – Biax sire ciers, por Diu, merci!
– Di va, chi n'est pas liex de querre
Allués ne fiés, honor ne terre:
Çou est ma cambre, ou je me gis.
– Par Diu, ki pardona Longis¹
1835 Ses peciés qant il feru l'ot,
De tel marcié ne soi je mot.
Sire, je sui chi Galerons,
Et vous si estes mes barons,
Que j'aim autant comme mon cors;
1840 Si fui oussiere par defors
Ier tote jor, et fuisse encore,
S'engiens ne fust; mes si est ore
Que je me sui ensi tenue
Que je sui devant vos venue.
1845 Or si me soit la raisons dite
Por coi m'est l'entree escondite,
Car je nel quic avoir forfait
En pensé n'en dit ne en fait.
– Si m'aït Dix, ma doce suer,
1850 Je vos aim tant comme mon cuer.
Tant estes france et debonaire
Que nus hom ne poroit mesfaire
Que g'eüsse vers vos haïne.
Ainc jor ne vos portai querine

1855 Ne ja ne ferai, se Diu plaist;
Vostre douçors del tot me paist.
– Por coi m'escondist on dont l'uis?
– Ma douce suer, car je ne puis
Feme veoir, que ne me double
1860 Li max qui si m'angoisse et torble
Si sai qu'il vos en peseroit
Se ma destrece me dobloit.
Ne vos puis veoir com je suel:
Çou est la riens dont plus me doel,
1865 Dont plus sui plains d'angosse et d'ire
Et cele entent bien qu'il veut dire:
Bien set toute s'entention,
Mais n'en veut faire mention,
Car ja ne dira rien, son voel,
1870 Dont ses amis ait grignor doel;
Trop l'a il grant, ce poise li.
Nus hom ne doit a son ami
Metre devant sa mesestance
Quant il le voit en tel pesance,
1875 Et Galerons est mout senee;
Tant li a dit la bele nee:
«Dous ciers amis, confortés vos
Por l'amor qui est entre nous,
K'a tenir m'avés en convent.
1880 As prex mesciet mout plus sovent
Qu'il ne fait a le gent fallie;
La preude gent est assalie
De mainte grant mesaventure:
Tex est proece et sa nature,

but rather believed that it was a man, for from head to toe he could make out nothing in her appearance which was not designed to give him a completely false impression. 'Come now!' he said, 'What are you doing here?' – 'Fair dear lord, for God's sake, have mercy!' – 'Come now, this is not the place to come asking for allods or fiefs, for a domain or a territory. This is my chamber, and I am ill in bed.' – 'By God, who forgave Longinus his sins after he had struck him,[1] I know nothing about such transactions. My lord, this is Galeron here, and you are my husband, whom I love as much as I love my own self; I was a door-keeper outside all day yesterday, and I would still be there now if it were not for trickery; but the fact is that now I have gone about things in such a way that I have been able to come into your presence. (1845) Now let me be told the reason why I am barred from the door, for I do not believe that I have done anything to deserve it, either in thought or in word or in deed.' – 'So help me God, sweet sister of mine, I love you as I love my own heart. You have such a good and noble nature that no-one's wrongdoing could make me feel hatred for you. I have never borne any ill-will towards you, and I never will, please God; your sweetness is all the sustenance I could wish for.' – 'Why then was I barred from the door?' – 'Sweet sister of mine, because I cannot set eyes on a woman without the affliction which is tormenting and troubling me doubling in intensity; and I know that it would grieve you if my distress were to be doubled. I cannot see you as I used to; this is the thing which grieves me the most, which fills me with most anguish and distress.' (1866) And Galeron understood clearly what he was trying to say: she was well aware of his full meaning, but did not want to refer to it, for she would never say anything, if she could help it, which might cause the man she loved more grief; he had enough already, and this grieved her. No-one should remind someone he loves of his mishap when he sees him in such a sorry plight, and Galeron was a woman of great good sense; this much and no more is what the fair creature said to him: 'Dear sweet love, take comfort, for the sake of the love we have for each other, which you have promised me to maintain. Ill fortune befalls the brave far more frequently than it does the race of cowards; the brave are assailed by many a great misfortune: this is in the very nature of courage,

---

[1] Longinus was the Roman soldier who struck Christ in the side with a spear while He was on the cross. This oath implies that Galeron is asking Ille's forgiveness for intruding into his sickroom, which underscores the irony of the situation. Ille is unable to see that Galeron values him for his qualities alone, and respects him so much that she will even ask his forgiveness for doing something which she has every right to do. The nature of Ille's injury may be a reflection of this moral 'semi-blindness'.

1885 Car cil qui mai[n]tenir ne l'osent
Sont a deduit et se reposent.
Totes les coses qui preus sont
Painent el siecle et pïeur l'ont
Que celes qui ne font nul preu.
1890 Icil est bien pris a droit neu
Qui a esté plains d'onnorance
Et puis, par une mesestance,
Pleure sa male destinee
Comme mescine encortinee.
1895 Ice ne doit nus preudom faire,
Mes, qant il a grignor contraire,
Lever se doit por deporter,
Por ses amis reconforter.
S'il ne mescaoit au prodome,
1900 Qui en porroit savoir la some
Ne la verté de sa proece?
Qui onques n'ot un jour destrece
N'anui de cors ne cousençon,
Qui set se il est preus u non?
1905 Esforciés vos, biax sire, un poi,
Se viax non por l'amor de moi
Et de la douce compagnie.
– Mout volentiers, ma doce amie.»
Assés i ot parlé et dit,
1910 Mais passer m'en voel a petit.
    Li jors s'en vait, la nuis repaire,
Et cele dame deboinaire[1]
Se part atant de son signor;
S'il a grant doel, ele a grignor.

1915 En l'autre cambre s'est tornee
Cele qui mainte aspre jornee[2]
Convenra traire a cuer mari
Ains que mais voie son ami.
Illes se pense, et si a droit,[3]
1920 «Sire Dix, comment avenroit
Que la tres douce creature,
Des qu'ele saroit m'aventure,
Ne m'eüst tos jors en despit?
Jou oï ja dire un respit
1925 Que feme a mout le cuer volage
Et mue sovent son corage.
Et ceste n'est mie endroit moi,
Car ele est suer au duc; si voi
Qu'il n'a si bele en tot le monde.
1930 Dix me destruise et me confonde
S'un seul jour mais sui ore ichi
Et se j'en tel liu ne m'en fui
Que mais n'orra de moi novele
La suer au duc, qui tant est bele!
1935 J'ai bien la cose aperceüe
K'ele a m'enferté conneüe.»
Son clerc apele isnelement,
Se li a dit mout belement:
«Va me tost jusque la aval,
1940 Met la sele sor mon ceval;
Ne me fai pas tenir por sot:
Garde que nus n'en sace mot.
Et qant jou ere alés ma voie,
Garde que nus hom ne te voie

1886 de reposent]W   1891 plus d'innorance]W (onerance)   1903 consencon]W
(quisencon)   1912 la pucele]W

64

for those who do not dare to uphold it amuse themselves and live a quiet life. All creatures of courage and worth toil in this world and have a worse time of it than those which do nothing worthwhile. A man is well and truly caught in the trap if he has been widely honoured and then, because of a single mishap, he bewails the fact that fate is against him, like a young girl in her curtained chamber. No gallant man should act like this, but even when he suffers a more serious setback, he should get up and enjoy himself, in order to comfort his friends. If ill fortune did not befall the gallant man, who could tell how great his courage was, or whether it was genuine? If a man has never known anguish or physical distress or burning care, who knows whether he is a man of courage or not? (1905) Bestir yourself a little, fair lord, if only for my sake and for the sake of your gentle companions.' – 'I shall do so very gladly, my sweet love.' Many things were spoken and said there, but I intend to make do with a few./

The day departed and night returned, whereupon the noble-natured lady left her lord;[1] if he felt great sorrow, hers was greater still. The lady who would have to endure many a harsh day's travelling[2] with a broken heart before she saw the man she loved again took herself off into the other chamber. Ille thought to himself, and he was not entirely wrong:[3] 'Lord God, how could it possibly be that this sweetest of creatures would not despise me for ever as soon as she knew what had happened to me? (1924) I once heard a proverb which said that a woman's heart is very fickle and she frequently changes her mind. What's more, I am not on a par with this woman, because she is the duke's sister; I can see, too, that there is not another woman as beautiful as her in the whole world. May God destroy and confound me if I now stay here a single day longer, and if I do not flee to a place where news of me will never again reach the ears of the duke's sister, who is so beautiful! I clearly perceived that she had recognised what sort of illness I had.' He immediately called his clerk, and said to him very quietly: 'Go downstairs for me right away and saddle my horse; do not make people think I am stupid: make sure that no-one knows a word of this. And when I have gone on my way, make sure that no-one sees you

---

[1] Galeron is now a married woman, and should be referred to as *dame* rather than *pucele*. The scribe used the correct title in l. 1733.

[2] *Qui* = the indirect object pronoun *cui*, governed by the impersonal verb *convenra*.

[3] W has 'Ylles est molt en grant destroit', which might appear to be the better reading: how can Ille be right to doubt Galeron? However, reading this passage against the background of *Eracle* suggests that P's 'et si a droit' may well be correct. The episode of the Bride Fair in *Eracle* demonstrates that most women are indeed unreliable. Ille is therefore right in the sense that his reaction conforms with the common wisdom expressed in the *respit*.

1945 Desque il soit tierce de jour;[1]
Çaiens t'encloras por m'amor.
Se nus de mon aler t'apele,
Par devers l'uis de le capele
Me sui emblés, ce poras dire;
1950 Ensi t'en poras escondire.»
Li clers l'a cier et bien se proeve
Et fait trestot canqu'il li roeve
A son signor et puis retorne,
Sel vest et quace et bien l'atorne
1955 D'un atour qui n'est pas pesans;
En s'aumosniere a .xx. besans,[2]
Issi com l'estore nos conte.
Vient au ceval et si i monte,
Qui l'a en maint besong porté,
1960 S'espee çaint a son costé.
Mout seroit lonc d'iloec son voel,
Car il cuide eslongier son doel;
Si va chaçant son grant anui,
Car son cuer laist deriere lui.
1965 Com plus esploite de sa voie,
Et plus s'eslonge de sa joie;
Com plus aproce ce qu'il veut,
Plus se dolouse et plus se deut.
Et li clers, qui remaint arriere,
1970 A l'uis fermé en tel maniere
Com li ot commandé se[s] sire.
Assés i ot et duel et ire
A l'eure qu'il entrer i porent:
Bien fu tierce quant il le sorent.

1975 Nus ne poroit conter la paine
Ne le doel que la dame maine:
Desi que son mari ravra,
Dist que jamais joie n'avra.
.M. mars emprunte sor sa terre
1980 Et puis si va son signor querre
Atout .xiiii. chevaliers;
Assés orent puis encombriers.
Illes s'en vait vers Normendie,
Et il passent mer a navie
1985 Et vienent en le grant Bretaigne;
En Gales a le grant montagne
Vienent, puis passent en Illande,
Puis revont en Nohuberlande;
Trestote Escoce ont puis cerquie,
1990 Puis ont Norouerge travescie,
Puis cerkent tote Danemarce
Et tante tere et tante marce,
Trestote Frise et Hongerie,
Saissone et tote Esclavonie;
1995 Mais por noient le quierent la,
Qu'en Normendie s'en ala,
De Normendie droit en France;
Illuec douta la connaissance,
A Lengres vint, outre passa,
2000 Ains dusc'a Rome ne cessa.[3]
Illoec trova l'empereour,
Qui mout estoit en grant freor:
Nus n'ot onques grignor destrece,
Que d'une part l'aqeut viellece,

1959-60 inverted in P]Lö   1990 auvergne]W

66

until terce;[1] shut yourself up in here for love of me. If anyone accuses you of letting me go, you can say that I slipped away towards the chapel door; this is how you can excuse yourself.' The clerk was fond of Ille and gave a good account of himself, doing everything that was asked of him for his lord, and then he came back, helped him on with his clothes and shoes, and equipped him with light-weight equipment; Ille had twenty besants in his purse,[2] so the story tells us. He went to his horse, which had carried him in many a battle, and mounted it; his sword was girded at his side. If he had had his way, he would have been far away from there, for he imagined that he could put a distance between himself and his sorrow; in fact, he was pursuing his own anguish, for he was leaving his heart behind. (1965) The further he succeeded in travelling, the greater the distance between him and his joy; the nearer he came to what he wanted, the more pain and sorrow he felt. And the clerk, who stayed behind, closed the door just as his lord had commanded him to. There was sorrow and dismay in good measure when the others were able to go inside: it was gone terce when they found out. The distress and the sorrow the lady displayed defies description: she said that she would never be happy again until she was re-united with her husband. She borrowed a thousand marks against her land and then she set out to search for her lord, taking fourteen knights with her; they subsequently experienced many difficulties. (1983) Ille went off towards Normandy, and they crossed the sea on board ship and arrived in Great Britain; they came to the great mountain in Wales, then crossed over to Ireland, then went back to Northumberland; then they searched the whole of Scotland, then rode through Norway, then searched all of Denmark and countless lands and marches, the whole of Frisia and Hungary, Saxony and all of Slavonia; but they sought him there in vain, because he went away to Normandy, and from Normandy straight to France; he was afraid of being recognised there, travelled to Langres, and beyond, and did not stop until he came to Rome.[3] There he found the emperor, who was in a state of great anxiety: no-one was ever in more desperate straits than he was, for on one side he was being beset by old age,

---

[1] Terce was the third of the twelve hours into which the medieval day was divided. It corresponds roughly to nine or ten a.m..

[2] Ille sets out with four besants in his purse, while Galeron borrows a thousand marks: this reinforces the idea of their social inequality. The besant was a gold coin originally struck in Byzantium, and which varied in value during the Middle Ages.

[3] Ille travels overland via neighbouring Normandy and France (i.e. the Ile-de-France area) to Langres and then directly to Rome. Galeron's initial decision to cross the Channel is not unrealistic, given the position of Brittany; the rest of her itinerary represents a plausible clockwise tour of northwestern and central Europe. The

2005 Et d'autre part li emperere,
Cil par dela, o son empere,
Por çou qu'il ert si foibles hom;[1]
Si l'eüst mené dusqu'en son,
Ne fust li senescax ses cors
2010 Qui s'esbanoie la defors.
    Li empereres se gisoit
Sor une chouce, si lisoit
Por soi deporter en un brief.
Sa fille seoit a son chief,
2015 Qui Rome et tot l'empire atent;
Assés i sont priveement.
Illes vint ens et si se mist
As piés le roi qu'iloeques gist:
«Sire, dist il Diex beneïe
2020 Vous et le vostre compaignie!
— Amis, et Dix te doinst grans biens!
Di que tu quiers et dont tu viens.
— Sire, je vienc de France droit.
Uns preudon qui me retenroit
2025 Feroit aumosne et cortoisie;
Jel serviroie sans boidie,
Mais qu'il me donast pain et dras:
Di moi se tu me retendras.
Je ne sui pas de grant afaire,
2030 Ne gaires ne promet a faire
Ne ne qier mie grant merite;
Por petit claim mon loier quite.
— Amis, se Dix me soit garans,
Tu n'en es mie mout parans:

2035 Se tu estoies de haut fait,
Autrement iroit qu'il ne vait.
Por qant, si as tu tel corsage,
Se tu avoies bon corage,
Assés pues estre prex de cors.
2040 Li senescaus est la defors,
Qui sous Diu nos garde et maintient;
N'est pas falis cui il detient.
Es tu sergans u chevaliers?
— Assés l'ai dit, biax sire ciers,
2045 Que onques chevaliers ne fui;
Il me pert mout bien qui je sui:
Assés ai soufert paine et mal.»
A tant es vous le senescal,
Que mout resanle bien prodome.
2050 Vient a l'empereour de Rome,
Et l'empereres li a dit
Tout en gabant, si qu'il en rit:
«Ja vos voel durement proier
De retenir cest saudoier:
2055 Il vous aquitera la terre
Et metra en pais ceste guerre,
Si ne quiert autre troveüre
Fors que viande et vesteüre.
— Sire, se Dix me face aïe,
2060 Por tant ne li faurons nos mie.»
Issi est Illes retenus.
Et quant li termes est venus
Que les .ii. os doivent combatre,
Qu'il se voelent par force embatre

2032 mon pooir]W   2043 Ers tu]W

68

and on the other by the emperor of Byzantium and his forces, because he was such a weak man;[1] and his enemy would have made short work of him, had it not been for the person of the seneschal who was enjoying the sport outside the city walls.

The emperor was lying on a couch, reading a letter to amuse himself. Sitting by his side was his daughter, who was to inherit Rome and all the empire; very few attendants were present. Ille came in and threw himself at the king's feet as he lay there: 'Sire,' he said, 'God bless you and your company!' – 'My friend, may God grant you great blessings, too! Tell me what you seek and where you come from.' – 'Sire, I come direct from France. (2024) A gallant man who would take me on would be doing a charitable and courtly deed; I would give him honest service, provided that he fed and clothed me: tell me if you will take me on. I am not a man of any rank, I do not promise to achieve a great deal, nor do I seek any great reward; I am satisfied with a small payment for my services.' – 'My friend, as God may be my protector, you surely do not look much like a nobleman: if you were a high-ranking noble, things would be different from the way they are. Nevertheless, with your physique, if you had the right temperament, you could display considerable physical prowess. The seneschal, who is our protector and defender on earth, is outside the city with the army; no-one he takes on is a coward. Are you a sergeant or a knight?' – (2044) 'I have explained at length, fair dear lord, that I was never a knight; you can see who I am quite clearly by looking at me: I have suffered a good deal of pain and hardship.' At this, up came the seneschal, who certainly did look like a gallant man; he approached the emperor of Rome, and the emperor said to him jokingly, so that he laughed at it: 'I want to beg you earnestly to take on this soldier: he will liberate the country for you, end this war and restore peace, and he is not looking for any reward other than food and clothing.' – 'Sire, so help me God, we will not fail him for so little.' This is how Ille was taken on. And when the time came for the two armies to do battle, when the eastern emperor's men tried to invade

---

widely divergent routes chosen by the two characters symbolise the psychological distance which has opened up between them as a result of Ille's reaction to his injury.

[1] Ille's second career in Rome closely parallels his first in Brittany: once again he comes to the aid of a weak ruler, and his military success wins him the love of the ruler's daughter. In this case, however, the motif of the *foible hom* is reinforced by the fact that the emperor is both physically and morally weak, unlike Conain, who was simply presented as a weak ruler. The emperor's moral weakness is illustrated by his mockery of the poor soldier who falls at his feet and asks to be retained.

2065 Cil a l'empereour de la
El païs cestui par deça,
D'Ille le preu, qui tant a fait,
Ne tient nus hom gaires de plait,
Car Romain sont vilain gaignon;[1]
2070 N'Illes n'a per ne compaignon,
Ne cambrelenc ne mariscal.
Venus en est au senescal:
«Sire, dist il, li autre en vont
Contre les Griex qui mal vos font,
2075 Et bien sai c'a mon pain fauroie
Se je derrier aus remanoie.
Biax sire, car me prestissiés
Unes armes povres et viés
Et un escuier qui les port;
2080 Un ronchi ai, ne qier plus fort.
Et se je muir, sire, as passages,
Ce n'ert ne prex ne grans damages.»
Li senescaus fait que cortois:
Unes viés armes as borgois,
2085 Qui erent mout enroellies,
Li a trestot esrant ballies
Et un escuier li carga.
La grans os puis ne se targa,
A grant bruit est de Rome issue;
2090 Tante ensegne a fin or tissue
I font porter li haut baron.
Illes i vait sans compaignon;
Li grant chevalier enbarni
L'ont mout gabé et escarni.

2095 Tant ont cevalcié les .ii. os
Que cil de la voient les nos;
La lor gent sont bien atornees
Et ont chevalcié .vii. jornees
En le tere l'empereour
2100 Por ce qu'il gist en tel langor.
Li sire de Constantinoble
I ot grant gent et bele et noble:
Si chevalier sont bel et jent,
Si a bien .vii. tans plus de gent
2105 Que n'a li senescaus de Rome.
Or orrés parler de prodome!
Les gens qui point ne s'entrameren
Isnelement et tost s'armerent.
Illes s'arma al mix qu'il pot
2110 De ses viés armes que il ot,
Et monte en son ceval d'Espagne
Qu'il ot amené de Bretaigne;
Si l'ot cevalcié por ronci.
Encor le trovera boin chi,
2115 Et por çou que Dix le garisse
Et il meïsmes ne perisse.[2]
Ensus se trait Illes li ber
De cex qui le suelent gaber,
En ses estriers est aficiés;
2120 Prodome sanle, ce saciés.
Li Romain sont desor un mont
Et li Griu en un val parfont:
Ne sont pas encor si prés trait
Qu'entr'ex demie liue n'ait.

2077 cor me pressissies]W (pretissiés)   2116 le perisse]W

the western emperor's country by force, no-one took very much notice of Ille the brave, who had achieved so much, because the Romans are despicable curs;[1] Ille had no comrade or companion-at-arms, neither chamberlain nor marshal. He approached the seneschal: 'My lord,' he said, 'The others are setting out against the Greeks, who are doing you harm, and I know that I would forfeit my keep if I were to remain here behind them. Fair lord, lend me a cheap old set of arms and a squire to carry them; I have an old nag, I am not asking for a stronger horse. And if I die, my lord, in the fighting, it will not be either an advantage or a great loss to you.' The seneschal behaved like a courtly man: he immediately gave him an old set of the burghers' arms, which were badly rusted, and entrusted a squire to him. Then the huge army delayed no longer, and the echoes rang as they rode out of Rome; the great barons had their men carry countless pennons woven with pure gold thread. Ille rode out companionless; the great noble knights made fun of him and mocked him unsparingly. The two armies rode on until the other side could see our men; their forces were well equipped and had penetrated seven days' ride into the emperor's territory because his debility kept him bed-ridden.

The lord of Constantinople had large, handsome, imposing forces there: his knights were handsome and noble, and his forces outnumbered those of the seneschal of Rome by a good seven to one. Now you are going to hear about a gallant man! The two armies, who had no love for each other, armed themselves swiftly and rapidly. Ille armed himself as best he could with the old set of arms he had, and mounted his Spanish horse, which he had brought from Brittany and had been riding as a nag. He would yet get good service from it here, provided both that God protected the horse and that he himself was not killed.[2] Ille the noble warrior drew aside from the men who were making fun of him, and settled himself firmly in his stirrups; he looked like a gallant man, I can assure you. The Romans were on the top of a hill, and the Greeks were in a deep valley: although they were drawing closer, there was still half a league between them.

---

[1] This is the first of a series of disparaging remarks about the Romans (see also ll. 4258, 4261, 4312-13 and 4359-60). The Romans were notorious in the Middle Ages for their bad character. Ille's rise to fame is made all the more impressive by the fact that he succeeds in winning over people who are not noted for their fair-mindedness.

[2] Both Löseth and Foerster posited a lacuna here. Delclos and Quereuil find the text of P unsatisfactory, even with *le* in l. 2116 emended to *ne*, since they see the *et* in l. 2115 as necessarily marking either the beginning or end of a sentence. If *et...et* is read as 'both...and', the text makes perfect sense.

2125 Illes fist bele contenance:
Saisist l'escu et prent la lance.
Li Grifon vienent aplovant,
Tot le grant tertre costiant.
Illes, ki veut le cop premier,
2130 Brandist le hanste de pumier
Et met devant soi son escu:
Ja en fera un irascu.
Le bai d'Espagne point et broce,[1]
Ens el pendant, les une roce,
2135 Encontre un Griu enmi sa voie:
Plaine se lance jus l'envoie.
Par les resnes prent le destrier
Et au plus povre chevalier
Que il coisist le guie et maine,
2140 Et se li done a bone estr[a]ine.
Li senescaus vit sa proece
Et vit de lui le grant largece;
A ceus qui l'ont issi veü
A dit: «Mout somes decheü:
2145 Par tous les sains que on apele,
Si preus ne monta hui en sele,
Et gabé l'avés entre vous;
Ricement s'est gabés de nous.
Avés veü com il le fist,
2150 Com il le bon cheval conquist?
Il n'en fu gaires covoitex,
Ains le dona al sofraiteus.
Faus est qui fait nului angoisse
Devant ce que il le connoisse,

2155 Ne ançois ne le doit nus faire,
Por que il soit de haut afaire;
Mais fel et fol sont plain d'anui,
Que il ne connoissent nului.
Felenie taut acointance
2160 Et la folie connaissance,
Et font lor signor orgillous,
Felon parlier et ramprosnous.
Cil les confonde qui les fist!»
A Ille vint et se li dist:
2165 «Amis, se Dix vos beneïe,
Qui estes vous? Nel celés mie!
– Sire, je sui uns povres hom;
C'est mes drois nons, issi me nom.
Des l'autre soir remés a vous
2170 Et fu convenant entre nous
Que pain et vesteüre avroie
Tos jors itant com vos sauroie.[2]
– Amis, se Dix me face bien,
Encor ne me repent de rien,
2175 Mais tous jors me repentirai
De ce que plus fait ne vos ai:
Ice me fist faire anemis.
Por Diu, biax sire, dous amis,
Et ke donastes vous si tost
2180 Le premerain gaang de l'ost?
– Biax sire ciers, jel vous dirai:
K'ainc mais ceval ne gaágnai,
Por çou si donai le premier
Por Diu au povre chevalier

2131 devant sor]Lf   2139 et maine et guie]W   2144 ont dit]W
2152 as sofraiteus]W

72

Ille adopted an impressive bearing: he grasped his shield and took up his lance. The Greeks came swarming all the way up the steep hill. Ille, who wanted the first blow, brandished the apple-wood shaft of his lance and covered himself with his shield: he would soon fill one of them with woe. He put the spurs to his Spanish bay horse and urged it on;[1] down the slope, next to a rock he encountered a Greek in his path; he sent him flying with the full force of his lance. He took hold of the war-horse by the reins, guided and led it to the poorest knight he could set eyes on, and presented it to him as a gift. The seneschal witnessed his prowess and also witnessed his great generosity; he said to the men who had likewise witnessed it: (2144) 'We have been seriously misled: by all the saints we call on, no-one as brave as this climbed into the saddle today, and you made fun of him between yourselves; he has seen to it that the joke is well and truly on us. Did you see how he performed, how he won that fine horse? He did not desire it for himself at all; instead, he gave it to that needy man. Anyone who gives a man a hard time before knowing who he is is a fool, and no-one should do so prematurely, in case he is a man of note; however, villains and fools are troublemakers, because they do not know who anyone really is. Villainy makes familiarity impossible, and folly makes knowledge impossible, and they make their owner arrogant, evil-tongued and insulting. May their Creator confound them!' (2164) He approached Ille and said to him: 'My friend, as you hope for God's blessing, who are you? Do not hide it from me!' – 'My lord, I am a poor man; this is my true name, this is what I am called. I have been attached to you since the evening before last, and we made an agreement that I should continue to receive food and clothing for as long as I discharged my duty to you.'[2] – 'My friend, as God may grant me His favour, I do not have any regrets about that yet, but I shall always regret not having done more for you: this was the work of the devil. For God's sake, fair lord, gentle friend, why were you so quick to give away the first spoils won by this army?' – 'Fair dear lord, I shall tell you why: I never won a horse before, and I gave my first winnings to the poor knight for God's sake, so that

---

[1] Spain was thought to produce some of the best horses in Europe. The reputation of Spanish horses was partly a result of the Moorish occupation, which introduced Arabian bloodstock into the country.

[2] *Sauroie* is a form of the conditional of *soldre/soudre*, used here in the sense of 'to pay back' or 'to fulfil one's duty to'. W's 'Itant con jo vos serviroie' reads suspiciously like a scribal *lectio facilior*.

2185 C'autre me doinst, par son plesir,
Qui de cestui me fist saisir.»
A tant se part du senescal,
Et l'os des Griex est lonc aval,
Mais cil qui envoisié estoient
2190 Montent le tertre et si costoient.
Illes voit un ki se desroie:
S'acorcier ne li puet sa voie,
Petit se prisera ja mais.
Vers le Grifon point a eslais,
2195 Et li Grijois, qui fiers estoit,
Broce vers lui a grant esploit;
Fier sont li vassal ambedui.
Li Grijois faut, et cil fiert lui
Por bien honir et por confondre:
2200 L'escu li perce et li esfondre
Et l'auberc li ront et desmaille;
Ne quic que ja mais home assalle:
Les arçons vuide de la sele.
Cil prent le destrier de Castele
2205 Sel done un chevalier Frison
Cui il tenoient a prison.¹
Li senescax forment l'esgarde,
Et Illes reporprent l'angarde
Trestot sans cri et tot sans noise,
2210 Et vit un Griu qui mout s'envoise:
N'ot plus vallant en tote l'ost.
L'uns point vers l'autre si tres tost
Que fu et flame font salir.
Li Griex, qui n'a song de falir,

2215 Le fiert et fraint en .ii. sa lance,
Et cil l'asene et puis s'avance,
Vient a celui et si l'embrace
Et tant forment l'estraint et lace
C'a poi que li cuers ne li crieve.
2220 Illes tout armé le souslieve,
Desor le col de son ceval
A mis devant soi le vassal;
Le bon ceval n'i laisse mie,
Mené l'en a par aramie.
2225 Au senescal en a fait don
Et del ceval et del prison.
    Or sont li malvais amusé
Qui l'orent ançois refusé.
Li senescaus qui en est sire
2230 Ne set sossiel que il puist dire;
Mais mout le mercie entresait
De cel present qu'il li a fait,
Et ti[e]nt grant plait de sa proece,
Et si est mout en grant destrece
2235 Qu'il ne li ot porté honor.
Se li a dit com a signor:
«Biax sire ciers, por Diu, merci!
Aidiés nos a geter de chi!
Se nos n'avons le vostre aïe,
2240 Ceste gens est morte et traïe,
Qu'il sont plus .x. tans par dela
Que nos ne somes par decha.
Franc chevalier, ne prenés garde
A le gent vilaine et coarde,

2205 chevalier prison   2206 a Frison   2220 tous armes]W (tolt armet)

74

He who put me in possession of this one might grant me others, at His pleasure.' Whereupon he left the seneschal, and the Greek army was far below, but those with a zest for battle were riding up and along the hill. Ille saw one racing ahead: if he could not cut his path short, he would never rate himself very highly again. He charged headlong at the Greek, and the Greek, who was an aggressive knight, spurred eagerly towards him; they were both aggressive fighters. The Greek missed his mark, and Ille struck him a blow designed to inflict shame and confusion on him: he pierced and smashed his shield and tore his hauberk and ripped it apart; I do not imagine that the Greek would ever attack an opponent again: he left an empty saddle behind. (2204) Ille took hold of the Castilian war-horse and gave it to a Frisian knight whom the Greeks were holding prisoner.[1] The seneschal watched him closely, and Ille resumed his position in the vanguard without any shouting or any noise whatever, and saw a Greek who was displaying a real zest for battle: there was none more valiant in the whole army. They charged towards each other with such great speed that they made fire and sparks fly. This Greek, who was not worried about missing his mark, struck Ille, breaking his lance in two, and Ille struck him and then rode forward, came up to the Greek, and took hold of him bodily, gripping and holding him so tightly in his arms that his heart nearly burst. Ille lifted him up fully armed and laid the man in front of him over the neck of his horse; he did not leave the fine horse behind either: he spiritedly led it away. (2225) He made a gift of both horse and prisoner to the seneschal.

Now the joke was on the cowards who had rejected him earlier. The seneschal, who was their leader, did not know what on earth to say; however, he immediately thanked him heartily for the present he had given him, and spoke at length about his prowess, and he was extremely distressed that he had not treated him with honour. He said to Ille, as if to his overlord: 'Fair dear lord, for the love of God, have mercy! Help us to get out of this! If we do not have your help, these men are dead and done for, for there ten times more of them on the other side than there are on ours. Noble knight, do not pay any attention to that pack of base cowards,

---

1 The Frisians inhabited the western part of the North German plain (nowadays the provinces of Friesland in the Netherlands and Ostfriesland in Germany), which formed part of the Holy Roman Empire, hence their presence in the Roman army. The original reading *cui il tenoient a Frison* is slightly odd, since it implies that the Greeks may be wrong about the knight's nationality, but Ille's action proves that the knight does belong to the Roman side. The emendation proposed here removes this logical difficulty. Interchanging the rhyme words on two adjacent lines is a common form of scribal error.

2245 N'a moi, qui point ne vos connui.
Li malvais qui sont plain d'anui
Tienent prodome a enuiex.
Sire, por Diu le glorïex,
Consilliés nos, car ne savons
2250 Conseil, se par vous ne l'avons;
Consilliés ceste baronie,
Qu'el(e) hui ce jor ne soit honie.
– Biax sire ciers, merci por Diu!
Je ne fui onques mais en liu
2255 Ou je veïsse estor ne gerre:
Vos ne me devés pas requerre
Rien nule el mont a maintenir
Dont je ne sace a cief venir.
– Amis, de vostre grant vaillance
2260 Avés ja fait tel demostrance
Que n'i a mestier coverture.
– Sire, ce fu par aventure.
I ciet bien tel a un assaut,
Quant on le reqiert, qui poi vaut;
2265 Ne mais proece est aduree
En cose bien amesuree.
– Amis, dont porés vos durer:
Bien vous savés amesurer
Et musart honir et confondre,
2270 Tot par bien faire sans respondre.
Bien ait cil Dix qui vos fist naistre!
Mout avés eü sage maistre.
Metés en nos votre conseil.
– Biax sire ciers, mout m'esmervel:

2275 Qui poroit consillier si tost
Ne adrecier trestot un ost?[1]
Ja le savés vos pieça, sire,
Que povres hom poroit mout dire
Ançois qu'il fust creüs de rien,
2280 Mais rices hom dist tos jors bien.
Et neporquant, qui ke m'en oie,
Vos mosterrai que je feroie,
Por tant que je l'eüsse a faire:
Ma gent feroie ariere traire.
2285 Un castel avés chi derriere,
Qui est mout fors de grant maniere:
Faites nos gens laiens entrer,
Car vos ne poés encontrer
Iceste fiere gent salvage
2290 Que n'i aiés mortel damage.
Il vos asserront, jel sai bien,
Mais assés tost n'i feront rien:
Bien nos tenrons une quinsaine,
Ou seviax non une semaine.
2295 Bien sai que l'os nos assaudra,
Ne mais viande lor faudra:
La tere est gaste tot entor;
Ne poront sofrir lonc sejor,
Car il ont a faire lonc cours,
2300 Et tost nos puet venir secors.
Et s'il vient Damediu a bel,
Faire lor porons tel cembel
Sovent a l'issir de la vile,
Dont en ploerront .iiii. mile.

2250 par nous]W (vos)

76

or to me, for my not recognising you. Cowards and troublemakers find a gallant man troublesome. My lord, for the sake of the God of glory, give us your counsel, for we are at a loss to know what to do, unless you counsel us; give these barons your counsel, so that they are not put to shame here today.' – 'Fair dear lord, have mercy, for God's sake! I have never been anywhere before where I have seen a battle or a war: you should not ask me to take responsibility for anything in the world which I cannot prove myself equal to.' – 'My friend, you have already given us such a demonstration of your great valour that there is no need for pretence.' – 'My lord, that was luck. A man may well fall on his feet in a single encounter, when he is attacked, and still be of little worth; only true courage is steadfast when the situation calls for great self-control.' – (2267) 'My friend, then you will be able to stay the course: you certainly know how to exercise self-control and put a fool to shame and confound him, just by fighting well without talking back. A blessing on the God who created you! You had a very wise teacher. Grant us your counsel.' – 'Fair dear lord, I am truly amazed: who could counsel or govern an entire army so quickly?[1] You have already known for a long time, my lord, that a poor man might say a great deal before anyone believed anything he said, but what a rich man says is always right. Nonetheless, whoever may hear me, I shall explain to you what I would do, supposing that it was up to me to do it: I would withdraw my troops. (2285) You have a castle here behind you which is immensely strong: get our men inside it, for you cannot engage these aggressive, ferocious forces without suffering mortal damage. I know for a fact that they will lay siege to you, but they will not achieve anything very quickly: we will hold out successfully for a fortnight, or if not, a week at least. I know for a fact that the army will mount an assault on us, only they will run out of food: the land has been laid waste all around, and they will not be able to endure a long siege, because they have a long way to travel for food, and help can reach us quickly. And if it please God, we shall be able to make frequent sorties from the town and give them a fight which will leave four thousand of them in tears.

---

[1] Elsewhere in the text *ost* is feminine (e.g. l. 2211).

2305   Mout lor porés nuire et grever
Et del siege faire lever
Ains que nos nuise lor assaus.
– Signor, ce dist li senescaus,
Avés oï ke il a dit?
2310 Je ne quier mais que Dix m'aït
Se il n'est haus hom en sa terre
Et s'il ne set assés de gerre:
Ainc ne vi chevalier si saige.
Venu fuissons a mal passage
2315 Hui en cest jor, se il ne fust,
Car il n'est hom qui nos seüst
Doner tel consel ne si sain.»
Grant joie en ont fait li Romain:
Li senescaus l'acole et baise
2320 Et maint des autres qui'n ont aise.
Retorner ont fait tote l'ost
Et au castel en vienent tost.
De prés les siuent li Grifon,
Ses assalent tot environ,
2325 Et li Romain bien se deffendent
Et dusc'au matinet atendent,
Qu'il onques les portes n'ovrirent;
Et l'endemain fors s'en issirent.
Ille, le baron Galeron,
2330 Honorent mout tuit li baron.
   Li senescaus l'onore et aime
Et tout adés signor le claime;
Mout par li vait sovent entour,
Se li a livré rice atour

2335 Et armes a se volenté
Et bons chevaliers a plenté,
Qui le serviront bonement.
Armé se sont mout ricement;
Tout par le consel au Breton
2340 S'en issent armé li baron.
Desarmés ont les Grix soupris;
Assés en ont et mors et pris.
Li preu s'armerent maintenant,
Si l'ont bien fait par avenant.
2345 Li estors est griés et pesans.
Or ne se prise .ii. besans
Illes li preus, qui tant a fait,
S'il as Grifons ne muet un plait.
Al maistre senescal s'eslaisse;
2350 A l'encontrer se lance abaisse
Si l'a si feru par defors
Que il li a cousu au cors
L'escu et l'auberc c'ot vestu:
Ne li valurent un festu.
2355 Sa lance trait aprés a soi
Et cil ciet mors ens el tornoi.
Tel doel fisent de lor signor
Onques nus hom n'oï grignor.
Illes s'en part et point a destre
2360 Et puis reguencist a senestre;
Tex .c. i fait seles vuidier
Dont on ne puet nul bien cuidier,
C'ainc puis a ceval ne monterent,
Ne lor convine ne conterent.

You will be able to do them a great deal of harm and damage and make them lift the siege before their assault can do us any harm.' – 'My lords,' said the seneschal, 'Did you hear what he said? I never want God to help me again if he is not a man of high rank in his own land and if he is not very experienced in warfare: I never saw such a knowledgeable knight. We would have come to a pretty pass today, if it were not for him, for there is no-one who would have been able to give us such good or such sound counsel.' The Romans expressed great delight with Ille: the seneschal embraced and kissed him, as did many of the others who had the opportunity. They made the whole army turn back and quickly arrived at the castle. (2323) The Greeks followed hot on their heels and assailed them from all sides; the Romans defended themselves well and waited until the early morning without once opening the gates; the next day they made a sortie from the castle. All the barons treated Galeron's husband Ille with great honour.

The seneschal treated him with honour and affection and constantly hailed him as lord; he was in very frequent attendance upon him indeed, and handed over to him splendid equipment and whatever arms he desired, and plenty of good knights who would serve him well. They armed themselves splendidly, and the barons rode out fully armed, all on the Breton's advice. They caught the Greeks unarmed and killed and captured a large number of them. The brave amongst them armed themselves right away, and fought well, as it befitted them to do. (2345) The battle was fierce and intense. Now Ille the brave, who had achieved so much, thought he was not worth tuppence if he did not start an action against the Greeks. He rode headlong at the chief seneschal; as they engaged each other he lowered his lance and struck him such a blow on the armour that he pinned his shield and the hauberk he was wearing to his body: they were of no more use to him than a straw. After this Ille pulled his lance free and the seneschal fell dead in the middle of the fighting. No man ever heard greater grief than that of the Greeks at the death of their lord. Ille left them and made a charge to the right and then wheeled round to the left again; he sent a hundred Greeks flying from the saddle there, and one cannot imagine that it did them any good, since they never mounted a horse or gave any account of themselves again afterwards.

2365   Li senescaus le fait mout bien,
Qui nes vait espargnant de rien;
Mais des que l'os est estormie,
Li Romain n'i arestent mie,
Car trop sont poi envers les lor.
2370 Partir s'en pueent par honor,
K'ocis i ont .m. de lor Griex,
Et tant dis com biax est li gieus
Se doit on de l'estor torner.
Qui veïst Ille trestorner
2375 Et en le grignor presse embatre,
Les uns navrer, autres abatre,
Tos jors poroit avoir matire
De bien parler et de bien dire,
Por que li nouvel chevalier,
2380 Qui de parler sont costumier,
Lors le vousissent creanter;
Mais il se voelent plus vanter
D'aus et de lour cevalerie
K'oïr d'autrui la signorie.
2385 Mais ja nen ert prodom entiers
Qui n'oë mout plus volentiers
D'autrui fais parler que des suens.
Illes vaut mix que rois ne quens;
Si est bien drois que on l'en oie.
2390 Il fait devant lui large voie:
.II. en abat a un trestour
Et, ains qu'il ait parfait son tour,
S'eslaisse au tierç et fraint sa lance
Et si l'abat mort d'acointance.

2395 Del tronçon qu'il tient en sa main
En fiert le quart et nient en vain,
Qu'il l'abat jus, ço est la voire.
Le bon ceval saisist en oire,
Celui al mort n'i laisse mie,
2400 K'ainc ne vit millor en sa vie:
Icelui retient a son oés;
Des autres se delivre lués.
Onques nus hom, si com je pens,
Ne pot conquerre en tant de tens
2405 Par sa proece tant d'amis
Ne tant de mortex anemis.
Mout endura paine et tormens
Ançois qu'il les mesissent ens.
A l'issir fu tous li premiers
2410 Et au rentrer tous li darriers.
Les portes, qui bien sont fermees,
Ont contre les Grijois serees
Et puis ne criement nul assaut.
Icil dedens, tuit li plus haut,
2415 Vienent a Ille, si l'onorent;
A grant esploit trestot i corent.
Tex joie ne fu faite d'ome
Com font de lui icil de Rome.
   «Sire, font il, Dix vos maintiegne,
2420 Dix vos honort, Dix vos sostiegne!
Maintenés nos, biax sire ciers,
Car il en est mout grans méstiers.»
Mout l'onorent tuit li Romain.
Ricement s'arment l'endemain

2367 fust e.]W   2376 Les uns abatre]W   2381 vausissent]Lö   2384 K'avoir]W
2392 son cours]W (tor)   2399 le ceval mort]W

The seneschal fought very well, not sparing his opponents at all; but as soon as the alarm was raised in the Greek army, the Romans did not stay on the field, for they were far too few in comparison with their opponents. They could leave the field with honour, having killed a thousand of the Greeks on the other side, and you should retire from battle while things are still going your way. Anyone who saw Ille doubling back to fight and charging into the thick of it, wounding some and killing others, could never run short of material for good stories and fine tales, providing that the newly-fledged knights, who are in the habit of doing the talking, would then agree to let him speak; but they are more willing to boast about themselves and their chivalry than to hear of anyone else's mastery of arms. (2385) However, no-one will ever be a truly gallant man if he would not much more willingly hear about someone else's deeds than about his own. Ille was worth more than a king or a count; so it is only right that people should hear what is said about him. He cut a wide path in front of him: on one occasion when he doubled back he struck two of them down and, before he had completed his turn, he dashed at the third, breaking his lance and striking him down dead as they met. With the stump which he held in his hand he struck the fourth – and not in vain, since the truth is that he felled him to the ground. He hastily seized the fine horse, and did not leave the dead man's horse either, for he had never seen a better in his life: he kept this one for his own use, but got rid of the others straight away. No-one, to my mind, had ever been able to win so many friends or overcome so many mortal enemies by his prowess in so short a time. (2407) He endured considerable toil and torment before the Greeks drove them inside the castle. He was the very first to ride out and the very last to return. They barred the gates, which were firmly closed, against the Greeks, and after that they did not fear any assault. All the greatest nobles inside the castle came to Ille and did him honour; they all ran up eagerly. No man had ever been greeted with such delight as he was by the Romans.

'My lord', they said, 'May God defend you, and honour and uphold you! Defend us, fair dear lord, for we are in very great need of it.' All the Romans did him great honour. The next day they armed themselves splendidly

2425 Et s'en issent mout lïement;
Mais mout lor avint malement,
C'au premier poindre que il firent
Tot le plus prodome i perdirent
Que on seüst en tout l'empire:
2430 Ce fu li senescaus, lor sire.
Mais Illes lor i fist confort,
Car le Grifon i geta mort
Qui l'ot ochis; et puis s'en vont.
Por le grant doel que il en font
2435 Les a fait Illes traire en sus;
A cele fois n'i ot fait plus.
El castel entrent maintenant
Et vont mout grant doel demenant.
Les portes del castel fremerent
2440 Et le senescal entererent,
Et se li fisent tel honour
Que on doit faire a tel signor.
    A Ille dient li baron:
«Ja n'arons de mort raençon
2445 Se Dix ne nos aïe et vous.
Biax sire ciers, consilliés nous.
Prenés ceste senescauchie
Que par vos soit Rome essaucie.
– Signor, je vail a ce trop poi
2450 Qu'ele ait essaucement par moi;
Ne sui si prous, ne sui si haus
Que jou en soie senescaus.
– Par certes, sire ciers, si estes.
Perdues sont en fin nos testes

2455 Demain, ains qu'il soit nuis oscure,
Se vos ne prenés de nos cure.
Or soiés nostres connestables,
Et senescaus serés estables
A tous les jours de vostre vie.
2460 – Signor, n'ai song de signorie;
Car il n'afiert pas a tel home
Qu'il ait tel signorie a Rome.
Se vos bien m'aviiés eslit,
Si me duerroit il petit:
2465 Li empereres, qui'n est sire,
I saroit mout bien autre eslire.
Mais por ce ne le di je mie
C'a mon pooir ne vous aïe.
– Sire, se Dix nos fait secours,
2470 Senescaus serés a tous jours,
Por que il en vos ne remaigne.
Ja l'emperere d'Alemaigne[1]
Ne sera la ou ce desdie
Dont cis barnages vos afie.
2475   – Signor, savés que je ferai?
En liu de senescal serai
Et, se Dix nos fait tant d'onor
Que nos veons l'empereour,
Lors si en face a son plesir;
2480 Car n'ai song d'autrui droit saisir.
– Sire, ce saciés vous por voir:
Mors est li senescaus sans oir.
N'en poés faire a nului tort.
– Signor, grans deus est de sa mort,

2454 vos bestes]W

82

and rode out in very high spirits; but they met with great misfortune, for during the first charge they made they lost quite the most gallant man known in the whole empire: this was the seneschal, their leader. However, Ille brought them some comfort, for he flung down dead the Greek who had killed him; and then they left the field. Ille made them withdraw because of the grief they felt for the seneschal; there was no more fighting on this occasion. They rode into the castle straight away, giving vent to their grief. They closed the gates of the castle, and buried the seneschal, and showed him the honour which should be shown to such a lord.

The barons said to Ille: 'We will never be ransomed from death without God's help and yours. Fair dear lord, give us your counsel. Take over the office of seneschal, so that Rome's cause may be advanced by you.' – 'My lords, I am far too unworthy for the task for Rome's cause to be advanced by me; I am not brave enough, nor am I of high enough rank to be its seneschal.' – 'Assuredly, you are, dear lord. Our heads are forfeit for good before darkness falls tomorrow, if you do not show some concern for us. Be our constable now, and you will be the acknowledged seneschal for the rest of your life.' – 'My lords, I am not interested in high office; for it is not fitting for such a man as I to hold such high office in Rome. (2463) Even if you had chosen me, it would be of little advantage to me: the emperor, who is the ultimate authority, might very well choose someone else. However, my saying this does not mean that I will not do my utmost to help you.' – 'My lord, if God comes to our aid, you will be seneschal for life, provided that you give your consent. The emperor of Germany[1] will never be in a position to refuse what this assembly of barons promises you.'

'My lords, do you know what I shall do? I shall stand in for the seneschal, and, if God grants us the honour to see the emperor again, then let him do as he thinks fit; for I am not interested in acquiring what belongs to someone else.' – 'My lord, let us tell you this for certain: the seneschal died without leaving an heir. You cannot wrong anyone by doing this.' – 'My lords, his death is a tragedy,

---

1 By the 12th century, the Holy Roman Empire, originally formed by the southwards extension of the Kingdom of Germany in the mid 10th century, included most of present-day Holland and Germany, plus Switzerland, parts of Belgium, Austria and the Czech Republic, as well as two-thirds of Italy, including Rome. Ganor's father, like the emperors of Gautier's own time, is therefore ruler of both Germany and Rome (he is referred to as *l'empereour de Rome* in l. 2050).

2485 K'ainc plus prodome ne connui,
Si me garisse Dix d'anui.»
Si reçoit Illes le ballie.
Li Griu lor font mainte asalie,
Si escrient en lor latin.
2490 Li Romain s'arment al matin;
Tot voelent metre en aventure,
Et issent fors en la couture
A .x. mil homes combatans;
Et cil de fors en ont .x. tans.
2495 Illes conduit se gent romaine,
Et mout sereement les maine;
Et bien lor mostre qu'il feront
Quant il a es des Grix seront,
Com il se devront trestorner
2500 Se il en vient as dos torner.
Et bien lor mostre en quel maniere
Il doivent sivir le baniere,
Com il iront sereement;
Car se il vont desreement
2505 Trestuit i morront a dolor,
Que cil sont trop envers les lor.
«Signor, fait il, mestier vos est
Que vous soiés garni et prest
De çou retenir par savoir
2510 Que cil voelent par force avoir.
Force vaut mout, et engiens plus,
C'on en vient sovent au desus.
Il n'i a noient de fuïr:
Ou ichi vivre u chi morir!

2515 Se nus de nos fuit en l'estor,
Ja au castel n'avra retour
Ne ne metra dedens les piés:
Ce voel que vous me fianciés,
U ja mais certes n'en ferai
2520 Rien nule avant que fait en ai.
– Sire, font il, mout volentiers.»
Prise a le foi des chevaliers
Illes li preus, et puis s'en vait.
Des .x. .m. dis escieles fait,
2525 Et cil de la en ont fait .xxx.,
Ses guient cil devers Otrente.[1]
Es .x. escieles dont je dis
A bons barons, et tresc'a .x.,
Et cascuns d'eus en guie l'une,
2530 Et Illes, sire de cascune.
Ille ordene ses chevaliers:[2]
Devant lui met .vi. des plus fiers;
Il se met en la sedme aprés;
Les trois le sivent mout de pres,
2535 Qu'il s'en iront sans contredit,
Et Illes les commande et di(s)t
Qu'il soient la ou il sera
Et facent çou que il fera.
Et qant ce vient a l'assanler,
2540 La tere font sos ex tranler;
Mainte ame font sevrer des cors:
Nes puet garir riens par defors.
Mout se sont tres bien adrecié:
Illoec ot maint escu percié,

2499 devroit]Lö   2504 Car cil]Lö   2533 s...e *illegible*]Lö   2534 le sive..
illegible]Lö   2535 iront sa.. *illegible*]Lö   2540 sor ex]W

for I never knew a more gallant man, as God may protect me from adversity.' So Ille accepted the leadership. The Greeks made numerous assaults on them, shouting out in their own language. The Romans armed themselves next morning; they were prepared to risk everything, and rode out into the fields with ten thousand fighting men; and their opponents had ten times as many men. Ille was at the head of his Roman forces, and led them out in very close formation; and he explained clearly what they would do when they came in contact with the Greeks, how they should double back if it came to retreating. He also explained clearly how they were to follow the standard, and how they would advance in close formation; for if they broke ranks as they advanced they would all die a painful death out there, because the enemy were too numerous in comparison with them. (2507) 'My lords,' he said, 'You need to be prepared and ready to use your intelligence to hold on to what the enemy want to take by force. Force can achieve a good deal, but cleverness can achieve more, as it often gives you the upper hand. There is no question of fleeing: we either live or die here! If any of us flees from the battle, he will never find refuge in the castle nor set foot inside it: I want you to give me your oath on this, or believe me I shall never do anything for you beyond what I have already done.' – 'My lord,' they said, 'Most willingly.' Ille the brave received the knights' oaths and then rode off. (2524) He made ten companies from his ten thousand men; and the enemy had made thirty from theirs and were leading them along the Otranto road.[1] In the ten companies I was talking about there were some worthy barons, ten of them, and each company was led by one of them, and by Ille, who was in overall command. He drew up his knights:[2] he placed six of the boldest companies in front of him, then himself behind them in the seventh; the other three followed very close behind him, so that they would ride out without being attacked, and Ille ordered and told them to go where he went and do what he did. And when they came to join battle, they made the ground shake under them; they parted many a soul from its body: no armour their opponents were wearing could save them. They aimed for each other with very great accuracy: many a shield was pierced,

---

1 The phrase *devers Otrente* is ambiguous. *Devers* can either be a simple alternative to *vers* ('towards Otranto'), or it can be read as *de* + *vers* ('from the direction of Otranto'). The translation attempts to preserve this ambiguity. Otranto is a port on the Gulf of Otranto, some 400 kilometres south-east of Rome as the crow flies. In Gautier's day it was part of the Norman Kingdom of Sicily.

2 Correcting the case error produces a hypermetrical line; Löseth emended *Ille* to *il*. W has 'Ylles ordone ses eschieles', which produces an unsatisfactory rhyme with *fieres* (W1837). Löseth's emendation is more plausible: a scribe taking dictation could easily have substituted *Ille* for its homophone *il*.

2545 Car d'ambes pars sont mout estout.
Illoeques ot fausé et rout
Tant maint auberc menu mallié,
Et maint pignon entretaillié
I veïssiés ens el sanc taindre;
2550 Tex .c. i veïssiés estaindre,
Qui sont keü en le grant presse,
Qu'il n'i quisent onques confesse.
La volent plus espessement
Tronçons que nois ne fait par vent.
2555 Li estors est mout angoissex,
Vers les Romains mout perilleus:
Trop par est grevex li mesciés.
Illes, qui d'aus est maistre et ciés,
Lor tarde huimés trop et demore;
2560 Mestier ont que il les secore,
Car cil ont .x. tans plus d'effors,
Et cuident bien k'Illes soit mors,
Por çou que il nel virent hui;
Et des qu'il n'ont regart de lui,
2565 Mort sont li autre finement,
Ce dient tuit communalment.
Atant i fierent mout a tire
Et font des Romains grant martire
Si qu'il les tornent de la place;
2570 Tant en ocient en la kace.
Li Romain vont sereement:
Au trestorner, qu'il font sovent,
Ont mout les Grix adamagiés
As fers de lor trencans espiés;

2575 Mais des que vint au trestorner,
N'i a or plus du retorner
S'il n'ont grant aïe de fors.
Entretant lor est Ille[s] sors,
Que mout lor ert par tans privés
2580 Et vient vers eus tous abrievés;
Mout se vaudra bien emploiés:[1]
Il lor corecera les liés.
A itant vient o sa baniere
A tot sa gent duite et maniere;
2585 Parmi ex se fiert en es l'eure.
Si com li leus, qui tout deveure,
Qui mais n'i cuide avoir retour,
Se contient Illes en l'estour:
Maint en i ocist et mehagne,
2590 Et bien le font cil d'Alemagne;
Li Romain sont de grant valor,
Si prendent garde a lor signor.
  Dinas estoit dus de Cartage;[2]
Venus estoit por faire estage,
2595 Qu'il le devoit l'empereour.
Les nos a mis en grant paor:
Mout adamage les Romains,
.XXX. en ochist a ses .ii. mains,
Qui mout erent de grant vallance.
2600 Li Griu ont en lui grant fiance:
Qui pris veut querre, au duc en vient,
O lui cevalce, a lui se tient;
Poi prise bacelers sa vie,
Se au duc ne prent compagnie.

2581 emploier

for they were quite fearless on both sides. Many indeed were the close-mailed hauberks damaged and torn on that field, and you would have seen many a swallow-tailed pennon dyed in blood there; you would have seen a hundred men who had fallen in the thick of the melée breathe their last there, without ever seeking confession. Splinters flew more thickly there than snow does in the wind. The battle was very intense, and fraught with danger for the Romans: they suffered extremely serious casualties. Now Ille, who was their commander and their chief, was too slow and was taking too long to reach them; they needed him to come to their rescue, for the enemy had ten times as many troops and were convinced that Ille was dead because they had not seen him that day; and once they did not have him to fear, the others were well and truly done for, so they all said with one voice. (2567) Whereupon they struck blow after blow in swift succession, and made such a massacre of the Romans that they forced them to retreat; they killed a large number of them in the chase. The Romans rode in close formation: when they doubled back, which they did frequently, they inflicted serious damage on the Greeks with their sharp iron lance-heads; but when once they had been forced into fighting on the run, there was no longer any chance of them turning back unless they had considerable support from elsewhere. Meanwhile, Ille had launched an attack on the Greeks, with whom he would soon be on very close terms, and was dashing towards them at full speed; he would be wanting to acquit himself well:[1] he would wipe the smiles off their faces. Then he rode up under his banner, with his skilled and able troops; he immediately flung himself into their midst. (2586) Just like a wolf, which devours everything, believing that it will never have a second chance – this was how Ille behaved in the melée: he killed and maimed large numbers of them; and the Germans fought well, and the Romans were men of great valour and took care of their leader.

Dinas was the duke of Carthage;[2] he had come to perform the military service which he owed to the Greek emperor. He struck terror into our side: he inflicted serious losses on the Romans, killing thirty extremely valiant men with his own two hands. The Greeks had great faith in him: anyone who wanted to seek renown joined the duke, rode with him and kept by his side; young noblemen felt that life was not worth living if they did not become the duke's companions.

---

1 Emending to *emploiés* is slightly awkward, but does allow the text of P to make sense. The alternative is to retain *emploier* and posit a lacuna of at least two lines after l. 2581. Scribes are more likely, however, to omit whole couplets than to leave out the second line of one couplet and the first of another with a different rhyme.

2 A possible historical reminiscence. The Exarchate of Carthage was a semi-

2605 Si troi .m. sont de se maisnie,
Qui nostre gent ont araisnie
Mout malement, si qu'il s'en plagnent,
Et ocient canqu'il ataignent.
Icil troi .m. o lor esfors
2610 En le kace en ont .iii. .c. mors:
Li dus lor fait mout grant anui.
Illes laisse corre a celui:
Mout li porte pesme novele,
Que tout l'escu li esquartele
2615 Et l'auberc li ront et desmaille,
Le cuer li perce et le coraille,
Et de tant lonc con lance estent
Le porte a tere entre sa gent.
La oïssiés estrange duel
2620 De gent qui morte i fust lor voel;
Pluiseur entendent al vengier
Et pluiseur au cors calengier,
Et qant defors [l]a presse l'ont,
Plorent, crient, grant doel en font.
2625 «Ahi! font il, Dinas, biax sire,
De quel pesance et de quel ire
Nous a cis traïtres maufés
Nos cuers espris et escaufés!
Mout par nos tient a recreans.
2630 Se il fust en Diu bien creans,
Ja ne nos osast envaïr;
Mais il fu nés por gent traïr,
Por gent confondre et por tenser.
Dous Diex, com l'osa il penser?

2635 Uns autres hom s'en fust fuïs
Et fust de paor amuïs.»
N'i sont plus longement remés:
Porté en ont le cors as nes
Qui a viande erent venues;
2640 Si l'esgardent les gens menues.
Le cors le duc portent al port,
Un maistre prient qu'il l'en port
Par haute mer dusc'a Cartage.
N'i firent mie lonc estage,
2645 Ains s'en revont en le bataille,
Cascuns lacie sa ventaille,
Le lance el puig, l'escu au col,
Et tienent celui mout a fol
Qui lor signor lor a toloit,
2650 Qui les biens faire lor soloit:
Mout li prometent grant anui.
Atant si laissent corre a lui.
Brandins i point, icil de Coine,
Et Estatins, li fiex Mado[i]ne,
2655 Et Torgins, li fiex Maraduc,
Et Gadifer, li fius al duc¹
Qui fu des orains asomés.
Cist .iiii. que j'ai chi només
Et .xx. dont ne sai bien les nons
2660 Sont a le mort Ille semons.
Cist .xxiiii. sont mout preu,
Tuit cousin germain u neveu;
N'i a maistre qui plus remagne.
Se cil de Rome u d'Alemagne²

2605 Li troi m.   2659 dont ie sai]W

88

There were three thousand of his followers, who took such fearsome issue with our troops that they made them groan, and they killed everyone they struck. By their sheer power, these three thousand men killed more than three hundred of them in the chase: the duke was causing enormous trouble for the Romans. Ille galloped at him: he brought him dire news, because he smashed his entire shield to pieces, and tore and ripped open his hauberk, pierced his heart and his entrails and hurled him a full lance-length to the ground amidst his troops. You would have heard extraordinary cries of grief from men who would have died there and then if they had had their way; a number of them strove to avenge him, others to rescue the body, and when they had him out of the melée, they wept and wailed and grieved for him. (2625) 'Ah!' they said, 'Dinas, fair lord, with what sorrow and anger this treacherous devil has kindled and inflamed our hearts! He takes us for complete cowards. If he was a true believer in God, he would never dare attack us; but he was born to betray men, to confound men and torment them. Gentle God, how did he even dare think of it? Any other man would have fled from us, and would have been struck dumb with fear.' They did not remain there any longer: they bore the body away to the ships, which had arrived with provisions; and the ordinary people looked on. They bore the duke's body to the port, and asked a sea-captain to bear it over the open sea to Carthage. (2644) They did not stay there for long, but rode back to the battle, each man with his ventail laced, his lance in his hand, his shield hung around his neck, and in their view the man who had deprived them of their lord, who used to reward them well, was a great fool: they promised him no end of suffering. Then they came at him full tilt. Brandin, who came from Coine, charged at him, as did Estatin, the son of Madoine, and Torgin, the son of Maraduc, and Gadifer,[1] the son of the duke who had just been struck down. These four men I have just named and twenty whose names I am not certain of were going to be present at Ille's death. These twenty-four were very brave men, all first cousins or nephews; not a captain amongst them held back any longer. If the Romans or the Germans[2]

autonomous province of the Byzantine empire in the late 6th and early 7th centuries.
[1] There are at least two Greek knights called Gadifer in *Ille et Galeron* : this individual, the son of the duke of Carthage, who may or may not be the Gadifer killed by Ille in l. 2809; and another Gadifer who is killed by Gerin del Mans during Ille's first battle after his return to Rome (l. 5893).
[2] See note on l. 2472.

2665 Ne li vienent plus tost aidier,
Mout se doivent bien apaier;
Car tos les maintient et adrece
Et esbaudist par sa proece.
«Signor, font il, ne vées vos
2670 Com Illes s'ocist la por nous?
Por nostre malvaisté se tue,
Sa car en a mout debatue.
Car li alegons son grief fais!
Mal ait qui mais i ert malvais!
2675 Qui son vil cuer ne puet donter,
Si peüst millor enprunter
Por nos sauver et por celui
Qui por nos tous trait tel anui!
Il suefre seus, bien le savons,
2680 Le malvaisté que nos avons;
Or perge Diu et sa luor,
Qui ne li rent bien sa suor.»
Lors n'i a nul qui cuer ne coelle;
Lors n'i a nul qui fuïr voelle.
2685 Lors i est grans li poigneïs,
Et esforce li fereïs:
.C. en ocient a cel poindre.
Et qant Illes les voit si joindre,
Proece acuet outre pooir
2690 Et vaut plus qu'il ne puet valoir,
Et devint outre pooir preus,
Com sel faisoit por ses neveus;
Et si n'a Illes nonperuec
Ne cousin ne parent illuec,

2695 Mais il i a assés amis,
Et plus de mortex anemis
Por li ochire et detrencier;
Mais cil ne sont pas esclenquier,
Ains trencent fies et pomons:
2700 Trestuit se sont a ce semons.
Or volent tronçon mout espés,
Or ont li Griu mout felon mes:
.M. en ocient li Romain.
Illes et tot li plus certain
2705 Outrent les mors et les tués,
Et ont par force remués
Les vis de la piece de terre.
Nus hom ne vit plus mortel guerre,
C'or n'i atent autre confort
2710 Qui pris est, mes c'a la mort.
Mout par doit on celui reprendre
Qui vif se laisse illoeques prendre;
C'autretant vaut illoec morir
Com estre pris et puis perir.
2715 N'i a mestier nes une triue:
Kaciés les ont plus d'une liue
Li Romain dusqes as destrois;
Illoec areste li tornois
Durement pesmes et mortex.
2720 Or garisse Ille Damedix,
Qu'il est mout durement haïs!
Or le gart Dix, ne soit traïs!
Agars le gaite, Agars l'espie,
Agars het durement sa vie;

2669 fait]Lö   2676 Qui p.]W   2709]W

90

did not come to Ille's assistance more quickly, they would certainly be forced to make peace; for he defended and organised and inspired them all with his prowess. 'My lords', they said, 'Can't you see how Ille is getting killed out there on our account? He is getting himself slain on account of our cowardice; he has taken a real battering. So let us lighten his heavy burden for him! A curse on anyone who is a coward any longer! If anyone is unable to master his faint heart, then he should borrow a better one to save us and the man who is enduring such hardship for all of us! He is paying single-handedly, as we well know, for our cowardice; now may God and His everlasting light be lost to anyone who does not pay him back in kind for the sweat of his brow.' Then there was no-one who did not take heart; then there was no-one who wanted to flee. (2685) Then there was a furious combat and the exchange of blows grew fiercer: they killed a hundred of them in that one charge. And when Ille saw how they joined with the enemy, he acquired superhuman prowess, and was worth more to them than he was capable of being, and his courage became superhuman, as if he were fighting for his own nephews; and yet, Ille had neither cousin nor relative on the field, but he had plenty of friends out there, and even more mortal enemies bent on killing him and hacking him to pieces; but the Romans were not cack-handed – no, they sliced up livers and lights and all urged one another on. Now splinters were flying thick and fast, now the Greeks were being served a poisonous dish: the Romans killed a thousand of them. (2704) Ille and the most confident of the Romans advanced beyond the dead and the slain and made the living give up their stretch of ground by force. No-one had ever seen more deadly combat, for now no-one who was taken prisoner could expect any relief apart from death. A man who let himself be taken alive on that field deserved to be severely criticised; for they might as well have died on the field as be taken prisoner and put to death later. There was no need for a truce at all: the Romans drove them back more than a league, as far as the defiles; at that point the fearsome and deadly tourney came to a halt. Now may the Lord God preserve Ille, for he was most bitterly hated! Now may God save him from treachery! Agar was watching him closely, Agar was spying on him, Agar bitterly hated the fact that he was still alive;

2725 Trop li vait prés, trop s'i amort.
Illes li a son frere mort;
Por çou le het de cuer Agar,
Se li entameroit sa car
Mout volentiers, se il pooit
2730 Et il aise et lieu en avoit,
Qu'il a le cuer mout irascu.
Desous le bocle de l'escu
Le fiert li Grix, Dix le destruie!
Si durement a lui s'apuie
2735 Que trestot l'eüst entrovert
S'ataint l'eüst a descovert,
Que desous l'arçon le sovine,
Si qu'il ne contast son convine
Grant piece aprés por .m. mars d'or.
2740 Li Romain n'ont autre tresor,
N'autre refuit, n'autre recet;
Bien le diroient en recet,
Bien s'en apercevront anqui.
Li Romain vienent dusc'a lui;
2745 Por sa dolor qui mout l'apresse
L'en ont mené hors de la presse
Por savoir se la bleceüre
Li tresalast par aventure.
    Or sont li Romain mout irié
2750 Or sont il mout empirié,
Des que li ciés lor est falis.
Li Griu les ont mout assalis,
Que ne se font de rien semonre
D'aus afoler et d'aus confondre.

2755 Ne prisent gaires lor esfors,
Ce dient, des que il est mors
Qui trestos les estoutioit
Et cascun jour les ochioit.
«Ferés, font il, sor le frapalle
2760 Et gardés bien que nus n'en aille.
Menés les a a le folie
Cil dont il n'aront mes aïe.
Mout estes preus, et vos et vos,
Et il ont deservi vers nous
2765 Que nos les doions encombrer.»
Tant en ont mors, nes puis nombrer;
Remués les ont de la place.
Et qant Illes coisist la kace,
Tote en oublie sa dolor;
2770 Rougist et taint, mue color.
A le maisnie qui li vient
A dit: «Signor, poi vos sovient
De ce que je vous dis orains,
Et des vix cuers falis et fains,
2775 Com malement il nos baillissent,
Com malement il nos traïssent!
Com mal en estes engignié!
Cil membre droit et aligné
Por coi se vont il estuiant?
2780 Vaut dont mix morir en fuiant
Que de morir honestement?
Or n'i ait nul arestement!
Pensés des Grijois desconfire,
Qui sont venu por nos ochire!

2730 Et il aaise il en avoit]Lö   2770 comme carbon]W   2774 A des v.]W
2782 Or ni a]W

92

he rode hard by him, he shadowed him closely. Ille had killed his brother; this was why Agar hated him with all his heart, and he would very gladly cut into his flesh if he could, and if he had the time and space to do so, because his heart was full of sorrow and anger. The Greek – may God destroy him! – struck Ille below the shield-boss and thrust at him with such force that he would have completely disembowelled him if he had caught him unprotected, and knocked him backwards below the saddle-bow, so that Ille could not have given an account of himself for a very long time afterwards, even for a thousand marks of gold. He was the Romans' only asset, their only refuge, their only shelter; they would certainly have said so in private, and they would certainly realise it that day. The Romans rode up to him; because he was overcome with pain they led him out of the melée, in order to find out whether there was any chance that his injury might wear off.

Now the Romans were deeply upset, now things were far worse for them, once they had lost their chief. The Greeks launched a fierce attack on them: they did not wait to be invited to slaughter and confound them. They did not rate the Romans' forces very highly, so they said, when once the man who had harried them all and slain them day after day was dead. 'Strike down that rabble,' they said, 'And make sure that no-one escapes. They have been led into folly by a man who will never come to their aid again. You are very brave men, every one of you, and we should crush them in return for what they have done to us.' (2766) They killed so many of them that I cannot count them; they forced them to retreat. And when Ille noticed the chase, he completely forgot his pain; his face reddened and flushed, and changed colour. He said to the followers who were approaching him: 'My lords, you have short memories for what I said to you just now about faint hearts, cowardly and craven hearts, how falsely they govern us, how falsely they betray us! What a false trick they have played on you! Why are those straight and well-formed limbs of yours heading for cover? Is it better, then, to die running away than to die with honour? Now let there be no holding back! Put your minds to defeating the Greeks, who have come here to kill us!

folio 301ᵛ d

2785 Vos avés millor occoison
Que n'aient li Grijois felon,
Qui sont venu a tort conquerre
Vostre païs et vostre tere.
Je sui por moi ichi endroit,
2790 Et vos i estes por le droit,
Et cil i sont venu a tort.
Bien sai, se nus d'aus en estort,
Que drois perdra son droit en vos
Par les vix cuers qui sont en nos.
2795 Or soiés preus: mestier vos est.
– Sire, trestot en somes prest;
Trestot somes entalenté
De faire vostre volenté;
Mout nos avés bien esbaudis.
2800 Or soit de Damediu maldis
Qui n'ert engrans d'aquerre honor
Puis que nos avons tel signor.»
Cex qui les siens ont plus outrés
A il les premiers encontrés
2805 Et si les fiert de tel vertu
C'ainc puis le tans le roi Artu
Ne fu si fiers encontres fais:
As Grix empire mais li plais.
Illes vait ferir Gadifer
2810 Si durement que de son fer
Li a son hauberc dessarti,
Le cuer del ventre en .ii. parti.
Sa lance estort et cil trebuce,
Et sa gens plore, crie et huce:

2815 «Biax sire Dix, par ta poissance
Donés moi hui ce jor venjance
Del traïtor qui fait nos a
Que nus hom mais penser n'osa.
Mal nos a fait: or del merir!»
2820 Atant i vont trestot ferir.
Bien sont .v. mile quis acoellent
Et li Romain bien les recoellent.
Or i est grans li fereïs
Et des lances li froisseïs;
2825 Or i a mainte lance fraite
Et mainte bone espee traite;
En mainte guise s'i assaient
Cascuns que il le mix en aient.
Illes se contient comme sire;
2830 Par tans vaura apaisier s'ire.
Agar coisist, merir li vait
L'outrage, l'orgoel et le lait
C'orains li fist voiant sa gent:
Mort l'a, quel virent plus de .c..
2835 Mervelles fist en cel estour
Ains qu'il eüst parfait son tour;
Mervelle fu, ce vos plevis,
Qu'il onques en escapa vis.
Icil des castel as Romains
2840 Tendent vers Damediu les mains
Et proient qu'il le maintiegne,
Que sains et haitiés en reviegne.
Les puceles qui sont as estres
Ont mout esgardé des fenestres

2807 ne fu si fais e.]W

94

You have a better cause than the treacherous Greeks, who have come to conquer your country and your territory unjustly. I am fighting for myself, and you are fighting for justice, and they have come here unjustly. I am convinced that if any one of them escapes from here justice will lose its just title in you because of these faint hearts of ours. Now, be brave: now is the time for it.' – 'My lord, we are all ready for it, we are all eager to do what you want; you have truly given us fresh heart. God's curse now on anyone who is not keen to acquire honour, since we have such a leader.' The Greeks who had ridden furthest past his own men were the first Ille encountered, and he struck them with such force that there had never been such a fierce encounter since the time of King Arthur: from then on things started to go badly for the Greeks. Ille went and struck Gadifer so hard that he shattered his hauberk and split the heart in his breast in two with his lance-head. He freed his lance and Gadifer fell, and his men wept and wailed and cried aloud: 'Dear Lord God, by your power grant me revenge today on the traitor who has done to us what no man ever yet dared to think of doing. He has done us wrong: now let us pay him back!' At this, they all went to strike him.

There were a good five thousand men in the attack, and the Romans stood up to them well. Now there was a fierce exchange of blows and a great shattering of lances; now many a lance was broken and many a trusty sword was drawn, each one of them trying in various ways to get the upper hand. Ille conducted himself like a true leader; he would soon let his anger subside. He picked out Agar, and went to pay him back for the outrage, the arrogant insult that he committed against him just now, in full sight of his men: he killed him, and more than a hundred knights witnessed it. He achieved wonders in the melée before he had completed his sally; it was a wonder, I give you my word on it, that he ever escaped from there alive. The people inside the Romans' castle lifted up their hands to the Lord God and prayed to Him to preserve Ille, so that he might return safe and sound from the field. The maidens who were sitting in the window-alcoves watched at length from the casements

2845 Com Illes vait, com Illes vient,
Com belement il se contient;
Diu proient qu'il le gart d'anui
Et ont grignor pité de lui
Que de lor freres qui i sont.
2850 Les dames grant pité en ont:
Mainte en i a, ce saciés bien,
Se il li mescaoit de rien,
Plus en aroit le cuer mari
Que de le mort de son mari.
2855 Quant il prenoit premiers son poindre,
Ces beles mains veïssiés joindre
Et metre ces genous par tere;
Diu oïssiés forment requerre
Plus por lui seul que por aus tous,
2860 Qu'il n'i a nul, tant soit estous,
Se il i muert, ja en escape.
Ne juënt mie desous cape
Ne li Grijois ne li Romain.
Illes i fait tant de sa main
2865 Que mainte place en est vermelle,
Et tous li mons s'en esmervelle
Comment alaine tant li dure.
La gens de Rome est aspre et dure:
Par force ont les Griex remués,
2870 S'en ont mout malmis et tués.
Ja les eüssent desconfis,
Ne fust Agenor et ses fis,
Li biax, li preus Emenidus,
Qui est d'Ataines sire et dus.

2875 Andoi manacent ricement
Et cevalcent mout fierement
A .v. .m. homes combatans:
Esmé[s] les ont li Griu a tans.
Or ont li Romain grant mestier
2880 Que li troi mile chevalier
Dont Illes fist l'arriere ban
Viegnent a sostenir l'ahan
Et le grant paine qu'il atendent.
Agenor et ses fius destendent
2885 Et laissent corre a nos Romains:
Tant en i ont ochis as mains!
Vers Ille poignent a plain cors:
Li Griu ont mestier de secors;
En mal an sont par Ille entré.¹
2890 Emenidus l'a encontré;
La ou li bers fu descovers
Le fiert en travers li quivers.
Mervelle qu'il n'est afolés,
Mais que li fiers li est coulés:
2895 Selonc le dos fist un escar;
Un poi l'entama en le car
Li fel, quant il retrait sa lance.
Bruns, uns Romains de grant vallance
Quant voit k'Emenidus a fait,
2900 En son escu ferir le vait:
Par tel aïr le rabat jus
Et le ceval ou il sist sus
Ans .ii. abati en un mont.
Illes lor dist: «Bruns vos semont

2878 a tant]W

96

how Ille came and went, how handsomely he conducted himself; they prayed to God to protect him from harm, and felt more compassion for him than for their brothers who were out there. The ladies felt great compassion for him: there was many a one, I can assure you, who would have been more heart-broken if any misfortune had befallen him than she would have been at her husband's death. When he was the first to make a charge, you would have seen those lovely hands joined in prayer and those knees falling to the ground; you would have heard more earnest entreaties to God for him alone than for all the rest of them, because if he died out there, none of them would escape, however daring he might be. Neither the Greeks nor the Romans were trying to disguise their intentions. (2864) Ille plied his hand so well out there that many a patch of ground turned scarlet, and everybody marvelled at how great his stamina was. The Roman troops were aggressive and tough: they had forced the Greeks to give ground, and had disabled and killed many of them. They would already have defeated them, had it not been for Agenor and his son, the handsome, the brave Emenidon, who was lord and duke of Athens. The two of them made a splendid challenge and rode very aggressively into battle with five thousand fighting men: that is the number the Greeks had reckoned for them. Now the Romans urgently needed the three thousand knights whom Ille had allocated to the rearguard to come and withstand the strain and the fierce struggle they were expecting. (2884) Agenor and his son dashed forward and galloped at our Romans: so many of them died at their hands! They charged at full gallop towards Ille: the Greeks needed their help; they found themselves in a parlous situation, thanks to Ille.[1] Emenidon encountered him; the wretch struck the noble warrior a sideways blow, where he was not covered by his shield. I am amazed that he was not critically injured, only the lance-head slipped past him: it grazed him across the back; the villain gave him a slight flesh-wound when he withdrew his lance. When Brun, a very valiant Roman, saw what Emenidon had done, he went and struck him on his shield: he knocked him to the ground with such violence, together with the horse on which he was sitting, that he knocked both of them down in a heap. Ille said to the Romans: 'Brun is inviting you

---

[1] Delclos and Quereuil suggest that the text is corrupt at this point, since Ille appears to be the one in need of assistance. This is a misreading: ll. 2888-89 are a comment on the situation which Ille has help to bring about, and which Agenor hopes to reverse by his intervention.

2905 Et vous envie et vos requiert:
S'en faites çou c'au jor afiert.
– Sire, font il, mout nos esmaie
Li sans qui del costé vos raie.
– Signor, dist il, çou est del mains;
2910 Pensés aillors, ferés a plains.
Li malvais sans soronde un poi;
Or ciet li malvaistiés de moi;
Perdre en vauroie mainte goute,
Par si qu'en fust issue toute.»
2915 Romain ont fait lor poindre ensanle;
La terre en tonbist tote et tranle.
Sor le duc sont tot aresté,
Mais il n'i ont riens conquesté,
Qu'en piés se met Emenidus;
2920 Sa bone espee trait li dus,
Si s'est desfendus come ber.
Et li sien n'ont song de gaber:
As Romains donent tex colees
Que jusq'es cars lor sont coulees,
2925 Et ont le duc fait tel bonté
Que maugré leur l'ont remonté;
Puis corent seure cex de Rome.
Or servent bien le duc si home;
Mout sont bon chevalier por voir:
2930 Les Romains ont fait removoir
Et gerpir la piece de tere.
Illes se sent mout de la gerre:
Li sans li raie contreval;
Descendus est de son ceval

2935 Lonc de se gent, les une haie,
Et fist la restraindre sa plaie.
As murs erent les damoiseles
Et les dames et les puceles,
Et voient navré lor signor:
2940 Duel ont, ainc mais n'orent grignor
Diu en ramprosnent durement
Qu'il est navrés si faitement;
Mout par en dient grans ranprosnes
Dient ne feront mais aumone[s]
2945 Se il est mors en tel maniere.
«Malvaise gent vil et laniere
Ne puet avenir se biens non!
Vrais Dix, par ton saintime non,
Aimes tu donques les malvais?
2950 Oïl, espoir, qu'il voelent pais.
Biax sire Diex, ja ses tu tout:
Ja sont li malvais plus estout
Que li prodome, s'il osoient
Et s'il les grans cols ne doutoient.
2955 Por coi mesciet il dont as buens?
Por coi mesciet il dont as tuens?
Mais nus ne puet a toi savoir:[1]
Tu veus les bons o toi avoir,
Por ce lor vient hastive mors.
2960 Prodom muert tost, ja n'ert si fors;
Mais li malvais ont longe vie,
Car n'a[s] song de lor compaignie.
Sire Dius, seceur dont cestui,
Car li malvais morront o lui;

and encouraging you and asking you to join him: so do what befits the day.' – 'My lord,' they said, 'We are very alarmed by the blood pouring from your side.' – 'My lords,' he said, 'This is the least of your worries; put your minds to other things, and strike home. This is just a little tainted blood overflowing; now the taint of cowardice is falling away from me; I should like to lose a good many drops, so that all of it might have left my body.' The Romans charged as one; the whole earth resounded and shook with it. They came to a halt where the duke was lying, but they did not take any prizes there, because Emenidon leapt to his feet; the duke drew his trusty sword and defended himself like a noble warrior. Moreover, his men were not interested in playing practical jokes: they dealt the Romans blows which buried themselves in their flesh, and they did the duke the service of remounting him in spite of the enemy; then they rushed at the Romans. (2928) Now the duke's men served him well; they were truly excellent knights: they forced the Romans to fall back and give up that stretch of ground. Ille was certainly feeling the effects of the war: the blood was streaming from him; he dismounted, far from his troops, next to a hedge, and had his wound bound up there. The damsels and the ladies and the maidens were on the walls, and saw their lord wounded: they had never known greater grief than they knew now. They reproached God severely for the fact that Ille had suffered such a wound; they uttered the harshest reproaches, saying that they would never give alms again if he died in such a fashion. (2946) 'Nothing but good ever comes to faint-hearted, lily-livered cowards! True God, by Your most holy name, do You love cowards, then? Yes, it seems, because they desire peace. Fair Lord God, You know everything already: cowards would soon be bolder than gallant men, if only they dared and if only they were not afraid of mighty blows. So why does misfortune befall the brave? So why does misfortune befall those who are on Your side? However, in comparison with You man knows nothing:[1] You want to have the brave with You, and this is why an untimely death is their lot. A gallant man dies before his time, however strong he may be; but cowards live long lives, for You do not care for their company. Lord God, come to this man's aid, then, for the cowards will die with him;

---

[1] A rather obscure phrase, which looks as though it may have been contaminated by 1. 2958. The use of the preposition *a* in the sense of 'in comparison with' is, however, well attested in Tobler-Lommatzsch, and occurs elsewhere in P (e.g. 1. 4771). Foerster suggested emending *a toi* to *ta loi*.

2965 Se il i muert, mort sont en oire.»
Atant es vos le grant estoire
Des trois mil chevaliers de Rome:
En le bataille a maint prodome;
Al parvenir le font mout bien.

2970 Ille, c'aiment sor tote rien,
Mout le verroient volentiers:
Ne pueent aler tans sentiers
Que d'Ille puissent trover mie;
Ne troevent qui voir lor en die.

2975 Mout en font mains et li Griu plus;
Ses ont remués bien ensus
D'iloec ou Illes fu bleciés.
Et il s'en est mout coreciés
Tantost com il le puet coisir.

2980 Il nen a mie grant loisir
Qu'il i demeure longement;
Saut el ceval isnelement.
Les puceles, qui sont as estres,
Plus l'ont esgardé des fenestres[1]

2985 Que lor parens ne lor cousins:
Prodom a tos jors bons voisins.
Tes .c. puceles a au mur,
Dont Illes puet estre asseür
Qu'eles l'aiment de fine amor.

2990 Des que le virent l'autre jour.
Mainte ramprosne i eüst dite,
Mais l'une claime l'autre quite,
Por le grant paor qui les tient.
Illes vers le batalle vient.

2995 Pluisor partoient ja de l'ost,
Et Illes les coisist tantost:
Brandist le hanste de pumier;
A poi n'en feri le premier.
Mout s'en aïre durement;

3000 Si lor escrie hautement:
«Malvaise gent, vix et laniere,
U fu(i)iés vos en tel maniere?
Alés vos noncier a la tour
Que vencu estes en l'estour?

3005 Alés vos noncier les noveles
As dames et as damoiseles?
Lasses, com mar vos virent onques!
Que lor volés vos noncier donques?
Icil vient trop tost a le porte

3010 Qui malvaise novele aporte.
Preu sont li malvais d'autre part
De çou que vos estes coart;
C'une vix riens de povre endroit
Selonc pïeur qu'ele ne soit

3015 Aqeut ensi cuer et valor
Por çou qu'ele est selon pïor.»[2]
Atant retornent tot ariere;
Ne quierent sente ne kariere,
Mes travers cans tot s'i eslaissent.

3020 Au parvenir les lances baissent
Et vont ferir el grignor tas.
Illes ne s'i espargne pas:
Mout i emploie bien sa main,
Et mout le font bien li Romain.

2974 vos en d.]Lö (lour)   2975 Mout ne sont ore li G.]W   2984 Si l'ont e.
2986 Pro..om (hole)]Lö   3003 Ales nos]W   3005 Ales nos]W   3007 mar nos]W
3016 quil est]W

if he dies out there, a speedy death is theirs.' At this, up rode the great army made up of the three thousand Roman knights: there was many a gallant man in this company; they fought very well when they closed with the enemy. They would very gladly have seen Ille, whom they loved more than anything: but no matter how many paths they took, they could not find any trace of Ille, nor could they find anyone who would tell them the truth about him. Because of this, they fought much less effectively and the Greeks much more so; the Greeks forced them back well beyond the spot where Ille had been wounded. And he became very angry at this, as soon as he was able to make out what was happening. He had little chance of staying there for any length of time; he leapt swiftly onto his horse. (2983) The maidens, who were sitting in the window-alcoves, watched him more closely from the casements than they watched their relatives or their cousins:[1] a gallant man always has good neighbours. There were a hundred maidens on the walls who Ille could be certain loved him with a true love from the moment they saw him the other day. There would have been many a harsh word exchanged there, but each forgave the other on account of the terror which gripped them all. Ille approached the Roman troops. Several of them were already forsaking the army, and Ille spotted them straight away: he brandished the apple-wood shaft of his lance, and came close to striking the first man. He was mightily angry with them and shouted to them in a loud voice: 'Faint-hearted, lily-livered cowards, where are you fleeing to like this? Are you going to announce to those in the tower that you have been defeated in battle? (3005) Are you going to announce the news to the ladies and the damsels? Unlucky women, what a pity that they ever laid eyes on you! What do intend to announce to them, then? The bearer of bad news arrives at the gate all too quickly. The cowards on the other side are brave men because of your cowardice; for a faint-hearted, worthless creature placed next to something worse than itself thus acquires heart and worth, just because it is next to something worse.'[2] At that, they all turned back; they did not look for a track or a road, but all galloped off across the fields. As they closed with the enemy they lowered their lances and went to strike them in the thick of it. Ille did not spare himself either: he put his right hand to good use there, and the Romans fought very well.

---

[1] Löseth and Foerster posited a lacuna after l. 2984. A simple emendation allows the text to make excellent sense as it stands.
[2] In W Ille's speech ends with the couplet: '«Ariere tost par cele foi/ Que vos devés et Deu et moi!»', which provides a rhetorically more satisfying transition to l. 3017.

3025 A un poindre k'Illes i fist,
Regarde; Emenidon coisist,
Sel fiert li ber par tel vertu
Qu'il li esfondre son escu,
L'auberc li desront et desmalle,
3030 Le cuer li perce et le coraille,
Sel fait trebucier contreval
Par son la crupe du ceval.
Et puis k'Emenidus est mors,
Est mout petis tos lor effors:
3035 Tornent les dos, la kace est fiere;
Desconfit sont en tel maniere.
   Li emperere estoit remés
O sa bataille prés des nes.
Quant il et cil qui o lui tienent
3040 Voient que cil ensi en vienent,
Es nes s'en entrent maintenant
Et vont mout grant dol demenant.
Griu vienent Ille merci querre:
Prodom est legiers a conquerre
3045 En tos les lius ou il sorpuet,
Que de franc cuer li naist et muet.
Lor avoir fait Illes saisir
Et prent trestous a son plaisir
Les plus haus barons qui i sont;
3050 Li autre cuite s'en revont.
Illes au castel s'en revient;
Maint salu rent, ce li convient,
Qu'Ille saluent .m. puceles,
.M. dames et .m. damoiseles,

3055 Et le mercient de lor vies,
Car toutes sont par lui garies.
Se il demorast .xv. jours.
Ne fust pas sofraitex d'amors:
Requis i fust de mainte amie.
3060 Mais il n'i pot demorer mie
Ne li baron qui od lui sont.
Grans est li deus k'eles en font;
Quant del departir fu li termes,
Si en plorerent mainte[s] lerme[s].
3065 Illes, li preus, li biax, li gens,
A conduit vers Rome ses gens.
Il es[t] pensis de l'aventure
Et de la douce creature
Dont il parti par se folie;
3070 Mais por rien nule ne l'oblie,
N'ele n'oblie mie lui,
Ains en a trait si grant anui
C'onques caitive n'en traist tant.
Tant l'a li bele alé querant[1]
3075 Que mort sont et enseveli
Tot cil qui vinrent avoec li.
A Lengres vint la douce cose;
En son cuer afice et prop(r)ose
Qu'el n'ira mais en son aé
3080 En Bretaigne, sa duceé,
Ains dist li lasse: «Or ait ma terre
Cil qui mix le pora conquerre.
Mes cuers me juge chi endroit
Que je n'ai en la tere droit;

3039 o lui vienent]Lö   3079 Quil]Lö

102

As he charged on one occasion, Ille looked up and spotted Emenidon: the noble warrior struck him with such force that he shattered his shield, tore his hauberk and ripped it open, pierced his heart and his guts and hurled him to the ground over his horse's quarters. And once Emenidon was dead, all their resistance amounted to very little: they turned tail and a fierce pursuit ensued; this is how they were defeated.

The Greek emperor had remained with his company close to the ships. When he and those who remained with him saw how the Greeks were quitting the field, they immediately boarded the ships, and gave vent to their grief. The Greeks came to beg Ille for mercy: a gallant man is easily won over, wherever he is the victor, because he is inspired and prompted by his noble heart. (3047) Ille had their treasure seized, and took the highest-ranking barons who were there as prisoners, exactly as he saw fit; the others departed free men. Ille rode back to the castle; he returned many a greeting – as he had to – for a thousand maidens, a thousand ladies and a thousand damsels greeted him and gave him thanks for their lives, for they had all been saved by him. If he had stayed for a fortnight, he would not have been short of love-affairs: he would have received advances from many a woman who loved him. However, neither he nor the barons who were with him could stay there. Great was the women's sorrow over this; when the time came for him to leave, they shed many a tear over him. (3065) Ille the brave, the handsome, the noble, led his troops towards Rome. He was deep in thought about the accident and the sweet creature he had left in his folly; but nothing could make him forget her, and she did not forget him either; indeed, she had suffered greater hardship for him than any unfortunate woman has ever suffered. This beautiful woman[1] had been searching for him for so long that all those who accompanied her were dead and buried. The sweet creature came to Langres; in her heart she swore and decided that she would never go back to her duchy of Brittany, as long as she lived; instead, the unlucky woman said: 'Now let my lands belong to whoever is best able to win them. Here and now the sentence of my heart is that I have no title to the land;

---

[1] Here and in l. 3081 *li* is the Picard form of the nominative of the feminine article. The transition from Ille's military exploits to Galeron's life in Rome is neatly handled, with an effective contrast established between his public glory and her private renunciation. Galeron's decision to seek penance from the pope not only solves the narrative problem of shifting the focus of both protagonists' lives to Rome, but also prepares for her eventual withdrawal to a nunnery by introducing a spiritual aspect to her character.

3085 Car ce mut tot par mon pecié
K'Illes se tint si a courcié
De ce qu'il ot perdu son oel.
Que Diex het mout en feme orgoel,
Ce parut bien a le premiere,[1]
3090 Et je suis assés costumiere
De traïner et vair et gris
Et dras de soie de grant pris,
De moi lacier et de bender:
Assés ai, lasse, a amender.
3095 Par moi fu k'Illes s'en fuï,
Par moi sont mort et enfoï
Cil qui o moi l'alerent querre.
Or m'estuet Damediu requere
Et l'apostole en passïence
3100 Que il me doigne penitence.»
    Vers Rome en vait la bele nee,
Et nuit et jor s'est tant penee
K'a l'apostole est parvenue:
Ne s'est plus longement tenue,
3105 Mais tos ses peciés li gehist,
Et li sains hom le beneïst.
Durement s'est humeliie
Cele qui pieça ne fu lie:
De son mari li conte l'estre,
3110 Com il perdi son oel senestre,
Et por l'orgoel qu'en li cuida
Trestot son païs en vuida,
Mais onques sen non ne li dist
Ne l'apostoles ne li quist.[2]

3115 Sa penitance li engoint
Itel qui ne li grieve point,
K'assés a el qui mout li grieve;
Et Galerons atant se lieve.
Illoec ot manant un haut home:
3120 N'ot plus vallant en tote Rome;
Nus hom plus loial ne savoit.
Sous son palais cambres avoit
Et povre gent i conversoient
Qui de lor mains se garissoient.
3125 La se trait cele maintenant,
Et lieue un ostel avenant;
Et si est itex sa pensee
Qu'envers tos velt estre tensee
Par le preudome qui la maint.
3130 Puis le requierent itant maint,
Mais n'i vient onques nus si ber
Qui au partir s'en puist gaber.
Li sire est de si haut afaire
Que nus n'i ose force faire:
3135 N'est pas ostex a peçoier
Ne la ou on doie forçoier.
De ce dont malvés hom le het
L'aime li prodom tant qu'il set
Qu'ele est si bone creature.
3140 Bien se garist de sa costure,
Et se riens nule li sofraint,
Li sire li peçoie et fraint
De son bel pain, qu'il li envoie;
Car il n'est jors qu'il ne le voie

3101 en vont]W   3127 Ensi]W   3136 Ne la ou doie]W

for it was by reason of my sin alone that Ille felt so afflicted by losing his eye. That God feels great hatred for pride in women can clearly be seen from the first woman,[1] and I am well accustomed to parading in furs and costly silken clothes, to wearing tightly-laced robes and braids: unhappy woman that I am, I have much to make up for. It was because of me that Ille fled, because of me that those who went with me to look for him are dead and buried. Now I must pray to God and meekly beg the pope to impose penance on me.'

This high-born woman set out towards Rome, and toiled night and day until she reached the pope: then she did not keep silent any longer, but confessed all her sins to him, and the holy man gave her his blessing. (3107) This woman who had not known happiness for a long while humbled herself completely: she told him about her husband's situation, how he had lost his left eye and had left his country altogether on account of the pride which he believed her to feel; but she never told the pope his name, and he did not ask her for it.[2] He imposed on her a penance which would cause her no distress, for she had many other things to distress her; and at this Galeron rose from her knees. There was a man of high rank living in that area: there was no-one more worthy in the whole of Rome; no-one knew a more loyal man than him. Beneath his palace he had rooms where poor folk dwelt, earning a living with their hands. (3125) Galeron took herself off there straight away and rented suitable lodgings; and her idea was that she would be protected from everyone by the gallant man who lived there. Subsequently, she received advances from a large number of men, but no-one who came was ever such a champion that he had anything to boast about when he left. The lord was of such high rank that no-one dared to use force there: it was not the sort of house to break into or to use force in. What made evil-minded men hate her caused the gallant man to love her when he learned that she was such a virtuous woman. She made a good living from her sewing; and if she did want for anything, the lord would break and tear off for her some of his fine bread, which he sent to her; for not a day passed without him seeing her

---

[1] The idea that Eve brought about the Fall through an arrogant desire for forbidden knowledge was commonplace in the Middle Ages.
[2] *Li = le li*

3145 Et a matines et a messe;
     Et fait a Diu mainte promesse
     De ce k'ele a vers lui mesfait;
     Ses eures ot, puis si s'en vait.
       Tierç jor ains qu'Illes et si home
3150 Venissent o lor gens en Rome,
     Vint uns mes a l'empereor
     Qui mout estoit en grant freor.
     «Sire, fait il, je vieng de l'ost.
     Demain ains midi au plus tost
3155 Vos porés tenir por bon né;
     Car vos verrés vostre barné
     Et les Romains et les Frisons,
     Qui nos amainent .m. prisons;
     De tote Gresse les plus haus;
3160 Mais mors est nostre senescaus.
     Mors nos eüst cil qui l'ocist,
     N'en escapast ne cil ne cist,
     Ne fust li biax, li preu, li ber
     Dont je vous oï tant gaber.
3165 Eslit [l']ont ore a senescal
     Et cambrelenc et marescal,
     Prince, baron, et canqu'il sont:[1]
     Lié pueent estre, quant il l'ont.
     C'est li chevaliers a un oel,
3170 Dont vos fesistes grant org[o]el
     Quant vos ramprosnes li deïstes,
     C'au plus prodom le feïstes
     Qui soit tant com li mondes dure.
     La gens vilaine et aspre et dure

3175 Prisent a vous example, sire,
     K'assés li sorent honte dire
     Ançois que il en l'ost venist.
     Nus hom, sans lui, ne se tenist
     Ne respondist aucune rien.
3180 Quant vint en l'ost, sel fist si bien
     Qu'il fuissent mort tot finement,
     Ne fust ses cors tot seulement.
     Quant besoins d'armes nel semont,
     Si est li plus sages del mont,
3185 As armes plus fiers que lupars.
     Ce n'est pas la centime pars
     De ce qu'en orrés encor dire.
     A tos jors mais serés plains d'ire
     Que vos ramprosne li deïstes
3190 El point que primes le veïstes.
     Sire, quels en sera li drois
     Quant vos al senescal vendrois?[2]
     Si m'aït Dix, li rois celestre(s),
     Ne sai cui li drois en puist estre;
3195 Mais ne le laissiés por nului
     Que vos n'ailliés encontre lui,
     Et si le mercïés, biax sire,
     De vostre honor et de l'empire
     Et de tout çou ke fait i a.
3200 – Par icel Diu qui tout crea,
     Puet c'estre voirs que tu m'as dit?
     – Biax sire, oïl, se Diex m'aït!
     Ne vos aroie awan conté
     Le disme part de sa bonté.

3166 mar..cal (hole)]Lf   3191 ques en sera]W   3194 ne sai qui
3202 Biax sire diex fait cil oïl]W (Dex)

both at matins and at mass; and she made many a vow to God as regards the sin she had committed against Him; she would hear her hours, and then leave.

Two days before Ille and his men arrived with their troops in Rome, a messenger came to the emperor, who was in a state of great apprehension. 'My lord,' he said, 'I come from the army. Any time after tomorrow forenoon you will be able to consider yourself a fortunate man; for you will see your barons and the Romans and the Frisians, who are bringing us a thousand prisoners, the greatest nobles in the whole of Greece; however, our seneschal is dead. The man who killed him would have done for us, not a soul would have escaped, had it not been for that handsome, that brave and noble warrior at whose expense I heard you make so many jokes. (3165) Both the chamberlains and the marshals, the princes, the barons and everyone there have now chosen him to be seneschal:[1] they are entitled to be happy, when they have him. He is the knight with one eye towards whom you behaved very arrogantly when you made gibes at him, for you did so to the most gallant man in the whole wide world. Your example was followed by uncourtly, cruel and hard-hearted men, sire, who found plenty of insults to throw at him before he joined the army. No man apart from him would have restrained himself from making some reply. When he joined the army, he fought so well that they would all have been well and truly dead had it not been for him alone. Away from the call of battle he is the most reasonable man in the world, but more ferocious than a leopard on the battle-field. (3186) This is not even one hundredth of what you are yet to hear about him. You will be eternally angry with yourself for making gibes at him on the first occasion you saw him. Sire, what will be the rights and wrongs of the situation, if you come out to meet the seneschal?[2] So help me God, the king of heaven, I do not know who will have right on his side; but do not let anyone stop you from going out to meet him, and give him thanks, fair lord, for saving your honour and the empire and for everything he has done out there.' – 'By the God who created everything, can what you have told me be true?' – 'Yes, fair lord, so help me God! If I took all year I could not describe one tenth of his virtues to you.

---

1 *Cambrelenc* and *marescal* could be either oblique singular ('the princes and barons have chosen him to be seneschal and chamberlain and marshal') or nominative plural ('the chamberlains, marshals, princes and barons have chosen him to be seneschal'). The second reading seems more plausible, given that there was no mention of Ille's being either chamberlain or marshal when the barons chose him to replace the seneschal (ll. 2457-59), and he is never subsequently referred to as holding any other office.

2 Going out to meet an incoming party was a mark of respect, normally reserved for feudal superiors. The messenger has doubts about what protocol would dictate in a

3205 Tuit le gaberent al premier
Com cil qui sont bien costumier.
Ainc respondre ne lor daigna.»
Et l'emperere s'en saina:
Tel mervelle a de ce qu'il ot
3210 Que il ne pot respondre mot.
    Ganors, la fille au roi, la bele,
Est mout lie de la novele.
Remembre li com simplement
Il se conti(e)nt premierement,
3215 Com il respondi sans desroi
Encontre le folie au roi,
Com il requist par grant mesure
Solement pain et vesteüre,
Com il se fist de povre gent,
3220 Com le vit bel, com le vit jent:
Tot ce recorde et ce retrait.
Amors un petitet l'atrait
A lui amer, car mout le prise;
Un petitet en est esprise.
3225 Li empereres mout s'esgot
Del rice mandement qu'il ot:
Mout durement li vint a bel
D'Ille, son senescal novel,
Mais que de l'autre mout li grieve.
3230 A l'endemain quant l'aube crieve,
Se fait en une chouce metre.¹
Cil qui s'en suelent entremetre
Ont bien la chouce aparillie
Et bien coverte et bien trellie.

3235 Quant vint a l'issir de la vile,
Si sont esmé a .iiii. mile.
    Si com cil de l'ost s'en reviennent,
Endroit l'empereor se tienent
Et dient a l'empereor:
3240 «Sire, faites celui honor
Qui de vos fu si mal venus;
Car il nos a tous soustenus
Et si nos a rendu l'empire.
Or tost encontre lui, biax sire!»
3245 Au roi ne vient ne quens ne dus
Qui ne l'en die autant u plus.
Quant il le voit, ses mains li tent,
Si le salue hautement,
Et cil qui mout li a valut
2350 Li rent encontre son salut.
Si tost qu'il ot et lieu et aise,
Vient l'emperere, si le baise,
Merci li qiert, merci li rent,
Tot selonc l'oevre et l'errement:
3255 Merci li quiert qu'il li dist lait;
Merci li rent de ce k'a fait.
Li emperere mout l'oneure
Et ben[e]ïe le jour et l'eure
Qu'il onques nasqui de sa mere.
3260 Grant feste fait li emperere,
Si font tot cil qui o lui sont:
Grans est la joie qu'il en font,
Qu'il sont par lui tout esclairié.
A Rome sont tout repairié.

3207 li daigna]W

108

They all made jokes at his expense to begin with, as is their usual way. He never saw fit to answer them back.' And the emperor crossed himself; he was so amazed by what he heard that he was unable to utter a word in reply.

Ganor, the king's lovely daughter, was very happy at the news. She remembered how modestly he had behaved at the first, how reasonably he had replied to the king's foolish words, how with great moderation he had simply asked for food and clothing, how he made himself out to be of humble origin, how handsome and how noble he had looked to her: all this she recalled and went over in her mind. Love drew her a little way towards loving Ille, for she held him in great esteem; a tiny flame of love was kindled. (3225) The emperor was overjoyed by the splendid message he had received: it gave him enormous pleasure to hear about his new seneschal, Ille, except that he was deeply distressed about the previous one. Next day, at daybreak, he had himself placed in a litter.[1] Those who normally saw to it got the litter fully prepared, and well provided with a roof and lattice-work. When the procession came to leave the town, it numbered four thousand people.

As the men from the army were returning, they gathered round the emperor and said to him: 'Sire, honour the man who received such a poor welcome from you; for he has defended us all and restored the empire to us. Quickly, now, go to meet him, fair lord!' (3245) Not a count or a duke came to the king who did not say as much to him, or more. When the emperor saw Ille, he held out his hands to him and greeted him in a loud voice, and the man who had been of great value to him returned his greeting. As soon as he had the opportunity, the emperor approached Ille, and kissed him, asked for his forgiveness and gave him thanks, in accordance with his actions and his deeds: he asked his forgiveness for having insulted him; he gave him thanks for what he had achieved. The emperor did him great honour, and blessed the day and the hour when his mother gave birth to him. The emperor gave him the warmest of welcomes, as did all those who were with him: they greeted him with great delight, since he had freed them all from care. They all made their way back to Rome.

---

situation like this, where the emperor is being asked to go to meet a man who is still technically only an ordinary soldier (and a poor one at that), but persuades his sovereign that Ille is worthy of the honour, regardless of his status.

[1] The emperor is old and infirm (see ll. 2004 and 2012), and unable to ride a horse. This detail creates a telling contrast between the ineffectual ruler and the triumphant young hero who is destined to replace him.

3265 Illes est volentiers veüs
Et a grant joie recheüs.
Or est il senescax de Rome,
Or est il sire de maint home;
Rice ostel prent, rice ostel tient:
3270 Mout est bien seürs qui i vient.
Hé, las! que Galerons nel set!
Caitive riens, que Dix le het!
Car mainte gens i sont a aise
De ce dont ele a grant mesaise.
3275 Or sont en la cité andui,
N'il ne l'i set ne ele lui;
Car Illes si n'est mie tex
Que il voist tracier les ostex,
N'ele n'est mie vilotiere:
3280 Bien passe la semaine entiere
Que n'est aillors c'a son mestier
Ou a ses eures au mostier;
.C. ans i poroit ensi estre
Ains qu'il seüst rien de son estre.¹
3285 Ganor, la fille au roi, la bele,
Ot conter d'Ille tel novele
Qu'enamé l'a sor tote rien,
Car tuit ensanle [en] dient bien:
Cascuns au sien entendement
3290 Le loe par amendement.
Illes est mout de rice ator,
Qu'il est saisis de mainte tour,
De maint castel, de mainte vile;
A son service a tel .v. mile,

3295 Qui rien ne doivent a nului
Fors que tot seulement a lui.
Cascun jor croist tote s'onor,
Mes ses cuers est adés aillor:
Ne l'esbaudist riens que il voie,
3300 Ançois l'eslonge de sa joie;
Com plus voit gent juër et rire,
Plus li sovient de doel et d'ire
Et de la douce creature
Et de sa grant mesaventure:
3305 Ainc hom ne fu si esgarés.
Un jour s'est vestu et parés
D'uns dras de soie a or tissus.
Quant de son ostel est issus,
Mout en embelist tote Rome,
3310 Que el monde n'a plus bel home.
A court vait veoir son signor.
Galerons n'est mie en grignor
De li veoir, si com je croi,²
Que Ganors, qui est fille au roi;
3315 Regarde a val, sel vit venir;
A paine se pot soustenir.
Voit qu'il est biax et ensigniés,
Et voit ces membres alignés,
Sa bele bouce et son bel vis.
3320 Tant a de bel en lui assis
Que de son oel ne li sovient:
Aillors entent, ce li convient;
Assés a aillors a entendre.
Amors li fait ses bras estendre

110

The people were happy to see Ille and gave him a very joyful reception. Now he was seneschal of Rome, now he was the lord of many men; he took splendid lodgings and his hospitality was splendid: anyone who visited him was very much at home. Alas that Galeron did not know of it! Poor creature, how God hated her! For many people were very happy about what was causing her great sorrow. Now the two of them were in the city, and he did not know that she was there, nor did she know that he was there; for Ille was not the sort of man to go cruising the lodging-houses, and she was not a woman of the streets: the whole week would pass without her being anywhere except at her craft or at her hours in the minster; she could have lived that way in Rome for a hundred years before Ille learned anything about her situation.[1] (3285) The king's lovely daughter Ganor heard the sort of reports about Ille which made her love him more than anything, for everyone, as one, spoke well of him: each according to his lights went one better in praising him. Ille was splendidly provided for, since he had been invested with many a tower, many a castle, many a town; he had in his service five thousand men who had no obligations to anyone apart from himself alone. His glory increased day by day, but his heart was constantly elsewhere: nothing he saw could put him in good spirits; instead, it widened the gulf between him and his joy; the more he saw people enjoying themselves and laughing, the more he was reminded of his sorrow and distress, of that sweet creature and his great misfortune: no man was ever so bereft. (3306) One day he dressed and decked himself out in silken cloth interwoven with gold. When he left his lodgings, the whole of Rome looked the lovelier for it, since there was no more handsome man in the world. He was going to court to see his lord. Galeron was no more eager to see him,[2] so I believe, than Ganor, who was the king's daughter; she looked down and saw him coming, and could hardly stay on her feet. She could see that he was handsome and well brought up, she could see those well-formed limbs, his handsome mouth and his handsome face. He was endowed with so much beauty that she forgot about his eye: her mind was on other things, as well it might be, for there were plenty of other things to occupy her mind. Love made her reach out towards him

---

[1] The irony of the situation is that it is their virtuous natures which keep them apart and allow time for the second love interest to develop. Suspense is also created, as the audience is left to wonder how – and indeed if – Ille and Galeron can be reunited.

[2] *Li* for *le*.

folio 303ᵣ a

3325 Et baaillier si doucement;¹
Encor li ira autrement.
Ganor la bele est as fenestres;
Illes descent et monte as estres;
Ele est encontre lui venue.
3330 Li uns l'autre mout bel salue;
Lors s'entreprenent main a main.
Arriere lonc sont li Romain,
Que nus n'entent ce que il dient;
De mainte rien gabent et rient.
3335 Ganors mainte parole i di(s)t
Qui touce a l'oevre mout petit:
Autres paroles va disant.
Les jangleors vait despisant:
«Amis, fait el, or aient honte
3340 Cil qui desfirent vostre conte!²
Mout sevent dire et petit faire.
– France pucele deboinaire,
L'en a sovent dit et retrait
Que mout a entre dit et fait.
3345 – Amis, li vostre fais me plaist.
Drois est que vostre bouce baist
Fille de roi et de roïne
Et k'ele soit a vous acline.»
Ganors li a dit mainte rien
3350 Par coi on puet entendre bien
K'ele vaurroit qu'il li queïst
K'ele s'amor en lui meïst.
Tout li a dit la fille au roi
Fors seulement: «Sire, amés moi!»

3355 Et se costume fust en terre
Que fille a roi deüst requerre
Nului d'amors premierement,
Ele le feïst esranment.
Durement vauroit qu'il fust suens,
3360 Por çou qu'il est et biax et buens,
Preus et cortois et afitiés.
Que donques, s'il fust bien haitiés,
Qu'il ne fust pensis de la bele
Dont il ne puet oïr novele?
3365 Ganors ne veut se Ille non,
Ne Illes el que Galeron,
Ne Galerons, qui est a Rome,
N'ameroit pas por rien autre home.
Illes si n'aime mie seus,
3370 Car il est amés d'eles .ii.,
Mais il n'en aime pas que l'une;³
K'amors n'a cose en soi commune,
Mais que largece et cortoisie,
Francise et jeu sans vilonie.
3375 C'est d'amors fine li commans,
Que on truist çou en tos amans,
Ne nus n'a çou entirement,
Que il n'aime parfitement.
Por çou que cis a en soi tout,
3380 L'aime Ganors la bele mout;
Mais Illes n'aime de li mie:
Ses cuers est a sa douce amie,
Qu'il set que l'est alee querre
Et ne revint puis en sa terre.

3339 fait il]W (ele)   3340 nostre c.]W

and yawn so sweetly;[1] but things would soon go differently for her. Ganor the fair was by the windows; Ille dismounted and went up to the window-alcoves; she came to meet him. Each greeted the other very courteously; then they joined hands. The Romans were a long way away from them, so that no-one could hear what they said; they joked and laughed about many things. Ganor said many things to Ille which had very little to do with the matter in hand: she was really talking about other things. She was condemning the slanderers: 'My friend,' she said, 'May those who tried to undermine your credit be ashamed now![2] They are all talk and no action.' – 'Noble high-born maiden, it has often been said and stated that there is a big difference between talk and action.' – (3345) 'My friend, your actions please me. Rightfully, your lips should kiss the daughter of a king and queen and she should be at your command.' Ganor said many things to him from which it could be clearly understood that she wanted him to ask her to grant him her love. The king's daughter said everything to him, with the one exception of: 'My lord, be my love!' And if it were the custom anywhere for a king's daughter to be the first to ask a man for his love, she would have done it straight away. She would dearly have liked him for her own, because he was handsome as well as worthy, brave, courtly and well-bred. And why not, if he had been in good spirits, and had not been lost in thoughts of the beautiful woman of whom no news reached his ears? (3365) Ganor wanted no-one but Ille, and Ille wanted no-one but Galeron, and Galeron, who was in Rome, would not have loved another man for anything. So Ille was not the only one to be in love, for he was loved by the two of them, but he only loved the one of them;[3] because there is nothing in love which can be shared around, except generosity and courtliness, nobility and fair play. This is true love's commandment, that this should be found in all lovers, and no-one who has this in its entirety can fail to love perfectly. Because Ille possessed all of this, Ganor the fair loved him deeply; but Ille felt no love for her: his heart belonged to his sweet love, for he knew that she had set out to look for him and had not returned to her country since.

---

1 *Baaillier* is difficult to translate in this context. The English verb *yawn* has connotations of boredom and fatigue which are entirely inappropriate here. As *baaillier* is often coupled with *sospirer* in descriptions of the physical manifestations of love, it may indicate an open-mouthed sigh rather than a yawn.
2 There is probably a play here on the two meanings of *conte* (financial and narrative). The expression *desfaire son conte* is also found in *Eracle* (l. 24).
3 The situation parallels that in *Eliduc*, where the hero is loved by two women, but only feels true love for one of them. The crucial difference is that Eliduc is a married man in love with another woman, whereas Ille's great love is his wife.

113

3385 Il parole a le fille au roi,
Mais mout li quiert mains de desroi
Que la pucele ne vaudroit.
Andoi en vont au roi tot droit,
Mais Ganors prise mout petit
3390 Tot canqu'il ont parlé et dit,
K'amors n'a nule entension,
Ne ja n'avra, s'a joie non.
Mais a le fois que se desroie,
Por plus aguisier cele joie,
3395 Amors i met douce ramprone;
Si fait grant bien et grant almosne,
Car ce n'est el k'aguisemens
D'amor et uns atisemens.
Ne di qu'il i conviegne ja
3400 Metre autre saveur qu'il i a;
Car nus ne le puet espuisier,
Tant en i a, mais aguisier.
Ganors seut estre adés mout sage¹
Et son sens metre en autre usage,
3405 Et lons usages par droiture
Vaut prés autant comme nature;
Mais trestot çou ne valt rien ci,
K'Amors le tient en se merchi.
Toute l'a mise en autre point;
3410 D'eures en autre li espoint
Si doucement par ces costés;
Mais ains que passe li estés
Li sanlera tout autrement.
N'i ont pas fait lonc parlement,
3415 Mais a Ganor sanle il mout lonc:

Plus de .c. pieces fait d'un jonc.²
Un jour li sanle bien d'une eure
Por son ami qui si demeure,
Car longe atente en fine amor
3420 Fait bien sanler d'une ore un jour;
Ganors a mout le cuer cangié.
Illes se lieve et prent congié.
Ganors cui Amors i envoie,
Revient a lui, si le convoie,
3425 Et pert qu'il soit outre son gré,
K'ançois qu'il soient au degré
Peüssiés ains avoir alee
Une grant liue longe et lee.
3428a Cil qui encontre cuer le fait
3428b Lentement vient, lentement vait;
Mais el le fait si volentiers
3430 Que cors li sanle li sentiers.
Por çou fait ele d'un pas .iiii.,
Car ne se set u mix enbatre.
Quant voit que departir l'estuet,
Si fait ce que faire ne puet,
3435 Car de son cuer se part illoec,
Si veut son ami nonperuec;
Et cors sans cuer ne puet voloir
Ne de rien joïr ne doloir,
Se ce n'est d'ami u d'amie:
3440 Icist ont cuer, si n'en ont mie,
Fors tant com li vilains entent,
Car del sorplus n'ont il noient;
C'o(u)me de mere né ne voi,
S'il aime bien, qui soit od soi:

3414 foit]W   3418 Par son a.]W   3423 qui A.]W   3436 Si vient]W (volt)
3443 ie ne voi]W (net)

He spoke to the king's daughter, but asked far less indiscretion of her than the maiden would have wished. The two of them went straight to the king, but Ganor thought very little of everything they spoke and said, for love pays no attention, and never will do, to anything other than joy. But at the same time as it is getting carried away, in order to make that joy more intense, Love adds a sweet snub to it; and this is an act of great bounty and great charity, for it is nothing other than a way of making love more intense and fanning its flames. I do not mean that it is ever appropriate to add any spice to love other than what is already there, for it has so much of its own that it cannot be exhausted, only made more intense. (3403) Ganor always used to be very sensible[1] and adopt other habits of mind, and a long-standing habit is rightfully almost a match for nature; but all of this was worthless now that Love had her at its mercy. It had placed her in a completely different situation; from time to time it put the spurs so sweetly to her flanks; but before the summer was out she would have quite a different impression of it. They did not have a long conversation, but it seemed very long to Ganor: she broke a reed into more than a hundred pieces.[2] An hour seemed just like a day to her because it was the man she loved who was lingering thus; for in true love long waiting does make an hour seem like a day; a great change had come over Ganor's heart. Ille stood up and took his leave. (3423) At Love's bidding, Ganor approached him again and accompanied him to the door, and it was clear that she did so against her will, since you could have travelled a good long league before they reached the staircase. *Anyone whose heart is not in it finds coming and going slow;* but she did it so wholeheartedly that the way seemed short to her. This is why she took four steps where one would have done, for she could not think of a better way of intervening. When she saw that they had to part, she did the impossible, for she parted company with her heart on that spot, but she still desired the man she loved; and a body without a heart cannot feel desire or joy or sorrow at anything, unless it is the body of a man or woman in love: these people have hearts, and yet have no hearts, except in so far as a churl would understand it, for they have none of Love's bounty; for I have never seen a living soul who is quite at one with himself if he is truly in love:

motif of heart being stolen

---

1 Love is conventionally described in medieval texts as a *folie*, which is diametrically opposed to the ideal of rational, moderate behaviour represented by *sagesse*. The power of Love is demonstrated here in its ability to transform the *sage* Ganor into an irrational and impulsive creature.

2 The stone floors of rooms in castles and palaces were usually strewn with reeds for comfort and warmth; Ganor has picked up a reed and plays with it while the two

3445 Ja soit çou qu'en le voie chi,
Ses cuers est illoec a merci.
Illes le cuer Ganor enporte.
Quant el le voit hors de le porte,
Si en cange tot son talent,
3450 Et pense: «Diex! com il vient lent;
Or s'en revait tel aleüre!»
Ganor riens nule n'aseüre,
Frote ses dois, frote ses mains,
Et de la rien se doute mains
3455 Dont ele devroit plus doter.
Cuide que cil n'ost debouter
Rien nule qu'ele voelle ja;
Poi set la bele qu'il i a:
Tout el i a k'ele ne cuide.
3460 N'a point de cuer, tote en est vuide:
Illes li ber l'enporte o lui.
Que vous diroie de celui,
Mais mout l'onore tote Rome,
A lui nen aiment il tant home,
3465 Ne roi ne conte ne baron?
Diex, quel pitié de Galeron!
Onques ne vait en liu la fole
Ou ele en puist oïr parole.
Que vos feroie plus lonc conte?
3470 Il n'a el païs duc ne conte
Qui ne port Ille autant d'onor
Comme le cors l'empereor.
Trestos li communs de l'empere
Valroient bien que l'emperere
3475 Le retenist en mariage.

Trestot li portent bon corage,
Et l'emperere plus que nus,
Estre Ganor, qui l'aime plus
Que riens el mont fors la caitive
3480 Qui l'aime plus que riens qui vive:
Toute Bretagne en a laissie,
Si s'est por lui tant abaissie
Qu'ele l'a quis comme mendie
En plus de liex que je ne die;
3485 S'en a emprise chasteé
A tous les jours de son aé,
Se Damedix por li ne velle
Qu'ele le truist. Mout se conselle
Li emperere a l'apostoile;
3490 De son consel rien ne li çoile.
«Sire, fait li a l'emperere,
Vos estes desous Diu mes pere,
Si est la droiture entre nos
Que consillier me doie a vous.
3495 Vos savés bien del senescal,
Cui Damedix destort de mal,
Qu'il n'a el monde plus prodome
Et par lui est sauvee Rome.
– Ce sai je bien, fait il, biax sire.
3500 Et que volés vos de çou dire?
– Por çou qu'il a si esploitié
Li vaurai doner le moitié
De canques j'ai a mon vivant,
C'aprés n'en voist nus estrivant.
3504a *Ma fille avra a son deport*
3504b *Et tolt l'empire aprés ma mort.*

3455 riens doter]W   3458 Sor set]W   3491 fait il a]Lö

116

even though you may see him here, his heart is over there at someone else's mercy. Ille carried Ganor's heart away with him. When she saw that he had gone through the door, her whole attitude changed and she thought: 'God! How slowly he came here; now he is leaving again so swiftly!' Nothing could reassure Ganor: she wrung her fingers, wrung her hands, and was least afraid of the thing she should have feared the most. She believed that Ille would not dare turn down anything she might ever want; little did the fair damsel know what the situation was: it was quite different from what she imagined. She had no heart at all, she was quite bereft of it: Ille the noble warrior carried it away with him. What can I tell you about him except that the whole of Rome did him great honour, and compared to him no-one was so well loved by them, be he a king or a count or a baron? (3466) God, what a pity about Galeron! The foolish woman never went anywhere where she might hear people speaking about him. To cut a long story short, there was not a duke or a count in the country who did not pay as much honour to Ille as to the emperor in person. All the inhabitants of the empire would have liked the emperor to keep him there by marriage. Everyone was well disposed towards him, the emperor more than anyone, apart from Ganor, who loved him more than anyone on earth did, except for the poor wretch who loved him more than any living soul: she had given up the whole of Brittany for him, and on his account she had demeaned herself to the extent of searching for him like a beggar in more places than I can tell; and she had undertaken to remain chaste for the rest of her life if God's will for her was that she should not find him. The emperor took counsel at length from the pope; he hid none of his thoughts from him:

'My lord,' the emperor said to him, 'You are my father under God, and the order of things between us is that I should take counsel from you. You are well aware that there is no more gallant man in the world than the seneschal – may God keep him from harm – and that Rome has been saved by him.' – 'I am well aware of this, fair lord,' he said. 'And what do you mean by saying this?' – 'Because he has been so successful, I mean to give him half of all I have during my lifetime, so that there may be no conflict over it later on. *He will have my daughter for his pleasure, and the whole empire after my death.*

---

men are in conversation. The walls of such chambers were hung with thick curtains or tapestries. Galeron hides between the wall and its hanging when she enters Ille's chamber surreptitiously (ll. 1766-69).

3505 Loés le vous qu'ensi le face?
— Oïl, se Dix me doinst sa grasse,
Biax sire ciers, jel lo mout bien.
Cil ne vos ameroit de rien
Qui vous desloeroit ce plait,
3510 Car il est mout de rice fait,
De haut consel et de franc cuer.
On ne le poroit a nul fuer[1]
Si bien emploier en nului,
En tot le monde, com en lui.
3515 Biax sire ciers, or m'escotés!
En' est ce donc li deboutés,
Li chevaliers plains de mesure
Qui onques ne requist usure
Des vilains jeus qu'i[l] li assisent
3520 Et des mesdis que il li disent,
Ains lor sauva la vie a tous
Ne onques n'en fu plus estous?
Mout lor eüst aidié en foi,
S'il eüst veü le porcoi;
3525 Quant il aprés lor felonie
Ne prist garde a lor vilonie,
Ains fist que preus, que faire dut,
Quant vit que faire li estut.[2]
Ce fu de par Diu qu'il vint chi
3530 Et par la soie grant merchi.
Cis salvera l'or et l'argent
Et maintenra le povre gent;
Cis souferra mainte hascie,
Par cui la tere ert alaskie

3535 De mainte persecution,
De mainte grant destruction.
Or ert ce que nos avons nostre;
Or mais sera l'empire vostre,
Or (m)ert il de bons murs enclos,
3540 Car jamais nus n'en ert si os
Qui contre Rome s'ost movoir.
Nos convenoit par estavoir
Que Dix nos donast tel eür;
Or porrons dormir asseür.
3545 Mout doit mix estre abandonee
L'onors celui qui l'a salvee
C'a l'orgillous empereour
Qui nous cuida tolir l'onour.»[3]
Puis que il nasqui de sa mere,
3550 Ne fu si liés li emperere;
Ce fait que cascuns faire seut:
Quant il li loe ce qu'il veut,
A l'apostole en set grant gré.
«Sire, fait il, par cel degré
3555 M'irés el prael la a val
Et manderés le senescal,
Et se li mosterrés ceste oevre.
Ne voel que autres li descoevre
Que tant me soit amis entiers.
3560 — Sire, fait il, mout volentiers,
Et de bon cuer le manderai
Et sa grant joie li dirai.»
Un mes envoia a celui
Et li mande qu'il viegne a lui,

3511 rice c.]W   3516 li deportes]W

118

Do you advise me to take this course of action?' – 'Yes, as God may grant me His grace, fair dear lord, I strongly advise it. Anyone who advised you against this proposal would show precious little love for you, for he is a man of splendid deeds, of lofty counsel and of noble heart. There is no way that your daughter[1] could be bestowed to such advantage on anyone in the whole world as on him. Fair dear lord, now listen to me! Isn't he that outcast, that knight full of self-control who never claimed interest on the low tricks they played on him and on the slanderous things they said to him, but instead saved all their lives and was never any the more arrogant for it? (3523) He would have given them much loyal support, if he had seen a reason to do so; but when, after their spiteful behaviour, he overlooked their lack of courtliness, then he acted like a gallant man, doing his duty, when he saw that he had to be the one to do it.[2] It was by an act of God and by His great mercy that he came here. This man will defend our gold and silver and protect the poor; this man will endure much suffering, and through him the land will be delivered from many a persecution and from many a great disaster. Now what we have will be ours; from now on the empire will be yours, now it will have strong walls to protect it, for no-one will ever be so rash as to venture marching on Rome. Of necessity, God had to grant us such good fortune; now we will be able to sleep safely in our beds. (3545) It is far better to hand the empire over to the man who has saved it than to the arrogant emperor who planned to dishonour us by taking the empire from us.'[3] The emperor had never been so happy since the day he was born; he did what people normally do: when the pope advised him to do what he wanted to do, he was very grateful to him. 'My lord,' he said, 'You will go down these steps into the courtyard for me and send for the seneschal, and explain this matter to him. I do not wish anyone else to reveal to him that he is such a peerless friend to me.' – 'Very willingly, my lord,' he said, 'And I will gladly send for him and tell him of his great joy.' He sent a messenger to Ille, bidding him come to him,

---

1 *Le* for *la*: the pope is referring to Ganor.
2 To make sense, the second half of this sentence has to be read as if *ains* preceded the temporal clause introduced by *quant*. In l.3527 the two phrases introduced by *que* are both dependent on the verb *fist*.
3 There is a play here on the two meanings of *onour* ('domain, empire' and 'honour') which it is impossible to capture in modern English.

3565 Et il i est mout tost venus;
Oiés com il s'est maintenus.
Li apostoles li a dit:
«Senescaus, oiés un petit:
Noncier vos vieng priveement
3570 Entre nos .ii. assés briement
La grignor joie qui en Rome
Fust onques mais noncie a home.
Et si est drois que mix m'en soit,
3573a *Car se uns gars le vos nonçoit,*
Rice et manans en devroit estre.¹
3575 – Sire, par Diu, le roi celestre,
Je ne puis en mon cuer savoir
Dont je tel joie doie avoir,
– Avés vos donc si povre cuer?
En' est Proece vostre suer?
3580 En' est Largece vostre amie
Et Malvaistés vostre anemie?
Savés quel preu vos en arois?
De canque vos sossiel sarois
Que tient cist emperere nostre
3585 Ert des or mais la moitié vostre,
Et si (l)arés avoec la rente
Ganor, qui si est bele et jente,
Et de par li tote l'onor
Aprés la mort l'empereor.
3590 En' a dont chi rice novele?
– Bel sire, oïl, et bone et bele.
J'aim mout et pris la fille au roi,
Mais il ne tai[n]t de rien a moi
Qu'ele soit moie ne je suens.

3595 D'autrui li otroit Dix ses buens!
Dix li otroit honor et joie
Si que je mie siens ne soie.
– Senscaux, laissiés le folie!
– Sire, ne puis, car trop me lie.
3600 Que valroit faire lonc estoire?
N'en prendrai mie, c'est la voire.
Raisons et drois le me deffent,
Et cil qui contre droit content,
Il n'en puet venir a nul preu.
3605 Plus bel assez et le plus preu
Avra la bele et doit avoir.
Je vos en ai dit tot le voir.
– Senescal, voir, ainc n'oï tel!
– Biax sire, encor orrés vos el.»²
3610 Li apostoles s'en aïre,
Revient au roi et dist: «Bel sire,
Se Damedix me face bien,
Je ne cuidai por nule rien
K'Illes ensi me respondist.–
3615 Comment, por Diu? – Ja m'escondist
Trestot ice que je li quis.
N'en fera riens, ce m'est avis;
Nel puis a mon voloir atraire.»
Or a li rois duel et contraire
3620 Et dist: «Comment a Dix soufert
Que je li ai mon regne offert?
Tel offre ne fist ainc mes nus,
Ne refusa ne quens ne dus.
Biax sire, encore l'atraiés

3574 J'en deveroie rices estre]W   3624 assaiés]W

120

and Ille arrived very swiftly; now hear how he conducted himself. The pope said to him: 'Seneschal, listen to me for a moment: I have come to announce to you very briefly, in private, between the two of us, the greatest joy which was ever announced to any man in Rome. And it is right and proper that I should benefit from it, *for if a page were to announce it to you,* he should be rich and wealthy as a result.'[1] – 'My lord, by God, the King of Heaven, my heart is at a loss to know what it is that should bring me such joy.' – 'Is your heart so unassuming, then? Is not Prowess your sister? Is not Generosity your friend and Cowardice your foe? Do you know how you will profit by them? (3583) One half of everything which to your earthly knowledge belongs to this emperor of ours will be yours from now on, and together with the revenue you will also have Ganor, who is so fair and noble, and through her the whole empire after the emperor's death. Are these not splendid tidings?' – 'Yes, fair lord, fine and fair indeed. I hold the king's daughter in great affection and esteem, but it is no concern of mine that she should be my wife or I her husband. May God grant her what she desires with someone else! God grant her honour and joy, provided that I am not her husband.' – 'Seneschal, have done with this folly!' – 'I cannot, my lord, it has too strong a hold on me. What would be the point of telling you a long story? I will have none of her; that is the truth. Reason and justice forbid me to, and a man who crosses swords with justice can derive no advantage from it. (3605) The beautiful maiden will marry – indeed, ought to marry – a much better-looking man than me, and the bravest of all. I have told you the whole truth of the matter.' – 'Seneschal, in truth, I never heard anything like it!' – 'Fair lord, you have heard nothing yet.'[2] The pope became angry at this, and returned to the king and said to him: 'Fair lord, as God may favour me, I did not for a moment imagine that Ille would answer me like this.' – 'How, for God's sake?' – 'He refused me everything I asked of him just now. He will do none of it, so it seems to me; I cannot bring him round to what I want.' Now the king was aggrieved and vexed, and he said: 'How did God put up with my offering him my kingdom? Such an offer was never made by anyone before, nor refused even by a count or a duke. Fair lord, draw him aside once more,

---

1 The pope's words echo ll. 1507-09, where Duke Conain playfully claimed a reward for furthering Ille's suit with Galeron, knowing full well that she had already declared her intention to marry no-one else. The pope is similarly convinced that he is dealing with a *fait accompli* which will result in a prestigious marriage for the hero.
2 It is difficult to convey the brusquerie of Ille's reply here without verging on the colloquial.

3625 A une part, si assaiés
Se ja le feroit por nul plet
Et, s'il nel veut, por coi le lest.
– Volentiers, sire.» Atant le mande:
«Amis, fait il, li rois vos mande

3630 Se mout ne vos est biax cis offres?
Altrement iroit a vos coffres,
Ains demi an, que or ne face,
Se Ganors a le clere face,
La tres bien faite, l'escavie,

3635 Vos estoit donee et plevie;
Kar Rome vos seroit donee
Et l'onors tote abandonee
Qui a la corone apartient.
Senescal por Diu, qui vos tient?

3640 Il a el mont maintes puceles,
Mais de trestotes les plus beles
Est Ganors la flors et la rose,
Et Rome est la plus doce cose
De totes les cités qui sont:

3645 Toutes ensanle en une sont.
Se Dix me doinst mes pain user,
Tel offre ai veü refuser
C'on ne vausist avoir laissié
Por .m. mars d'or; car abaissié

3650 En vit on puis tot le parage.
Cor atemprés vostre corage,
Et si orrés consel d'ami,
S'en aront doel vostre anemi
Quant il verront Rome essalcie(r),

3655 Cui tante fois ont encaucie.
– Dix li doinst, sire, essaucement
Qui lui puist durer longement.
Vos m'avés chi tel cose quise
Que ne feroie en nule guise,

3660 Se tos li mondes ert avoec;
Et si vos di je nonperuec
Que tex offres ne fu mais onques.
– Por coi le refusés vos donques?
– Biax sire, assés i a por coi.

3665 – Quel cose donc? Dites le moi.
– Biax sire, je sui Bres naïs;
Si pris ja feme en mon païs
Qui mout par ert cortoise et bele,
Et si estoit ma damoisele.

3670 Suer ert al duc Conain, por voir,
Qui de Bretagne le fist hoir:
Li dus vit tant en sa seror
Com li dona sauve s'onor.
Contes et dus li vi requerre,

3675 Mais por li plus que por la terre;
Onques de tous ne li plot nus.
Ne sai que vit en moi li dus:
Moi le dona; mervelle fist,
Et ele grignor, qui me prist.

3680 L'an que le pucele espousai
Perdi mon oel; grant doel en ai.
Por çou que je si bas hom ere
Envers la fille al duc son pere,
Cremi ne montast en orgoel

3634 La tres clere et la bien faite]W   3650 En vit .i.]W   3674 com li nonca]W

and sound out whether he would ever agree to it on any account, and, if he will not, why he is declining it.' – 'Willingly, my lord.' Whereupon he sent for Ille: 'My friend,' he said, 'The king desires to know whether this offer is not very much to your liking? Within six months, your coffers would be in quite a different state from now if the radiant, the shapely, the elegant Ganor was given and pledged in marriage to you; for Rome would be given to you, and all the territory which belongs to the crown would be handed over to you. Seneschal, for God's sake, what is holding you back? There are many maidens in the world, but Ganor is the flower and the rose of the loveliest of them all, and Rome is the most pleasant of all the cities in existence: Rome is all of them rolled into one. (3646) As God may grant that I eat bread again, I have seen you refuse the sort of offer which no-one would have wished to decline for a thousand marks of gold; for afterwards his whole lineage is seen to be discredited. So moderate your attitude, and listen to a friend's advice, and your foes will grieve when they see Rome, which they have assailed so many times, in the ascendant.' – 'My lord, may God grant her long-lasting ascendancy. You have asked something of me here which I would in no way agree to, even if the whole world went with it; yet I will tell you nonetheless that such an offer was never made before.' – 'Why are you rejecting it, then?' – 'Fair lord, there are good reasons why.' – 'What, then? Tell me.'

'Fair lord, I am a Breton by birth; recently, in my homeland I took a wife who was extremely courtly and beautiful, and she was also my liege-lady. The truth is that she was the sister of Duke Conain, who made her the heir to Brittany: the duke saw so much good in his sister that he gave her his duchy in its entirety. I saw counts and dukes ask for her hand, but more for herself than for the land; of all of them, not one was ever to her liking. I do not know what the duke saw in me: he gave her to me, which was an astonishing thing to do, and she did something even more astonishing by accepting me. The same year I married this maiden I lost my eye; it grieves me a great deal. Because I was a man of such low estate in comparison with the duke's daughter (her father was a duke), I was afraid that she would stand on her dignity

3685 Et me deboutast por men oel;
Si m'en afuï de ma terre
En aventure de pain querre.
Mix aim desüer mon mangier[1]
Que la soufrir malvés dangier
3690 Ou je suel estre sire et ciés;
Car nule cose n'est si griés
Com illueques viex devenir
Ou on seut home cier tenir,
Com estre a cele gent sougis
3695 De cui on doit estre servis.
et je n'oc pas le cuer si sage
Que je seüsse son corage,
K'ele por moi querre et cerquier
Daignast les terres travescier.
3700 Cerkie en a mainte contree:
Jou ai ja tel gent encontree
Qui la verté m'en ont retraite.
Trestuit cil dont ele est estraite
Ne sevent de li vent ne voie.
3705 Dix me doinst que j'encor le voie!
Car pleüst Diu et sa merchi
Que jou or le tenisse chi,
Quele qu'ele soit, u morte u vive!
Que fera m'ame la caitive
3710 Se je ne voi encor la bele?
– Savés ent vos nule novele?
– Sire, je sai bien qu'il est si
Que de son [païs] s'en issi,
Et k'ele n'i repaira puis;

3715 Rien avant ce savoir ne puis.
Mais ce sai je dusques en son
Que j'en sui li plus dolans hom
Qui soit tant com li mondes dure;
Ma destinee est aspre et dure.
3720 – Amis, laissiés le dementer.
Ce fait maufés por vos tenter,
Qui a maint home muet contraire
Quant il le veut a doel atraire;
Mout se paine d'ome torbler
3725 Et de son doel adés doubler.
Quant il el grignor doel l'a mis,
Savés que fait li anemis?
Tant fait que cil s'ocist et pent
U noie ou art. – Or m'en repent,
3730 Et si kerrai vostre casti.
Bien croi que maufés m'a basti
Et mon damage et mon grant doel,
K'ocis fuisse pieça mon voel:
En maint liu me sui mis sovent,
3735 Et si le fis par tel convent
Que je perdisse illoec la vie.[2]
– Amis ce fait cil par envie
Qui fist pecier le premier home.
Par tos les sains qui sont en Rome,
3740 Senescal, cor vos porvoiés!
Prendés un mes, si l'envoiés
En vostre païs por enquerre
Se vostre feme est en la terre;
Et s'on el païs ne la troeve,

and spurn me on account of my eye; and so I fled from my lands to take my chances winning my bread. I prefer to earn my keep by the sweat of my brow[1] than to have to put up with abuse where I used to be lord and master; for nothing is so hard to bear as becoming an object of contempt in a place where people used to hold you dear, as being under the thumb of the sort of people who ought to be doing your bidding. And my heart lacked the wisdom to understand her feelings, to know that she would think fit to travel through the lands to seek and search for me. She has searched many a country for me: I have recently met people who have told me the truth about it. None of her family has the remotest idea where she is. (3705) God grant that I may see her again! Would that it pleased God and His mercy for me to have her here now, in whatever state she may be, dead or alive! What will become of my poor soul, if I do not see that beautiful woman again?' – 'Do you not have any news of her?' – 'My lord, I do know that the situation is that she left her country and that she did not return there subsequently; beyond that, I am unable to find out anything. But this I do know with a vengeance, that it has made me the saddest man in the whole wide world; my fate is cruel and harsh.' – 'My friend, stop this lamenting. The Evil One is doing this, in order to tempt you; he stirs up trouble for many people when he wants to bring them to grief; he strives hard to confound an individual and then to double his sorrow straight away. (3726) When he has plunged him into the deepest sorrow, do you know what the Common Enemy does then? He goes on to make the man kill himself by hanging or drowning or burning.' – 'I repent of it now, and I shall seek correction from you. I do indeed believe that the Evil One plotted both my injury and my great sorrow, for I would have been killed long before now if I had had my way: I have frequently put myself in dangerous situations, and did so with the avowed intention of losing my life there.'[2] – 'My friend, the one who caused the first man to sin does this out of envy. By all the saints in Rome, seneschal, give this matter some thought! Take a messenger and send him to your country to enquire whether your wife is in the land; and if she is not to be found in the country,

---

[1] There is no need to emend to *deservir* here, as both Löseth and Lefèvre do. Tobler-Lommatzsch glosses *desüer* as 'durch Schweiß erringen' and gives a number of examples of its use in contexts similar to this.

[2] This comment sheds a new light on Ille's determination to be in the forefront of the fighting against the Greeks (cf. l. 2129), and introduces a subtle irony into the situation: the hero's deliberate courting of danger as a result of his estrangement from Galeron is directly responsible for the new 'woman problem' represented by the proposed marriage to Ganor.

3745 Si faites çou que on vos roeve.
Se faites rien contre la loi,
Trestot le pecié preng sor moi.
3747a – *Sire, par Deu qui tolt porvoit,*
3747b *Jo voel molt bien c'on i envoit.*»
Li apostoles s'esgoïst:
Je ne quic mie qu'il oïst
3750 Rien pieça dont il fust si liés;
Durement s'est esleeciés.
Dist li: «Por ceste afaire nostre
Ira mes mes avoec le vostre.
Tant com la cose ert plus creüe,
3755 Ert vo honors plus acreüe.
– Sire, se Dix me face bien,
Ice ne me desplaist de rien.»
Eslit sont li doi messagier.
Li sire vait assoagier
3760 L'empereor, qui se plaignoit
K'Illes sa fille n'adaignoit.
Li apostoles tot li conte
Et de son oel et de la honte
Qu'il ot de ce qu'il perdi l'oel,
3765 Com s'en afuï par l'orgoel[1]
Qu'il cuida que sa feme eüst,
K'ele despire le deüst,
Por çou qu'ele ert sa damoisele;
Et se li conte que la bele
3770 Le sivi maintenant aprés
Et qu'il n'est hom ne lonc ne prés
Qui sace sossiel ou ele est,
Et que li mesagier sont prest

Qui cerqueront destre et senestre
3775 Se el païs qui siens doit estre
Revint ainc puis, ou ele est morte.
Li apostoles le conforte,
Et sont la par l'otroi de lui
Li messagier tramis andui
3780 Et s'on ne troeve la celi,
Ceste avra Ille et Illes li.
Li mes aceminé se sont;
Le cemin vers Bretagne vont.
Savés que fait le senescax?
3785 Les nus conselle et les descax,
Les povres et les orfenins;
Ainc mais ne fu si bons voisins.
Quant il cevalce par ces rues,
Ces povres gens qu'il a vestues,
3790 Cil orfenin qu'il a aidié,
Ces veves por qu'il a plaidié,
Escrient tot communalment:
«Vesci nostre maintenement
Veschi le salu des Romains
3795 Cui Dix fist a ses beles mains!
Vesci nostre deffention!
De cele sainte Assention,
Quant li Fiex monta en son Pere,
Soit beneois li fix sa mere!»
3800 Il et Honors, c'est bien tot un,
Et canqu'il ont lor est commun;
Ele est adés a son cochier,
Ne autres n'ose a lui tocier.
.II. choses a li chevaliers,

3754 Tant que]W   3759 voit]W   3765 Com sen fui par son orgoel]W
3769 li conte la novele]W   3775 Que el p.]W   3793 vostre m.]W
3802 chocier]W (colcier)

then do what is being asked of you. If you do anything unlawful, I will take all the sin upon myself.' – *'My lord, by God who ordains everything, I am very happy for someone to be sent.'* The pope was overjoyed: I do not believe that he had heard anything which made him so happy for a long time; he was highly delighted. He said to Ille: 'For this business of ours, my messenger will go with yours. The more faith people have in this matter, the more your honour will be enhanced.' – 'My lord, as God may grant me His favour, this is entirely to my liking.' The two messengers were chosen. The pope went to appease the emperor, who was bemoaning the fact that Ille was spurning his daughter. (3762) The pope told him the whole story, both about Ille's eye and about his shame at having lost the eye, and how he fled on account of the pride he imagined his wife to feel,[1] how he imagined that she would look down on him because she was his liege-lady; and he told him that the fair lady then followed after him and that no-one far or near knew where on earth she was, and that the messengers were ready to search far and wide to find out whether she ever returned again to the country which should be hers, or whether she was dead. The pope comforted him, and with the emperor's permission, the two messengers were dispatched to Brittany, and if the lady was not to be found in that country, Ganor would be Ille's wife and Ille would be her husband.

The messengers went on their way; they travelled along the road towards Brittany. Do you know what the seneschal did? He brought aid to the naked and the barefoot, the poor and the orphans; never before had there been such a good neighbour. When he rode through the streets, the poor folk to whom he had given clothes, the orphans he had helped, the widows whose case he had pleaded all cried out collectively: 'Here is our protection! Here is the salvation of the Romans, whom God created with His own fair hand! Here is our defence! May his mother's son be blessed by the Holy Ascension, when the Son was taken up into His Father!' Ille and Honour were indeed one and the same, and everything they had belonged to both of them; Honour was always present when he retired to bed, and no-one else dared to lay a finger on him. This knight had two qualities:

---

[1] This line clearly does not make sense in P: Ille has already explained that it was his fear of Galeron's pride which caused him to leave Brittany. The verb *s'en afüir* occurs in Ille's speech (l. 3686), immediately after an *oel/orgoel* rhyme, which further suggests that W's reading is correct, since the pope is repeating Ille's explanation for the emperor's benefit.

3805 Qu'il est piteus et justiciers;
Et s'il est cose ke Justice
L'argüe un petit et atise
De faire ce c'a li afiert,
Dont vient Pitiés, se li requiert
3810 Por Diu et por sa bele face
C'un petit a son gré le face;
Et met i une atempreüre,
Si com del fruit qui si meüre,
Qui n'estoit mie trop en l'ombre
3815 Ne li solex trop ne l'encombre.
A l'une l'autre ensi acorde,
Que ne s'en plainst Misericorde
Ne Justice n'i a damage.
Si faitement les aestage
3820 Que il en fait ce que il veut
Et nule d'eles ne s'en deut.
Illes par est si debonaire
Que pluisor laissent mal a faire
Mout plus por lui que por pecié.
3825 Icil se tient mout a trecié
Qui por lui ne laisse aucun visse,
N'i a si fol, n'i a si nice,
Tant comme Rome est large et ample,
Qui n'i prengne aucun bon example;
3830 Rome le vait tot enclinant.
Li mesagier vont ceminant
Tant que il vienent en Bretaigne.
N'i a valee ne montaigne
Ne bourc ne castel ne chité

3835 Ou il n'aient andoi esté,
Et quierent Galeron la bele.
Mais ne puent oïr novele,
Car en Bretaigne n'en a mie:
A Rome estoit la Diu amie.[1]
3840 Mors est pieça li dus ses frere,
Que des le tans le premier pere
Ne fu tes deus en nule terre:
Tote est destruite de la gerre,
Car païs u li drois oirs faut
3845 Assalent tuit, et bas et haut.
Li mesagier vont mout cerquant,
Tot le païs vont reversant
Et troevent gastes ces contrees,
Dolantes gens et esgarees,
3850 Qui leur dient: «Mors est li dus
Illes li preus, et Elidus.
La suer au duc, qui si ert bele,
Nos n'en poons oïr novele.
Nos ne savomes qu'il devinrent;
3855 Ne ne savons quel voie il tinrent.
En Ille estoit nostre atendance,
Nostre refuis, nostre esperance;
Ne savons por coi s'en fui,
Ne Galerons qui le sivi
3860 Atout .xiiii. chevaliers.
Dix lor soit verais consilliers
Et de lor ames ait pitié!·
Mout i convenroit lonc ditié,
Qui toutes nos destructions,

3811 griu]W   3820 il ne fait]W   3838-9 inverted   3864 Que t.]W

he was compassionate and just; and if there was a case where Justice was bringing a little pressure to bear on him and urging him to do what befitted her, then along came Pity and begged him for the sake of God and His fair countenance to act a little in accordance with her wishes; and he established a happy medium, just like the fruit which becomes fully ripe because it was not in the shade for too long, and is not over-exposed to the sun. In this way he reconciled one with the other, so that Compassion had no cause for complaint, and Justice suffered no harm. He accommodated them both in such a fashion that he had his own way with them and neither of them felt aggrieved. Ille's nature was so noble that a number of people renounced evil-doing, inspired far more by him than by the thought of sin. (3825) Anyone who failed to renounce some vice on his account considered himself sorely cheated, and no-one in the length and breadth of Rome was so foolish or so simple-minded as not to learn something by his good example; he had the whole of Rome at his feet. The messengers continued on their way until they arrived in Brittany. *Words of people in direct speech* There was not a valley or a mountain, not a town or a castle or a walled city which the two of them did not visit, looking for Galeron the fair. However, they could not find any news of her, for there was none to be had in Brittany: the God-fearing woman was in Rome.[1] Her brother the duke had died some time ago, with the result that no land had ever known such distress since the time of our first father: the whole land was ruined by war, for everyone, low-born and high-born alike, will attack a country which is without its rightful heir. (3846) The messengers searched long and hard, they scoured the whole country and found the countryside laid waste and the people disconsolate and destitute, who told them: 'The duke is dead, and Ille the brave, and Eliduc. We have no news of the duke's sister, who was so beautiful. We do not know what became of them; nor do we know which road they took. We put our faith, our trust, our hope in Ille; we do not know why he fled, nor Galeron who followed him along with fourteen knights. May God be a true counsellor to them and have pity on their souls! It would need a very long ballad, if anyone wanted to put down on parchment all the destruction,

---

[1] Lines 3838 and 3839 appear in reverse order in both P and W. The simple process of transposition produces such a compelling improvement in both sense and syntax that I have chosen to emend, despite the agreement of the two MSS. An error common to both MSS would be possible if the version represented by W was adapted from a MS of P which already contained the mistake. If Gautier had dictated his text to a scribe as he composed it, as was not uncommon, these lines could well have been written down in the wrong order in the original MS.

folio 304ʳ b

3865 Toutes nos persecutions
Vauroit escrire en parcemin.»
Cil se remetent au cemin.
Tant ont alé c'a Rome sont:
L'empereour trové i ont,
3870 L'apostole et le senescal
Au cors jentil, au cuer loial.
    «Bel signor, font li mesagier,
Ce vos doit bien assoagier
Et alegier de grant anui,
3875 Ice que vos orrés anqui.
Tote Bretaigne avons alee,
Quise et requise et reversee;
De Galeron, seror au duc,
Et d'Ille le fil Eliduc
3880 N'en set nus hom ne vent ne voie.
N'i a ne ju, feste ne joie:
Trestos li païs se demente
Et est en duel et en tormente.»
Quant Illes l'ot, si en lermoie
3885 Et tint un baston qu'il paumoie
Et fait bien sanlant d'ome irié:
En poi d'eure l'a empirié
La pitiés qui del cuer li muet.
U voelle u non, plorer l'estuet¹
3890 L'apostole, et l'empereour.
Il n'a el mont si roubeour
Qui ne plorast, s'il le veïst,
Et cui ses deus ne desseïst:
Trop est grans pitiés tres qu'il pleure.

3895 A bien poi qu'il ne maudist l'eure
Qu'il onques nasqui de sa mere;
Mout a grant doel li fix son pere.
Il pense: «Dix, que ferai ge?
Je voi et sai bien ke tot ce
3900 Est avenu par me folie.
Il ne me vaut pas une alie
Trestot ice c'on m'a offert,
Tres puis que Dix a tant sofert
Que je tolue m'ai ma joie
3905 Et la riens que je mix amoie
U autant com mon cuer demaine.
E las! quel jour et quel semaine,
Quel mois, quel an et quel novele!²
La mors me semont et apele,
3910 Et ge le devroie apeler.
Je voel, et si nel puis, celer
M'ire, mon duel et mon martire;
Je sai bien que je doins matire
De moi gaber mes a tos jours.
3915 Chevalier gabent mais d'amors
Et tornent tout a jouglerie;
Si fu peruec cevalerie
Par amors primes maintenue
Et avoee et retenue,
3920 Et furent par amor espris
D'aquerre honor et los et pris;
Ce fu l'ocoisons premeraine.³
Mais or est si que gens vilaine
Ont amors tote refusee;

3871 au cors loial]W   3889 plorer lestuet   3903 Quel mal   3917 Ce fu]Lö

130

all the persecution we have suffered.' The messengers set out on the return journey. They travelled until they were in Rome: there they found the emperor, the pope and the seneschal, who had a noble body and a loyal heart.

'Fair lords,' said the messengers, 'What you will hear in a moment should indeed bring you comfort and relief from great anxiety. We travelled through the whole of Brittany, searched, re-searched and scoured it; no-one has seen either hide or hair of the duke's sister Galeron and Ille, the son of Eliduc. There is no fun, no merry-making, no joy there: the whole country laments in grief and torment.' (3884) When Ille heard this, tears filled his eyes and he ran his hands up and down a stick which he was holding, and looked like a man in real distress: it had not taken long for the pity which welled up from his heart to make a sad spectacle of him. Like it or not, the pope was forced to weep, as was the emperor.[1] There is no-one in the world who is such a brigand that he would not have wept if he had seen him, and would not have been moved by his grief: it was a very pitiful sight indeed to see him weep. He came very close to cursing the hour when his mother gave birth to him; his father's son experienced great grief. He thought: 'God, what shall I do? I can see and I know for sure that all this has happened because of my folly. Everything I have been offered is not worth a fig to me since God has allowed me to deprive myself of joy and of the woman I loved better than, or as much as my very own heart. (3907) Alas! what a day, what a week, what a month, what a year, and what tidings![2] Death summons and calls me, and I ought to be calling him. I want to hide my distress, my grief and my suffering, and I cannot; I am well aware that I am providing fodder for jokes at my expense for ever and a day. Knights make a joke out of love now and turn everything into a jest; and yet to begin with chivalry was love's dependant, her protegé and her retainer, and knights were fired by love to acquire honour and praise and renown; this was the initial reason for it.[3] But now things are such that uncourtly folk have quite rejected love;

---

[1] Lines 3891-94 make it clear that the focus has shifted to the spectators' reactions to Ille's grief, hence my emendation. W also has *l'estuet*, but this represents such a simple scribal error, and the resulting construction is so peculiar, that I have chosen to emend despite the agreement of the MSS.

[2] The parallel constructions involving the terms *jour, semaine* and *an* suggest that the series originally contained a fourth temporal noun. *Mois* in close proximity to *quel* and *an* could easily have been miscopied as *mal*.

[3] A variation on the nostalgia motif introduced in ll. 1227-33: here a second literary motif, the chivalry topos, is embedded in the first. Ille regrets the passing of the good old days, while himself embodying a renewal of their core values.

131

3925 Si voi mais gent acostumee
De faire honte et vilonie,
Qu'estainte ont par lor felonie.[1]
Amors gabent et les amans;
Cil est plus gabés c'Alemans[2]
3930 Qui cortois est et velt amer.
On ne s'en set a cui clamer
Fors seul a Diu, qui tot adrece,
Qui des amans set le destrece;
En lor cuer sont fin et verai.
3935 Poi sevent cist ce que je sai,
Com ert bien faite, jente et bele
La suer au duc, ma damoisele,
Com jou envers li bas hom ere.
– Senescal, fait se l'emperere,
3940 Il est ensi com vous oés.
Mais or voel je, se le loés,
Que vos selonc le convenance
Me faciés la reconnissance
Que l'apostoles vos requist
3945 Ensi com il le me redist.
– Biax sire ciers, et je l'otroi;
Et cil qui est et uns et troi,
Sains Esperis et Fiex et Pere,
L'otroit ensi que nel compere
3950 L'ame de moi al jugement,
Quant on venra au parlement.»
Jour ont mis en le Maselaine,[3]
Qui estre doit a le quinsaine;
Car lors seront a cief mené

3955 Li plait dont tant se sont pené,
Qu'ensanle ajosteront ses .ii..
Ensi le dient il entr'eus;
Et sont semons le plus haut home
K'a jor nomé soient a Rome.
3960 Bon loier a qui la novele
Ala conter a le pucele.
Cele semonse n'entent nus,
Ne haut ne bas, ne quens ne dus,
Qui ne dient apertement
3965 Que trop l'ont fait sodainement.
Assés les oïssiés jurer
Que .iiii. mois poroit durer
Li bans al mains, qu'il fust seüs
Et par trestout ramenteüs.
3970 Mais a Ganor est il mout lonc:
On les deüst avoir semons,
Ce dist la bele, tres antan;
Lors se feïssent un lonc ban.
Ganors a tos ceus en despit
3975 Qui metent le plait en respit.
Des que la feme bien le veut,
Ne mal ne sent ne ne se deut;
Et quan le plait doit metre a ués,
Ce dist: «Por coi nel fist on lués?»
3980 Li jors vint tost, cui qu'il anuit.
Grant joie i ot mout cele nuit:
Par Rome cantent ces puceles,
Cil damoisel, ces damoiseles,
Cil jougleor trompent et rotent,[4]

3939 fuisse de l'empere]W

now I see people who are accustomed to shameful and uncourtly deeds, who have quenched love's fire with their wickedness.[1] They make jokes about love and lovers; a man who is courtly and wishes to love has more jokes made about him than a German.[2] You do not know who to appeal to, with the one exception of God, who judges all things, who knows the anguish that lovers go through; in their hearts they are true and sincere. Little do these people know what I know, how shapely, noble and beautiful was the duke's sister, my liege-lady, and how lowly I was compared to her.'– 'Seneschal,' said the emperor, 'Things are as you hear. But now, with your approval, I want you, in accordance with the agreement, to give me the formal consent which the pope asked you for, as he recounted it to me.' – (3946) 'Fair dear lord, I give my consent; and may He who is One and Three, Father, Son and Holy Spirit, give His consent, so that my soul does not have to pay for it on the Day of Judgement, when we come before the assembly.' They fixed the date for the feast of Mary Magdalene,[3] which was to be in a fortnight's time; for then the plans over which they had taken such pains would be brought to a successful conclusion, as they would join these two in marriage. So they said between themselves, and the greatest nobles were summoned to be in Rome on the appointed day. Whoever went to recount the news to Ganor was well paid for his trouble. No-one, either high or low, count or duke, heard this summons without saying openly that they had gone about it too hastily. (3966) Time and again, you would have heard them swear that the proclamation should have been in force for four months, at least, in order for it to become known and to be acknowledged by all. However, Ganor found it very long indeed: they should have been summoned very much earlier, so the beautiful maiden said; then they could have given themselves a long deadline. Ganor felt scorn for all those who were for putting the matter off. Since it was what this woman really wanted, she felt neither pain nor sorrow; and as she was about to turn this business to her advantage, she said: 'Why was it not done straight away?'

The day soon came round, whoever might have been put out about it. The night before, there was very great rejoicing: throughout Rome the maidens, the young noblemen and the damsels sang, the jongleurs played trumpets and rottes,[4]

---

[1] If *que* is a relative pronoun, its antecedent has to be *amors* in l. 3924, rather than either of the two feminine nouns in l. 3926. Foerster posited a missing couplet after l. 3927; Delclos and Quereuil suggest amending to *Qu'estainte l'ont par felonie.*

[2] Germans frequently figure as the butt of humour or disparaging comments in Old French literature. Strong expressions of anti-German feeling are to be found in some of the *chansons de geste* in particular.

[3] July 22nd.

[4] The name *rotte* (or *rote*) was loosely applied to various kinds of stringed

3985 Vïelent, cantent et si notent.
Que vos diroie? A l'endemain
Se lievent matin li Romain;
A ex acesmer tot entendent
Por cele joie qu'il atendent.
3990 Ganors s'est vestue et paree.
Las de le caitive esgaree!
Que Damedix li puis maintiegne,
Qu'ele nel set ains qu'il aviegne!
Tuit li Romain communement
3995 Se sont acesmé ricement;
Grans est la joie que il font,
Vers le mostier Saint Piere vont
Et s'i mainent la damoisele.
Par tote Rome est la novele
4000 Qu'Illes li senescax le prent.
Li uns Romains l'autre reprent
Quant il ne cort a cele joie.
Galerons est enmi la voie
Devant son uis et si orelle:
4005 De cele noise a grant mervelle,
Escoute et ot Ille nomer.
Si bien le peüst asomer
Qui le noma, qu'ele s'en pasme;
Devine, cuide, croit et asme
4010 Que malvais max l'ait si sosprise.
Entre lor bras le dame ont prise;[1]
Si longement l'i ont tenue
C'un petitet est revenue.
D'iaue froide l'ont arousee,

4015 Et content li de l'espousee
Del senescal, qui le doit prendre.
«Mout faites, font il, a reprendre,
Qui tous jors estes en tristrece;
Ce vos a mis en tel destrece,
4020 Ice vos fait muer coulor
Et renoveler vo dolour.»
Tous li monde le blasme et cose
Et dist: «Tristrece est male cose.
Riens ne nos doit hui destorber;
4025 Trestuit devons joie mener.
Hui n'est pas jors, ore ne termes
De faire doel, d'espandre lermes,
Mais de mener joie et baudor
Por la fille l'empereour,
4030 Qu'Illes li ber doit espouser,
Li Bres qui tant fait a loer,
Qui tote ceste tere aquite.
De Diu et de Sainte Esperite
Soit beneïs qui l'engenra!
4035 Trestote Rome convenra
Que facent joie hui al mains,
Car il a salvé les Romains.
Bele, venés a ceste feste.»
Restraindre li ont fait sa teste,
4040 Car la dolors l'ocist et tue.
Al mix qu'ele puet s'esvertue,
Vers le mostier Saint Piere vait;
Deriere l'uis tant i estait
K'ele voit venir son mari.

3985 vieles]W (viielent)

played fiddles, sang and made music. What is there to tell you? The next day the Romans rose early; they were all intent on dressing elegantly for the joyful occasion they were expecting. Ganor dressed herself and put on her finery. Alas for poor forlorn Galeron! May God preserve her afterwards, if she does not learn about it before it happens! The Romans had dressed in rich and elegant clothing, one and all; great was their rejoicing as they went towards Saint Peter's church, taking the damsel with them. The news that Ille the seneschal was marrying her spread through the whole of Rome. One Roman took another to task if he did not rush to this joyful occasion. Galeron was standing in the middle of the street outside her door, listening: she was astonished at the commotion, and listened, and heard Ille's name mentioned. (4007) The person who mentioned Ille's name might just as well have knocked her out, for she fell down in a dead faint; he guessed, imagined, believed and supposed that what had suddenly come over her like this was an epileptic fit. They took the lady in their arms[1] and held her there for so long that she began to come round. They splashed cold water on her face, and told her about the seneschal's bride and how he was about to marry her. 'You really deserve,' they said, 'To be taken to task for always being sad; it is this which has caused you such distress, which is making you turn pale and making your pain worse.' Everyone chided and scolded her and said: 'Sadness is a bad thing. Nothing should be troubling us today; we should all be rejoicing. (4026) This is not the day, nor the hour, nor the time to be sorrowful or to shed tears, but to rejoice and be cheerful, for the sake of the emperor's daughter, who is about to be married to the noble warrior Ille, the Breton who deserves such praise, who is bringing peace to the whole of this land. The blessing of God and the Holy Spirit on the man who sired him! The whole of Rome will have to rejoice, for today at least, for he has saved the Romans. Fair lady, come to this celebration.' They put a bandage round her head, for she was racked with pain. She bestirred herself as best she could and went towards Saint Peter's church; there she stood behind the door until she saw her husband approaching.

---

instruments at different times. Here it probably indicates a Germanic lyre, which was usually held on the knee and plucked, but could also be played with a bow like a *viele* (fiddle).

[1] A slightly awkward transition from a singular to a plural subject. In W l. 4009 reads 'Ses visnés cuide et croit et asme' ('the people of her neighbourhood imagined, believed and supposed'). The re-appearance of the *visnés* in both MSS in l. 4414 provides some evidence to support W's reading here.

4044a *Se la biele a le cuer mari*
4045 Ne s'en doit nus hom mervillier;
Ne se set mie consillier.
De la parole mout se doute,
Que ses maris ne la deboute,
Qu'il ait de li vergoigne et honte;
4050 Ice desfait trestot son conte:
Ne set que puisse devenir.
Et s'el le laisse convenir
Que ses maris espeust celi,
Crient que li peciés tort sor li.
4055 Comment que soit de l'escaper,
Vers Diu se vaudra descouper,
Non por atente qu'ele i ait,
Car il est trop de rice fait,
Car rice plait a entre mains
4060 Icil qui sire est des Romains
Et a cui tote Rome acline.
Lasse, caitive, miserine!
Et repense: «Dix, que ert çou?
Comfaitement li dirai jou:
4065 Biax sire, je sui la caitive
Qui tant ai esté ententive
De vos cerquier de tere en terre
Ou je vos sui alee querre?
N'en daignera oïr parole.
4070 Si me tenront tot cil a fole,
Qui me verront a lui toucier,[1]
Et ne m'i lairont aprochier,
Car g'i voi mout felons Romains,
Et portent bastons en lor mains.

4075 Et se cil me font, voiant lui,
Por m'engresté, lait et anui,
Honte i avrai et deshonor,
Et il n'i avra nule honor,
Car je sui fille et suer al duc
4080 Et Illes fu fiex Eliduc.[2]
Trop par ai pensé grant folage
Quant j'ai pris garde a son parage!
Ques hom sossiel que fust ses pere,
Si vaut il mix c'uns emperere.
4085 A lui pert mout bien qui il est:
De rice cuer rice conquest,
Rice parole et rice fait:
A cascun pert mout bien qu'il fait.
Ahi! fleurs de cevalerie
4090 Et mireoirs de signorie,
Mout plus me peseroit por toi,
S'il me feroient, que por moi.
Cil Dix qui set que mes cuers sent
Me doinst d'a to[i] parler present
4095 Qui en ai forment grant mestier!»
Atant et cil entre el mostier.
Li lasse qui illoec l'atant[3]
Se met avant et si s'estant
As piés celui, et il le lieve;
4100 Et as wisciers anoie et grieve:
Salent avant, ferir le voelent
Si com li huissier faire suelent.
«Fuiiés! dist il, vilains vos voi:
Ferriés vos dame devant moi?

4052 Et fol]W (ele)   4058 Car ele est]Lö   4061 R. avive]W   4062 messerine]W
4066 entaitive]W   4072 atoucier]W   4076 maigrete]W   4080 Elidus]W
4090 m. et s.]W

No-one should be surprised *if the fair lady's heart was stricken*; she did not know what to do for the best. She was terrified of speaking, in case her husband drove her away and was embarrassed and ashamed of her: this thought threw all her calculations into confusion; she did not know what would become of her. And yet, if she allowed her husband's marriage to this woman to go ahead, she was afraid that the sin would be upon her. Whatever the outcome might be, she wanted to clear her conscience before God, not because she expected anything from Ille, for he was too great a noble for that, because the man who is lord of the Romans and has the whole of Rome at his command finds himself in a noble situation. Poor wretched, unfortunate woman! And then she had second thoughts: 'God, how can this be? How can I say to him: (4065) "Fair lord, I am the wretched woman who has been so intent on searching for you in each and every land where I went to look for you"? He will not think fit to listen to a word of it. And all these people will take me for a mad woman, if they see me touch him,[1] and will not let me get near him, for I can see some very villainous Romans there, and they are carrying sticks in their hands. And if they injure and ill-treat me in full view of him, on account of my forwardness, I shall be shamed and dishonoured by it, and no honour will accrue to him, for I am the daughter and the sister of a duke, and Ille was only the son of Eliduc.[2] What an incredibly foolish thing for me to have thought, to have attached importance to his birth! Whoever his father was on this earth, he himself is more worthy than an emperor. (4085) It is quite obvious from what he is now what kind of man he really is: noble conquests, noble words and noble achievements come from a noble heart: what each man can achieve is quite obvious from what he is. Ah, flower of chivalry and shining example of lordship, it would grieve me much more deeply for your sake, if they were to strike me, than for my own. May the God who knows what my heart is feeling grant me the boon of speaking to you, for my need is very great indeed!' At that moment, Ille entered the church. The poor woman who was waiting for him there[3] stepped forward and threw herself at his feet, and he raised her up; and this vexed and upset the door-keepers: they leapt forward, intending to strike her, as door-keepers are in the habit of doing. 'Get back!' said Ille, 'I can see that you are no better than peasants: would you strike a lady in my presence?

---

[1] Galeron is probably thinking of catching Ille by the sleeve to attract his attention.

[2] As Delclos and Quereuil point out, the opposition between the present tense (*je sui*) in l. 4079 and the past (*Illes fu*) in l. 4080 is significant: Ille is no longer simply the son of a minor nobleman, but a future emperor.

[3] *Li* for *la*.

4105 Poi savés, espoir, qui li nuist.
Il n'est hom sossiel qui trop puist
Consillier gens le lor contraire;
Tos jors est saisons de bien faire,
De conseil doner, de bien dire.
4110 Amie, ç'a dit li bons sire,
Or me dites vostre plaisir,
Car je n'ai d'estre chi loisir.
– Sire, il n'est pas ne bel ne jent
Que je tot die oiant la gent,
4115 Qu'il en poroient bien gaber.»
A une part se trait li ber.
«Biax sire ciers, ce dist la bele,
Ja sui jou Galerons t'ancele,[1]
Qui m'en issi de mon païs
4120 Le mois aprés que t'en issis,
Noient por autrui que por toi.
Chevaliers menai avoec moi,
Qui tot sont de ce siecle alé.
Maint grant tertre ai puis avalé,
4125 Maint pui monté, maint mal sofert
Et maint denier por toi offert,
Et tout içou me sanle poi.
Quant vi que trover ne te poi
Et que mort furent tot mi home,
4130 Ving m'ent a l'apostole a Rome;
Descovri lui ma conscience,
Et il m'enjoin[s]t ma penitence.
En ceste vile ai puis esté,
.IIII. ans aroit en cest esté.

4135 Si m'aït Dix, a cui je sui,
Onques de toi dusc'al jor d'ui
Ne fu qui m'en deïst novele;
Mais or le sai je bone et bele
A toi et a tous tes amis.
4140 Bien ait li bons cuers qui t'a mis
A tel honor, a tel hautece,
Et Dix maintiegne ta proece
Et ton grant sens et ta biauté,
Ta bone foi, ta loiauté!
4145 Sire, je voi benignement
Que je te tieng trop longement:
Espouser dois la fille au roi.
Por Diu, soviegne vos de moi,[2]
Que l'apostoles tant me face,
4150 Por Diu et por la soie face,
Qu'il me mete en une abeïe.
Que Dix te saint et beneïe!
Proier voel Diu et nuit et jor
Qu'en paradis vos doinst sejor
4155 Quant les armes istront des cors,
Que li felon seront dehors.
Si m'aït Dix et si saint non,
Je nel te quier se por Diu non,
Que il te gart et te maintiegne. –
4160 Dous cuers, fait il, Diu en sovie[g]ne!
Et Dix, dont tot li bien descendent,
A cui tot li pardon apendent,
Me pardoinst al jor du juïse
La paine ou vos en estes mise,

You have little idea, it seems to me, who or what is vexing her. There is no man on earth who can do too much to help people with their problems; it is always the right time to do good deeds, to give counsel, to say good words. My friend,' so said the good lord, 'Now make your wishes known to me, for I do not have the time to stand here for very long.' – 'My lord, it is neither fitting nor seemly for me to tell you everything within earshot of these people, for they could well make fun of it.' The noble warrior moved off to one side. 'Fair dear lord,' so said the fair lady, 'I am in fact your servant Galeron,[1] who left my country the month after you left it, on account of no-one other than you. I took with me some knights, who have all departed this world since. (4124) Since then I have climbed down many a great hill, and up many a mountain, suffered many a hardship and offered up many a coin for your sake, and all of this strikes me as very little. When I saw that I could not find you and that all my men were dead, I came away to the pope here in Rome; I bared my conscience to him, and he imposed a penance on me. I have been in this town ever since: it will be four years this summer. So help me God, whose servant I am, there was never anyone who gave me any news of you until today; but now I have news which I know is good and welcome to you and all your friends. A blessing on the noble heart which has brought you to a position of such honour and such eminence, and may God preserve your bravery and your great good sense and your good looks, your good faith, your loyalty! (4145) My lord, I can see very well that I am keeping you too long: you are due to marry the king's daughter. For God's sake, may I be in your thoughts and your wife's,[2] so that for the sake of God and His countenance the pope may do this much for me, and find a place for me in an abbey. May God sanctify and bless you! I intend to pray God night and day to grant you a place in paradise when our souls leave our bodies, when evil-doers will be left outside. So help me God and His holy names, I am only asking you this for God's sake, so that He may defend and preserve you.' – 'Gentle heart,' he said, 'May God remember this! And may God, from whom all good things proceed, to whom all forgiveness belongs, forgive me on the Day of Judgement for the toil and trouble this has caused you,

---

1 Nothing could be better calculated than this humble mode of address to convince Ille of how mistaken he was to fear her aristocratic pride after his injury.

2 Throughout her speech, Galeron addresses Ille as *tu*; *vos* here indicates the future royal couple. Galeron implies that it is still possible for the wedding ceremony to go ahead once she has finished talking to Ille, providing he and Ganor have agreed to help find her a place in a suitable abbey. There is a certain amount of poetic licence in this: it is difficult to imagine the pope celebrating a second marriage which took place *before* the first wife had actually retired from the world.

4165 Et la mesaise et la poverte
Que vous avés por moi soferte.
Avés vos .iiii. ans chi esté?
– Oïl, se Dix me doinst santé.
– Quel part, amie, ert vostre uis,
4170 Qu'i ne me veïstes ainc puis?
– Sire, j'ai mes ciés un prodome,
N'a plus loial en tote Rome:
Maint bien m'a fet icil bons sire.
Li visnages le set bien dire,
4175 Quele vie g'i ai menee,
Se j'ai esté fole u senee:
Savoir en pués la verité.
Por Diu, por sainte carité,
Selonc ice qu'il t'ert conté
4180 Fai moi encontre la bonté
Que je requier por amor Diu:
Metre me fai en un bon liu.
Tu as a grant cose a entendre;
Si me convenra tant atendre
4185 Que tu puisses entendre a moi.
Je ne porrai parler a toi
A piece mais, si com je quit.
Biax sire, por Diu, ne t'anuit
Que t'ont chi avoec moi veü;
4190 Li desiriers que j'ai eü
D'a toi parler a mon vivant
Me fist hardie maintenant.
Et, por Diu, ne m'oblier mie,
Car je fui ja ta bone amie.¹

4195 – Comment, ne m'amés vos encore?
– Biax sire, se je disoie ore
Comment je t'aim, quel qui me prenge
On i poroit noter losenge:
Quant on voit povre vanteor,
4200 On le tient a losengeour.
Com plus dist povre[s]: «Je vos aim»,
Mains i tent rices hom son aim²
Et mains s'i croit et mains s'i fie,
Qu'il cuide adés c'on le desdie,
4205 Qu'il face tot por recovrer.
Mais penst prodom de bien ovrer:
U tempre u tart c'est cose aperte,
Bien fais ne puet torner a perte.
Et neporqant, biaus tres dous sire,
4210 Te puis je sans losenge dire
Que mix m'alast une grant masse
Se je de fin cuer ne t'amaisse.
Mors est pieça li dus mes frere,
Qui tint Bretaigne aprés mon pere,
4215 Et sans calenge de nului
Le deüsse avoir aprés lui;
Et si eüsse jou por voir,
Mais sans toi ne le ruis avoir.
Tote Bretaigne ait qui le veut,
4220 Çou que mes pere tenir seut.
Je ne quier ja sans toi avoir
El que je t'ai fait assavoir:
Un vol et une blance gone
Comme rencluse et comme none,

4194 je sui chi le vostre amie]W   4202 son ain

and the deprivation and the poverty which you have endured for my sake. Have you really been here for four years?' – 'Yes, as God may grant me health.' – 'Where was your home, my love, that you never saw me here again?' – 'My lord, I live in the house of a gallant man, the most honourable in the whole of Rome: this good lord has done me many favours. The people in the neighbourhood can vouch for what kind of life I have been leading there, whether I have behaved foolishly or sensibly: you can find out the truth about it from them. For the sake of God and holy charity, in accordance with what you are told, do me the kindness that I am requesting for the love of God: have a place found for me in some good house. You have important business to attend to, and I shall have to wait until you can attend to me. (4186) I shall not be able to speak to you for a good while yet, so I imagine. Fair lord, for God's sake, do not let it upset you that they have seen you here with me; the desire I felt to speak to you while I was still alive made me bold on this occasion. And, for God's sake, do not forget me, for I was once your true love.'[1] – 'What, don't you love me any more?' – 'Fair lord, if I were to say now how much I love you, regardless of who might lay hands on me, it might be taken for flattery: when a poor man is seen to make great claims, he is considered to be a flatterer. The more a poor man says "I love you", the less a rich man is inclined to keep him in tow,[2] the less confidence he has in him, the less he trusts him, because he believes that he will be proved a liar straight away, that he is doing it all for gain. (4206) However, let a man of worth put his mind to good works: sooner or later it becomes obvious; a good deed cannot go to waste. Nevertheless, fair and most gentle lord, I can tell you without a hint of flattery that things would have gone a good deal better for me if I had not loved you with a true and heartfelt love. My brother the duke, who ruled Brittany after my father, died some time ago, and I should have held the duchy after him, without anyone disputing my claim; and so I would have done, in truth, but I do not wish to have it without you. Let the whole of Brittany, the lands my father used to rule over, belong to whoever wants it. Without you, I no longer ask for anything other than what I have given you to know: a veil and a white habit as a recluse and as a nun,

---

[1] W's reading is better here, because Ille's next question makes sense only if Galeron's words have implied that her love is a thing of the past, and up to this point Galeron has addressed Ille exclusively as *tu*, which makes P's *vostre* suspect. Despite his new status in Rome, Ille addresses Galeron as *vous*, suggesting that he still regards her as his superior.

[2] Literally 'the less the rich man dangles his hook (or 'angles') for him'. The phrase *estre pris a l'aim* is used in l. 1688, where it also provides a rhyme for the

4225 Com feme qui n'a d'el mestier
Que seulement de Diu proier
Et d'estre en grans aflictions,
De faire tos jors orisons
Que il nos mece en paradis;
4230 Ice li proierai tous dis.
Ce tient a moi, biaus sire ciers,
Et jel ferai mout volontiers.
Proierai Diu, le creatour,
Que li sires par sa douçour
4235 Mece nos armes a sa destre;
Des que li cors ne pueent estre
Ensanle d'une compaignie,
Diu proierai, le fil Marie,
Que nos ames le soient viax.
4240 Frans chevaliers fins et loiaus,
La graindre paors que jou ai
Et dont je sossiel plus m'esmai
C'est qu'en ton cuer aies vergoigne
Por ma poverte et ma besoigne;
4245 Mais por noient, se Dix m'aït,
Car ja por moi ne sera dit
A home el siecle qui or vive
Que j'onques fuisse fors caitive.
La graindre honours que j'onques oi
4250 Est que tu daignes chi a moi
Parler, n'a tel besong veoir:
Ice dirai, se dirai voir.
Dix le te puist merir et rendre
Que tu daignes a moi entendre,

4255 N'en tel liu tenir parlement.»
Ciex le baisast isnelement,
Mais il doute la felonie
Des Romains pleins de vilonie.
Jamais ne mangeroit de pain
4260 Se or le savoient li Romain;
Se la gent felenesse et fiere
Savoient tote le maniere
De l'oevre que il cuide faire,
La france riens, la debonaire
4265 Seroit depicie en .c. pieces,
Qu'ele n'i a nevex ne nieces,
Parent, ami, ne nule aïe,
Qu'ele ne fust lués envaïe.
Dix le consaut, Dix li aït![1]
4270 Illes, ses maris, li a dit:
«Amie, ne me decevés!
Par cele foi que m'i devés
Se je laissoie tot ce plait
Por vostre amor, qu'en seroit fait?
4275 Averiés me vos contre cuer
Por m'aventure, douce suer?
– Sire, se Dix me doinst s'amor,
Que l'amours ne descrut ainc jour
D'aventure qui t'avenist,
4280 Ne por çou ne te convenist
Aler aillors qu'en ton païs,
Ce pert a çou que t'ai si quis:
Des que tot me desplot sans toi,
Dont n'i a pas raison par coi

4261 de la g.]W

142

as a woman who has no need of anything other than simply to pray to God and to live in great humility, to offer up prayers every day that He may set us in paradise; this will be my prayer to Him each day. This is for me to do, fair dear lord, and I shall do it with great pleasure. I shall pray to God the Creator that the Lord in his gentleness may set our souls at His right hand; since our bodies cannot keep company together, I shall pray to God, the son of Mary, that our souls may at least. Noble, true and loyal knight, my greatest fear, and the thing that frightens me most in the world, is that you may feel shame in your heart on account of my poverty and my straitened circumstances; but so help me God, there is no need, for it will never be said of me to any man now living in this world that I was ever anything but a wretched woman. (4249) The greatest honour I ever had is that you see fit to speak to me here, and to see me at a time like this: I shall say this, and I shall be speaking the truth. May God reward you and repay you for seeing fit to listen to me and to hold a discussion in a place like this.' Ille would have kissed her there and then, but he feared the spitefulness of the churlish Romans. He would never eat bread again if the Romans found out about it now; if that spiteful and violent crowd knew the full details of the deed which he planned to do, the noble and good-natured creature would be torn into a hundred pieces, because she had no nephews or nieces, relatives, friends or any assistance there to prevent her being set upon forthwith. (4269) God counsel her and help her![1] Her husband Ille said to her: 'My love, do not lie to me! By the faith you owe me now, if I were to abandon this marriage altogether for love of you, what would happen? Would you resent me on account of my accident, gentle sister?' – 'My lord, as God may grant me His love, that my love never once diminished because of any accident which happened to you, and that there was no need for you to go anywhere other than your own country because of it, this is clear from the fact that I went looking for you as I did: since I took no pleasure in anything without you, then there are no grounds

---

first person singular of *amer*. Emending *ain* to *aim* is preferable to adopting W's *lectio facilior* 'mains i tent rices hom la main'.

[1] I have taken both *le* and *li* here to be Picard forms of the feminine pronoun, since Galeron appears to be the one most in need of divine help. However, *le* could also refer to Ille, giving an alternative translation 'God counsel Ille and help Galeron'.

4285 On puist prover que mendre soit
L'amors del cuer qui estre i doit;
Ains i est or l'amors trovee
Et mix enquise et mix provee.
Je n'aim pas ta mesaventure,
4290 Mais toi sor toute creature,
Et ferai tant com j'ai a vivre;
Et celui tieng je mout a ivre
Cui ne desplaist, cui ne messiet
Quant il a son ami msciet;
4295 Mes ne l'en doit mesaesmer,
Ne plus haïr ne mains amer.»
  Cil le regarde enmi la ciere,
Se li a dit: «Amie ciere,
Si m'aït Diex li glorïeus,
4300 Ja ne serai autrui espeus
Et si n'arai d'autrui envie
Por tant que vos soiés en vie.
Contes refusastes et dus
Por moi; je ferai por vos plus,
4305 Car j'en refuserai l'onor
Et le fille l'empereour,
Ganor, qui tant est jente et bele,
Qui dolante ert de la novele;
Et se li Romain le savoient,
4310 Grant felonie vos feroient.»
Derier le grant autel le maine
Por cele fiere gent romaine,
Por le gent felenesse et fiere,
Qu'il crient forment c'on ne le fiere.
4315 Derier le grant autel le met,

Et por l'apostole tramet;
Ne s'ose movoir de celi,
4317a *Qu'aucuns de çaus ne vigne a li*
Ki li face honte et anui.
Li apostoles vient a lui;
4320 Cil se laist caoir a ses piés,
Et il l'en lieve tous iriés:
Bien set c'a lui li cose taint.[1]
Illes parfons souspirs ataint.
«Sire, fait il, por Diu, merci!
4325 Veés ma damoisele chi,
Que nos avons tant faite querre
Et tant alé de tere en tere.
Ele a en ceste vile esté;
.IIII. ans avra en cest esté.
4330 Ce dist k'a vous se confessa,
Et puis cele eure ne cessa
De mener bone vie et sainte.
Por moi a mainte larme atainte
Et vescu de povre despense.»
4335 Li apostoles se porpense
De ce que il li a gehi:
Sovient li qu'il l'a ben[e]ï
Et qu'il l'asolst de ses peciés.
«Senescax, fait il, ce saciés
4340 C'or me sovient de l'aventure
Que ceste bone creature
Me descovri l'autr'an de vous;
Par icel Diu qui maint sor nous,
Je ne cuic millor feme el monde.

4288 esquise]W   4318 Que aucuns ne li face a.]W

144

for anyone to argue that the love which is supposed to fill my heart is any less than it was; no, now the existence of that love has been proved and more clearly ascertained and more clearly demonstrated. I do not love the accident which happened to you, but I do love you above all others, and shall do so for as long as I live; and I regard as a drunken fool anyone who is not upset and who is not disturbed when misfortune befalls his friend; but he should not despise the friend for it, not hate him more nor love him less.'

Ille looked her full in the face and said to her: 'Dear love, as the God of glory may help me, I shall never be anyone else's husband, and I shall never want anyone else for as long as you are alive. (4303) You refused counts and dukes for me; I shall do more for you, for I shall refuse the empire for you, and the emperor's daughter Ganor, who is so noble and beautiful, and who will be disconsolate at this news; and if the Romans knew it, they would commit some outrage against you.' He led her away behind the high altar, for fear of that violent crowd, for fear of the spiteful and violent crowd, because he was sorely afraid that they would strike her. He placed her behind the high altar, and sent for the pope; he did not dare leave her side, *in case one of them approached her* and did her insult and injury. The pope came to him; Ille let himself fall at his feet, and the pope raised him up in great dismay: he was well aware that the matter concerned him.[1] (4323) Ille heaved deep sighs: 'My lord,' he said, 'For God's sake, have mercy! You see here my lady, for whom we had our men search and travel from land to land at such length. She has been living in this town; it will be four years this summer. She said that she made her confession to you, and since that time she has lived a good and holy life without interruption. For my sake she has shed many a tear and lived on slender means.' The pope thought over the disclosure Ille had made to him: he remembered that he had blessed Galeron and had absolved her of her sins. 'Seneschal,' he said, 'Let me tell you that I now recall the story which this good woman revealed to me a few years ago in connection with you; by the God who dwells above us, I do not believe that there is a more virtuous woman in the world.

---

[1] *Li* for *la*.

4345 En cele crote plus parfonde
Vauroie que se fust emblee
Dessi a tant que l'assanlee
De ces Romains se fust esparse,
Qu'il vauroient qu'ele fust arse.
4350 Onques mais si dolans ne fui
Com del plait qui remanra hui,
Car Rome en ert desconsillie,
Morte, destruite et escillie.
Bien quic que vos ne lairés mie
4355 Cesti por avoir autre amie.
– Biax sire, non, ne poroit estre,
Si m'aït Dix, li rois celestre.
Or trovés aucune occoison,
Car plus sont ardant d'un tison
4360 Romain, quant ire les esprent.»
Li senescax le dame prent
Entre ses bras et si le baise.
Li sire cele gent apaise,
Qui ja s'aloient coreçant
4365 De ce que il demeure tant:
Li apostoles bien lor dist
C'au senescal convient respit,
Que il est de grant mal soupris.
Et cil s'en revont d'ire espris,
4370 Lor damoisele ont remenee,
Qui mout se tient a enganee.
Au roi en vont andui parler
Li apostoles et li ber,
A qui sa joie renovele.

4375 Au roi acontent le novele,
Com la dame a esté en Rome
.IIII. ans entiers ciés un prodome,
Com ele a vescu saintement,
Et dient li com faitement
4380 Ele calenge son mari.
Li rois en a le cuer mari
Et mout parfons sospirs en fait:
De canques cil li ont retrait
Ne lor sot il gaires de gré.
4385 Icil avalent le degré.
Ganor nule riens n'atalente,
Ains est si durement dolente
Que nus hom n'ose a li parler;
Ne il n'i voelent mie aler
4390 A cele fois, ains s'en revont,
Et Galeron porter en vont
Ciés son mari el grant palais.
Joie ot la nuit plus c'onques mais,
Qu'el mont n'a rien si bien ovree
4395 Qui vaille joie recouvree;
Car a cascun qui la desire,
De tant com il plus se consire,
De tant li est li delis graindre
Com il sa joie puet ataindre.
4400 «Biax sire Dix, font li Romain,
Com poi nos cuidiiens hui main
Qu'ele fust feme au senescal,
Qui trait a .iiii. ans tant de mal!»
Li ostes l'a mout honeree,

4369 s'en revient]W

146

I should like her to conceal herself in this crypt, which is deeper underground, until the time when the Romans who have gathered here have dispersed, because they would like to have her burned to death. Never before has anything saddened me as much as this marriage which will not take place today, for Rome will be left as good as dead, ruined and defeated as a result. It is my firm belief that you will not leave this woman in order to take another love.' – 'No, fair lord, that could not be, so help me God, the king of heaven. Now, come up with some excuse, for the Romans are more fiery than firebrands when their anger is kindled.' The seneschal took the lady in his arms and kissed her. (4363) The pope calmed the people, who were already getting angry at the fact that Ille was taking so long: the pope told them that the seneschal needed to postpone the wedding, because he had suddenly been taken seriously ill. And they went home seething with anger, taking their liege-lady back with them, who felt that she had been sorely deceived. The two of them – the pope and the noble baron whose joy was being restored to him – went off to talk to the king. They told the king the news of how the lady had been in Rome for four whole years, living in the house of a worthy man, how she had lived a saintly life, and told him how she was claiming her husband. This made the king sad at heart and he sighed very deeply over it: he felt precious little gratitude towards them for everything they had recounted to him. (4385) The two men left by the main staircase. Ganor could find no pleasure in anything; no, she was so dreadfully upset that no-one dared to speak to her; Ille and the pope had no wish to go and see her at this point; instead, they went back, and had Galeron brought in a litter to her husband's lodgings in the great palace. That night Ille experienced greater joy than ever before, since nothing in the world, however finely crafted, is worth as much as joy regained; for each man who longs for it finds that the more he is deprived of it, the greater his pleasure when he is able to attain his joy.

'Dear Lord God,' said the Romans, 'How little did we imagine this morning that she might be the seneschal's wife, she who has endured such suffering for four years!' Her landlord had done her great honour,

4405 Mais que a cascune denree
Que mise i a, si vauroit il
Qu'ele cousté li eüst mil.
Li senescax por lui envoie:
Grant feste en fait et mout grant joie;
4410 De ce qu'a fait a sa mollier
Mercis li rent plus d'un miller;
Mout li a bien gerredoné
Tout canqu'il a celi donee.
Li visnés ou ele estre seut
4415 La voie vers la court aqeut:
N'i a celui qui la ne keure,
Et li sire mout les honeure.
La dame tent a cex sa main
Qui li suelent doner du pain;
4420 Ne mains de cent et dis et noef
A fait revestir tot de noef,
Qui mainte mesaise ont soferte
Avoec la dame en sa poverte.
Ainc tex compaigne ne fu mais,
4425 Ne tex compains ne fu jamais
Com ses amans li a esté.
Qui s'eüst illoec aresté
Ou il arestut por s'amor?
Mervelle fist por li le jour:
4430 Si dut li sire mout bien faire,
Car ele ert mout de haut afaire
Quant por s'amor povre devint,
Et il fist bien qant l'en sovint.
Itex li set mal gré, je croi,

4435 Que il ne prist le fille au roi,
Qui en son cuer l'en aime et prise
Mout plus que s'il l'en eüst prise.
Tes veut autrui en mal embatre,
Si l'en requiert trois fois u .iiii.,
4440 Que cil crient Diu et nel veut faire;
Et cil n'ert ja de si mal aire
Que plus nel pri[s]t en son corage.
On doit mix sofrir son damage
Que faire por home estreloi
4445 Et contre Diu et contre soi,
Car tex est del requerre engrés
Que on aroit plus vil aprés;
Si aroit Dix, qui mout est plus
Que ne soit rois ne quens ne dus.
4450 Illes entent et set mout bien
Que il mesoirre d'une rien,
C'est ce dont plus se desconforte:
Set que Bretaigne est tote morte
Et que li dus Conains est mors,
4455 Et taut au foible li plus fors
Canques bons sires doit tenser.
Illes se prent a porpenser
Des felons jeus qu'il a veüs,
Des encombriers k'il a eüs:
4460 Si est tout a recommencier.
«Tex, fait il, n'a song de tencier
Ne ne vait pas grant bruit faisant
Qui trait assés mal en taisant;[1]
Car tel ot on grant noise faire,

4410 de ce que fait]W   4420 .I. mains]W   4431 ele est]W
4434 le sert malgre]W (seut)   4462 vont]W (va)

148

only for every denier's worth he had given her he would have preferred her to cost him a thousand. The seneschal sent for him: he greeted him warmly and with great delight; he thanked him more than a thousand times for what he had done for his wife; he compensated him very handsomely for everything he had given her. The people of the neighbourhood where she used to live made their way to the court: there was not one who did not rush there, and the lord did them great honour. The lady held out her hand to those who used to give her bread; she had complete new sets of clothing given to no less than one hundred and nineteen people who had endured many a discomfort with the lady during her poverty. (4424) Never before had there been such a companion for a man as her; never before had there been such a companion for a woman as her lover had been to her. Who else would have stopped at the point where he had stopped for love of her? He did an extraordinary thing for her that day; and yet it was the lord's bounden duty to do it, for she was a woman of very high rank when she became a pauper for love of him, and he did well to remember it. Some people who bore him ill-will, I believe, because he did not marry the king's daughter, felt much greater affection and esteem for him in their heart of hearts because of it than if he had married her. Some people are keen to push others into wrongdoing, and have to urge them three or four times to do it, because the others are God-fearing and do not want to; and the first ones are never so evil-natured that they do not inwardly esteem them more highly for it. (4443) It is better to bear one's loss patiently than to commit a crime against God and against oneself for someone else, for someone who is eager to encourage wrongdoing would be held the cheaper for it afterwards by others; and by God, who is much more important than a king or a count or a duke. Ille understood and was well aware that he was guilty of one thing, and this was what made him most disconsolate: he knew that Brittany was in a state of total ruin, that Duke Conain was dead, and that the strong were dispossessing the weak of all the things that a good ruler should defend. Ille began to cast his mind back over the evil tricks that he had witnessed, the troubles he had had: it would all have to be done again. 'Some people', he said, 'Who avoid conflict and do not make a lot of noise suffer a good deal as a result of keeping quiet;[1] while others, who are heard to make a great row about things,

---

[1] To make sense, this passage has to be read as if ll. 4461-62 formed the relative clause and l. 4463 the main clause. Even so, it is not entirely clear whom Ille has in mind here. Is he thinking of his enemies in Brittany, who are evoked in the previous lines, some of whom suffered in silence when he was in power, while others who drew attention to themselves by opposing him were destroyed?

4465 Miex li venroit sofrir et taire
Et atendre eure, liu et tans.
Mout sui dolans, quant me porpans
Com Bretaigne ert et bone et bele
Au jour que pris ma damoisele,
4470 Qu'il orent tuit entendement
D'avoir par moi amendement.
Or l'ont destruite por m'amor[1]
Et le destruisent nuit et jor
Icil ki onques ne m'amerent,
4475 Que grant piece a qu'il espererent
Que je fuisse del siecle alés.
Por ç'ont assalie a tous lés
La tere por l'amor de moi.
Congié m'estuet prendre du roi,
4480 C'aler m'en vaurai en ma tere.»
Le soir vait au roi congié querre,
Et l'apostole maine od lui;
Devant le roi vienent andui.
Illes li ber le roi apele,
4485 Sel fist venir en sa capele.
«Sire, ce dist li senescaus
Il est ensi que des plus haus
Qui sont en toute vostre honor
M'avés fait aprés vos signor.
4490 Grés et mercis en aiés vous
De Damediu qui maint sor nous.
Ce que m'avés offert et fait
Vos rende Dix au rice plait,
Quant ert del tot a son commant.

4495 Congié vos quier, sire, et demant,
Et si vos renc ceste ballie;
C'une vix gens fausse et fallie,
Qui maint home ont mort et traï,
Ont le mien et moi envaï:
4500 Çou est Bretagne la petite.
Je le deüsse tenir quite,
Car oirs en est ma damoisele.
J'en a[i] oïe tel novele
C'aler m'i estevra sans faille;
4505 Je ne puis laissier que n'i aille
Sans moi honir et abaissier.
– Comment? Me volés vos laissier?
Qui avra mais pitié de soi
Quant vos n'avés pitié de moi?
4510 Ma tere est vostre plus que moie
Et le riens que je mix amoie
Vos estoit plevie et donee.
Or mais ert terre abandonee,
Or ira ma tere a escil
4515 Et a dolour et a peril.[2]
– Biax sire ciers, or entendés!
Par bone ensegne me mandés,
Se vos avés mestier d'aïe,
Que vostre gens soit envaïe:
4520 Lués m'averés, ce vos plevis,
Por que je soie sains et vis.
Aussi me face Dix merchi,
Isnelement m'arés ichi
Si me doinst Dix rien que je quiere,

4491 sos]W

150

would do better to be patient and keep quiet and wait for the right moment, the right place and the right time. It makes me very sad when I think back to how fine and fair Brittany was the day I married my lady, and how they were all of the opinion that I would make things even better. Now, for love of me,[1] it has been destroyed, and is still being destroyed night and day by those who never had any love for me, and had been hoping for a long while that I had departed this life. This is why they have attacked the land on all sides, for love of me. I must take my leave of the king, as I mean to go back to my own land.' That evening, he went to take his leave of the king, taking the pope with him; the two of them came before the king. Ille the noble warrior greeted the king and drew him into his chapel.

'Sire', so said the seneschal, 'It is the case that you have made me lord and master, after yourself, of the greatest nobles in the whole of your empire. May you receive gratitude and thanks for this from God who dwells above. May God reward you for what you have offered me and done for me at the glorious judgement, when everything will be at his command. I ask you, sire, and request you to give me leave to depart, and I also surrender this office to you, because a base, treacherous and cowardly race, who have caused the death and downfall of many, have attacked me and my territory: that is, Brittany. I should be its unchallenged ruler, for my lady is heir to it. (4503) I have heard such news of Brittany that I must go there, without fail; I cannot refuse to go there without dishonouring and disgracing myself.' – 'What? Do you mean to abandon me? Who will ever feel pity again, even for himself, when you have no pity for me? My land is yours more than it is mine, and the one I loved best was promised and given to you. Now it will be a forsaken land, now my land will go to rack and ruin, suffering and danger.'[2] – 'Fair dear lord, now listen to me! If you are in need of help, if your people are being attacked, send someone for me, with reliable identification: I will be with you straight away, I promise you, provided that I am alive and well. As God may have mercy on me, I will be here with you immediately; as God may grant me anything I ask of Him,

---

1 The phrase *por m'amor* is ambiguous: is Ille saying that his enemies have taken their revenge on the inhabitants who loved him, or that Brittany's plight is the result of Galeron's love for him, which caused her to abandon her duchy?

2 The hero of *Eliduc* does not face the same kind of political problems as Ille: he returns home to save Brittany, confident that Guilliadun's father will face no further opposition (*Eliduc* ll. 609-10). His predicament is a purely emotional one, stemming from his reluctance to leave his beloved in England (see Introduction, pp. xlvi-xlvii).

4525 Ja mençoignieres vers vos n'ere.»
Et l'apostoles li a dit:
«Çou est assés, se Dix m'aït;
Ne quic que Rome ait ja estrif
Por tant com il le sacent vif.
4530 Diex le conduie, s'il li plaist,
Et li doinst cuer qu'il ne vos laist.
Ichi ne monte pas lons plais:
Li senescax est trop parfais,
Trop est de grant afaitement
4535 Por vilener si faitement.»
    Li empereres li a dit
Que il se fille pas n'oublit,
Qu'il le conseut, qu'en pregne cure.
Et cil li dist mout bien et jure
4540 Qu'il le fera mout lïement:
Consel i metra(i) bonement.
Li empere mout l'onore,
Car il l'acole, baise et plore,
Et l'apostoles autretel.
4545 En le capele les l'autel
Se prent li rois a un mairien:
Ne se tenist por nule rien
Qu'il ne caïst, se ce ne fust.
Li rois devint plus rois d'un fust:
4550 Il doi l'ont saisi de .ii. pars;
Ne sont que troi, Dix soit li qars!
En le kaiere l'ont assis;¹
N'i a celui ne soit pensis.
Revenus est li emperere;

4555 Sospire et dist: «A! Dix, biax pere!
Trop par est grevex li mesciés,
Cui faut li cuers, cui faut li ciés,
Cui falent ambedoi li pié,
Qui pert s'espee et son espié,
4560 Ses armes, dont il seut porfendre
Ses anemis et soi deffendre.
Biax sire ciers, c'or te ramembre:
Ja me sont fali tot li membre,
Li bastons ou je me tenoie
4565 Et a cui je me soustenoie.
Hui en cest jor ai perdu plus
C'onques ne fist ne quens ne dus,
Rois n'emperere n'amiraus.»
Quant çou entent li senescax,
4570 Si s'est escrevés a plorer,
Com s'on le deüst acorer.
Mout plor li ber tenrement,
Et l'apostoles ensement:
Bien ont espeneï tot troi
4575 Icel congié et cel otroi.
Cil de la sale oent le plor,
Si s'en esfroient li pluisor:
Lieve la noise par la sale,
Muent color, devienent pale,
4580 De grant angoisse lor sovient,
Quant il ne sevent dont ce vient.
De mout plus grant lor sovenra
Quant la novele lor venra.
Ne tarde gaires c'on le set;

152

I was never untrue to my word with you.' And the pope said to the king: 'This is good enough, so help me God; I do not believe that Rome will ever find herself at war, for as long as they know that he is alive. May God be his guide, if it please Him, and grant him the courage not to abandon you. There is no point in having a long discussion here: the seneschal is too admirable a man, and has far too many fine qualities to act so dishonourably.'

The emperor told Ille not to forget his daughter, to counsel her and to take care of her. And Ille assured him and swore that he would be very happy to do so: he would gladly give her his counsel. The emperor did him great honour, for he embraced him, kissed him and wept for him, and the pope did the same. (4585) In the chapel, next to the altar, the king grasped hold of a wooden pillar: there was no way that he would have been able to prevent himself from falling, had it not been for that. The king went as stiff as a post: the other two men took hold of him, one on each side; there were only the three of them there – may God make a fourth! They sat him in the priest's chair;[1] both of them were deeply worried. The emperor came round, sighed, and said: 'Oh God, dear Father! What a terrible calamity it is for a man when his heart fails him, when his mind fails him, when both his legs fail him, when he loses his sword and his lance, his arms, with which he used to cut through his enemies and defend himself. Fair dear Lord, do not forget me now: now all my limbs have failed me, and so has the staff I used to lean on and on which I used to support myself. (4566) Today I have lost more than any count or duke, king or emperor or emir ever lost.' When the seneschal heard this, he broke down and wept as if he were about to be disembowelled. The noble baron wept very tenderly, and the pope did the same: Ille's leave-taking and the king's consent cost the three of them dear. The people in the hall heard the weeping, and many of them were alarmed by it: a commotion arose in the hall, the colour drained from their faces, they turned pale; their minds were filled with great anguish, since they did not know the reason for it. They would be filled with far greater anguish when the news reached them. It was not long before they learned it;

---

1 Even in a royal chapel, the congregation would have sat on benches; only the priest had a high-backed chair with arms, which could have been used for propping up a person who had suffered some kind of seizure. Line 4551 reminds us how unusual it was for a king or emperor not to have numerous attendants in the same room, even if he was engaged in a private conversation.

4585 Cascuns despit sa vie et het:
E vos gent morte et confondue!
Se Rome estoit tote fondue,
N'i aroit grignor doel, je quit.
Dient entr'ex: «Mort somes tuit!
4590 Mors nos deüst avoir soupris
Ains qu'eüssiens a vivre apris!»
Quant çou entendent les puceles,
Les dames et les damoiseles,
Ganor racontent la novele,
4595 Cui ele est mout amee et bele,
Qu'ele set bien tout entresait
Qu'il morront tot se il s'en vait.
Ce vauroit ele mout tres bien,
Si l'ameroit sor toute rien;
4600 Et toute ice li vient d'Envie,
Car mout het durement sa vie.
Il est costume d'envieus
Qu'il vauroit estre al bien tous sex,
Et qant li fel n'a se mal non,
4605 Lors si vauroit maint compaignon:
Tos jors le bien trestot par lui
Et le mal partir a autrui.
Se Ganors eüst esploitié
A ce k'ele avoit covoitié,
4610 Ja n'i quesist avoir compagne;
Mes de cest mal qui li engragne
Morroient tuit o li son voel
Por vengier s'ire et son grant doel.
Escrie: «Dix, sainte Marie,

4615 Com or m'a ceste mors garie!
Seule cuidoie bien morir;
Or verrai Rome o moi perir.
Or ert la mors plus avenans,
Car povres ert li remanans.
4620 Or ne me poront mais gaber
Ne rois ne dus ne quens ne ber,
Car cil qui Rome a deffendue,
De cui ma mors est descendue,
Les metra mais al convenir.
4625 Dix doint que tost puist avenir!¹
Jou ai mal dit, or m'en repent.
Je sanle celui qui on pent,²
Qui veut a tote gent anui
Et c'on les pendist avoec lui.
4630 Fole amors, qui est plaine d'ire
Me fist cele folie dire;
Folie m'issi de la geule:
Mix doi voloir a morir seule,
Que tote Rome acompaignier
4635 Sans rien conquerre et gaagnier.
Mout doit bien avoir sa deserte
Qui sans gaang veut autrui perte.
Mais fille sui d'empereour,
Qui sui menee a deshonor,
4640 Car cil el mont qui mix me sist
A l'uis du mostier me despist:
Ce m'a fait dire tel desroi.»
Illes a pris congié del roi;
A le pucele vait parler,

4588 je quic

then each man despised and detested his own life: these were people who thought they were dead and done for! If Rome had been totally destroyed, I do not believe there would have been greater sorrow. They said to one another: 'We are all dead men! Death should have come upon us before we had learned to live!' When the maidens, the ladies and the damsels heard this, they told the news to Ganor, to whom it was very welcome and agreeable, because she immediately knew for sure that they would all die if Ille left. This is what she would dearly wish, and what she would like more than anything; and this was all Envy's doing, for she hated her own life with a vengeance. It is normal for an envious person to want to be the only one to enjoy the good things, but when the wretch experiences nothing but trouble, then he would like plenty of company: he always wants to have the good all to himself and to share the bad with other people. (4607) If Ganor had succeeded in getting what she desired, she would never have asked for company; but if she had her way now, they would all die with her from this affliction which was tormenting her, in order to avenge her anger and her grief. She cried out: 'God and the blessed Mary, this death knell is my salvation! I truly believed that I would be the only one to die; now I shall see Rome perish with me. Now death will be the more attractive, for what is left behind will be worthless. Now neither king nor duke nor count nor baron will be able to mock me any more, for the man who has been Rome's defence, and the cause of my death, will leave them to their own devices from now on. (4625) God grant that it may happen quickly![1] These are sinful words; I repent of them now. I am like a man who is about to be hanged,[2] who wishes harm to everyone, and wants them to be hanged with him. Foolish love, which is full of anger, made me say these foolish words. Foolish words came out of my mouth: I ought to prefer to die alone than to accompany the whole of Rome, without achieving or gaining anything. Anyone who wills someone else's destruction for nothing should indeed get his just deserts. But I am the daughter of an emperor, and I have been treated dishonourably, for the man who suited me best in the world turned his back on me at the church door: this is what made me say such senseless things.' Ille had taken his leave of the king; he went to talk to the maiden,

---

1 There is considerable psychological truth in Ganor's reaction, but one can appreciate that this petulant portrait of a future empress might not have struck Beatrice of Burgundy as particularly flattering. The same can be said of Ganor's lament after Ille's departure (ll. 5205-77), in which self-pity, sexual frustration and jealousy mingle with outright hatred for her rival Galeron.
2 *Qui* for *que*.

4645 A paines qu'il i ose aler.
Mout a grant honte de celi:
Crient que n'ait vilené vers li,
Et si a il mout durement,
Mes il ne puet estre altrement;
4650 Ensi est or la cose prise.
Il set bien k'ele l'aime et prise,
Mais Galerons l'ama ançois,
E si a el, car drois et lois
Et fine raisons et li prestre
4655 Tesmoignent qu'ensi doit il estre.
Prestre, raisons, drois et lois
Font les amans sovent destrois.
Feme et Amors desfont sovent
De tous ces .iiii. le convent;
4660 Feme et Amors ont tel nature
Que sovent font contre droiture,
4661a *Contre loi, contre raison voire*
4661b *Et contre boce de provoire.*¹
Amors est mout de rice pris,
Vers tous ces .iiii. a entrepris:
Faite lor a mainte envaïe.
4665 Et puis que feme est en s'aïe,
Qu'eles sont ans .ii. d'une part,
Mervelle est grans se nus les part
De cose qu'eles voellent faire,
Qu'eles sont mout de haut afaire.
4670 Amors et Ganors, la pucele,
Sont bien a un de la querele:
Bien dient d'Ille plainement
Qu'il a esré vilainement
Et qu'il ert vilains encontrés.

4675 Illes est en le cambre entrés.²
Ele est encontre lui venue;
De plorer ne se fust tenue,
Qui li donast .m. mars d'argent;
Ensus se traient por le gent.
4680 Illes voit plorer la pucele,
Qui tant par est bien faite et bele;
Se il grant gré ne l'en savoit
Et il grant pitié n'en avoit,
Outrages seroit et orgeus:
4685 Les larmes lor vienent as ex.
«Por amor Diu, ma douce amie,
Fait cil a li, ne plorés mie.
– Biax sire ciers, que ferai donques?
Mais fu il fille a vilain onques
4690 Qui si grant honte eüst soferte,
4690a *Que ne se fust al vent oferte*
Ou qui ne fust aprise en l'onde,
Ou la riviere est plus parfonde,
Ou en un fu ne se fust arse?
Trop ai esté de moi escarse,
4695 Quant je pieça nen ai el fait
Aprés tel honte, aprés tel lait.
De nul grief torment ne m'esmai,
Quant fui de tel honte a l'essai.
– Si m'aït Dix, ma douce suer,
4700 A tort avés si gros le cuer.
Ce vos devroit esleecier
Dont je vos voi si corecier,
Car je vos di bien que mes pere
Ne fu ne rois ne emperere

4687 fait sil]Lö

156

but he hardly dared go to her. He was very much ashamed on her account: he was afraid that he had acted dishonourably towards her, and so he had, very dishonourably indeed, but it could not be otherwise; this was how things stood now. He was well aware that she loved him and held him in high esteem, but Galeron had loved him before her, and this was not all, for justice and law and pure reason and the church bore witness that this was how it should be. The church, reason, justice and law often throw lovers into confusion. Woman and Love often undo what these four have agreed upon; the nature of woman and Love is such that they often act against justice, *against the law, against reason even, and against the teaching of the church*.[1] Love is of very high renown, and has waged war on all these four: she has launched many an attack on them. (4665) And when once she has woman as her ally, and they are both on the same side, it is a great wonder if anyone manages to make them give up something they want to do, for they are extremely powerful. Love and the maiden Ganor were in full agreement in this dispute: they said quite openly of Ille that he had acted dishonourably, and that he was patently no better than a peasant. Ille entered the chamber.[2]

She came to meet him; she could not have prevented herself from weeping if someone had given her a thousand marks of silver; they withdrew to one side on account of the other people there. Ille saw that the maiden, who was so very shapely and beautiful, was weeping; it would have been insulting and arrogant of him if he had not been very grateful to her for it, and if he had not felt great compassion for her: both of them had tears in their eyes. (4686) 'For the love of God, sweet friend', he said to her, 'Do not weep.' – 'Fair dear lord, what else can I do? Was there ever a peasant's daughter who would have suffered such deep disgrace *without jumping to her death* or throwing herself into the water where the river runs deepest, or burning herself to death in a fire? I have been too lenient with myself, not doing something like this long before now, after such disgrace, after such dishonour. No dire torment holds any fear for me, since I was subjected to such disgrace.' – 'So help me God, gentle sister, it is wrong for your heart to be so heavy. What I see you so bitterly upset over ought to make you glad, for I assure you that my father was not a king or an emperor,

[*handwritten margin note:* still courtly]

[*handwritten note:* trying to make Ille feel guilty]

---

1 The repetition of *drois, lois, raisons* and *prestre* in ll. 4653-54 and 4655-56, together with the references to *ces quatre* in ll. 4559 and 4663, indicates that this couplet almost certainly figured in the original.
2 This laconic description of Ille's arrival intensifies the expectation of a dramatic encounter with Ganor, whose present state of mind was so skilfully illustrated in the previous scene. For further discussion of this scene, see the Introduction, p. xlii.

4705 Ne il ne fu ne quens ne dus,
Ains fu de Bretagne Elidus,
Qui soufri mainte grant besoigne:
Sa teneüre le tesmoigne
Qui gaires lonc n'est estendue.»
4710 Cele a le parole entendue
Et dist: «Por Diu, le roi celestre,
Que t[a]int a moi de vostre ancestre?
Je ne voi gaires home amer
Por ce c'on l'ot roial clamer,
4715 Ne nul qui vive comme rois
Ne vaille un roi, s'il est cortois;
Et vostre pere soit vilains,
Ja por ce ne vaurés vos mains.
A cascun en son cuer demore
4720 Por coi on l'aville u honore:
Ne li vient mie de plus long;
On ne li quiert autre tesmong.
Oïstes me vos ainc requerre
Se vostre pere ot povre tere
4725 U s'il ert besoignex d'avoir?
Mais voel je vostre pere avoir
Ou vos amer por vostre pere?
Plus ameroie, biax dous frere,
Por vous les vos, faus et estous,
4730 Que vos tot seul por aus trestos.
De vostre pere a moi que taint?
Sont dont por vostre pere ataint
Li sospir qui de parfont vienent
Et qui si prés del cuer me tienent?

4735 Onques de lui ne me sovint
Quant ceste volentés me vint
De vos amer, de vos joïr.
Il ne me tint pieça d'oïr
De vostre pere ne du mien.
4740 Assés a en cascune rien
Por c'on le doit amer por lui
U haïr, plus que por autrui.
Onques qant j'ai conté vo estre
Ne me sovint de vo ancestre.
4745 Par icel Diu qui maint sor nous,
Amé vos ai trestot por vous,
Nient por autrui, ce sace Diex,
Mais por ce que vos estes tiex
Com tous li mons set et entent.[1]
4750 Lasse celi ki si atent
Com jou ai lonc tans atendu!
Vix cuers, ou as tu entendu?
Mout a grant duel qui aperçoit
Que s'esperance le deçoit:
4755 Je quic morir de mon damage.[2]
Comment ai je le cuer si sage
Que je vos puis ma dolor dire?
N'est pas de sens, ains me vient d'ire.
Qui le cuer me destraint et lie,
4760 Si me fait dire tel folie:
Dit ai maint mot fel et estout
Por çou que j'ai perdu le tout.
Cele neïs qui est partie
D'une seule bone partie

4745 sous]W   4747 ce sai je bien]W (Dex)   4749 sert et atent]W   4755 marir]Lö
4764 dune seule qui est partie]W

158

nor was he a count or a duke; no, he was Eliduc of Brittany, who suffered many a tribulation: his land-holdings bear witness to this – they were never very extensive.' She heard what he said, and replied: 'In the name of God, the King of Heaven, what has your father got to do with me? I seldom see a man being loved just because he is said to be of royal blood, nor may anyone who lives like a king be the equal of a king, if the king is a courtly man; and even if your father was a peasant, you would be no less worthy because of it. Each man's heart holds the key to whether he is treated with contempt or with honour: it is as close to home as that; no-one asks him for any other proof than that. Did you ever hear me ask you how small your father's lands were, or whether he was short of money? (4726) Do I mean to marry your father or to love you for your father's sake? Fair gentle brother, I would rather love your whole family, traitors and heroes alike, for your sake, than you alone for the sake of all of them. What has your father got to do with me? These sighs which well up from deep inside and which grip me so close to the heart, are they heaved for your father? He was never in my thoughts when I found myself wanting to love you, to make much of you. It did not concern me in the past to hear about your father, or mine for that matter. There are good enough reasons in every person for loving or hating him for his own sake, rather than for someone else's. Your father was never in my thoughts when I rehearsed your qualities. By the God who dwells above us, I have loved you entirely for your own sake, not for anyone else's, as God is my witness, but because you are the sort of man everyone knows and understands you to be.[1] Unhappy the woman who waits as I have waited, and for so long! Shameful heart, what were you thinking of? Anyone who realises that his hopes are playing him false feels very great sorrow: I believe that I shall die from the loss I have suffered.[2] How can I be so reasonable as to be able to describe my sorrow to you? It is not reason which is responsible, but anger, which oppresses and grips my heart, and makes me say such foolish things: I have spoken many a wicked and reckless word because I have lost everything. Even a woman who has been deprived of a single good thing

[handwritten marginal note:] Gautier shows importance of personal merit, not also your father was.

---

1 Ganor's words echo those of Galeron in ll. 4081-88. The degree of repetition here serves not only to express the intensity of Ganor's feelings, but also to foreground the theme of individual merit being more important than lineage, which will find its ultimate expression in Ille's coronation as emperor.
2 Both P and W have *marir*, but I have adopted Löseth's emendation to *morir* in the light of the repeated references to Ganor's death in ll. 4799, 4823, 4854 and 4890. *A* for *o* is a common scribal error.

4765 A(i) le cuer mat et esperdu;
Et je qui ai le tout perdu,
Com retenroie jou la vie,
Qui n'est del tout c'une partie?
Ja por si poi de cose, sire,
4770 Ne voel qu'al tot ait rien a dire:
Que poroit faire a si grant perte?
Trop par est parans et aperte
Iceste perte que je fas.»
A tant se pasme entre les bras
4775 Le senescal qui le reqeut,
Qui mout tres durement s'en deut.
Illes par est de tel nature
Qu'el mont n'a millor creature,
Plus france rien ne plus piteuse,¹
4780 Ne qui plus aint de cuer s'espeuse,
Car ele est bele et mout loiaus.
Mais ceste pucele est roiaus,
Si est autresi bele u plus.
Se li peres celi fu dus,
4785 Ceste est fille d'empereour,
Et si atent mout bele honor.
Por le pitié de lui se pasme:
Par tant cuide il et croit et asme
Que Ganors l'aint de cuer verai.
4790 «Sire Dix, fait il, ke ferai?
Com par me puet li cuers doloir
Del desirier et del voloir
Et de l'amor que je voi chi.
Bien m'a alé dusques en chi:

4795 De tos les max que j'ai soufers
Est chi icis li plus quivers.
De Ganor senc et sai et voi
Que trop a mis son cuer en moi
Et k'ele morra finement,
4800 Se Damedix pitiés n'en prent.
Mout me fait hui d'angoisse avoir,
Mais ne l'en doi mal gré savoir,
Ains dist Pités que je le pregne,
Salve l'onor de ma compaigne.
4805 Assés i a raison por coi
Pitiés ne puet partir de moi.
Ahi! fait il, ma douce suer,
Com j'ai grant pité en mon cuer
De la dolor qui si vos blece
4810 Et qui vos tient en tel destrece!
Mais plus n'i puet il avoir mie,
Car ne puis partir de m'amie,
Se lois ne le veut desmentir
Et ele ne s'en veut soufrir.
4815 N'en partiroie, je ne puis;
Partir n'en quier, partir n'en ruis:
Ne le souferroit amors fine.²
Amors ne cesse ne ne fine
De tenir celi envers moi
4820 Cui jou aim tot si com je doi;
Mais s'ele n'estoit, vraiement
Vostres seroie quitement.
Dix doinst que ja por çou ne muire
Et Damedix vos puist conduire

4766 du tout]W   4770 quel tot]W   4774 ses bras]W   4809 nos blece]W

160

is down-hearted and distraught; and I, who have lost everything, how should I retain a hold on life, which is only one part of that whole? I do not mean the whole to be found wanting for lack of so small a thing, my lord: what difference could it make, in comparison with so great a loss? The loss I am suffering is far too obvious and clear for all to see.' / With this, she fainted in the arms of the seneschal, who caught her as she fell, and who was enormously distressed by it. Ille's nature was indeed such that there was not a better person in the world, not a more open or compassionate soul,[1] nor one who loved his wife more deeply, for she was beautiful and very faithful. However, this maiden was of royal blood, and just as beautiful, if not more so. (4784) If his wife's father had been a duke, this woman was the daughter of an emperor, and heir to a very fine domain. She fainted because of her sorrow over him: this was enough to make him suppose and believe and reckon that Ganor's love for him was true. 'Lord God', he said, 'What shall I do? How much my heart aches at the sight of this longing and this desire and this love. Things have gone well for me up to this point: of all the ills I have suffered, this one is the most treacherous. I sense and know and see that Ganor has set her heart too dearly on me, and that it will kill her in the end, if the Lord God does not take pity on her. She is causing me great anguish here today, but I should not bear her any ill-will because of it; rather, Pity tells me to marry her, if it could be done without prejudice to my wife's honour. (4805) There are plenty of good reasons why Pity cannot leave my side. Ah! gentle sister, how my heart is full of pity for the sorrow which cuts you to the quick and so oppresses you! However, my heart can feel nothing more than pity, for I cannot leave the woman I love, unless the law was willing to dissolve our union, and she was willing to allow it. I would not leave her, I cannot; I do not seek to leave her, I do not ask to leave her: true love would not tolerate it.[2] Love constantly and unceasingly keeps her true to me, and I in turn love her exactly as I should; but if it was not for her, in all honesty I would be yours without reservation. God grant that she may not die because of this! And may the Lord God be your guide

[margin note: comparison with what happens in Elidic]

[margin note: loyalty + love.]

---

1 Ille's capacity for pity has already been demonstrated in his response to the messengers' report on the plight of Brittany (l. 3888). The motif of the pity he feels for Ganor is skilfully used by Gautier to explain the transfer of the hero's affections from Galeron to Ganor after the former's retirement to a convent. His second love develops out of the instinctive compassion which Ganor's distress inspires in him, and which he recalls after Galeron's retirement.

2 Lines 4814-16 could also be punctuated 'Et ele ne s'en veut soufrir,/ N'en partiroie; je ne puis./ Partir n'en quier...'. I prefer to place the sentence break at the

4825 Et m'otroit que je vos revoie
Un jor encor a plus grant joie!
De vos ai pitié mervillose,
Si aim de cuer verai [m']espouse.
De l'amor qui est entre nous,
4830 De la pitié que j'ai de vous,
Me destraint si l'angoisse et grieve
A poi que li cuers ne me crieve.
Amors et Pitiés me justicent
Et mout diversement m'atisent.
4835 Amors me veut partir de chi,
Et Pitiés me reqiert merchi,
Que je por Diu pregne conroi
Que ne muire la fille au roi;
Et je ne voi sossiel secours
4840 Que ce ne soit encontre Amors.
Ne voel k'Amors die a le gent
Que fas vers li vilainement,
Mes que mout grans peciés seroit
Se Ganors la bele en moroit.
4845 Dix! que ferai por çou ataindre?
Ou por Pitié ichi remaindre
Et envers Amors vilener,
U laissier ceste chi pener
Et faire ce k'a Amor taint?
4850 Doubles pitiés mon cuer ataint
Et me tormente et vait entor:
Une pitiés qui vient d'amor,
Et autre qui de chi me vient
Que il cesti morir convient

4855 Se je m'en vois, car mout se deut:
Pitiés chi me demande et veut.[1]
Doble pitiés mon cuer desment
Et si m'angoisse durement.
Ja vint por pitié Dix en tere
4860 Home perdu cerquier et qerre:
Li mons n'a rien par sa desserte
Qui tot ne soit livré a perte
Se Pitiés seule nel delivre.
Que ne me lait dont Pitiés vivre,
4865 K'a un jour fis por Pitié plus
C'onques ne fist ne quens ne dus,
Quant por celi qui pain queroit
Fis çou c'a Pitié aferoit?
Rome en laissai et iceli
4870 Por cui Pitiés m'a recoelli.
Pitié de cha, Pitié de la:
Ainc por mon bien ne commença.»
De pasmison revint la bele;
Illes a dit a le pucele:
4875 «Por amor Diu, ne plorés mais!
Cuidiés vos dont que je vos lais?
Naje certes, ne vos tués!
Or voi je bien que vous [m']amés;
Mais n'en plorastes onques lerme
4880 Qui ne vos soit rendue a terme
Por que de moi aiés besong.
– Sire, li termes n'est pas long
Que j'en aroie grant mestier
D'avoir tel home a consillier.

4842 Que ie vers li]Lö   4856 P. qui me   4864 Qui ne me laist de pite vivre]W
4869 R. laissa et il celi]W

162

and grant that I see you again some day under more joyful circumstances! I feel extraordinary pity for you, and yet I love my wife with a true love. The anguish I feel because of the love she and I have for each other and the pity I feel for you oppresses and torments me so that my heart is close to breaking. Love and Pity have me on the rack, and are pulling me in very different directions. Love wants to take me away from here, and Pity is begging me to have mercy and see to it for God's sake that the king's daughter does not die; and I can see no earthly way out which does not involve going against Love. I do not want Love to say to people that I am acting dishonourably towards her, except that it would be a very great sin if Ganor the fair were to die because of it. O God! What shall I do to achieve this? Stay here for Pity's sake and act dishonourably towards Love, or leave this woman here to suffer and do what Love requires? My heart is stricken and I am tormented and beset by a double pity: one kind of pity which comes from love, and another which comes from the fact that this woman will have to die if I leave, for she is in great pain: Pity demands and wants me here.[1] A double pity rends my heart and causes me terrible anguish. In days gone by, God came down to earth for Pity's sake to search and seek for fallen man: this world has nothing on its own merits which is not doomed to perish unless Pity alone comes to its rescue. Why doesn't Pity let me be, since on one day I did more for Pity's sake than any count or duke ever did, when I did what Pity required for the woman who had to beg for her bread? Out of pity, I gave up Rome and this woman for whose sake Pity has opened her arms to me again. Pity on one side, Pity on the other: this situation never arose for my benefit.'

The beautiful maiden came round from her faint; Ille said to her: 'For the love of God, do not weep any more! Do you imagine, then, that I am abandoning you? Not so, I assure you, do not torment yourself! Now I can clearly see that you love me; but you never shed a tear for me which will not be paid back one day should you have need of me.' – 'My lord, that day is not very far off, when I may be in dire need of such a man to give me counsel.

---

end of l. 4814, which gives a clearer sequence of ideas. Moved by pity for Ganor, Ille recognises his inability to help her: even if he were willing to leave Galeron, there would be legal obstacles to overcome; as it is, their mutual love precludes any possibility of giving Ganor what she wants.

[1] Both P and W have 'qui me demande et veut', which makes *Pitiés* the subject of *se deut*, and creates an awkward break in the middle of l. 4855. Given the degree of confusion in P between *qui*, *ki* and *chi*, and the stress on *chi* in l. 4853, I have chosen to emend *qui* to *chi*, which gives a more logical sequence of clauses.

4885 Vos en alés, jel sai mout bien,
Et se vous oés nule rien
Qui soit encontre cest empire,
Venés nos aidier, biax dous sire!
Mais por moi ne le di je mie,
4890 Car je quic ains perdre la vie.
Jel di por Rome et por honor,
Et por sauver vostre suor
Et les travax et les grans paines,
Les mois, les jors et les semaine[s]
4895 Que vous avés mis el service
Mon pere et cex de sa justice.
Mais mains hom pert legierement
Ice qu'il a conquis griement.
A Diu de la sus vos commanc,
4900 Mais revenés se je vos manc,
Que par vos serons apaisié.»
Al congié prendre l'a baisié.
    Ganors remaint, Illes s'en vait.
Icele nuit grant joie (ont) fait
4905 De ses amis qu'il a mandés,
A Diu les a tous commandés.
Grant doel i ot puis cele nuit,
Et l'endemain s'asanlent tuit.
El senescal n'ot qu'ensignier;
4910 N'est pas legiers a enginier:
Par son consel en est alee
La dame ains jor a recelee;
Ne veut de rien li mesaviegne
Ne c'on a force le detiegne.

4915 Quant vient a l'eure que il monte,
Plorent li roi, plorent li conte,
Pleurent li duc, li castelain,
Et li borgois et li vilain,
Cil damoisel, ces damoiseles,
4920 Et ces dames et ces puceles,
Et pleurent cele[s] gens menue[s],
Qui a son monter sont venues;
Escrient tuit: «Ou alés vos
Biax sire? Que ert il de nous?
4925 A! bone joie! A! bone pais!
Qui vos verra des ex jamais?
A! Rome fiere et felenesse,
Com es vilaine et peceresse!
Par ta merite et ta desserte
4930 Avons nos hui iceste perte.
Par quemun pecié de l'empire
Avient sovent que muert bon[s] sire
Et vit li malvais longement.
Nos ne savons sossiel comment
4935 Nos aiemes longe duree.
Et com Rome ert bien enmuree
Et environ fermee et close,[1]
Et hui n'est c'une povre cose!»
Illes s'en vait et cil remainent,
4940 Qui por s'amor grant doel demainent.
Illes en maine bele gent
Et assés a d'or et d'argent,
De dras de soie en son tresor
Et de vaisselemente d'or:

You are leaving, I am very well aware of that, and if you hear of any threat to this empire, come to our aid, fair gentle lord! However, I am not saying this on my own account, for I believe that I shall lose my life before then. I am saying it for Rome's sake and for honour's sake, and so that your sweat and the toil and the torment, the months, the days and the weeks which you have devoted to the service of my father and those who live within his jurisdiction may not be wasted. Yet many men lose with ease what they won at great cost. I command you to God on high, but return if I send for you, for you will restore peace to us.' She kissed him as he took his leave.

Ganor stayed behind, and Ille departed. That night, he received his friends, whom he had sent for, with great joy, and commanded them all to God. There was great sorrow later that night, and they all gathered again the next day. There was nothing you could teach the seneschal; he was not easily outwitted: on his advice Galeron had left secretly before daybreak; he did not want any misfortune to befall her, or for her to be detained by force. When the time came for him to mount his horse, the kings wept, the counts wept, the dukes wept, and the castellans, the townspeople and the peasants, the young noblemen and the damsels, the ladies and the maidens, and the common folk who had come to see his departure; all of them cried out: 'Where are you going, fair lord? What will become of us? (4925) Ah, a fine celebration this is! Ah, a fine peace this is! Which of us will ever set eyes on you again? Ah, Rome, cruel and wicked city, what a low-born sinner you are! It is because of what you have merited and deserved that we are suffering this loss today. It often happens that because of the collective sins of the empire good lords die and bad ones live long lives. We do not know how on earth we can survive for any length of time. And how strong the city wall was, and how well Rome was fortified and enclosed,[1] and today it is just a worthless thing!' Ille departed, and the people who were displaying great grief because of their love for him remained behind. Ille took a fine company with him, and he had plenty of gold and silver, silken cloths and gold plate in his coffers:

---

[1] The 'strong wall' is Ille himself, whose departure, the people fear, will leave the city as defenceless as if its fortifications had been destroyed. The same metaphor is used by the pope in l. 3539 to express the Romans' confidence in their new leader.

4945 Il est garnis de grant avoir,
De canques princes doit avoir.
.X. chevaliers a de maisnie,
Mout bone gent bien enraisnie,
Biax sergans et bons escuiers,
4950 Et bons cevax a remuiers:
Vont s'ent com gent bien atornees.
Tant vont cevalcant lor jornees
Qu'il sont venu prés de la terre
Dont cele mut por celui querre.
4955 Vont s'ent avant li mesagier
Por les barons assoagier
Ou Illes ot grignor fiance
Et plus d'atente et d'esperance.
    Qant cil entendent la novele,
4960 Mout par lor est et bone et bele;
A maint home plait sa venue.
Grant joie en font li gent menue:
A mout grant paine qu'il le croient,
Tant par desirent qu'il le voient.
4965 Ce mostre raisons et droiture
C'on aint le droit oir par nature:
N'est mie bien preudom naïs
Qui het le droit oir del païs.
A maint avient de cuer felon
4970 Que il le het, u voelle u non;
U voelle u non, haïr l'estuet,
Des que de felon cuer li muet:
Tex hom est bien mors et traïs.
Illes est amés et haïs,

4975 Car nus hom n'est, mon essïent,
De tous amés onnïement.
Tuit si ami grant joie en ont
Et a grant joie encontre vont.
Et qant ce vint a l'encontrer,
4980 K'Illes dut en la tere entrer,
Plorent de pitié et de joie,
Si s'arestent enmi la voie.
Qui lors veïst cel baiseïs,
La joie et cel acoleïs,
4985 Ne peüst laissier a nul fuer
Qu'i[l] n'eüst pitié en son cuer
Et qu'il ne plorast tenrement.
Mout i pleurent espessement,
Et sevent tuit que ce sont cil
4990 Et s'en i a peruec tex mil
Qui ne le pueent mie croire.
Ainc cose c'on tenist a voire
Ne cose si tres bien seüe
Ne fu si forment mescreüe.
4995 Il sevent lor ami illuec
Et si mescroient non peroec
Et sont de voir en sospeçon.
Lors dient: «Dix, par ton saint non,
Que est ce que nos veons chi?
5000 Qui puet desservir la merci
Que Dix nos a ichi mostree?»
Plorant corent a val l'estree,
Com s'a cevax erent detrait
Trestuit cil dont il sont estrait,[1]

4995 sivent]W   4949 bans e.]W   4983 Que lors]W

he was well supplied with treasure, with everything a prince should have. He had ten knights of his household, who were very able and well-spoken men, fine sergeants and able squires and good reserve horses: they set off like a well-equipped company. They put in so many days' riding that they came close to the land from which Galeron set out in search of Ille. The messengers rode on ahead to reassure the barons in whom Ille had more confidence and of whom he had greater expectations and hopes.

When these men heard the news, it was very welcome and very much to their liking; Ille's arrival pleased many people. The common folk were overjoyed at it: they longed to see him so much that they found it almost impossible to believe. (4965) Reason and Justice teach us that it is natural to love the rightful heir: anyone who hates the rightful heir to the country is not a man of worth by birth. Many a black-hearted villain finds himself hating the rightful heir, whether he likes it or not; whether he likes it or not, he has to hate him, since his black heart prompts him to: death and damnation surely await such a man. Ille was both loved and hated, for no man, to my mind, is unanimously loved by all. All his relatives were overjoyed at his return and went joyfully out to meet him. And the time came for them to meet Ille as he was due to enter the country, they wept with pity and joy, and came to a halt in the middle of the road. (4983) Anyone who had seen the kissing, the joy, and the embracing then would not have been able, at any price, to prevent his heart filling with pity or to stop himself weeping tenderly. The tears fell thick and fast there, and they all knew that it was them, and yet there were a thousand people there who could not believe it at all. Nothing which was thought to be true, nothing which was so very widely known was ever met with such intense disbelief before. They knew that their relative was there, and nevertheless they disbelieved it and were truly in doubt. Then they said: 'Oh God, by Your holy name, what is this we are seeing here? Who can deserve the grace which God has shown us here?' They rushed weeping down the road, as if every member of their family had been tied to four horses and dismembered,[1]

---

[1] This is the punishment inflicted on the traitor Ganelon in the *Chanson de Roland*.

5005 Et dient: «Dix, biax sire pere,
Sainte Marie, douce mere!
Hui ert la dolors esclusee,
Que nos avomes tant usee.»
Lors veïssiés Diu aourer,
5010 Lors veïssiés barons plorer
Por la joie de cele païs
Qu'il espoirent a tos jors mais.
«Biax sire Dix, font cil de Rome,
Com est grans joie de cest home,
5015 Com il doit Damediu amer,
Que par tout s'ot sire clamer!
Rome ot de son departement
Pesance, doel et mariment;
Or se tient si a retenue
5020 Ceste terre de sa venue.
Mains hom est mout mix assenés
Aillors que la dont il est nés,
Qui aroit povre remanance
El païs ou il prist naissance;
5025 Mais s'Illes est a Rome amés
Et maistre senescax clamés,
Ichi li mostrent plus d'amor
C'on ne fist onques [l]a nul jour,
Et cil li portent plus d'onour
5030 C'on ne faisoit l'empereour
Et grignor joie font de lui.
Et l'en a dit tresc'al jour d'hui
Que los de voisin passe tout:
S'on me tient aillors por estout

5035 Et mes voisins me loe et prise,
Cis los fraint tot le blasme [et] brise
Mais li afaires est si pris
Que cil est par tout de grant pris
Et plus servis c'uns emperere.
5040 Or nos otroit Dix et saint Pere
K'a Rome puissons dire encore
La joie que nos veons ore.
Dix le nos doint illoec retraire
Et celui encor la atraire!»
5045 De Galeron grant joie font
Tuit li Breton qu'iluekes sont:
Tote la joie renovele
Por amor de la damoisele.
Les damoiseles des contrees
5050 Que cele gent ont encontrees
Ont mout la dame conjoïe,
Volentiers veüe et oïe.
Toutes les dames de la terre
Le vienent comme saint requerre,
5055 Presentent li maint rice ator.
De maint castel, de mainte tor
Est saisis li fiex Eliduc;
Bien l'ont reconneü a(u) duc.
Cil qui le païs orent ars,
5060 Par cui li home sont espars,
Ont ore assés lait et anui:
N'i a un seul encontre lui
Qui ne soit livré a martire.

5036 tous le b.]W   5056 Et m. c. et m. t.]W

and said: 'Oh God, fair Lord and Father, holy Mary, gentle mother! Today the floodgates will be closed on the sorrow we have experienced for so long.' Then you would have seen people praising God, then you would have seen noblemen weeping for the joy which they hoped the country would enjoy for ever more. 'Fair Lord God', said the Romans, 'How overjoyed people are to see this man, how much he must love God, to hear himself being hailed as lord everywhere! Rome suffered heartache, sorrow and chagrin at his departure; now his arrival makes this country feel so secure. (5021) Many a man who would have been of little substance in the country of his birth is far more successful elsewhere than where he was born; but if Ille is loved and hailed as chief seneschal in Rome, the people here are showing him more love than he was ever shown there, and they are treating him with greater honour and greeting him with greater joy than people used to show the emperor. And it has always been said until today that a countryman's praise outdoes any other: if elsewhere I am regarded as a reckless fool, and my countryman praises and esteems me, then his praise breaks down and destroys all the blame; but the situation is such that this man is held in high esteem everywhere and served better than an emperor. Now may God and Saint Peter grant that we may yet describe in Rome the joy that we are seeing now. God grant that we may tell of it at home and draw him back there again!' (5045) All the Bretons who were there greeted Galeron with great joy: their joy redoubled for love of their liege-lady. The damsels from the regions whom the company encountered welcomed the lady joyfully, and were delighted to see her and hear what she had to say. All the ladies of the country came to visit her as they would a saint, and presented her with many a splendid garment. The son of Eliduc was invested with many a castle and many a tower: they fully acknowledged him as duke. Those who had put the country to the torch, and scattered its people, now had damage and injury done to them in good measure: not one of his opponents escaped the sternest punishment.

---

1 Folio 306 verso has columns of 59 lines, as compared with 60 lines for folios 296-305.

Illes li ber les desatire,
5065 Premiers celui, puis l'autre aprés.
Cil qui plus a esté engrés
De la tere honir et nuire
Premierement se voit destruire.
De tous se venge onnïement,
5070 Ne mie soursalïement,
Mais tout par sens et par mesure.
Mout lor fait rendre ciere usure
Des tors, des hontes et des lais
Que il ont en la tere fais:
5075 Mout lor sont or li dé cangié.
Et cil de Rome ont pris congié:
Il lor otroie bonement,
Del sien lor done largement.
Par eus salue la pucele,
5080 Ganor, la bien faite, la bele,
L'empereour et ses barons.
Mout est cortoise Galerons:
As Romains done ses joiaus,
Rices et jens et bons et biaus;
5085 Et mout lor a doné li sire
Et grant onor en poront dire.
Icil se misent au cemin,
Ne cessent ne ne prenent fin
Entrués qu'il sont venu a Rome.
5090 Novele enquierent du prodome,
Comment li Breton le reçurent.
«Certes, font il, si com il durent,
Com le plus vaillant qui soit nés.

Onques de Rome li barnés
5095 Ne l'onera en .v. ans tant
Com firent la petit et grant.
N'i ot si fier qu'il ne convint
Le premier jour que il i vint
Rendre les castiax et les tors,
5100 U sostenir mortex estours.
Tote Bretaigne la petite
I tient de par se feme quite.
Mout durement nos honererent
Trestot cil qui illueques erent,
5105 Car en la tere n'ot celui
Qui ne le veïst bien en lui:
Por s'amor firent au menor
De nos trestous plus grant honor
Que bouce d'ome ne puet dire.
5110 Beneois soit por ce li sire!
Sa feme mout nos honera:
Li joiel k'ele nous dona
Valent .iiii. .c. mars d'argent.
Ainc ne vi mais si bone gent:
5115 Grant sont li bien ke Dix i mist.
Si voirement com Diex les fist
Les maintiegne il et beneïe!»
Cil qui la novele ont oïe
Ne le vont mie despisant,
5120 Ançois vont mout entr'ex disant:
«Tex hom devroit porter corone.»
Et dient bien: «Se Dix tant done

5064 Isles]W   5069 omniement]Lö   5086 en poroit]W

Ille the noble warrior overwhelmed them, first one, then the other. Those who had been most eager to inflict dishonour and damage on the land were the first to find themselves being destroyed. He took revenge on all of them equally, without being at all reckless, but showing good sense and moderation all round. He made them pay a hefty rate of interest on the wrongs, the shameful deeds and the outrages which they had committed in the land: now the dice were loaded heavily against them. And the Romans took their leave: Ille courteously gave them leave to go, and gave them generous gifts from his own coffers. He sent greetings by them to the noble, shapely and beautiful maiden Ganor, to the emperor and to his barons. (5082) Galeron was a very courtly lady: she gave the Romans gifts of her own splendid, attractive, fine and beautiful jewels; and the lord gave generously to them, and they would be able to speak very highly of him. They set out, and did not stop or end their journey until they had arrived in Rome. The Romans asked for news of the gallant Ille, and of how the Bretons had received him. 'Indeed', they replied, 'Exactly as they ought, as befitted the most valiant man alive. All the barons of Rome never did him as much honour in five years as the people, great and small, did him there. No man was so haughty that he did not have to surrender his castles and towers to him the first day he arrived, or else endure mortal conflict. He is the unchallenged ruler of the whole of Brittany through his wife. (5103) All the people who were there treated us with extreme honour, for there was not a man in the land who would not gladly be like him: for love of him they did the least of us more honour than the human tongue can tell. A blessing on the lord for this! His wife did us much honour: the jewels she gave us are worth four hundred marks of silver. I never saw such good people before: great are the virtues with which God has endowed them. As truly as God created them, may He preserve and bless them' Those who had heard the news were far from despising Ille; rather, they were continually saying to one another: 'Such a man should wear a crown.' And indeed they said: 'If God in His bounty

171

Qu'il revigne, si fera il.»
Ce ne sont mie li plus vil
5125 Qui ce dient, mes li plus haut
Et li plus lié et li plus baut,1
Et tout li plus rice baron
De tote Rome et d'environ:
Ne cuident dire nul desroi.
5130 Et cil s'en vont tot droit al roi:
De par le duc l'ont salué,
Et mout se sont de lui loé
Et de la ducoise ensement
Et de tous ciaus communement
5135 Qui en Bretaigne ont rien a faire.
«Sire, font il, ne fait a taire
Comment li dus fu recheüs
Et a quel joie il fu veüs,
Mes nus ne puet le moitié dire
5140 De cele honor que ot li sire.
Grans fu l'onors que on li fist,
Et sa venue desconfist
Tos ciaus qui onques mal li fisent,
Car a ses piés trestot se misent.»
5145 Et l'empereres lor a dit:
«Foi que devés Saint Esperit
Ot dont la tant d'onor li dus?
– Oïl, biax sire, tant et plus.
– Et je vous di que la novele
5150 M'est durement et laide et bele.
J'aim mout l'onor que li dus a,
Mais qu'il l'eüst aillors que la:

Mout le vauroie ameement
Qu'il fust receüs altrement.
5155 Je ne vauroie pas son lait,
Mais c'on li eüst la tant fait
Que li païs li despleüst
Ou que remanoir n'i peüst;
Et fust .m. aunes desous terre2
5160 Qui en cest païs le vint querre,
Si que li dus eüst Ganor
Et en son cief corone d'or.
– Sire, cil Diex qui tot adrece
Doinst a Ganor joie [et] leece,
5165 Si que ne muire Galerons.»
Li rois respondi as barons:
«Vencu[s] vos a tous covoitise!
– Sire, mes faites: «grant francise»!3
Celui het Dix sor tote rien,
5170 A cui on fait honeur et bien
Et ki ne l'ose dire avant.
Et cil se vait tot decevant,
Qui voit c'on fait autrui honor
Et por le gré de son signor
5175 Le laist a dire et si s'en taist
Et dist adiés ce que lui plaist.
Por voir saciés, c'a un bien fait
Que nos volomes que cele ait,
Volomes nos a Ganor .m.;
5180 Mes li hom a le cuer trop vil,
Qui le bien çoile, s'il le voit.

5123 Quil remagne si sera]W   5154 hautement]W   5172 vont]Lö

172

allows him to come back, so he will.' It was not the meanest of men who were saying this, but the noblest, those with most cause to be glad and cheerful,[1] and all the mightiest barons in the whole of Rome and the surrounding areas: they did not believe that they were saying anything unreasonable. And the others went straight off to the king: they greeted him on the duke's behalf, and sang his praises at length, and the praises of the duchess likewise, and the collective praises of all those who had any connection with Brittany. 'Sire', they said, 'How the duke was welcomed and how joyful they were to see him is not something to be kept quiet, but no-one can describe even half of the honour which was given to this lord. Great was the honour done to him, and his arrival subdued all those who ever did him wrong, for they all threw themselves at his feet.' (5145) And the emperor said to them: 'By the faith you owe the Holy Ghost, was the duke really treated with so much honour there?' – 'Yes, fair lord, so much and more!' – 'And I tell you that this news is both extremely unwelcome and extremely welcome to me. I cherish the honour which the duke enjoys, but if only he enjoyed it somewhere other than there: my fondest wish would be for him to receive a different kind of welcome. I would not wish him harm, but if only he had been treated in such a way there that he took a dislike to the country or felt unable to stay there; and if only the person who came to look for him in this country was a thousand ells under ground,[2] so that the duke could marry Ganor and wear a golden crown on his head.'

'Sire, may the God who decides everything grant Ganor joy and happiness, so long as Galeron does not have to die.' (5166) The king replied to the barons: 'You have all been won over by greed!' – 'Sire, say rather: by great generosity![3] More than anything, God hates the man who is treated with honour and generosity and dare not say it out loud. And that man is a complete traitor to himself who sees someone else being treated with honour and forebears to say so and keeps quiet in order to please his lord, and says instead what his lord wants to hear. Let us tell you the truth, which is that for each blessing we wish Galeron to have, we wish Ganor a thousand; but a man is thoroughly base at heart if he sees good and keeps it quiet.

---

1 W has 'li plus fier et li plus baut', which may be the better reading, given that P also has *fier* in ll. 6163-64, which are an almost exact repetition of ll. 5125-26.

2 The *aune* or ell was the universal measure for woollen cloth in Europe in the Middle Ages. Despite its widespread use, the ell was not standardised, and could vary in length from well under to well over a yard depending on the location. The *aune* of Champagne was accepted by many of the great cloth-making cities of Northern Europe, including Arras, in the later 12th and 13th centuries.

3 W has 'Sire, ne mais sa grans francise' an obvious *lectio facilior*.

173

– Signor, tant voel et tant covoit
D'Ille la joie et la venue
Que jou en dis desconvenue
5185 Por endroit de Ganor ma fille.
– Sire, mal fait qui trop aville
L'autrui voloir et l'autrui bien
Et veut c'on prist adés le sien.»
A tant en vont a le pucele
5190 Et saluent lor damoisele
De par celui qui l'aime et prise;[1]
Et s'ele fu ançois esprise,
Tant li ont dit k'ele s'en deut
A c. doubles plus que ne seut.
5195 Malade se sent de petit,
D'une parole, s'on li dist,
Et il en orent dit tex cent
Qui li greverent durement.
A tant ont laissié le parler,
5200 Car vespres est et tans d'aler.
De la pucele ont pris congié,
Qui rien n'a cele nuit songié,
S'ele ne songa en villant:
Amors le vait mout travillant.
5205 «Lasse, fait ele, k'ert de moi,
Que me desplaist canques je voi?
Çou qui me plaist de moi s'eslonge,
Fors que del cuer, qui me tesmoigne
Qu'i[l] est od li, quel part k'il aille.
5210 Li cors se sent, si se travaille
Quant mes cuers me dist rien de lui,

Si me fait angoisse et anui:
Toute sa biauté me retrait
Et tous les biens que il a fait.
5215 Com plus me dist, et plus me grieve,
Quant autre choce o lui et lieve!
Sans autrui chocier et lever
Me poroit il assés grever.
Endroit de ce que jel desir,
5220 A desmesure me consir;
Je m'en consir, por ce m'en duel.
Et c'autre prent ce que je voel,
Ice me double mon torment
Et me tormente doublement.
5225 L'uns me poroit assés torbler,
Et qant vint que l'estut doubler,
Plus me tormente et plus me paine
Que ne feroit double tierçaine.[2]
Qui contre fievre estrive et tence,
5230 Bien puet garir par astinence;
Ou se il veut de gré morir,
Se puet la fievre bien norir.
Mais je n'en sai a cui tencier
N'envers qui tençon commencier
5235 Por garison ne por merchi.
Ne puis morir, se ne m'ochi,
Mais Dix ne claime nule part
En celui qui se noie o s'art;
Mix voel dont languir longement
5240 Que morir pardurablement.

5202 Que rien]W   5208 del que c.]W   5238 qui se vie]W

174

– 'My lords, so greatly do I desire and long for the joy which Ille's coming would bring that I spoke unbecomingly about her out of regard for my daughter Ganor.' – 'Sire, anyone who casts too many aspersions on another's wishes and another's virtues, wanting people to think well of his own instead, is guilty of wrongdoing.' At this, they went to see the maiden and greeted their liege-lady on behalf of the man who held her in affection and esteem;[1] and if she was in love before, they said so much to her that her suffering became a hundred times greater than it used to be. It took very little – one word someone might say to her – to make her feel ill; and they said a hundred words to her which hurt her terribly. At that they left off talking, for it was evening and time for them to leave. (5201) They took their leave of the maiden, who dreamed no dreams that night, unless she dreamed while she was awake: Love was torturing her cruelly. 'Unhappy woman', she said, 'What will become of me, as everything I see causes me displeasure? What gives me pleasure is far away from me, but not from my heart, which lets me know that it is with him, wherever he goes. My body feels it and is tormented when my heart tells me anything about him, and causes me anguish and suffering: it recounts all his good looks to me, and all the good deeds he has done. How much more it has to tell me, how much more it hurts me, when another is sleeping and waking with him! It would cause me enough pain without another's sleeping and waking. As for the desire I feel for him, my deprivation knows no bounds; I am deprived of him, and this is why I am suffering. (5222) And the fact that another is taking what I want, this redoubles my torment and torments me doubly. The one would cause me enough distress, and then when it had to be redoubled, it torments and tortures me more than a double tertian fever would.[2] Someone who is struggling and fighting against a fever may indeed be cured by starving it; or if he wishes to die of his own volition, then he may feed the fever well. But I do not know who to fight over this, or who to pick a fight with to find a cure or mercy. I cannot die unless I kill myself, but God claims no part in someone who drowns or burns himself to death; so I prefer a long illness to eternal death.

---

1 W has 'De par celui qu'ele aimme et prise', which may be the better reading. Mistranscription of the abbreviations for *qui* and *que* is a common scribal error. There is, however, a certain logic to P's 'qui l'aime et prise', which reminds the audience of Ille's positive feelings towards Ganor, and prepares the way for their evolution into love.

2 A tertian fever is characterised by the occurrence of a paroxysm every third day, counting the day of the previous episode as one (in other words, every other day). In a double tertian fever, which is more severe, there are two sets of paroxysms, each recurring every third day.

N'est pas d'amor mes de la mort,
Car amors fait aucun confort:
D'amor est hom en tel balance
Qu'il ne vauroit autre esperance.
5245 Mais je n'ai sossiel tant d'espoir
Que jel puisse jamais veoir.
Mais li veoirs que me vauroit,
Quant lui de moi ne li caurroit?
Et, s'il l'en caloit mout tres bien,
5250 Ne me poroit il valoir rien.
Ice n'est pas cose avenans,
C'autre en est vestue et tenans
Qui grignor droit de moi i claime,
Et que il veut et prise et aime.
5255 Feme a le loy l'enfant qui pleure:
Ce k'avoir puet n'aime une meure,
Ains veut içou qu'estre ne puet.
Ice dont consirer m'estuet
Pris et desir et aim et voel;
5260 Et por ice que je m'en duel
L'aime autre assés plus que ne seut.
Quant feme set c'autre s'en deut
De son ami, plus l'aime et prise
Et plus forment en est esprise.
5265 N'ai song de rien que j'avoir puis,
N'en Ille nul confort ne truis
Se Galeron n'est morte avant.
Mais or me vois je decevant;

Mors que on veut vient a envis;
5270 Ançois muert amés que haïs.
Mais li que caut, se je la hé
Trestos les jors de son aé?
Joie ne bien plaines ses mains,
A son vivant nen ara mains
5275 Por cose que je dire doie.
Mais nen a(i) mie tant de joie
Que je de duel nen aie autant.»
De Ganor lairons or atant,
Si vous dirai de Galeron.
5280 .II. biaus fiex a de son baron,
Tant a esté o son mari:
Illes s'en tient mout a gari.
    Li enfant ont bel home a pere,
Et bele feme est mout lor mere:
5285 El mont plus biax enfans nen a.
Nature un point ne s'en pena
Ne au former ne au polir,
Car sans le matere tolir
Ichi nen a un point a dire;
5290 Fols est qui bone cose empire.
On puet de mainte cose oster
Un poi por aillors ajouster;
Mais ains que l'oevre fust mostree²
Ne qu'ele parust en l'estree,
5295 Peüst bien soufrir en quemun
Ce que Nature mist en l'un

I am not love-sick, but sick unto death, for love provides some comfort: love keeps a man in such a state of suspense that he would not wish for any other source of hope. But I have no earthly hope of even seeing him ever again. But what good would seeing him be to me, when he for his part would not care about me? And even if he really cared about me a great deal, it could be no good to me. This is not a proper thing to be thinking, for another woman has been invested with him, and has tenure, a woman who has a greater right to him than I have, and whom he desires and prizes and loves. A woman is just like a crying child: she doesn't care tuppence for what she can have, but wants what is impossible. (5258) I prize and desire and love and want what I have to do without; and because I am heart-broken on his account, another loves him much more than she used to. When a woman knows that another is heart-broken over the man she loves, she loves and prizes him more, and is more passionately in love with him. I am not interested in anything that I can have, and I can find no comfort in Ille unless Galeron dies beforehand. But now I am deluding myself, because if you wish for someone's death, it is unlikely to happen: the one you love dies before the one you hate. But what does it matter to her, if I hate her for the rest of her days? With all the joy and prosperity she could ask for now, she will not have any less as long as she lives because of anything I have to say. But however much joy she has, I have just as much sorrow./ (5278) Now let us leave Ganor at that, and I shall tell you about Galeron. She lived with her husband long enough to have two fine sons by her lord: Ille thought himself a very lucky man.

The children had a handsome man for a father, and their mother was a very beautiful woman: there were no better-looking children in the world. Nature did not put herself to the slightest trouble either in forming or in finishing them, for unless some material were to be removed, nothing whatever was lacking in them; anyone who makes a good thing worse is a fool. There are many things where you can remove a little from one and add it to another, but before this creation was put on show,[2] and before it appeared in the open, the beauty of face and form with which Nature endowed one could well have been made to do for both,

---

1 Folio 307 has columns of 56 lines, except for 307ᵛ d which has 57.

2 *Oevre* refers to both sons. Lines 5286-92 are somewhat elliptical: the sense is that it is possible to make small modifications to many artefacts without spoiling them, since they are not perfect to start with; however, if Nature had put herself to the trouble of trying to make minor improvements to Ille's children she would only have spoiled her own handiwork, since they came out perfect first time.

Et de biauté et de faiture;
Car tes les veut avoir Nature.
Acarins ot l'aisnés fiex non,
5300 Et l'autre apelent Garsion.
Nus ne puet Ille corecier,
Nus ne se puet vers lui drecier
Que lui en soit ne c'une bille.
Cele conçut puis une fille.
5305 Quant vint que delivrer en dut,
Confessa soi, ce li estut.
Morir cuida; none devint,
Les dras vesti, ce li convint:
Tes fu ses veus et sa promesse,
5310 Ains que d'enfant alast a messe.¹
Galerons est none velee –
Sa fille Ydone a apelee:
Ja tant n'irés a val n'a mont
Que vous truisiés plus bele el mont –
5315 Ne mais li dus en ot tel doel
Q'il en morust le jor sien voel.
Por ce grant doel et por cel'ire
Ot puis maint jor mestier de mire:
Ne li vaut puisons ne mecine,
5320 Car autre en estoit la racine.
Cil cui la teste deut de vin,
S'il en veut garir, al matin
De vin se doit desjeüner
Por sa dolour desaüner;

5325 Et qui ses bones amors pert,
Si puet bien morir en apert,
Se fine amors ne le delivre
De la grant dolor qui l'enivre.
Vins est legiers a recovrer
5330 Et puet legierement ovrer;
Mais amors est griés a trover
Qui gaires bien se puist prover
A le dolor ki est si drue
Quant on pert s'amie et sa drue.
5335 Illes forment se desconforte.
Se Galerons s'amie ert morte,
Mains l'en sovenroit, bien puet estre;
Mais or i vient adés li prestre,
Car ce besoigne qu'il i viegne.²
5340 Que Dix le gart, Dix le maintiene,
Entruesque la qu'il soit en voie
Qu'encontrer puist aucune joie
Et c'ait aucun alegement,
Qu'il ne muire si faitement.
5345 La cose qui plus le sostient,
Çou est li deus dont li sovient
Que Ganors fist al congié prendre.
Pitiés li fist cel duel reprendre:
Cil deus qui lores commença
5350 Aliege le duel par deça.
Cil deus de la le duel aliege
Qui en son cuer a fait le siege;

5341 Et truesque]W (entrosque)

178

for this is how Nature wanted them. The elder son's name was Acarin, and they called the other Garsion. No-one could do anything to anger Ille, and it did not matter a jot to him if anyone opposed him. Galeron then became pregnant with a daughter. When the time came when she was due to give birth, she made her confession; this was her Christian duty. She thought she was going to die; she became a nun and donned the habit; she had no choice: this was what she had vowed and promised to do before she went to her first mass after childbirth.[1]

Galeron had taken the veil – she called her daughter Ydone: however far you travelled up hill and down dale you would never find a more beautiful girl in the world – only, the duke was so heart-broken at this that he would have died that very day if he had had his way. (5317) On account of his grief and his dismay he needed a doctor for many a day afterwards: no potion or medicine was of any use to him; the root cause of his illness was quite different. If a man has a hangover and wants to be cured of it, he should have wine for breakfast next morning to relieve his headache; and a man who loses the love of his life may well die before your very eyes unless true love delivers him from the great pain which clouds his mind. Wine is easy to come by, and can do its work easily; but it is very difficult to find a love which can be at all effective against the pain of losing one's lady and one's love, which is so potent. (5335) Ille was in extreme distress. If Galeron, his love, had been dead, it might well have been the case that he would have thought of her less often; but now the priest came without delay, for his presence was certainly needed.[2] God guard and preserve Ille until he is in a position to meet with some joy and find some relief, so that he will not die this way! The thing which did most to keep him going was the grief he remembered Ganor displaying when he took his leave of her. Pity had made him take her to task for her grief: the grief which had begun at that moment relieved the grief he felt here and now. That other grief relieved the grief which had laid siege to his heart;

---

1 After giving birth, a woman would convalesce for a certain period of time, and then attend a service of thanksgiving, which marked her return to 'normal' daily life. The parataxis of ll. 5307-10 makes it difficult to establish the exact sequence of events: does Galeron actually take the veil before attending the service, or does she take the opportunity of her convalescence to confirm a vow made during a difficult labour, and retire to a convent after churching? My translation attempts to preserve the ambiguity of the original. Galeron's vow would not have seemed extraordinary to Gautier's audience, for whom childbirth was a very dangerous experience, which often resulted in the deaths of both mother and baby.
2 Ille's condition gives so much cause for concern that the priest is summoned to hear his confession and to be ready to administer the last rites.

Cil deus aliege la dolor
Qui li a fait muer coulor.
5355 Dix li aliege son grant doel,
Dont il fust mors pieça son voel.
Oés del duc qui dist une eure:
«A! Galeron, Dix te sekeure,
Et Dix me doinst guerredon faire
5360 A le pucele deboinaire
Qui se pasma ja en un jour
Que por pitié, que por amour,
Et Diex me mece encor en aise
De faire cose qui li plaise.
5365 Biax sire Dix, que poroit estre?
Jamais n'ere, je quic, en l'estre
Que je la voie n'ele moi,
Qu'ele a mari si com je croi:
Bon mari doit avoir la bele;
5370 Mout i a noble damoisele.
Mout sui keüs en bas degré:
Bien presist mon service a gré,
N'a pas .v. ans, non mie .iiii..
Maint grant orgoel voit on abatre:
5375 D'u[n] mui vient on a un sestier¹
Et puis a nient, si n'a mestier.
Bien me voloit la bele nee,
Lors cuida bien estre assenee;
Mais or sui cil qui tot avroit
5380 Por faire canques li plairoit,

Et son mari, se ele l'a.
Et Dix, com ricement m'ala
A cel jour que je muç de li!
Dix en soit garde de celi
5385 Por cui je Ganor refusai,
La plus tres bele que je sai,
Et laissai le corone avoec,
Que otroïe m'ert illuec,
Et Rome avoec et tot l'empere
5390 Que a cel jor tenoit ses pere.
Et Dix me puist ore avoier!
Espoir qu'ele a maint soldoier
Assés millor que je ne soie.
De canqu'ele a, Dix li doinst joie,
5395 Et Galeron gart et sekeure!»
Ille[s] se plaint et Ganor plore,
Cis en Bretaigne et cele a Rome,
Qui mestier aroit d'un prodome.
Mors est pieça li rois ses pere,
5400 Si le requiert li emperere,
Cui Ille[s] fist ja tel laidure;
Mais ele dist tres bien et jure
Que ja nen ert en sa saisine,
Qu'il ot a feme sa cousine
5405 Et tant li fist et lait et honte
Que morte en fu la fille au conte.
Et cil en a mout grant desdang,
Et dist li fel: «Se je me faing

that grief relieved the pain which had caused his colour to drain away. God relieved his grief for him, which would have killed him long before, if he had had his way. Listen to what the duke said at one point: 'Ah, Galeron, may God be your help, and may God grant that I may repay the noble maiden who fainted one day not so long ago out of pity, out of love, and may God yet give me an opportunity to do something to please her. Dear Lord God, how could that be? I do not imagine that I shall ever be in a position to see her, or for her to see me, because she has a husband, or so I believe: the lovely girl must have a good husband now; she is a very noble damsel. (5371) I have really come down in the world: she would have accepted my service very gladly, not five years, or even four years ago. You often see great pride being humbled: you go from a bushel down to a peck,[1] and then down to nothing, if there is no use for it. The lovely creature certainly wanted me, and thought she had been well provided for then; but now I am the one who would have a job doing whatever might please her, and her husband, if she has one. Oh God, how splendidly things were going for me the day I rode away from her! May God be the guardian of the woman for whose sake I rejected Ganor, who is quite the most beautiful woman I know, and refused the crown that came with her, which had been granted to me there, and Rome with it, and the whole empire that her father ruled over at that time. (5391) And may God be my guide now! She probably has many a knight on her payroll who is considerably better than I am. Whatever she has, God grant her joy of it, and may He be Galeron's guardian and help!' Ille cried and Ganor wept, he in Brittany and she in Rome, who was likely to be in need of a gallant man. Her father the king had died a while ago, and the emperor on whom Ille once inflicted such disgrace was asking for her hand; but she said very clearly and swore that she would never allow him to take possession of her, because he had taken her cousin to wife and had done her such violence and dishonour that the count's daughter had died of it. And the emperor took very great offence at this, and the villain said: 'If I am half-hearted

---

1 The *mui* was a measure of volume equivalent to the English bushel (8 imperial gallons). The *sestier* was a variable measure, but always smaller than the *mui*. I have translated it as 'peck' (2 gallons), in order to convey the idea of progressive reduction in size.

D'abatre l'orgoel a le fiere,
5410 Ja Dix n'otroit rien que je quiere!»
Li emperere les tormente
Et tout li païs se demente.
Requierent Ganor li plus sage
Qu'ele refraigne son corage;
5415 Et ele dist que ja nen ert
Ce que li rois velt et requiert.
　Rome est dolante, triste, morne,
Et mains pesmes jors li ajorne.
Cil prent les castiax et les tours,
5420 Les rices viles et les bours,
Abat les murs et les chités
K'Illes lor avoit aquités;
Tos li païs fremist et bruit.
A Rome vienent li destruit:
5425 N'i troevent conseil ne confort;
Tos jors aprocent li plus fort.
E vous gent morte et mal tensee!
Ganors [s']est un jour porpensee
Del convenant k'Illes li fist
5430 A icel jor que congié prist
Et k'il en Bretaigne en ala,
Et pense: «Dix! irai je la
Savoir s'il me tenra convent
De ce que tant me dist sovent,
5435 Car Rome s'atent tote a moi?
Bien sai se j'autrui i envoi,

Que il n'i daignera venir,
Qu'il a mout grant tere a tenir,
Et feme qui l'acole et baise,
5440 Et aime le repos et l'aise.[1]
Encor espoir se jou i vois,
Nen ert il pas trop a mon cois;
En aventure ert s'il i vient
Et se del convent li sovient.
5445 Dix m'en avoit et doi[n]st consel!»
Il .x. qui plus li sont feel
Muevent od li celeement,
Que nus ne set qant ne comment.
Nus ne set sossiel les noveles,
5450 Mais lor sergant et lor puceles
Qui vont avec sans plus de gent:
Grant plenté ont d'or et d'argent,
Vers Bretagne s'en vont tot droit.[2]
Ganors est mout en grant destroit:
5455 Mout se doute que la ducesse
Ne soit vers li trop felenesse,
Et durement s'en vait doutant
Que ses maris li dus l'aint tant,
Et li et s'aise et son delit,
5460 Que il le convenant n'oublit;
Et pense: «Diex, sainte Marie,
Com je me tenroie a garie
Se je trovoie la merchi
Por coi je sui venue chi,

5435 Rome sacent tot]W

about humbling this arrogant woman's pride, never again may God grant anything I ask for!' The whole country groaned under the punishment the emperor inflicted on them. The most prudent men asked Ganor to moderate her attitude; and she replied that what the king desired and asked for would never be.

Rome was disconsolate, sad and mournful, and many an evil day dawned for the city. The emperor captured the castles and the towers, the rich towns and the burghs, and razed the fortifications and the walled cities which Ille had delivered for them; the whole country shuddered and rang with it. The dispossessed came to Rome: they found no counsel or comfort there. Every day the emperor's superior forces came closer to the city. Here were doomed and defenceless people for you! (5428) One day Ganor's thoughts turned to the promise which Ille had made her on the day he took his leave and went off to Brittany, and she thought: 'Oh God! Shall I go there and find out whether he will keep his promise to me about what he said to me so many times, for the whole of Rome is looking to me for help? I know for sure that if I send someone else, he will not deign to come, because he has a very large dukedom to rule over, and a wife to embrace and kiss him, and he enjoys a life of ease and pleasure.[1] And yet, perhaps, if I go there, things will not be quite as I would like; it will be a question whether he comes here and whether he remembers the promise. (5445) May God be my guide and give me counsel!' The ten men who were most loyal to Ganor set out secretly with her, so that no-one knew when or how they left. No-one on earth knew what was happening, except for their sergeants and their maidens, who were the only people who went with them; they had a large amount of gold and silver, and headed straight for Brittany.[2] Ganor was in dire straits indeed: she was very much afraid that the duchess would act very cruelly towards her, and she was mightily afraid that her husband the duke loved her so much, both her and the pleasure and enjoyment she gave him, that he would forget his promise; and she thought: 'Oh God, holy Mary, how lucky I would think myself if I were to find the mercy for which I have come here,

---

1 I take il, rather than feme, to be the subject of aime.

2 There are close parallels between the journeys undertaken by Ganor from Rome and Brittany, and subsequently by Ille from Brittany to Rome (ll. 5506-687), and those taken by Ille and Galeron earlier in the story. In both cases, secret departures precede a fruitless search by the woman, and the ultimate destination of both parties is Rome, where a reunion eventually takes place. In both cases, too, the fact that the couple's paths fail to cross reflects a psychological distance between them: in the first instance, Ille's inability to understand Galeron's true nature; in this case, Ganor's doubts as to Ille's willingness to keep his word.

5465 Et la ducoise fust ensi
Comme je fui jadis por l(u)i
En la cité le roi mon pere
Devant l'uis del mostier saint Pere.»
Pelerin qui del païs sont,
5470 Qui mout sovent vienent et vont,
Retraient Ille la novele
Que li emperere revele
Encontre Rome o son effors
Por çou que l'emperere est mors
5475 Et qu'il ne puet sa fille avoir:
Ele n'a song de lui por voir,
Tant l'a sor cuer et tant le het,
N'ele consel de soi ne set.
«Diex, pense Illes, qu'en ert il?
5480 Mout me pora tenir por vil
Se je ne vois Ganor secorre
Ains que me verté laisse encorre.¹
Ses pere grant honor me fist
Et en plorant le me requist
5485 Que je tout issi le feïsse
Et que je consel i mesisse,
Si fist la pucele ensement;
Et je lor dis veraiement
Que je tout issi le feroie
5490 Lués maintenant que je verroie
K'ele aroit mestier de m'aïe.
Mout par l'aroie en fin traïe
Se li faloie en cest besoing.

5493a Por coi li sui ge donc si loing?»
Poi sot li dus com ele ert prés.
5495 Mout par s'en daura chi aprés
Que ne so(i)t ançois sa venue.
Illes sans nule retenue
S'est ricement aparilliés;
Ses trois enfants a consilliés,
5500 Ce que lui plest lait a cascun:
Ne veut qu'il aient pas commun.
A trois barons les laist en garde.
Trop li demore et trop li tarde
K'ajorner voie l'endemain.
5505 Congié a pris de le nonain.
    Al congié prendre et au parler
Dist c'a saint Jake en velt aler,
Et Galerons congié lui done:
N'i entent el que bien la none.²
5510 Entre Bretons et Poitevins,
Fait movoir comme pelerins
Entrosc'a trente cevaliers:
El mont n'a millors ne plus fiers.
Noeves armes a cascun[s] d'eus
5515 Et bons cevax, qui un qui deus.
Mais por les Bretons desvoier
Les ot li dus fait convoier
Fors del païs et fors de voie.
Ançois qu'il moeve les envoie
5520 .VII. jors tos plains; il .xxx. sont

5482 laisse corre]W   5512 Et trosca]W (entrosqu'a)   5516 avoier]W

and if the duchess were the same as I was for her in the past in my royal father's city, outside the door of Saint Peter's church.' Pilgrims from Brittany, who were travelling to and fro very frequently, reported the news to Ille that the emperor was in revolt against Rome with his troops because the old emperor was dead and because he could not have his daughter: the truth was that she did not care for him, because she resented him and hated him so much, and she did not know what she should do for the best. 'Oh God,' thought Ille, 'What will become of her? Ganor may indeed think me the lowest of the low if I do not go to her rescue before I allow my integrity to be impugned.[1] (5483) Her father did me great honour and asked me with tears in his eyes to do exactly the same for her and to give her my counsel; and the maiden herself did the same; and I told them in all sincerity that this is exactly what I would do the moment that I saw she was in need of my help. I would have proved a complete traitor to her if I were to fail her in this emergency. *Why then am I so far away from her?*' Little did the duke know how close she was. He would be quite heart-broken afterwards that he had not known about her arrrival beforehand. Without any hesitation Ille equipped himself splendidly; he counselled his three children, leaving each of them what he pleased: he did not wish them to have possessions in common. He left them under the guardianship of three barons. He could not see the next day dawn soon or swiftly enough. He took his leave of the nun.

When he was taking his leave and talking to her, he said that he intended to go to Santiago de Compostela, and Galeron gave him leave to go: the nun could see nothing but good in it.[2] He had as many as thirty knights, both Bretons and Poitevins, set out as if they were pilgrims: there were no better and no more aggressive knights in the world. Each of them had a new set of arms and fine horses; some had one, some two. However, in order to throw the Bretons off the scent, the duke had them escorted out of the country off the beaten track. He sent them on their way a full week before he set out; there were thirty of them,

---

1 Löseth emended *verté* to *vertu*, but in a context where the keeping and breaking of promises is being emphasised *verté* is surely the correct reading .
2 Lefèvre sees Ille's dissimulation of his true destination as proof that he is 'un mari plein de délicatesse', who does not want to upset Galeron by reminding her of Ganor (p. 239). I would interpret his actions rather differently, given the particular choice of lie: pulling the wool over a nun's eyes with a story of a fake pilgrimage smacks more of deceit (and a guilty conscience?) than of delicacy. We should perhaps see in this a reflection of the web of broken loyalties in which the hero of *Eliduc* finds himself ensnared. Gautier's reworking of the tale so as to legitimise

Et dient tot c'a Rome en vont,
Et Illes k'a saint Jake en vait.
Li dus si cointement le fait,
Que bien le cuident tot si home
5525 Qu'aut a saint Jake et cil a Rome.
Et qant ce vint al jor qu'il muet,
Tot le païs plorer estuet:
Li uns le plaint, l'autre le plore.
Li dus en vait, cui Dix secore!
5530 Et se maisnie en est alee,
Et vient li dus a recelee
La ou atendre se rova:
Cevax et armes i trova
Tot si com il devisé l'ot.¹
5535 E Dix, que Ganor n'en set mot,
Que vers Bretagne en vient adés!
Trover le poroit mout plus prés.
Le cemin vait par le montagne
Et ele un autre vers Bretagne.
5540 Plus tost que pot i vint la bele
Et si enqiert del duc novele.
Cil qui li cuide tot voir dire,
Dist c'a saint Jake en va li sire
Et que la ducoise est rendue.
5545 Cele a le parole entendue:
De duel et d'ire esprent et art,
A poi que li cuers ne li part.
Li deus mout prés del cuer li point,

Noient por la ducoise un point;
5550 Ains li sostient içou sa vie,
Car autrement en fust partie:
Se tant n'eüst d'alegement,
Illoec morust tot quitement;
Mais ce l'aliege et reconforte.
5555 «Lasse! fait ele, com sui morte,
Quant je le duc n'ai chi trové,
Çou que a Diu ai plus rové.
Mes d'autre part m'estait si bien
Que plaindre ne me voel de rien;
5560 Si m'esta bien en autre endroit,
Qu'esleecier m'en doi par droit
Et l'un encontre l'autre metre,
Por lui envoier et trametre
Et mander lui que je sui chi
5565 Et ke il ait de moi merchi.
Ja si durs n'ert, mon essïent,
C'a moi ne viegne isnelement.»
Son mes vers saint Jake en envoie;
En vain li fait aler grant voie.
5570 Un jor sans plus illoec sejorne;
L'endemain par matin s'en torne.
Li dus cevauce durement
Et si est ja mon essïent
.XV. jornees bien avant;
5575 Noveles va plus entervant
Qu'il n'ait escrit el parcemin.²

5525 qant a S. J.]W   5530 A se m.]Lö

and they all said that they were going to Rome, and Ille said that he was going to Compostela. The duke managed it so cleverly that all his men really believed that he was going to Compostela and the others to Rome. And when the day came for him to set out, the whole country was forced to weep: some cried for him, others wept for him. The duke left, God come to his aid! The knights of his household had left, and the duke also came secretly to the place where he had asked them to wait for him: there he found a horse and a set of arms, just as he had arranged.[1] Oh God! That Ganor knew nothing about it as she was heading for Brittany at that very moment! She could have found him much closer at hand. Ille took the road over the mountains, and she took a different road towards Brittany. (5540) The beautiful damsel arrived there as soon as she could, and asked for news of the duke. A man who believed that he was telling her the whole truth said that the lord was on his way to Compostela, and that the duchess had taken the veil. Ganor heard what he said, and was consumed by searing grief and dismay; her heart nearly broke in two. The grief stung her very close to the heart, but not one jot of it was on account of the duchess; rather, it was this which kept her alive, for otherwise she would have departed this life: if she had not had this much relief, she would have died on the spot without any resistance at all; but this brought her relief and comfort. 'Alas!' she said, 'I am doomed, since I have not found the duke here, which is what I have asked God for the most. (5558) But in other respects things are going so well for me that I have no desire to cry over anything; things are going so well for me in other ways that I ought by rights to rejoice over it and let one compensate for the other, send for him, and inform him that I am here and ask him to have mercy on me. I cannot believe that he will be so hard-hearted as not to come to me immediately.' She sent her messenger off towards Compostela; she made him travel a long distance for nothing. She stayed in Brittany for just a single day; the following morning she left for home. The duke was riding hard, and he was already, so I believe, a good fifteen days' ride ahead of her; he was seeking news of her more keenly than is written in this parchment.[2]

---

the hero's love for the second woman does not entail the total sanitising of his protagonist. Ille remains a flawed hero, whose political success is interwoven with moments of personal weakness.

[1] In order to maintain the pretence that he was going on a pilgrimage to Santiago de Compostela, Ille would have had to leave his court dressed as a pilgrim, unarmed, and on foot.

[2] In other words, in Gautier's text itself. There is a similar reference in ll. 748-51 to the hero's activities outstripping the clerk's ability to record them.

Endroit Viane entre el cemin;
La se herberge cele nuit.
Avoec son oste se deduit;
5580 Aprés souper a dit: «Biax sire,
Savés me vos noveles dire
De cex de Rome, u laide u bele?
– Oïl, sire! Leur damoisele
Se herberga chi l'autre soir.
5585 – Puet c'estre voirs? – Oïl, por voir.
Au duc de Bretaigne est alee
Tout coiement, a recelee.¹
– Que quiert ele? – Biax sire, aïe,
Si com en l'ome u plus se fie.
5590 Morte est se n'a consel de lui,
Car n'a sossiel autre refui.
    – Biax ostes ciers, quel feme est cié?
– Sire, que vos diroie gié?
Se Damedix me puist aidier,
5595 C'est la plus bele, au mien cuidier,
Qui soit tant com li mondes dure.
Longe voie a et aspre et dure.
Maleois soit de Diu le Pere
De Romenie l'emperere
5600 Qui a tel tort l'a travillie!
De Diu soit ele consillie!
Bien sai que consillie en ert
Se li dus fait ce que li quiert,
Car il est mout de rice fait;

5605 Ce dist la bele qui la vait
Et tos li mons le dist avoec.
– Biax ostes, bien ait il peroec!»
Dormir se vont cil chevalier
Qui sont anoié de villier.
5610 Illes est las et si se chouce:
Amors le point, Amors le to[u]ce.
Ceste amors l'autre li aliege,
Mes mix i a l'autre son siege,
Que ceste amors encore n'ait,
5615 Qui confort et soulas li fait
Et l'autre aliege, qui li grieve,
Qui adés choce o lui et lieve.
Et tant a plus ciste que ceste,
Com cil qui trait a l'arbaleste
5620 Lasus en une haute tour
Envers celui qui vait entour
Et est dehors et si l'assaut.
Mes a celui ses fais que vaut?
Comment conquerra par son cors
5625 Celui dedens icil dehors?²
Mout li convient que il soit sages
Por entor gaitier les passages
Et por enginier et destraindre,
Que cil ne puist viande ataindre,
5630 Et por mostrer bien par raison
Que cil n'a droit en le meson.
Ensi est de ces .ii. amours:

5582 bone u bele]W   5612 si aliege]W   5618 Et tant de ceste a plus que ceste]W
5625 Icil dedens celui dehors]W

He came on to the main road near Vienne, and lodged there for the night. He amused himself in conversation with his host; after supper he said to him: 'Fair lord, can you tell me any news, good or bad, about the people of Rome?' – 'Yes, my lord! Their liege-lady lodged here the other evening.' – 'Can this be true?' – 'Yes, in truth. She has gone off very quietly, in secret, to the duke of Brittany.'[1] – 'What does she want from him?' – 'Help, fair lord, as she would from the man in whom she has the greatest faith. She is doomed if she cannot get counsel from him, for she has nowhere else on earth to turn to.'

'Fair dear host, what sort of woman is she?' – 'What shall I say, my lord? As the Lord God may help me, she is the most beautiful woman, to my way of thinking, in the whole wide world. (5597) She has a long, hard and difficult journey in front of her. May God the Father curse the emperor of Byzantium who has tormented her so unjustly! May God come to her aid! I do know that He will come to her aid if the duke does what she wants of him, for he is a man of very noble character. So says the fair damsel who is on her way there, and the whole world agrees with her.' – 'Fair host, a blessing on him for that!' The knights, who had had enough of staying awake, went off to sleep. Ille was weary and went to bed: Love pricked him, Love put the spurs to him. This love brought him relief from the other, but the other was more firmly ensconced than this love was as yet, this love which brought him comfort and solace, and relief from the other, which was afflicting him, which always slept and rose with him. (5618) And the first love was in as much stronger a position as regards the second as is a man wielding a crossbow on the top of a high tower in comparison with the man riding around, who is outside attacking him. But what good is the second man's prowess to him? How will the man outside overcome the man inside on his own?[2] It is very important that he should be wise enough to keep watch on the approaches on all sides, and to outwit and blockade the first man, so that no supplies can reach him, and to demonstrate beyond any doubt that the first man has no title to the fortress. This is how it was with these two loves:

---

[1] The host recognised Ganor, despite her precautions, but does not recognise Ille. If Gautier was consciously or unconsciously identifying Ganor with the empress Beatrice, this would be quite natural: as heiress to the county of Burgundy, the empress would be well known to the inhabitants of Vienne.

[2] W has the better reading here: it is clear from ll. 5626-31 that the situation is being described from the point of view of the besieger.

Li cuers Ille est la haute tours.
Dedens qui est? L'amors premiere,
5635 Qui del tenir est costumiere;
Ne mais l'amors de la pucele,
Qui est dehors, sovent l'apele,
Dist li c'a tort est la dedens
Et veut mostrer par argumens
5640 Et prover k'amors de nonain
N'a droit en cuer de castelain,
De duc, de conte ne de roi,
Ains torne mout a grant desroi
C'on l'i suefre, c'on l'i consent.
5645 Illes s'en deut, Ille[s] s'en sent.
L'autre amors est fors a confondre
Ne ne set soussiel que respondre,
Mais itant dist qu'ele est tenans
Par droit; tex est ses convenans;
5650 Et ceste, que a noient vint
Des lors qu'ele none devint:[1]
De castel c'a a faire none?
Mais fille a roi qui taut et done,
Et la none son sautier lise
5655 En l'abeïe et en l'eglise!
Illes li dus n'a nul deduit,
En tel torment est tote nuit:
«Ha! Ganor, bele douce suer!
Com poi le cuidai en mon cuer
5660 Que por tel home com je sui
Daignissiés ja passer tant pui,

Tant mont, tant val et tante plagne.
Mout criem que vostre cuers se plaɡ
De moi qant ne me troverés;
5665 Mais, se Diu plaist, vos me verrés
Et je vos autrement encore.
N'en poons mais, ensi est ore:
Mout a grans teres entre nos.
U ke soie, je sui a vous:
5670 Mon oirre m'estuet acointier,
Et se je puis rien esploitier
De vostre afaire, m'ert mout bel.
Por vos quic faire maint cenbel
A l'issir de la forterece.
5675 Et Dix qui tot le mont adrece
Le m'otroit faire a son plesir,
Et que je puisse dessaisir
L'empereor, le fier, le fort,
Qui issi nos demaine a tort,
5680 Et se cuide de nous gaber.»[2]
Devant le jour lieve li ber
Quant l'eure vient que lever velt;
Oïe ot messe com il seut.
Vers Rome droitement cemine
5685 Et puis ne cesse ne ne fine
Desi qu'il vint droit a la guerre
Ou l'emperere assiet la terre.
Bien a .v. jours, ne sai, ou .vi.
Qu'en un castel les a assis.

5650 qui noiens devint]Lö

Ille's heart was the lofty tower. Who was inside? The first love, which held it by force of custom; except that his love for the maiden, which was outside, frequently accused her, saying that she had no right to be there inside, and intended to demonstrate logically and prove that love for a nun has no title to the heart of a castellan, a duke, a count or a king, and that it is on the contrary wholly unreasonable that it should be allowed, that it should be permitted to be there. It was Ille who suffered, Ille who felt the effects of this. The first love was difficult to overcome, and did not know what on earth to reply, but what she did say was that she was the rightful occupant; this is what her title deed said; and the second replied that it was null and void from the moment she became a nun:[1] what use does a nun have for a castle? (5653) But a king's daughter does, who has the power to give and to take away, and let the nun read her psalter in the abbey and in the church! Duke Ille was not enjoying himself at all: this was the sort of torment he was in all night long: 'Ah! Ganor, fair sweet sister! How little I imagined in my heart that you would ever think fit to cross so many hills, so many mountains, so many valleys and so many plains for a man such as I. I am very much afraid that your heart will reproach me when you do not find me; but, please God, you will see me and I shall see you again in different circumstances. There is nothing we can do about it; this is how it is now: there are vast lands between us. (5669) Wherever I am, I am yours: I must address myself to my journey, and if I can achieve any success in this business of yours, I shall be very pleased about it. For your sake I plan to undertake many a joust when we ride out from the fortress. And may God who governs the whole world grant that I may do it according to his wishes, and that I may oust the violent and powerful emperor who is unjustly mistreating us like this, and plans to make a laughing-stock of us.'[2] The noble warrior rose before daybreak, at the hour when he felt like rising; he heard mass, as he normally did. He travelled straight towards Rome and then did not pause or stop until he arrived right where the fighting was, where the emperor was besieging the country. He had been besieging them in a castle for perhaps a good five or six days.

---

1 Lines 5646-55 represent a debate between the two loves: Ille's love for Galeron is hard pressed by his feelings for Ganor (*l'autre amors*), but nonetheless states her claim to his heart; this claim is then refuted by the second love (*ceste*), who puts forward a counterclaim. The subject of the verbs in ll. 5647-48 is *l'amors premiere*; *dist* is understood after *ceste* in l. 5650. See the Introduction, pp. xvi-xviii.
2 W has *vos* in both lines. *Nos* is more satisfying in terms of the development of Ille's love for Ganor, indicating as it does his complete identification with the Roman cause and with the reputation of the empire which Ganor represents.

5690 Les gens a mout mal atornees
Et est venu bien .x. journees
En le tere la damoisele
Cui il de mariage apele.
Romain n'en sevent vent ne voie;[1]
5695 Onques mais n'orent mains de joie:
Ne sevent qu'ele est devenue,
Quel voie ele a sossiel tenue;
Que puissent cuidier ne que croire?
A poi que ce nes fait mescroire
5700 De la grant guerre que il ont
Contre les gens qui sor eus sont.
Entr'ex ont pris jor de combatre
Al mains, ou .ii. ou .iii. ou .iiii.;
Mix voelent a un cief venir,
5705 Tost trespasser ou tost fenir,
Que sofrir tel lime et tel mort.
En un castel mervelles fort
A .ii. liues de l'ost romain
Avoit un preude castelain:
5710 Nus hom qui fust deça la mer
Ne soloit Ille(s) tant amer.
   Li castiax ert en une roche:
Nus n'i avient, nus n'i aproce,
Nus home n'i puet siege tenir
5715 Ne aprocier ne avenir;
Li castiax ert en un destor.
Au castelain de cele tour
Mande li dus tout coiement
Qu'il viegne a lui celeement.
5720 Cil vient a lui en une lande

Par entresegnes qu'il li mande.
Cil le connut si com il seut
Com l'ome que il amer veut;
De parler ne s'est plus tenus,
5725 Ains dist : «Bien soiés vos venus!
Sans vos ne poiemes nos plus.
Grasses en ait Diex de lasus!
5727a *Grasses en ait Dex nostre sire!*
Ne sai que je vous puisse dire,
Mais que Ganor avons perdue.
5730 Demain nos ert mout cier vendue,
Car nos atendons le bataille
Qui ert demain sans nule faille.»
Li dus a dit: «Or est assés.
Parmi le forest nos passés
5735 Tot coiement et en .i. angle
Quant il seront trestot ensanle.
O vous demoërrai hui mes;
Mais or le faites si par pais
Que nus ne sace qui je soie.
5740 – Biax sire ciers, ce soit a joie.»
En son castel les a menés
Et d'aus servir s'est mout penés;
Mout lor fu bele cele nuis.
Li castelains s'est mout deduis:
5745 Tout issi l'a li dus trové
Com il li ot dit et rové.
A l'endemain, qant l'aube crieve,
Li dus s'esvelle et si se lieve;
Messe li dist ses capelains,

5694 Romain ne sevent ne ne voient]Lö   5699 ce ne fait a croire]W
5711 Le soloit]W

192

He had brought the people to ruin and had advanced a good ten days' ride into the territory of the damsel whose hand he was claiming in marriage. The Romans did not have the remotest idea where she was;[1] they had never been less joyful in their lives: they did not know what had become of her, which earthly way she had gone; what were they to think or to believe? This almost made them lose faith in the great war they had on their hands against the forces which were assailing them. The two sides had agreed between them on a day for the battle, one day at least, or perhaps two or three or four; they preferred to have it over and done with, to be cured at once or die at once, than to endure such a death by attrition. (5707) In a wonderfully strong castle two leagues away from the Roman army there lived a gallant castellan: no man on this side of the sea used to love Ille so much.

The castle was on a rock: no-one could approach it, no-one could come near it, no man could lay siege to it or come near it or approach it; the castle was in an out-of-the-way place. The duke covertly sent a message to the castellan of this tower to come to meet him in secret. The castellan came to meet him in a wooded area, using secret identification which Ille sent to him. He recognised Ille as he used to, as the man he willingly loved; he did not refrain from speaking any longer, but said: 'Welcome! We could not go on any longer without you. Thanks be to God on high! *Thanks be to God our Lord!* I do not know what to tell you, except that we have lost Ganor. (5730) Tomorrow we shall be made to pay very dearly for her, for we await the battle which will take place tomorrow without fail.' The duke said: 'Enough of this. When they are all together on the field, you lead us very secretly through a corner of the forest. I will stay with you from now on, but go about it so discreetly that no-one knows who I am.' – 'Fair dear lord, may it bring us joy.' He led them into his castle and went to great pains to serve them; that night was very agreeable for them. The castellan enjoyed himself greatly: the duke found everything exactly as he had told him and asked him. The next morning, as dawn was breaking, the duke awoke and then got up; his chaplain said mass for him,

---

[1] I have chosen to emend here, following Löseth, rather than adopt the W reading 'Romain n'en sevent nule voie' on the grounds that Gautier twice uses the expression *ne saveir vent ne voie* to describe Galeron's disappearance (ll. 3704 and 3880), which closely parallels the situation here. This phrase is also used again of Ganor in l. 6116.

5750 Puis vait devant li castelains.
Monte li dus, montent li suen
Por son plaisir et por son buen.
Il dui cevalcent prés a prés
Et li chevalier trente aprés,
5755 Et les cevax font traire en destre,
Les escus covrir a senestre;[1]
Pieç'a qu'il ont esté covert,
Mais sempres verront li quivert
Com fait il sont, u lait u bel:
5760 En cascun ot un lioncel.
Ne sont pas chevalier a gas
Car Illes nes amenast pas.
Cascuns des .xxx. vaut .i. roi
Por commencier un grant desroi,
5765 Car tex gent va li dus querant.
Tant vont parmi le bos errant
Qu'endroit le castel sont venu
Que li Romain ont tant tenu,
Et voient les cevax brocier;
5770 L'un oïssiés l'autre aprocier.
El bos parfont tantost descendent
Et ces armes par tere estendent;
Armé se sont isnelement.
Li dus lor dist mout belement
5775 Par grant consel et par esgart:
«Je nen ai sossiel nul regart
Que cuers vos faille plus c'a moi
Por mout de tel gent com je voi:
De tot içou nen ai je song,

5780 C'uns hom valt .m. a tel besoing.
Mes ne vos caut a el entendre
Que seulement as testes prendre.
Qui de lonc vient avoec signor
Qui ne veut querre el que honor,
5785 Ne l'aime pas de bone amor
Se il le gerpist en estour
Vilainement por gaaignier;
Mix ne se puet il mehagnier
Ne plus honir ne mix haïr
5790 Ne mix son bon signor traïr.
Mout est malvaise Covoitise:
Mar fu qui est en sa justice,
C'adés le fait a ce tenir
Dont plus se puet au lonc honir.
5795 Mais por vos ne le di je pas:
Ne poés aler un seul pas
C'Onors ne soit a vo[s] compagne.
Ce parra ja en le campagne.
   – Sire, font il, trop nos demeure.
5800 Bien en est hui mes tans et eure.»
D'iloec les voient assanler;
La tere bondir et tranler
Oent d'iluec benignement
Et voient tot apertement
5805 Ces chevaliers droit adrecier
Et ces escus fraindre et percier,
Ces haubers rompre et desconfire,
Chevaliers navrer et ochire,
Sele[s] vuidier et anstes fraindre,

5765 tex Gent   5774 li dist]W   5780 tel beson]W

194

and then the castellan attended on him. The duke mounted, and his men mounted to do his pleasure and carry out his wishes. The two men rode side by side, and the thirty knights rode behind them, their squires leading their chargers behind them on the right, and carrying their shields covered up on the left;[1] they had been covered up for a good while, but the traitors would soon see what they were like, whether they were foul or fair: each one had a lioncel on it. They were not knights for fun, for Ille would not have brought such men with him. Each of the thirty was as good as a king for causing havoc amongst the enemy, for these were the sort of men the duke was looking for. They went riding through the wood until they came close to the castle which the Romans had defended for so long, and they could see the horses being spurred on: you could have heard one charging at another. (5771) They dismounted at once in the dense wood and laid their arms out on the ground; they swiftly armed themselves. The duke spoke to them very quietly, showing great wisdom and discernment: 'I am not in the least bit apprehensive that your hearts will fail you any more than mine will on account of large numbers of the sort of men I can see here: I am not worried about any of this, because one man can be worth a thousand in such a fight. But the only thing that matters for you is to concentrate on cutting off heads. Anyone who comes from afar with a lord whose only wish is to seek honour does not love him with a true love if he deserts him dishonourably in battle in order to acquire booty for himself; there is no better way to disfigure himself, no way he could dishonour himself more, no better way to hate himself, no better way to betray his good lord. (5791) Greed is a very evil thing: unlucky for anyone who is subject to it that he was ever born, for it makes him intent on having at once something which may bring greater shame upon himself in the long run. However, I am not saying this on your account: you cannot take a single step without Honour being your companion. This will soon be obvious on the field.'

'My lord', they said, 'It cannot come quickly enough for us. From now on the time is surely ripe for it.' From where they were, they could see the others join battle; from there they could distinctly hear the ground echo and shudder and they could clearly see the knights charging straight at one another and the shields being shattered and pierced, and the hauberks being torn and ripped apart, knights being wounded and killed, saddles being emptied and lance-shafts shattered,

---

[1] The knights set out from Brittany with brand new arms (l. 5514), including shields which were protected by covers while they were travelling; the covers are removed before combat (l. 5852) Ille's men's shields bear a device of a single lioncel (ll. 5760 and 5854); Ille himself has a shield with a lion painted on it in l. 546. No

5810 Ces espees trencans ataindre;
Voient ces hiaumes enbarer,
Voler de cief et enterer,
Et voient bien qui mix i oevre
Et qui mix fiert et mix recoevre;
5815 Les uns fuïr, les uns kacier,
Et puis les fuians rakacier;
Voient maint caoir en la kace
Qui ainc puis n'ot song de manace.
Aler i voelent tuit des ore.
5820 «Nou ferés, mi ami, encore,
Mes quant vos verrés les Romains
Alasqier de bras et de mains,
Las et anoiés de combatre
Et en leur forterece embatre,
5825 Quant vos verrés çou avenir,
Lors ne vos voel je plus tenir.»
Ne tarda gaires que c'avint
Que les Romains fuïr convint
Et que il quierent lor adrece
5830 Por fuïr vers la forterece.
Li Griu en font mout grant martire;
A tas i fierent et a tire.
Escrient tuit: «A ce besong
Vos ert huimes li Brés trop long.
5835 Espenir vos convenra hui
Canqu'il onques nos fist d'anui.»
Quant Illes voit cele dolor
Et ces ensegnes de coulor
Müer et taindre en sanc vermel,

5840 «Signor, fait il, or au solel!
Trop avés mais esté en l'ombre
Car l'emperere nos encombre
Nos gens de Rome mortelment.
Or vous tenés sereement;
5845 N'espargniés pas vos noeves armes,
Prenés escus par les enarmes,
Desploiés confanons au vent.
Mal ait qui mout cier ne s'i vent!
Aidiés la gent que j'ai amee.»
5850 Atant issent de la ramee,
Mostrent ces armes as quivers
Et ces escus ont descovers,
Qui mout sont reluisant et bel;
En cascun ot un lioncel.
5855 Poignent vers l'ost lance levee(s).
Le gent de Rome est mout grevee:
Gardent amont, venir les voient
Et cuident qu'anemi lor soient,
Qui soient o les Grix venu,
5860 Et k'aient ens el bos tenu
Por tout destruire al daerain.
Et dient lors li premerain:
«Ne vinrent pas d'assés si bel.
Dix, com lor destrier sont isnel,
5865 Com noeves armes et com beles,
Com sont reluisans et noveles,
Com vienent acesmeement!
Mort somes tuit communement,
Vrais Dix, se tu ne nos confortes.»

5830 les la f.]W   5848 ne li vent]W   5856 a mout g.]W   5858 que venir]W

the sharp swords being drawn; they could see the helmets being split open, flying off men's heads and burying themselves in the ground, and they were well able to see who was performing the best there, and who was striking the best and parrying best; they could see one side fleeing and the others pursuing them, and then those who were fleeing turning and doing the pursuing; they saw many a man fall in the pursuit who was never worried about threats again afterwards. They all wanted to join in at once. 'You will not do so yet, my friends, but when you see the Romans' arms and hands slacken, when they are weary and tired of fighting and are being forced back into their fortress, when you see this happening, then I do not intend to hold you back any longer.' Very soon after this it came about that the Romans were forced to flee and looked for the shortest route to flee towards the fortress. (5831) The Greeks were massacring them; they were striking them thick and fast. The Greeks all cried out: 'In this emergency the Breton will be too far away to help you from now on. You will have to make amends today for all the harm he ever did us.'

When Ille saw their suffering and saw the coloured pennons changing colour and being dyed in scarlet blood, 'My lords', he said, 'Quick, out into the sunlight! Now you have been in the shade too long, for the emperor is inflicting fatal damage on our Roman troops. Now keep in close formation; do not spare your new arms, grasp your shields by the arm-straps, unfurl your banners to the wind. A curse on anyone who does not make them pay dearly for him out there! Go to the aid of the people I have loved.' (5850) At this, they rode out from under the branches, displayed their arms to the traitors, and carried their shields uncovered: they were gleaming and handsome, and each one had a lioncel on it. They charged towards the army, lances raised. The Roman forces were suffering serious casualties: they looked up, saw them coming, and thought that they were enemy forces who had come with the Greeks, and which they had kept in the wood in order to finish everything off at the end. And then those at the front said: 'Those who came first were nothing like as handsome as these. God, how swift their chargers are, what fine new arms they have, how gleaming and fresh they are, how disciplined their advance is! We are doomed to die, all of us, true God, if you do not give us comfort.'

---

other devices are mentioned in *Ille et Galeron* (Hoel's shield bears a number of lioncels in l. 674; a Greek knight has a device of a lion in l. 5884), suggesting that Gautier's knowledge of heraldry was limited.

folio 308^r d

5870 Li coart se sont mis as portes
Fuient laiens garir lors cors,
Et li preudome sont dehors
A mout grant paine et a mescief.
Cil ne se traient mie au cief
5875 De la bataille, mais en mi.
Li felon, li Diu anemi,
Ocient Romains et estonent,
Que nule garde ne s'en donent
Des Bretons ne des Poitevins
5880 Qu'il les aient si prés voisins.
Tant com ceval porent aler
Les vont ferir sans aparler:
En ex se fierent a desroi;
Qui abat un, qui .ii., qui troi.
5885 Illes vait ferir un Grifon,
Parmi l'escu paint a lion
Li met le fer de Cornualle,[1]
L'auberc li ront et li desmalle,
Le fer li conduist sos l'aissele,
5890 Mort le trebuce de la sele.
Et de cel poindre abat Maurin:
Cil doi furent germain cousin.
Gerins del Mans fiert Gadifer,
Parmi l'escu li met son fer,
5895 L'auberc li ront et li desment
Si que par tere mort l'estent.
Et Lanselins, cil de Poitiers,
D'un poindre ocist .ii. chevaliers;
Ponces de Nantes le garnie

5900 I ocist Lot de Commenie;
Paris de Resnes la cité
S'a de deus Grijois aquité,
Et por la mort qui cex soubite
Ne sont de rien li autre quite.
5905 Li Breton sont chevalier buen:
Cascuns al mains ocist le suen;
Or sont li Griu en grant freor.
Uns mes vint a l'empereour;
Devant les portes de la vile
5910 S'escrië oiant .iiii. mile:
«Sire, fait il, por Diu, merci!
Romain ne perdent pas tant chi
Que vos ne perdés .c. tans plus
En le batalle cha desus.
5915 A cex de Rome vient secors
Qui de la forest lor est sours:
Malement mainent nos Grijois.
Il n'orent c'un seul Ille ançois,
Mais or en ont il plus de .m.»
5920 Ce dist li mes et ce cuide il.
Preudom, en leu u cier se vent,
Se torne menu et sovent
Et sanle d'un qu'en i ait .iiii.,
Et cil les ot veüs combatre,
5925 S'en i cuide bien .m. sans falle.
Or ne puet müer que n'i aille
Li empereres por l'onour;
Li Grijois vont o lor signor.
Romain coisissent a droiture

5870 sest mis]W   5927 par l'o.]W

198

The cowards made for the gates, fleeing inside the castle in order to save their skins, while the gallant knights were outside suffering severe punishment and hardship. These men did not take themselves off to the fringe of the battle, but into the heart of it. The evil enemies of God were killing and battering the Romans, and were quite oblivious to the fact that they had the Bretons and Poitevins for such close neighbours. They went to strike them as fast as their horses could go, without addressing a word to them: they charged into them pell-mell; some struck one man down, some two, some three. Ille went to strike a Greek and thrust his lance-head of Cornish iron through the man's shield,[1] which had a lion painted on it, tore his hauberk and ripped it apart, drove the lance-head below where the arm joins the body and hurled him dead from the saddle. (5891) And in the same charge he struck down Maurin: these two were first cousins. Gerin of Le Mans struck Gadifer, thrusting his lance-head through his shield, tearing and ripping open his hauberk so that he laid him out dead on the ground. And Lanselin from Poitiers killed two knights in one charge; Ponçon from the well-fortified city of Nantes killed Lot of Comenia out there; Paris from the walled city of Rennes settled accounts with two Greeks, and the sudden death which overtook them did nothing to discharge the others' debts. The Bretons were skilful knights: each of them killed his man, at least; now the Greeks were terrified. A messenger came to the emperor; in front of the gates of the town he cried out, and four thousand people heard him:

(5911) 'Sire', he said, 'For God's sake, have mercy! However many men the Romans are losing here, you are losing a hundred times more in the battle up there. The men of Rome have reinforcements who have sprung out of the forest to join them: our Greeks are getting rough treatment from them. They only had a single Ille before, but now they have more than a thousand of him.' So said the messenger, and so he believed. When a gallant knight is in a situation where he is making his enemies pay dearly, he wheels round with such speed and frequency that it seems as if there were four of him rather than one, and the messenger had seen them in action, and really and truly believed that there were a thousand of them. Now nothing could stop the emperor going there in search of honour; the Greeks went with their lord. The Romans correctly made out

---

[1] A curious reference. Cornish tin was well-known in the Middle Ages, but there does not seem to have been any iron-working in the county (no forges are recorded in the Domesday Book). The nearest iron-working areas were the Forest of Dean and Glamorgan. It is possible that Gautier had limited knowledge of British geography, and that for him the term 'Cornwall' covered the whole of the Celtic

5930 La sus lor grant bone aventure
Et dient: «Diex! qui sont cil la?
Onques puis k'Illes s'en ala
N'eümes nos mais tex amis:
Diex les nos a en fin tramis.
5935 Biax sire Dix, qui puet cil estre
Qui si emploie bien sa destre,
A cel escu d'or, qui si fiert?
Com vistement il les requiert!
Il en a ochis plus de cent.
5940 – Foi que je doi a saint Vincent,[1]
Fait li uns d'eus, .m. mars vos doi
Se ce n'est Illes que je voi.»
Lors respondent communalment:
«Qui poroit cuidier seulement
5945 Que ce fust il, bien nous iroit:
Ja l'orgillous ne s'en riroit.
Or le cuidon por nos garir
Et por nos anemis ferir.»
Recoevrent cuer et hardement,
5950 Et sont de bel contenement;
Arriere s'en revont tantost
Et vont ferir en cex de l'ost.
Illes besoigne mout tres bien
Que soient preu il et li sien:
5955 Il sont a grant mescief illuec.
Ensi le font, et neperuec,[2]
C'onques por eus ne se remuent,
Ains en ocient mout et tuent.
      Jonas s'eslaisse et fiert Ponçon

5960 Si que son fer et un tronçon
Del fust qu'il tenoit a se destre
Li laisse en la quisse senestre.
Illes en a mout grant anui;
Bien pert que Ponces est a lui.
5965 Jonas vait ferir en l'escu,
Que d'eur a autre l'a fendu:
Plaine sa lance jus l'envoie
Navré a mort. Quil veut, se l'oie!
Illoec ot un estor mout fort
5970 Por le navré et por le mort;
Mout i ont fait et mout soufert:
Durs est li drois qu'il ont offert.
Breton les metent a dolor,
Mais trop sont poi envers les lor.
5975 Gerins del Mans i fiert Madan,
Paris de Resnes Madian,
.II. Grius qui mout par furent noble
Puis les plora Constantinoble.
Illes se torne mout menu.
5980 Un chevalier novel venu
I gete mort; la ot grant plor,
Car il ert niés l'empereour.
A lui vengier ot mout grant bruit:
A le vengance poignent tuit.
5985 Lores s'escrient cil de Rome:
«Dix! com nos somes malvés home
Quant nos n'alomes cex aidier
Cui nos veons ensi plaidier,

5987 nos volomes]W

200

the great good fortune which was theirs further up and said: 'God! Who are those men over there? Never since Ille left have we ever had such people on our side: God has sent them to us in the last resort. Dear Lord God, who can that man be who is putting his right hand to such good use, the man with the golden shield, who is striking such blows? How swiftly he goes for them! He has killed more than a hundred of them.' – 'By the faith I owe to Saint Vincent',[1] said one of them, 'I owe you a thousand marks if that isn't Ille I can see.' Then they all replied as one: 'If only we could believe that it was him, things would go well for us: that arrogant man wouldn't find it very funny. So let us believe it, so as to save ourselves and strike our enemies.' (5949) Their courage and daring returned, and they conducted themselves handsomely; they turned back at once and went to strike the men of the Greek army. Ille was making every possible effort to ensure that he and his men fought gallantly: they were in dire straits there. And nonetheless they fought in such a way that they never gave ground on their account,[2] slaying and killing many of them instead.

Jonas dashed out and struck Ponçon, so that he left his lance-head and a section of the shaft he had been holding in his right hand embedded in Ponçon's left thigh. This caused Ille very great distress; it was quite obvious that Ponçon was one of his men. He went and struck Jonas on the shield and split it from edge to edge: he hurled him down with the full force of his lance, mortally wounded. Let whoever wants to, hear the rest! (5969) A very fierce battle took place there over the wounded man and the dead man; they performed great deeds and suffered greatly: harsh was the justice they meted out. The Bretons inflicted punishment on them, but there were too few of them in comparison with their opponents. Gerin of Le Mans struck Madan, and Paris of Rennes struck Madian, two extremely noble Greeks, and Constantinople wept for them afterwards. Ille was wheeling round with great rapidity. He hurled down dead a newly-arrived knight; there was great weeping on that spot, for he was the emperor's nephew. There was a great commotion over avenging him: they all charged to join in the revenge. Then the men of Rome cried out: 'God! What cowards we are, not to go to the aid of the men we see arguing their case like this,

---

south-west, including South Wales, which was known for its iron industry. There may be some support for this in l. 1986, where *Gales* seems to be identified with North Wales (the *grant montagne* is Snowdonia).

[1] Vincent of Saragossa (d. 304 AD), the most celebrated of the early Spanish Martyrs, whose fame was widespread in Europe in the Middle Ages.

[2] The very similar construction in ll. 6017-18 suggests that P's reading is correct.

Et por nous est canques il [f]ont,
5990 Si ne savomes ki il sont.»
Lors les requierent mout de prés,
Et sont del ferir mout engrés:
n'i espargnent jovenes ne viex;
Onques mais gens nel firent miex.
5995 La gens de Rome est mout haitie:
Outre Ille plus d'une traitie
Ont ja les Grius mis et kaciés.
Ponces de Nantes est bleciés,
Por çou remest li dus arriere.
6000 En un destor les le kariere
Descent li ber prés d'une haie;[1]
Illuec restraint Ponces sa plaie.
Grans est l'angoisse et griés la tence
Et mout est dure la bestence
6005 Des gens de Grece a nos Romains:
De la'n a plus et de ça mains.
Li Griu qui sevent plus de guerre
Lor tolent la piece de tere,
Ses ont remués de la place.
6010 Mortex eüst esté la kace,
Ne fust li ber qui çou coisist.
Saut el ceval, l'escu saisist
Et prent le lance de pumier.
Trestot sont fres com de premier
6015 Et montent od leur avoué,
Se li ont plevi et voué
Qu'en peril sont et neperuec
Ne voelent estre aillors qu'iloec.

«Signor, fait Illes, je vous di,
6020 Demain, se Diu plaist, ains midi
Vos ert mout bel que vos chi estes.
Pluisor qui ont humaines testes
Sont assés home por nombrer
Et por le païs encombrer.[2]
6025 Cil de la sont mort et traï,
Mais qu'il soient bien envaï;
Car cist s'esbaudiront por nous.
Faites honeur et moi et vous!
– Sire, par Damediu le voir,
6030 Cascuns i metra son pooir.»
Trestot ensanle ont pris leur poindre
Et vont as Grius joster et joindre.
Li Breton sont chevalier buen,
Par tere met cascuns le suen:
6035 As fers des lances lor presentent
Un tel present dont mout se sentent.
Illes n'ataint sossiel celui
Qui se puisse loer de lui.
Griu voient lor malaventure
6040 Et resortissent a droiture,
Tornent les dos et li renc ploient,
Et li Breton qui les convoient
Mout en ocient et mehagnent:
N'escape riens de cank'atagnent.
6045 Et li Romain, qant il ce voient,
Cui li Grijois kacié avoient,
Lor retornent enmi les vis

6032 as preus]W

and everything they are doing is for us, and yet we do not know who they are.'
Then they attacked them at very close quarters and were very keen to strike; they
spared neither young nor old there; no men had ever fought better before. The
Roman forces were full of vigour: they had already forced the Greeks back and
chased them more than a bow-shot beyond where Ille was. Ponçon of Nantes was
injured, and this is why the duke remained behind. The noble warrior dismounted
near a hedge in a secluded spot near the highway;[1] there Ponçon bound up his
wound. There was great anguish, fierce fighting and a very hard contest between
the Greek forces and our Romans: there were more men on their side and fewer on
ours. The Greeks, who were more experienced in warfare, ousted them from that
stretch of ground and forced them to retreat. (6010) It would have been a deadly
pursuit, had it not been for the noble warrior, who noticed this. He leapt onto his
horse, grasped his shield and took up the apple-wood lance. All his men were as
fresh as they were at the outset, and they mounted with their leader, and they gave
him their word and swore that although they were in danger they did not want to be
anywhere else but there. 'My lords', said Ille, 'Let me tell you, before noon
tomorrow, if it please God, you will be well pleased that you are here. Many
creatures who have human faces are men enough to make up the numbers and
ravage the countryside.[2] Our opponents are dead and done for, if only we launch a
good attack on them, for the Romans will take heart on our account. Do me and
yourselves honour!' – 'My lord, by the true Lord God, each of us will do his
utmost.'

(6031) They all made a charge together and went to joust and do battle with the
Greeks. The Bretons were skilful knights, and each of them unhorsed his man: with
their lance-heads, they presented them with a present whose effects they really felt.
No-one Ille hit could possibly congratulate himself for it. The Greeks saw the
misfortune which was befalling them and rode straight out of the melée again, they
turned tail and broke ranks, and the Bretons who escorted them on their way killed
and maimed many of them: of all those they caught up with, not one escaped. And
when the Romans whom the Greeks had been pursuing saw this, they turned around
and faced them head on,

---

[1] Here and in l. 6011 *li ber* refers to Ille, who dismounts in order to help the injured
Ponçon, and then rejoins the fray. W's *Ponçon* implies that Ille binds up Ponçon's
wound for him. This may represent the better reading, since in a parallel situation
in ll. 2935-36 the injured Ille has his wound dressed for him.
[2] The implication is, of course, that when it comes to serious fighting they will
prove to be less than men.

Et bien le font, ce vous plevis.
D'aus desconfire s'entremetent
6050 Et tote lor entente i metent.
Li Griu lor ont torné les dos;
Je n'i quic mie trois si os
En tos les Grius, non mie .ii.,
Qui s'ost retorner devers eus:
6055 En fuies tornent tot ensanle.
Or sevent tuit et bien lor sanle
C'on les ait menés a folie.
Li empereres ne s'oublie,
Or n'a il joie ne deport:
6060 Passer se fait endroit un port,
Et puis qu'il est a autre rive,
Il ne crient nul home qui vive.
Mais ce ne dient pas si home:
Mout lor font mal icil de Rome,
6065 Illes li ber qui tous les prent,
Et as Romains les livre et rent.
    Or ont achievé li Romain
Ce qu'il douterent si hui main
Et leurs prisons bien assenés,
6070 Quis ont hui si a mort pené[s]:
Sans bone garde un sol n'i laissent.
Au desarmer le duc s'eslaissent,
Sel baisent trestot li plus haut.
«Biax sire, font il, Dix vos saut!
6075 Mout par soiés vous bien venus
Et a grant joie recheüs,
Com Damedix vos puet doner!

N'eüstes song d'abandoner
Vo gent de Rome a deshonor:
6080 En vos avomes boin signor.
Prenés l'onor, prenés l'empere,
S'en soiés sire et commandere.
Perdue est nostre damoisele:
Se mais revient a nos la bele
6085 Prenés le a feme, biax dous sire;
Nos ne vos savons el que dire.
Trestuit avons par vos confort,
S'en somes gari de la mort.
– Bel douç signor, bien aiés vous
6090 De Damediu qui maint sor nos!
Mout bonement vous en merchi
De ce que vos m'ofrés ichi.
Je nel refus ne je nel prenc,[1]
Mais gré[s] et mercis vos en renc.»
6095 Li Romain mout grant joie font
Des compagnons qui o lui sont;
Trestot ensanle s'entrebaisent,
As ostex vienent, si s'aaisent.
Lor harnois font venir manois
6100 Et l'oste qui remest el bois.
Tuit li Romain, petit et grant,
Honorent le duc autretant
Com s'il avoit, od la corone,
Canqu'emperere taut et done.
6105 As millors castiax k'a coisis,
Que l'empere avoit saisis,

6062 Il ne criement home quil vive]W

204

and they fought well, I promise you. They applied themselves to defeating them, and turned all their attention to it. The Greeks had turned tail; I do not believe there were three men, or even two, amongst all the Greeks, bold enough to dare to turn back and face them: they all turned and fled together. Now they were all aware and had the distinct impression that they had been led into folly. The emperor did not waste any time, there was no joy or amusement for him now: he crossed the sea close to a port, and when once he was on another shore, he did not fear any man alive. But this was not what his men were saying: great pain was being inflicted on them by the men of Rome and by the noble warrior Ille, who was taking them all prisoner and delivering them up and handing them over to the Romans.

Now the Romans had achieved what they had been so doubtful about that morning, and they had made good provision for their prisoners, who had inflicted such mortal punishment on them that day: they did not leave a single one there unguarded. They rushed to disarm the duke, and all the noblest barons kissed him. 'Fair lord', they said, 'God save you! You are very welcome indeed, and may you be given as joyful a reception as the Lord God can grant you! You did not care to abandon your people of Rome to dishonour: we have a good lord in you. Take the realm, take the empire, and be its lord and commander. Our liege-lady is lost: if the fair damsel ever returns to us, take her to wife, fair gentle lord; we do not know what else to say to you. (6087) You have brought comfort to all of us, and you have saved us from death.' – 'Fair gentle lords, may the Lord God who dwells above us bless you! I thank you most kindly for what you are offering me here. I am neither refusing nor accepting it,[1] but I give you my grateful thanks for it.' The Romans gave a very joyful welcome to the companions who were with him; they all kissed one another, then went to their lodgings and rested. They immediately sent for their belongings and for their host who had remained in the wood. All the Romans, great and small, did the duke as much honour as if the crown and all that an emperor has the power to give and to take away were already his. The duke went off to the strongest castles he had identified, which the emperor had seized,

---

[1] Ille's careful response recalls his reaction to the offer of the seneschalcy made by the barons in the Roman army (ll. 2460-80). The hero is portrayed throughout as a man who respects other people's rights and privileges, even though doing so may be to his own disadvantage. On the previous occasion he would not accept the seneschalcy because it was not the barons' to give; here he will not commit himself to marrying Ganor without her express consent. The contrast between Ille and the emperor of Byzantium, who intends to marry Ganor against her will, could not be more explicit.

folio 308ᵛ d

En vait li dus et si les prent:
Cascuns s'otroie a lui et rent.
Trestuit i vienent a plain cours,
6110 Car il n'atendent nul secours.
Lonc fu de Rome que ç'avint;
Si a maint jor ne l'en sovint
De ju, de ris ne d'autre joie,
Qu'encor ne set on vent ne voie
6115 De cele grant bone aventure
Ne de la bele creature
Qui vient vers Rome canque puet.
Mout pense adés, ce li estuet:
Onques cil jor[s] ne li ajourne
6120 Qu'ele ne soit pensive et morne.
Mais encor n'est ce se gas non,[1]
Se Dix nel fait par son saint non;
Tot autrement en ert encore,
Se Dix nel fait, qu'il n'en est ore.
6125 A Rome en vient un jor la bele
Et si enqiert de l'ost novele.
«Bele, font il, rien n'en savons,
Mes que de vos grant joie avons,
Quel que de cex de l'ost aviegne,
6130 Car il n'est hom qui les maintiegne,
Se Damedix n'en prent conroi,
Et vous, car n'avons autre roi,
N'empereour n'empererris.
Mout nos avés trestous garis;
6135 Mais de l'aler si faitement
Fesistes vos mout malement.
6136a *N'est mervelle se cil meserre*

6136b *Qui sans segnor sostient grant gerre*
Rome l'a mout grant sostenue.
Bele, bien soiés vos venue!
– Signor, et Dix vos beneïe!
6140 Por querre a vos trestos aïe
Me sui penee et travillie,
Et si n'en sui preu consillie.
J'ai en Bretaigne puis esté,
Mais je n'i ai rien conquesté
6145 Fors que traval et paine et mal:
Trover cuidé le senescal,
Nel trové pas, ce poise moi.
A Saint Jake est alés, je croi,
Issi le dient el païs.
6150 Mon mes d'ilueques li tramis,
Mout li rovai qu'il se coitast
Et du revenir se hastast.
Et se li dus cha revenoit
Et vers les Grius nos maintenoit,
6155 Tost en feroie le conseil
De vous qui estes mi feel,
Mi home liege et mi juré.
– Damoisele, ç'a trop duré»
Font se li .x. qui mout sont fier[2]
6160 Et ont eü del Griu loier,
Et lor a promis grant tresor
S'il le sesissent de Ganor;
Cist sont de Rome li plus haut
Et li plus fier et li plus baut.
6165 Nes puet destraindre tote Rome,

6137 grans]Lö   6146 troeve]Lö (trouvai)   6162 fesissent]W (saisiscent)

206

and captured them: every defender gave himself up and surrendered to him. They all came to him at top speed, for they were expecting no help. It was far from Rome that all this took place, and for many a long day Rome had not turned its thoughts to fun or laughter or any other delight, because no-one yet had the faintest inkling of this piece of great good fortune, or of the whereabouts of the lovely creature who was heading for Rome as swiftly as she could. She was constantly pre-occupied, as well she might be: the day never dawned when she was not pre-occupied and despondent. However, what had happened so far was just fun and games,[1] unless God intervened, by His holy name; things would yet go quite differently for her, unless God intervened, from the way they were now.

The fair damsel arrived in Rome one day and asked for news of the army. (6127) 'Fair one', they said, 'We know nothing about it, except that we are overjoyed to see you, whatever happens to the men in the army, for there is no-one who can defend them, unless the Lord God takes care of them, and you do, for we have no other king or emperor or empress. You have indeed saved us all; but you acted very wrongly to go off in the way you did. *It is not surprising if people behave wrongly if they are going through a great war without a leader.* Rome has been going through a great war indeed. Fair damsel, welcome!' – 'My lords, God bless you, too! I have put myself through pain and torment in order to seek assistance for you all, and yet I have precious little help to show for it. I have been in Brittany since I left, but I achieved nothing there apart from torment, pain and suffering: I thought I would find the seneschal, but I regret that I did not find him. (6147) He has gone to Compostela, I believe, so they say in his country. I sent a messenger to him from there, and begged him to hurry and make haste to come back. And if the duke came back here and defended us against the Greeks, where he is concerned I would readily do what you advise me to do, you who are my loyal subjects, my liege men and my sworn vassals.' – 'Damsel, this has gone on too long', ten men said to themselves:[2] they were very arrogant men, and had received money from the Greek emperor, who had promised them a fortune if they put him in possession of Ganor; they were the highest-ranking, the most arrogant and the most presumptuous men in Rome. The whole of Rome could not control them,

---

1 Another example of ellipsis: 'compared with what was going to happen' has to be understood after this phrase.

2 It is clear from ll. 6166-77 that these are not the same ten knights who set out with Ganor on her fruitless journey to Brittany: these traitors had remained in Rome when the army marched out to do battle during Ganor's absence.

Ains le destragnent cil .x. home.
De l'ost remesent li felon,
Savés par quel entension?
Que qant li Grius aroit vencu,
6170 Que cascuns eüst son escu
Desor sa tour par connissance,
Por faire as Grijois demostrance
Al quel tour traire se devroit,
Et cascuns d'aus le recevroit;
6175 U s'ele revenoit ançois,
Qu'il la menroient au Grijois,
S'ele estoit hors de la cité.
Tans est qu'il soient aquité[1]
Selonc l'oevre et le mesprison.
6180 Et por covrir le traïson
Dient illoec voiant le gent:
«Il n'est pas drois ne bel ne jent
Que Rome voist a dolenté
Por vostre seule volenté.
6185 Car aiés viax, por Diu, merci
De ces caitis que veés chi,
Que l'emperere a mehagniés
Por çou que vos ne l'adagniés.
– Signor, loés le vos en foi
6190 Por çou qu'il les ocist por moi,
Que jou au malvais me marie?
Chi a bele cevalerie
Por apaisier cuer de pucele

Et d'une haute damoisele!
6195 Doi je donc soie devenir,
Qui se paine de moi honir?
Se n'estoit por el que por cié,
Certes, si le harroie gié.
Com bel dosnoiement chi a!
6200 Par icel Diu qui tout cria,
Ja n'ere soie ne il miens
Ne ja nen ere en ses liiens,
Por tant com Illes li dus vive;
Ançois seroie .xi. ans caitive,
6205 Et ains me doinst Dix que je muire.
– Comment? Nos volés vos destruire
Por un tel home com il est?
Et nos somes ichi tot prest
De mande[r] a l'empereour
6210 Qu'il viegne chi por vostre honor.
– Ja n'i puist il venir nul jor
Ne por m'onor ne por m'amor!
– Ne mais quels hom est dont li dus?
– Ja nos valut il un jour plus
6215 Que l'emperere ne fist onques.
Et por coi l'avilliés vos donques?
– Car envers lui estes trop noble,
Si averiés Constantinoble
Se l'emperere vous avoit.
6220 – Signor, cuidiés que je covoit
Un malvais home por avoir,

rather, these ten men controlled Rome. These traitors had not gone with the army – do you know what they had in mind? It was so that when the Greek emperor had won the battle, each of them would place his shield on the top of his tower as a signal, to show the Greeks which tower he should make for, and each of them would receive him; or else, if Ganor returned beforehand, they would take her to the Greek, if she were outside the city. It was time for them to act and be rewarded according to their criminal plan.[1] And in order to cover up their treachery, they said to Ganor, in front of the people of Rome: 'It is not right or proper or seemly that Rome should be condemned to suffer simply on account of your wishes. (6185) For God's sake, at least have mercy on these poor wretches you see here, whom the emperor has maimed because you do not think him worthy of you.' – 'My lords, are you seriously proposing that I should marry that evil-minded man because he is killing them on my account? A fine display of chivalry this is, to win over the heart of a maiden and a noble damsel! So I must belong to a man who is striving to dishonour me? I would certainly hate him, if for nothing other than this! A fine courtship this is! By the God who created everything, I shall never be his, nor he mine, and I shall never be tied to him so long as Duke Ille is alive; I would rather be a prisoner for eleven years, and God grant that I may die before it happens,' – (6206) 'What? Do you intend to destroy us for the sake of a man like him? And here we are, ready and waiting to send for the emperor to come here to bring you honour.' – 'May he never come here, ever, either to bring me honour or to ask for my love!' – 'But what manner of man is this duke, then?' – 'In the past, he was worth more to us on one day than the emperor ever was. So why do you belittle him?' – 'Because you are too noble in comparison with him, and Constantinople would be yours if you were the emperor's.' – 'My lords, do you imagine that I would desire an evil man on account of his wealth,

---

1 There is a play here on *estre aquité*, which can mean both 'to fulfil an obligation' and 'to receive one's just reward'. It is difficult to convey this double meaning in modern English.

Qui cest empire puist avoir
Et en baillie toute Rome?
Mout ai por avoir un prodome,
6225 Et je ne sai ne bas ne haut
Qui vaille tant com li dus vaut,
Ne qui tant soit cortois ne biax:
Mout par est sire et damoisiaus
En tos les lius ou il converse.
6230 Mais costume est de gent perverse
Tos jors encontre poil aler.
– Bele, que vaut tant a parler?
Li dus est or en autre terre;
Ançois qu'il viegne a vostre guerre,
6235 Orrés espoir autre novele.
– Dix le m'otroit et bone et bele!»
Et ce ne dient li felon,
Li traïtre, se por ce non
Qu'il le cuident livrer au gré
6240 L'empereour outre son gré;
Puis qu'il sevent qu'il s'entreheent,¹
Grant pecié font qui a ce beent.
Tex ne het point au commencier
Qui puis ne fine de tencier
6245 Et het se feme mortelment,
Et ele lui tot ensement,
Ne pais ne bien n'ont puis entr'ex.²
«Signor, ce dist Ganor a cex,
Je vous commanc que vos venés

6250 O moi seur qanque vos tenés;
S'irai novele oïr de l'ost.
– Volentiers,» dient il tantost,
Que ne queroient autre cose.
Ganor mout petit se repose
6255 Icele nuit, ains se demente
Et dist: «Com chi a longe atente,³
Biax dous amis! Que ferai gié
Et comment souferrai je chié?
Une bataille ai par dehors
6260 Et une au cuer dedens mon cors,
Mais cele est menre de cesti.
Lasse, quel bliaut me vesti
Amours, qant Ille m'acointa!
Ele coisi, ele enpointa,
6265 De dolor fist la gironee
Qui m'a trestote avironee;
De lons sospirs, de griés espointes
Fist les coustures et les pointes;
Le cors du bliaut de pesance,
6270 Qui me destraint sans esperance;
Amors meïsme le tissi.
Onques puis de mon dos n'issi
Que jel vesti premierement:
Mout ot chi dur acointement,
6275 Ne nul'aïde n'ai de vous,
Amis, ne convent entre nos
Que vos doiés miens devenir

a man who could then have this empire and the whole of Rome in his possession? I am quite wealthy enough to marry a man of worth, and I do not know anyone, high or low, who is as worthy as the duke, nor who is as courtly or as handsome: he is without question lord and prince in all the places he frequents. But it is customary for corrupt people always to go against the grain.' – 'Fair damsel, what is the point of so much talk? The duke is now in another country; before he comes to help in your war, you will likely hear other news.' – 'God grant me good and pleasant tidings!' And the villains, the traitors, only said this because they were planning to hand her over to the emperor against her will, for him to do as he pleased; since they knew that they hated each other,[1] the people who aimed to do this were committing a great sin. (6243) Even a man who feels no hatred to begin with may be constantly fighting later on, and feel mortal hatred for his wife, and she may feel the same for him, and there is no peace or affection between them thereafter.[2] 'My lords', Ganor said to these men, 'I command you, by every fief you hold, to come with me; I shall go to find news of the army.' – 'Gladly', they replied at once, because this was exactly what they were seeking. Ganor had very little rest that night; instead, she lamented and said: 'How long I am having to wait, fair gentle love![3] What shall I do, how shall I endure this? I am involved in one battle outside, and another inside me, within my heart, but the first is less intense than the second. (6262) Alas, what a tunic Love gave me to wear when she introduced Ille to me! She chose it, she made it ready; out of suffering she made the skirt which has wrapped itself all around me; out of long sighs, out of stinging pain she made the seams and the stitches; the bodice of this tunic, from which I have no hope of freeing myself, she made of sorrow; it was woven by Love herself. It has never left my back since I first put it on: a very harsh introduction this was, and I have no support from you, my love, nor any agreement between us that you should become mine

---

[1] Ganor has made no secret of her hatred for the emperor (ll. 5469-78); his reaction to her refusal to marry him (ll. 5407-10) indicates that the animosity is mutual.

[2] Lines 6243-47 can be read as a comment on the marital difficulties of Henry II of England, who was in open conflict with his wife Eleanor of Aquitaine over their eldest son Henry from March 1172 onwards, and eventually had her imprisoned on the Continent in the summer of 1173. In 1174 she was moved to Old Sarum near Salisbury, where she effectively remained in captivity for the next ten years.

[3] *Longue atente* is a common motif in lyric poetry, where the poet gently chides his lady for keeping him waiting too long for his reward. There is another reference to this motif in ll. 3419-20.

Ne a Rome mais revenir.
Por vos ont a mi estrivé
6280 Mi home lige et mi privé,
Et il n'est hom, ne max ne buens,
Qui pior guerre ait que des suens.
Je souferroie assés, je croi,
Ceste bataille dedens moi
6285 Et cele que me font li Griu,
Se mi home erent simple [et] piu
Envers moi, que tant m'obeïssent
Et a me volenté feïssent.»
Ganors la bele est en grant pe[i]ne;
6290 Mais ains que past cele semaine
Avra plus de pesance et d'ire
Que jou or ne vos voelle dire.
    La nuis en vait et l'aube crieve;
Lievent li prince et Ganors lieve.
6295 Montent trestot, vers l'ost en vont,
A lor sergans commandé ont
Les escus sor lor cols tenir,
Quant il verront le Griu venir.¹
Or oiés com grant mesproison!
6300 On ne puet celer traïson
Ne murdre, que on ne le sace,
Car mis i a Dix une estace
U li diables les espie,
Et nus ne puet plus male [es]pie
6305 Ne plus noiseuse recovrer;

Car de ce qu'il fait home ovrer
Le descoevre puis et acuse.
Celui deçoit, celui amuse
Qui l'aime et sert et croit de rien,
6310 Car il honist tos jors le sien.
Ganors cevalce mout dolante,
D'eures en autre s'espoante:
Grant droit a, que si compagnon
Ne li vont querant se mal non,
6315 Mais que un preudome i avoit
Qui cele traïson savoit.
Hardement prent et cuer recoevre:
Mix velt morir por dire l'oevre
K'aler o cele gent haïe
6320 En liu u Ganors soit traïe.
Tot li descoevre et tot li conte
Et des escus et de la honte
Dont cele gens illoec se paine,
Qui a l'empereour l'en maine.
6325 Dist li: «Ceste oevre savés ore,
Ne mes, por Diu, celés le encore,
Qu'il m'ociroient lués manois,
S'il le savoient; par ces bois
Je m'enblerrai, s'a bel vos vient,
6330 Et la tot droit u l'os se tient
Me trairai lués, se j'onques puis.
Tot lor dirai, se je les truis.»
Ganors li dist: «Por Diu, merci!

or ever return to Rome. On your account my liege-men and my intimates have striven against me, and no man, be he good or evil, knows worse strife than with his own people. I believe I would be able to endure doing battle with myself and with the Greeks quite well, if my men were sufficiently honest and devoted to me to obey me and act according to my wishes.' Ganor the fair was in great distress; but before the week was out she would know greater sorrow and dismay than I intend to describe for you at this point.

The night came to an end and dawn broke; the princes rose and Ganor rose too. They all mounted and rode off towards the army, having ordered their sergeants to keep their shields hung round their necks when they saw the Greek emperor coming.[1] (6299) Now hear how great their crime was! Neither treason nor murder can be kept secret, so that no-one knows of it, for God has set up a post, from which the devil spies on them, and no-one can find a more evil or malevolent spy than him, for after the event he informs against and accuses a man for the deeds he has made him do. He deceives and plays games with anyone who loves and serves him and has any faith in him, for he always brings dishonour on those who are his. Ganor rode along disconsolate, and every now and again she was overcome by fear: her fear was quite justified, because her companions were seeking to do her nothing but harm, except that there was one man of worth there who knew about the treason. (6317) He summoned up his courage and recovered his spirit: he preferred to die for revealing the plot than to accompany those hated men to a place where Ganor would be betrayed. He disclosed everything to her and told her all about the shields, as well as the shameful deed which these men were eager to commit there, who were taking her off to the emperor. He said to her: 'Now you know about this plot, only for God's sake keep it a secret as yet, because they would immediately kill me on the spot, if they found out; I shall steal away through these woods, if that meets with your approval, and I shall make at once straight for the place where the army is stationed, if I possibly can. I shall tell them everything, if I find them.' Ganor said to him: 'For God's sake, have mercy!

---

1 Shields were carried on the forearm only during combat or when there was a likelihood of combat; when travelling, they were hung around the neck by means of a long strap, so leaving the hands free. This gesture is designed to indicate to the Greeks that the approaching Romans are not hostile (and that the party therefore includes the traitors).

Se tu me pués geter de chi,
6335 Gete m'ent par tel convenant:
Rice te ferai et manant.»
El bos se part de la pucele
Cil qui li conta la novele.
Durement vait, ce li estuet,
6340 Vers l'ost se trait plus tost qu'il puet.
Ganors a dit as max senés:
«Signor! A destre me menés,
Que trop vos tenés a senestre.¹
– Par Damediu, le roi celestre,
6345 Vos venrés a l'empereour.
– Ahi! Com estes traïtour
Et plain de maise felonie!
Il n'est hom qui se gardast mie
De traïson por rien del monde.²
6350 Dix vos destruie et vos confonde
Et il me doinst le jor veoir
Que j'aie sor vos tous pooir.
– Ne savons or qant ce sera,
Mais li Grijois nos vengera
6355 De vostre cors novelement:³
Vos le verrés premierement.
– Ja Dix ne doinst que je le voie,
Mes que jou saine et sauve soie!
Se il me voit, je nel vaudroie. –
6360 Por coi? – Car plus vil m'en tenroie.
– Ne sai qui vous en tenra vil.

Toutes voies vos verra il,
Et pleüst Diu et son saint non
Que nos tenissons le Breton
6365 Por seul itant que vous l'amés.
– Voire, par si qu'il fust armés
Et seüst tout çou que je sai!
Ja venriiés tost a l'assai
Li quels vaut mix, ou il tous seus
6370 Ou vos tuit, felon orgilleus.
Je sui hardie de parler,
Car ne poroie pis aler
[N']en pieur liu que j'ore vois.⁴
Que ert il de moi, sire rois?
6375 Hé! O vois jo, lasse, mendie?
Si ne me kaille que je die!
A! Jentix dus, com estes long!
Or me falés vos au besong:
N'est pas si com vos ja deïstes.
6380 Ice que vos as Grix feïstes
Ert a moi seule cier vendu.
Illes, trop avés atendu!»
Lors maine un duel et un martire
Et ront ses cavex et detire,
6385 Son vis depece, crie et pleure;
Ja s'ocesist en icele eure,
S'ele seüst sossiel de coi.
Tot belement et en recoi
Se departent el bos si home

6364 Que vos tenissies]W   6373 que je revois]W   6375 Nen pior liu lasse m.]W

214

If you can get me out of here, then get me out of here on this understanding: I shall make you a rich and wealthy man.'

The man who told the maiden this piece of news parted from her in the wood. He rode hard – as well he might – and made for the army as quickly as he could. Ganor said to the unscrupulous men: 'My lords! Lead me over to the right; you are keeping too far to the left.'[1] – 'By the Lord God, the King of Heaven, you will come to the emperor.' – 'Ah! What traitors, what out-and-out villains you are! Not for anything on earth would anyone have suspected you of treason.[2] May God destroy and confound you, and may He grant that I live to see the day when all of you are in my power.' – (6353) 'We do not know when that will be now, but the Greek emperor will soon take revenge for us on your person:[3] you will be seeing him first of all.' – 'God forbid that I should see him, unless I am safe and sound! If he sets eyes on me, it is not of my wishing.' – 'Why?' – 'Because I would hold myself cheaper for it.' – 'I do not know who will hold you cheap for it. In any case, see you he will, and would that it had pleased God and His holy name for us to have our hands on the Breton, for the simple reason that you love him.' – 'Yes indeed, provided that he was armed and knew everything I know! You would soon be put to the test, we would see who is worth more, either him on his own or all of you arrogant villains together. I am bold enough to speak out, for I could not be going to a worse fate or a worse situation than I am now.[4] What will become of me, Lord and King? (6375) Ah! Alas, where am I going, poor creature that I am? Let me not care what I say! Ah, noble duke, how far away you are! Now you are failing me in my hour of need: it is not as you once said it would be. I alone shall be made to pay a heavy price for what you did to the Greeks. Ille, you have waited too long!' Then she gave vent to such grief and suffering, and rent and tore her hair, gouged her face with her nails, cried out and wept; she would already have killed herself at this point, if she had known what on earth to use. Her men split up very quietly and secretly in the wood,

---

1 *Senestre* (which is related to English 'sinister') has overtones of evil and misfortune which are clearly being brought into play here.

2 I interpret this line differently from both Foerster and Delclos and Quereuil.

3 Apart from the obvious sexual innuendo, this threat recalls the fate of the emperor's first wife, Ganor's cousin, who died as a result of being ill-treated by him (ll. 5404-06).

4 The first hemistich of l. 6373 was inadvertently, but accurately, copied onto l. 6375, while the first letter was carelessly omitted from l. 6373.

215

6390 Por querre l'ost, mes cil de Rome
U se prova bone nature
L'encontra ains par aventure.
Ce ne fu pas le jor meïsme,
Mais l'endemain assés ains prime.¹
6395 Noveles vait mout demandant
Et cil li ont fait entendant
K'a nule gent si bien n'estait,
Et dient k'Illes a tout fait,
Qu'il fuissent mort ne fust ses cors.
6400 «Or a vencus et pris et mors
Et maubaillis tos cex dehors.
Il a tot fait par son effors.
– Est dont li sire en ceste terre?
– Qui finast donques nostre gerre?
6405 Qui les eüst dont mors et pris?
Mes qu'en ont il a Rome apris?
– Il n'en sevent encor novele.
– Et ke de nostre damoisele?
– Vos le sarés assés a tans.»
6410 Ainc ne fina parmi les rans,
Si vint au duc, si le salue
De par Ganor, qu'il a perdue,
Se Damedix ne li aïde,
«Et nos, dist il, mes ele cuide
6415 Que vos soiés mout lonc de chi.
Or en aiés por Diu merchi,
Que c'est por vos k'ele est en paine.
– Qui li fait ce? – Sa gens demaine:

Vendue l'ont l'empereor.
6420 N'en sevent mot li traïtor
Que vos si prés lor soiés ore;
Nel set ma damoisele encore.
Por vos, cui ele tant desire,
Dont ele a paine se consire,
6425 Li vient devant canqu'il li font,
Et por l'avoir que il en ont.
– Amis, qant en partistes vous?
– Ersoir, par Diu qui maint sor nous.
Asseür sont et vont a joie:
6430 N'ont song que nus venir i doie
Qui lor deïst pis de lor nons.
Tant entendi je des felons
Qu'il cuident mout tres bien pieça
Tot soient mort cist par deça.
6435 Tot vont cantant, mes Ganor plore,
Ne croit que nus hom le secore:
Vers l'ost m'envoia por aïe,
Por dire com ele est traïe.
Aiés merci de la pucele!»
6440 Li dus ses compaignons apele;
A ceus de l'ost a dit itant
Qu'il aillent belement avant.
Part s'en avoec sa compagnie,
Et li mes qui les maine et guie
6445 Les fait par un destor guencir
Por les felons adevancir.

6424 Com ele]W   6434 Tant soient]Lö (Tuit)

216

to go and look for the army, but as luck would have it, the Roman in whom nature proved its worth encountered them first. This was not the same day, but the following morning, well before prime.[1] He went eagerly asking for news, and they gave him to understand that things were going as well as they possibly could for them, and they said that Ille had done it all, that they would have been dead men, had it not been for his presence. 'Now he has defeated all our opponents and taken them prisoner and killed them and ruined them. He did it all by his own efforts.' – 'Is the lord in this country, then?' – 'Who else would have brought our war to an end? Who else would have killed them and taken them prisoner? But what have they learned about this in Rome?' – 'They know nothing about it yet.' – 'And what about our damsel?' – You will know about it soon enough.' (6410) He continued through the ranks and came to the duke, and greeted him on behalf of Ganor, whom he had lost unless God came to her aid. 'And we do', he said, 'But she believes that you are a very long way from here. Now have mercy on her, for God's sake, since it is on your account that she is in distress,' – 'Who is doing this to her?' – 'Her own men: they have sold her to the emperor. The traitors do not have the faintest idea that you are so close at hand at the moment; and my lady does not know it yet, either. Everything they are doing to her is happening to her because of you, whom she longs for so much, whom she finds it so painful to do without – and because of the money they have received for it.'

(6427) 'My friend, when did you leave her?' – 'Yesterday evening, by God who dwells above us. They are confident and riding joyfully along: they are not worried that anyone may come along and say anything worse to them than their own names. I heard enough of what the villains were saying to know that they are absolutely convinced that all the men on our side are long dead. They are riding along singing, but Ganor is weeping, and does not believe that anyone will come to her rescue: she sent me off to the army to get help, and to tell them how she has been betrayed. Have mercy on the maiden!' The duke called his companions to him; he told the men in the army to go quietly on ahead. He parted from them with his own company, and the messenger who was leading and guiding them took them on a detour off the beaten track in order to get ahead of the villains.

---

1 The first hour of the medieval day; before prime indicates very early in the morning.

Tant ont icel destor tenu
Qu'il sont outre un mal pas venu
Bien une liue, et cil les voient:
6450 Ne sevent pas quels gens ce soient.
Armé se sont isnelement
Et li nostre tout ensement.
Illes li bers vait tot devant,
L'escu a or a trait avant;
6455 Tant com cevax le pot porter
Fiert le premier, sel fait voler
Plaine sa lance contre val.
Li sien i font assés de mal:
Cascuns i vait le sien requerre,
6460 Mort o navré l'abat a terre.
Ganors mout durement se deut,
Mes mains se doute qu'el ne seut.
Sospire et dist: «Biax sire pere!
Sainte Marie, douche mere!
6465 Ja me vienent ichi rescorre!
Or me puist Damedix secorre,
Que cist chi soient de nos gens!
Si biaus chevaliers ne si gens
Ne vi ainc puis en cest païs
6470 K'Illes s'en ala, mes amis,
Qui est si biaus, com Diex le fist;
Si cevauce aussi comme cist
A l'escu d'or, au bai cheval:
Mout par i avoit bon vassal!
6475 Car fust ce li fiex Eliduc,

Ou amast autretant le duc
Comme je l'aim d'amor entiere,
Si me ramenroit viax ariere.»
Uns en velt mener la pucele:
6480 Li dus s'eslaisse et si l'apele
De traïson, de felonie.
Escus ne li vaut une alie,
Ne li haubers, tant soit treslis,
Que il ne soit tous desconfis:
6485 Le cuer li perce et le pomon,
Sel porte a val par son l'arçon.
Des leur refont cil autretel:
Doné lor ont le cop mortel.
Traïtres n'ert ja de grant pris:
6490 Cist i sont tuit et mort et pris
Fors ne sai qans, qui s'en fuirent,
Qui en le forest se perdirent.
    Li dus vient a le fille au roi,
Qui forment est en grant esfroi:
6495 Ne set que cuidier ne que croire.
Les uns voit morir et recroire,
Les autres voit et baus et liés.
Li dus [s']est mout humeliiés
Vers le pucele et se li dist:
6500 «Amie, et Diex vos aït!
Je sui li dus, ne vos cremés.
Je vos aim mout et vos m'amés,
Et Diex vos doinst joie et deport!

6448 Qui sont]Lö   6460 Mort et navre]W   6462 quil ne seut   6497 et biax et lies]W
6501 li d. qui vos ames]W

218

They followed this detour until they came out a good league beyond a marshy area, and the others saw them: they did not know whose forces they were. They swiftly armed themselves and our men did exactly the same. Ille the noble warrior rode right at the front, and drew his golden shield in front of him; he struck the first man as fast as his horse could carry him, and sent him flying to the ground with the full force of his lance. His men did considerable damage there: each of them went to attack his man and knocked him to the ground dead or injured. Ganor was extremely distressed, but she was less afraid than she was before. She sighed and said: 'Dear God, our Father! Holy Mary, gentle mother! Let them be coming to rescue me here! (6466) Now may the Lord God come to my aid, and let these men here be some of ours! I never saw such a handsome or such a noble knight in this country since the departure of Ille, the man I love, who is so handsome, as God made him; and he rides just like this man with the golden shield on the bay horse: what an excellent knight he was! If only this was the son of Eliduc, or someone who loved the duke as much as I love him with a wholehearted love, at least he would take me back.' One of them tried to lead the maiden away: the duke dashed at him, accusing him of treason and felony. His shield was not worth a fig to him, nor was the hauberk; no matter how closely-mailed it was, it could not prevent him from being totally overcome: Ille pierced his heart and his lung and threw him down dead over the rear of the saddle. (6487) The others did likewise with their opponents; they dealt them the same fatal blow. A traitor will never be of great renown: all of them were killed or taken prisoner, apart from some – I do not know how many – who fled and got lost in the forest.

The duke approached the king's daughter, who was in a state of extreme terror: she did not know what to think or to believe. She could see one side being killed and giving in and the others cheerful and in high spirits. The duke greeted the maiden very humbly and said to her: 'My love, may God be with you! I am the duke, do not be afraid. I love you dearly and you love me, and may God grant you joy and pleasure!

Bones noveles vos aport:
6505 Desconfis est li emperere
Et trestot cil de son empere
Sont mort et pris et retenu;
Mout par vous est bien avenu.
– Biax dous amis, estes vos ce?
6510 – Oïl, amie, ce sui ge.
– Dont me baisiés, biax dous amis!»
Ses bras li a a son col mis.
Li uns acole l'autre et baise,
Qu'il en ont bien et lieu et aise.
6515 Ainc tant de joie n'ot mes nus
Que Ganors n'ait .c. tans et plus,
Car cex voit mors dont plus se claime,
Celui que plus desire et aime
Acole et baise tot por voir,
6520 Et du sorplus a bon espoir.
La joie est grans qu'il vont faisant,
Et li a dit tout en baisant:
«Amis, com petit je cuidoie
Ja mes recovrer si grant joie!
6525 Sire, je n'ai autre signor:
De moi, de tote ceste honor
Vos faç le don et ravest chi.
– Ma bele suer, vostre merci!»
Ens el cemin se metent tost;
6530 Ainc ne finerent jusc'a l'ost.
Cist de l'ost oent la novele
C'a Rome vint lor damoisele,

Oent com cil traïr les durent
Qui avoec li de Rome murent,
6535 Et com li dus, lor boins amis,
L'a bien rescousse et cex ochis.
Grans est la joie qu'il en ont:
Li Romain mout grant joie font.
A Rome vienent maintenant
6540 Et vont grant joie demenant.
Ganors fait lués les tors abatre
As traïtors, la .iii., la .iiii.;
Lor gens fait Ganor dekacier.
En grant sont tuit de porkacier
6545 K'Illes li ber ait la corone;
Bien sevent que sa feme est none.
Illes li dus le veut mout bien,
Et Ganor ne desplaist il rien;
Li apostoles le porkace;
6550 Dont n'i a el, mes c'on le face.
Li apostoles les espeuse,
Rome en est lie et joieuse.
   De Rome est Illes emperere
Et rois et sire et commandere.
6555 Les chevaliers noviax venus
A en la tere retenus,
Et les marie ricement,
Estre les .iiii. seulement
Qui femes orent en la terre
6560 Ou Ganor fu por Ille querre.

6520 en bon e.]Lö   6531 Dist]Lö

I bring you good tidings: the emperor has been defeated and all the forces of his empire have been killed and taken prisoner and captured: it has turned out extremely well for you.' – 'Fair sweet love, is it really you?' – 'Yes, my love, it is I.' – 'Then kiss me, fair sweet love!' She threw her arms around his neck. Each of them embraced and kissed the other, as they had plenty of time and opportunity to do so. No-one had ever felt so much joy but that Ganor felt a hundred times as much, and more, for she could see that those she had most reason to accuse were dead, and she was really and truly kissing the man she most desired and loved, and she had high hopes of something more. Great was the joy they felt, and she said to him, even as she kissed him: (6523) 'My love, how little I imagined that I would ever find such joy again! My lord, I have no other lord but you: I make you the gift of myself and the whole of this realm and invest you with them here and now.' – 'Fair sister, I thank you!' They quickly set off along the road, and did not stop until they reached the army.

The men in the army heard the news that their liege-lady had arrived back in Rome, they heard how the men who had set out from Rome with her had tried to betray them, and how their good friend the duke had duly rescued her and killed the others. They were overjoyed at it: the Romans rejoiced mightily. They came to Rome straight away, and let their great joy be known. Ganor immediately ordered the demolition of the towers which belonged to the traitors, three here and four there; Ganor had their men banished. (6544) All the Romans eagerly endeavoured to see to it that Ille the noble warrior should have the crown; they were all well aware that his wife was a nun. Duke Ille wanted it very much, and the prospect did not displease Ganor in the least; the pope used his best endeavours; so there was no alternative but for it to be done. The pope celebrated their marriage; Rome was glad and rejoiced at it.

Ille was the emperor of Rome, and its king and lord and commander. He kept the newly-arrived knights with him in the country, and arranged splendid marriages for them, with the one exception of the four men who had wives in the country where Ganor had gone to look for Ille.

Ceus abandone son tresor:
Assés lor done argent et or,
Envoie les liés et joians,
Par eus salue ses enfans
6565 Et le nonain et ses amis;
Assés lor a joiaus tramis.
Li dus a sofert puis grant paine
Por Rome, sa cité demaine:
Ne la veut veoir despoillier.
6570 .III. fiex ot puis de sa mollier
Et une fille mout tres bele.
Akarins entent la novele,
Et Garsions, ses aisnés frere;[1]
A Rome en vienent a lor pere
6575 Et a leur freres qui i sont,
Qui mervillose joie en font.
Li uns des .iii. freres romains
A non Morins, li uns Germains,
Li tiers a non Oriadés;
6580 Il firent puis proëce assés.
Des .ii. enfans a son signor
Fist Ganor feste mout grignor
Qu'ele ne fait de son demaine;
Li pere grant joie en demaine.
6585 Mout furent puis de haut afaire,
Mes ne voel pas lonc conte faire;
Ce ne tient pas ichi a dire.
O Ganor vesqui puis li sire
A joie tant dis com Dix vaut,
6590 Ne en l'estore plus n'en aut,
Ne plus n'i a, ne plus n'i mist
Gautier d'Arras qui s'[en] entremist.[2]

Explicit d'Ille et de Galeron

He threw his coffers open to these men: he gave them large sums of silver and gold and sent them home happy and rejoicing, and sent greetings by them to his children and to the nun and to his kinsmen; he sent them considerable quantities of jewels. Afterwards, the duke endured great tribulations for the sake of Rome, his domanial city: he was not willing to see it ransacked. Subsequently, he had three sons by his wife, and a very beautiful daughter. Acarin heard the news, and so did his elder brother Garsion;[1] they came to Rome to see their father and the brothers they had there, who gave them a wonderfully joyful reception. (6577) The first of the three Roman brothers was called Morin, the second Germain and the third Oriadés; they subsequently performed considerable feats of prowess. Ganor made a great deal more of her husband's two children than she did of her own; their father displayed great joy at this. They were men of great note later on, but I do not want to make this a long story; this is not the place to tell of it. The lord lived joyfully thereafter with Ganor for as long as God wished him to, and let no more go into this story about him; there is no more to it, and no more was included by Gautier d'Arras, who undertook it.[2]

Here ends the story of Ille and Galeron

---

[1] In ll. 5299-300 Akarin (Acarin) is the name of the elder son, and Garsion that of the younger. Despite the agreement of the two MSS, there would seem to be a good case for following Löseth, who simply swapped the names over here. W has an additional couplet after l. 6580 which gives the name of Ganor's daughter as Ydone, the same name as Galeron's third child.

[2] The final line of P is unsatisfactory as it stands. The emendation proposed here is based on a very common type of scribal error, but has the disadvantage of producing a hypermetrical line. Alternatively, the first line of W's epilogue ('D'Eracle, ains qu'il fesist ceste uevre') could be added in order to complete the sense of the sentence. This would create a parallel with the prologue, which also ends with an apparently incomplete couplet in P. There might then be grounds for emending to 'D'Eracle, ains qu'il ceste uevre fesist', which would give a more satisfying triple rhyme in -ist (there are four successive lines with the same rhyme shortly before this, at ll. 6399-402).

TABLE OF PROPER NAMES

The first form listed is normally the oblique singular, which is in many cases identical to the nominative plural (and occasionally the nominative singular as well). Where this is the form used in the English translation, no English equivalent is given. If only nominative forms occur in the text, this is indicated, as is the form of the name used in the translation.

ACARINS nom. 5299, Akarins 6572, Acarin, elder son of Ille and Galeron

AGAR 2727, 2831; nom. Agars 2723, 2724, Greek knight, killed by Ille

AGENOR 2872, 2884, Greek knight, father of Emenidon

AGOULANS nom. 1612, Agolant, Saracen hero of *La Chanson d'Aspremont*

ALEMAGNE 48, 2590, 2664; Alemaigne 2472, Germany

ALEMANS nom. sing. 3929, a German

ANGAU 1494, Anjou, area of western France bordering on Brittany

ANGEVINS obl. plur. 1554, (inhabitants of Anjou)

ARTU 2806, King Arthur

ATAINES 2874, Athens

BRANDINS nom. sing. 2653, Brandin, Greek knight

BRETAGNE 135, 1549, 1683, 3481, 3671, 3783, 4706, 5453, 5536, 5539; Bretaigne 147, 261, 305, 334, 1192, 2112, 3080, 3832, 3838, 3876, 4214, 4219, 4453, 4468, 5135, 5397, 5431, 5586, 6143, Brittany; Bretagne la petite 1205, 4500, Bretaigne la petite 5101, Brittany; le grant Bretaigne 1985, Britain

BRETON obl. sing. & nom. plur. 139, 588, 2339, 5046, 5091, 5905, 5973, 6033, 6042, 6364; nom. sing. Bres 3666, 4031, 5834; obl. plur. Bretons 625, 5510, 5516, 5879, Breton(s)

BRUNS D'ORLIENS nom. 556, 622, 634; Brun obl. 578, 638; Bruns nom. 583, 590, 598, Brun of Orleans (q.v.), French knight

BRUNS nom. 2898, 2904, Brun, Roman knight

CADOR 556, 563; nom. Cados 354, 531, Breton knight, nephew of Hoel and cousin of Ris, killed by Brun of Orleans

CARTAGE 2593, 2643, Carthage (see note to l. 2593)

CASTELE 2204, Castile, kingdom in central Spain

COINE 2653, city in the Byzantine empire, possibly ancient Iconium (modern Konieh) in Asia Minor

COMMENIE 5900, Comenia, land between the Byzantine empire and Russia

CONAIN 867, 889, 968, 3670; nom. Conains 140, 1186, 1191, 1408, 1473, 1475, 1514, 4454, duke of Brittany, brother of Galeron

CONSTANTINOBLE 2101, 5978, 6218; Constantinople

CORNUALLE 5887, Cornwall

224

DANEMARCE 1991, Denmark

DINAS 2593, 2625, duke of Carthage

ECTOR 612, Hector, Trojan hero, eldest son of Priam

ELIDUC 133, 915, 1702, 3879, 4080, 5057, 6475; nom. **Elidus** 148, 3851, 4706, father of Ille

EMENIDON 3026; nom. **Emenidus** 2873, 2890, 2899, 2919, 3033, duke of Athens, son of Agenor

ENGLOIS 137, the English

ESCLAVONIE 1994, Slavonia, area inhabited by the Slavs (probably here the lands between the Oder and the Elbe and/or Bohemia)

ESCOCE 1989, Scotland

ESPAGNE 2111, 2133, Spain

ESTATINS nom. 2654, Estatin, Greek knight

ESTOUS DE LENGRES nom. 628; **Estous** 635, Estout de Langres (q.v.), French knight

FRANCE 159, 260, 269, 457, 486, 1997, 2023

FRANÇOIS nom. plur. & obl. plur. 312, 346, 360, 446, 520, 568, 616, 633, 664, 806, 824, 1014, the French

FRISE 1993, Frisia (see note to l. 2205)

FRISON 2205; obl. plur. **Frisons** 3157, Frisian(s)

GADIFER (1) 2656, 2809, Greek knight, son of the duke of Carthage, killed by Ille during the first Greek war

GADIFER (2) 5893, Greek knight, killed by Gerin of Le Mans during the second Greek war

GALERON 132, 156, 931, 1723, 2329, 3366, 3466, 3836, 3878, 4391, 5045, 5279, 5358, 5395; nom. **Galerons** 141, 872, 895, 910, 1188, 1218, 1374, 1425, 1472, 1527, 1837, 1875, 3118, 3271, 3312, 3367, 3859, 4003, 4118, 4652, 5082, 5165, 5267, 5311, 5336, 5508, sister and heiress of duke Conain, later first wife of Ille and duchess of Brittany

GALES 1986, Wales

GANOR obl. & nom. 3285, 3327, 3415, 3447, 3452, 3478, 3587, 3970, 4307, 4386, 4594, 4797, 5080, 5161, 5164, 5179, 5185, 5278, 5385, 5396, 5413, 5481, 5535, 5658, 5729, 6162, 6248, 6254, 6412, 6435, 6543, 6548, 6560, 6582, 6588; **Ganors** nom. 3211, 3314, 3335, 3349, 3365, 3380, 3389, 3403, 3421, 3423, 3633, 3642, 3974, 3990, 4608, 4670, 4789, 4844, 4903, 5347, 5428, 5454, 6289, 6294, 6311, 6320, 6333, 6341, 6461, 6516, 6541, daughter and heiress of the Roman emperor, later second wife of Ille and empress of Rome

GARSION 5300; nom. **Garsions** 6573, second of Ille and Galeron's two sons

GAUTIER D'ARRAS nom. 6592; **Gautiers** (also nom.) 23, 96

GERINS DEL MANS nom. 5893, 5975, Gerin of Le Mans (q.v.), French knight

GERMAINS nom. 6578, Germain, second (?) of Ille and Ganor's three sons

GRECE 6005; **Gresse** 3159, Greece

GRIFON obl. sing & nom. plur. 2127,

2194, 2323, 2432, 5885; obl. plur. **Grifons** 2348, Greek(s)

GRIJOIS (all cases) 2195, 2198, 2412, 2783, 2786, 2863, 5902, 5917, 5928, 6046, 6172, 6176, 6354, Greek(s)

GRIU obl. sing. & nom. plur. 2122, 2135, 2210, 2488, 2600, 2702, 2752, 2878, 2888, 2975, 3043, 5831, 5907, 6007, 6039, 6051, 6160, 6285, 6298; nom. sing & obl. plur. **Grius** 5977, 5997, 6032, 6053, 6154, 6169, **Grix** 2341, 2498, 2573, 2733, 2808, 5859, 6380; nom. sing & obl. plur. **Griex** 2074, 2188, 2214, 2371, 2869, Greek(s)

HOEL 670, 854, 858, 876, 954, 1152, **Hoiel** (W graphy) 851a; nom **Hoiaus** 352, 566, 684, 837, **Hoiax** 576, 785, 839, 866, 985, 1040, 1134, 1137, 1146, 1180 **Oiaus** 152, Breton knight, enemy of Ille, uncle of Cador, Ris and Rogelion

HONGERIE 1993, Hungary

ILLANDE 1987, Ireland

ILLE 133, 148, 155, 364, 371, 565, 678, 686, 931, 1085, 1095, 1110, 1138, 1174, 1393, 1475, 1519, 1540, 1573, 2067, 2164, 2329, 2374, 2415, 2443, 2531, 2660, 2720, 2887, 2889, 2970, 2973, 3043, 3053, 3228, 3286, 3365, 3471, 3781, 3856, 3879, 4006, 4672, 5183, 5266, 5301, 5471, 5633, 5711, 5918, 5996, 6263, 6560; nom. **Illes** 150, 172, 185, 187, 231, 241, 256, 265, 326, 336, 344, 433, 440, 485, 656, 694, 700, 706, 732, 742, 743, 744, 745, 746, 747, 783, 787, 813, 832, 834, 874, 884, 887, 937, 956, 966, 1004, 1022, 1035, 1038, 1059, 1112, 1132, 1151, 1165, 1178, 1183, 1200, 1202, 1217, 1373, 1414, 1526, 1548, 1561, 1563, 1585, 1596, 1603, 1606, 1621, 1632, 1634, 1643, 1649, 1680, 1761, 1919, 1983, 2017, 2061, 2070, 2092, 2109, 2117, 2125, 2129, 2191, 2208, 2220, 2347, 2359, 2388, 2431, 2435, 2487, 2495, 2523, 2530, 2536, 2558, 2562, 2578, 2588, 2612, 2670, 2688, 2693, 2704, 2726, 2768, 2809, 2829, 2845, 2864, 2881, 2904, 2932, 2977, 2988, 2994, 2996, 3022, 3025, 3047, 3051, 3065, 3086, 3095, 3149, 3265, 3277, 3291, 3328, 3366, 3369, 3381, 3422, 3447, 3461, 3614, 3761, 3781, 3822, 3851, 3884, 4000, 4030, 4080, 4270, 4324, 4450, 4457, 4484, 4643, 4675, 4680, 4777, 4874, 4903, 4939, 4941, 4957, 4974, 4980, 5025, 5064, 5282, 5335, 5396, 5401, 5422, 5429, 5479, 5497, 5522, 5610, 5645, 5656, 5762, 5837, 5885, 5932, 5942, 5953, 5963, 5979, 6019, 6037, 6065, 6203, 6382, 6398, 6453, 6470, 6545, 6547, 6553, son of Eliduc, later duke of Brittany, then Roman emperor, husband of Galeron and Ganor

JONAS 5959, 5965, Greek knight, killed by Ille

LANSELINS nom. 5897, Lanselin of Poitiers (q.v.), knight in Ille's company

LE MANS 5893, 5975, town in Anjou (q.v.)

LENGRES 628, 1999, 3077, Langres, town in eastern France, north of

Dijon

LONGIS 1834, Longinus, Roman soldier supposed to have wounded Christ on the cross with his lance

LOT DE COMMENIE 5900, Lot of Comenia (q.v.), knight in the Greek army, killed by Ponçon of Nantes

MADAN 5975, Greek knight, killed by Gerin of Le Mans

MADIAN 5976, Greek knight killed by Paris of Rennes

MADOINE 2654, father of Estatin

MARADUC 2655, father of Torgin

MARCEL 955, 1100; nom. **Marciax** 766, Breton knight, cousin of Ponçon (1), brother of Rogelion, killed by Ille

MARIE 586, 4238, 4614, 5006, 5461, 6464, the Virgin Mary

MASELAINE 3952, the feast of Mary Magdalen

MAURIN 5891, Greek knight, one of two cousins killed by Ille

MORINS nom. 6578, Morin, eldest (?) of Ille and Ganor's three sons

NANTES 5899, 5998 town in western France, near the mouth of the river Loire

NOHUBERLANDE 1988, Northumberland

NORMANS obl. plur. 1554; **Normant** nom. plur. 138

NORMENDIE 1496, 1983, 1996, 1997, Normandy

NOROUERGE 1990, Norway

OLIVIERS nom. 1612, Oliver, companion of Roland in *La Chanson de Roland*

ORIADÉS nom. 6579, youngest (?) of Ille and Ganor's three sons

ORLIENS 556, 622, 634, Orleans, town on the river Loire, south of Paris

OTRENTE 2526, Otranto, town in southern Italy

PARIS DE RESNES nom. 5901, 5976, Paris of Rennes (q.v.), Breton knight in Ille's company

POITEVINS 1553, 5510, 5879 (inhabitants of Poitou)

POITIERS 1495, 5897, town in western France, capital of Poitou

PONÇON (1) 756, 759; nom. **Ponces** 756, Breton knight, cousin of Marcel, killed by Ille

PONÇON (2) 5959; nom. **Ponces de Nantes** 5899, 5998, **Ponces** 5964, 6002, Ponçon of Nantes, Breton knight in Ille's company

RESNES 5901, 5976, Rennes, former capital of Brittany

RIS nom. 522, 544, 563, Breton knight, nephew of Hoel, cousin of Cador, killed by Ille

ROGELION 950, 1127, 1169; nom. **Rogeslions** 954, 993, 1081, 1089, Breton knight, nephew of Hoel, brother of Marcel, rejected suitor of Galeron, seriously injured by Ille

ROLLANS nom. 1611, Roland, nephew of Charlemagne, hero of *La Chanson de Roland*

ROMAIN nom. pl. 2069, 2121, 2318, 2325, 2368, 2423, 2490, 2571, 2591, 2703, 2717, 2740, 2744, 2749, 2822, 2863, 2879, 2915, 3024, 3332, 3987, 3994, 4260, 4309, 4360, 4400, 5694, 5768, 5912, 5929, 6045, 6067, 6095,

6101, 6538; nom. sing. & obl. plur.
Romains 2556, 2568, 2597, 2839, 2885, 2898, 2923, 2930, 3157, 3794, 4001, 4037, 4060, 4073, 4258, 4348, 5083, 5821, 5828, 5877, 6005, 6066, Roman(s)

ROME 19, 60, 69, 71, 74, 77, 90, 92, 2000, 2015, 2050, 2089, 2105, 2418, 2448, 2462, 2664, 2868, 2927, 2967, 3066, 3101, 3120, 3150, 3264, 3267, 3309, 3367, 3463, 3498, 3541, 3571, 3636, 3643, 3654, 3739, 3828, 3830, 3839, 3868, 3959, 3982, 3999, 4035, 4061, 4130, 4172, 4352, 4376, 4528, 4587, 4617, 4622, 4634, 4869, 4891, 4927, 4936, 5013, 5017, 5025, 5041, 5076, 5089, 5094, 5128, 5389, 5397, 5417, 5424, 5435, 5473, 5521, 5525, 5582, 5684, 5843, 5856, 5915, 5985, 5995, 6064, 6079, 6111, 6117, 6125, 6137, 6163, 6165, 6183, 6223, 6278, 6390, 6406, 6532, 6534, 6539, 6552, 6553, 6568, 6574

ROMENIE 5599, the Byzantine empire

SAINT JAKE 5507, 5522, 5525, 5543, 5568, 6148, Santiago de Compostela, major pilgrimage site in northern Spain

SAINT PIERE 3997, 4042; **S. Pere** 5040, 5468, Saint Peter

SAINT VINCENT 5940, Saint Vincent of Saragossa, early Christian martyr

SAISSONE 1994, Saxony, area of northern Germany bordering on Denmark and Frisia (q.v.)

TORGINS nom. 2655, Greek knight, son of Maraduc

VIANE 57, 5577, Vienne, French town in the Rhône valley, south of Lyons

YDONE 5312, daughter of Ille and Galeron

KING'S COLLEGE LONDON

MEDIEVAL STUDIES

ISSN 0953-217X

General Editor: Janet Bately *Executive Editor:* David Hook

I: James E. Cross, *Cambridge Pembroke College MS 25: a Carolingian sermonary used by Anglo-Saxon preachers.* viii + 252 pp., 1987. ISBN 0 9513085 0 5.

II: *The Sacred Nectar of the Greeks: the study of Greek in the West in the Early Middle Ages,* edited by Michael W. Herren in collaboration with Shirley Ann Brown. (10) + xii + 313 pp., 24 plates, 1988. ISBN 0 9513085 1 3.

III: *Cultures in Contact in Medieval Spain: historical and literary essays presented to L.P. Harvey,* edited by David Hook & Barry Taylor. xvi + 216 pp., 1990. ISBN 0 9513085 2 1.

IV: *Eleven Old English Rogationtide Homilies,* edited by Joyce Bazire and James E. Cross. xxxii + 143 pp., 1989. ISBN 0 9513085 3 X.

V: *Chaucer and Fifteenth-century Poetry,* edited by Julia Boffey and Janet Cowen. x + 174 pp., 1991. ISBN 0 9513085 4 8.

VI: Lynne Grundy, *Books and Grace: Ælfric's theology.* viii + 290 pp., 1991. ISBN 0 9513085 5 6.

VII: *Richard Coeur de Lion in History and Myth,* edited by Janet L. Nelson. xiv + 165 pp., 1992. ISBN 0 9513085 6 4.

VIII: Frank W. Chandler, *A Catalogue of Names of Persons in the German Court Epics. An examination of the literary sources and dissemination together with notes on the etymologies of the more important names,* edited by Martin H. Jones. xxxi + 319 pp., 1992. ISBN 0 9513085 7 2.

IX: *Evangelista's 'Libro de cetrería': a fifteenth-century satire of falconry books,* edited by José Manuel Fradejas Rueda. liv + 87 pp., 1992. ISBN 0 9513085 8 0.

X: *Kings and Kingship in Medieval Europe,* edited by Anne J. Duggan. xv + 440 pp., 17 plates, 1993. ISBN 0 9513085 9 9.

XI: Jane Roberts and Christian Kay, with Lynne Grundy, *A Thesaurus of Old English.* xxxv + 1555 pp., in 2 volumes, 1995. ISBN 0 9522119 0 4 (complete work).

XII: *Roland and Charlemagne in Europe: essays on the reception and transformation of a legend,* edited by Karen Pratt. x + 217 pp. + 34 plates, 1996. ISBN 0 9522119 4 7.